Dearest Anna
A LOVE STORY

By Carol Allis

FUZIONPRESS
Minneapolis, Minnesota

ISBN: 978-1-946195-52-4

Library of Congress Control Number:2019918974

FUZIONPRESS
www.fuzionpress.com
Manufactured in the United States of America

DEDICATION

To my beloved family,
and to everyone who has letters
hidden in the attic

Dear Jean,
Oh, the stories you could tell,
Jean - and I hope - some day -
I can help get them down.
Thank you, thank you, for being
in my life - a book about you
would be a best seller!
Love,
Carol

"We will write as often as we must,
for we are never going to be tired of each other,
if we live a thousand years."
Anna to Roy: October 14, 1898

PREFACE

Finding Anna

Before my grandmother, there was Anna – a family legend and a buried mystery none of us dared talk about while my grandmother was alive.

I first heard about Anna, my grandfather's first love, when I was only 19 – about Anna's age when she and my grandfather began exchanging hundreds of love letters after they graduated from Rochester High School in 1894.

In 1898, at age 24, Anna died suddenly and tragically. My grandfather was devastated. Even after he married my grandmother, every year on the anniversary of Anna's death he went to "Lovers' Point" – their place – to grieve, much to my grandmother's despair. He hid Anna's pictures and the letters – both sets – for years, until my aunt was old enough to marry and have her own home, and he entrusted the letters to her for safekeeping. He never forgot Anna. In my father's words, "Your grandmother always had to endure that shadow."

Who was Anna – this woman my grandfather loved so deeply that he kept memories of her all those years, even after his 63-year marriage to my grandmother?

The letters lay hidden for almost 80 years. After both my grandparents died, my aunt felt it was safe to bring the letters out of hiding and turn them over to me. They languished again for decades until I retired in 2012 and finally had time to open and read them.

And what letters they are – lyrical, passionate, full of utter trust and faith in each other. They were young – a hopeless romantic yearning to be a writer, and a fierce, headstrong bookworm determined to be a teacher – finding their way in a time of stunning change. The letters are laced with the history, social revolution and political turmoil of the times. And books! How they loved to read! Their love affair played out in words on paper across the miles.

This is Anna and Roy's story – a snapshot in time, told through their eyes, in the waning years of the Gilded Age. Most of all, it is a love story, finally brought out of the shadows.

Rochester High School graduating class of 1894:
(back row) Roy Allis, Nellie Ottman, Walter E. Bowers,
Minnie Fordice, Martin Beatty.
(front row) Anna L. Barnard, Prof. Henry Adams (teacher),
Jennie Clark, Edwin Hagaman, Mabel E. Peck (teacher).
Photo courtesy of the History Center of Olmsted County

CHAPTER 1

A Little History

1854:
> White settlers found Oronoco, Minnesota, by the Zumbro River. They name the town after the Orinoco River in South America.

1855:
> The first dam and mill are built on the river, creating a lake. Abraham Delancy Allis and his wife Maria build their house on the lake, next to the river.

1863:
> Abraham takes over operation of the dam and mill.

SEPTEMBER 20, 1874:
> Roy Wirt Allis is born in the house in Oronoco.

NOVEMBER 11, 1874:
> Anna Leuella Barnard is born in Granville, New York.

AUGUST 21, 1883:
> A monstrous tornado devastates Rochester, Minnesota – 11 miles south of Oronoco – precipitating the very real need for a hospital.

SEPTEMBER 30, 1889:
> Rochester Hospital – the beginning of the Mayo Clinic – opens. The first surgery – for a malignant lesion of the eye – is performed by all three of the Mayo doctors – the father and two sons.

1894:
> Korea and Japan declare war on China and defeat the Chinese at Port Arthur.
>
> Czar Alexander III dies and is succeeded by son Nicholas II.
>
> Rudyard Kipling publishes *The Jungle Book*.

Bernard Shaw publishes *Arms and the Man*.

Claude Debussy's "Afternoon of a Fawn" is performed.

Louis Lumiere invents the cinematograph.

20-year-old Roy Allis walks from Oronoco to high school in Rochester every day. School lasts six hours – 9 to 12 and 1 to 4. Classes start with "morning exercises." Courses include English, social studies, geometry, algebra, foreign languages. Latin is the most common language course. There are few extra-curricular activities – no sports, no wrestling team. Roy is active in sports outside of school. No organized drama. Traveling acting troupes come to town and ask for extras. Roy joins ("I was the only local talent").

JUNE 15, 1894:

Roy Allis and Anna Barnard graduate from Rochester High School (Anna with honors) – a graduating class of eight – four girls and four boys.

Rochester Post Bulletin newspaper article:

> **"Another Graduating Class Enters the Running Tide of Life's Stream.**
>
> "Another class of eight young people was graduated with all due honors last evening from the high school. . . . 'The Old Man Eloquent,' an oration by Roy W. Allis, was one of the most pleasing of the evening. Much of the history of Gladstone, with his private traits of character and mental strength, was set forth in a masterful style. Mr. Allis has the power of personal magnetism so essential to a public speaker – unusually well developed for one so young – and will make a record for himself should he enter some profession where he can use his powers to advantage.
>
> "The last of the graduates to take a part in the program was Miss Anna Barnard, and she entertained the audience with the class prophecy, taking as her date of prophesying the year of 1919. The different members of the class were shown honoring the various professions to which the prophetess assigned them.
>
> "The annual alumni meeting and banquet was held at the Cook House. The first toast very fittingly was the 'Class of 1894' and was responded to by Roy Allis, who drew inspiration for his remarks from a large cabbage head, which he described as representing the composite head of the class."

Very little college is needed for occupations. Students interested in medicine or law "read" with a doctor or an attorney as sort of an apprentice. After a year or two, they take state exams, and if they pass, they become professionals. Teachers usually take at least one year of college, but it's not required. After school, most young people get married and go into business farming.

Picnickers at the Allis resort Camp Comfort, Oronoco, Minnesota;
June 23, 1894

CHAPTER 2

A Civilized Being

(To the reader: For reasons we'll never know, Anna's letters to Roy for the first few months are missing. Be patient … they commence soon.)

JULY 18, 1894
(To) Miss Anna L. Barnard in Eyota, Minnesota
(From) The Point, Under-our-birch, Oronoco, Minnesota
Sweetheart:

Excuse me for my long delay in writing. I confess that 62 hours have rolled over my head since I saw you, but I know you will pardon me when you think of my deeply ingrained tendency to put off very disagreeable things to the last minute, in the vain hope that my time may come to my rescue.

Mother was very sorry that she didn't see you to say good-bye. It was her birthday, you know, and we went over on Trout Brook on a picnic. We didn't think you would be there before we started, but we found *Three Men in a Boat* and knew you had been there.

I think I saw you and the girls as I went down to the barn for the horses. We had a pleasant, quiet day. Fred and Volney *(Roy's older brother and brother-in-law)* and Mr. Reifsnider fished and I read some to the folks out of *The Witch's Head*. It's a nice place in Trout Brook – a little clear stream of the coldest spring water running down through hills and rush and woods. Sometime when I have you again we'll go over there. One place where a great elm bends clear over the brook and makes a pretty little woodsy glen, Mother said, "Anna ought to be here to see that."

Yesterday I got up early and went up on the farm to help Joe Heins stack. It was barley, and I pitched in the field. New work, it was, and I was a wee bit tired when night came. But it was not old woman's work. My! How a fellow eats when he works hard. For supper it doesn't seem that he is hungry so much as that he wants fuel for his furnace. But those Germans were stacking right near the house and didn't get a jug of fresh water all afternoon. They sent the jug out in the field twice to me. The last time it was like dishwater. Some people don't know how to enjoy themselves though – how a drink of fresh water or lemonade when a fellow's mouth and lips are dry and hot is worth half a life-time.

If I were a farmer I would try and have such things a little more comfortable and do the same work easier and quicker. There – what do you care for all this?

I took a big sleep last night and have been doing not much of anything all day. Did you see in the paper that Nellie *(Nellie Ottman – a fellow graduate – she's in the graduation photo)* was quite sick with typhoid fever? I'm sorry for Nellie – that the fever would take hold of her in this hot weather – she is so strong and excitable and restless.

A night or two ago there came a letter from Miss Peck *(one of Anna and Roy's high-school teachers and a beloved advisor – she's also in the graduation photo)* and one from Mark, wanting to see me about school. He is going to Northwestern and would like me to go with him. Miss Peck heard from Walter that I was likely to go to Hamline, and she wrote me a good little letter – one that showed she thought a fellow might amount to something – and she asked me what the summer had brought me, and I told her *Anna – you* are the best thing it has brought me.

Well, I must go. Write. I'm not blue, but I wish you were where I could reach out and touch your soft hair.

Good-bye,

Roy

You won't care if my letters are queer and rambling? I'll probably improve after a bit.

The Allis mill and homestead in Oronoco.

AUGUST 9, 1894
Oronoco to Eyota

My Dear Anna:

I'm very sorry I can't be with your folks tomorrow. Fred is going to Rochester in the afternoon for a band and orchestra practice, and I'll have to be miller. Almost any time I can get away, though, I am coming to see you *sure* this vacation.

You won't be disappointed, I hope – no, I take that back – perhaps with your sick people, such an inroad of barbarian Goths all at once would trouble you. I'll see you soon anyway.

Roy

I received both your letters. Never mind the number – the more the better.

Fred Allis (Roy's brother)

AUGUST 10, 1894
Oronoco to Eyota

Dear sweetheart:

Here I am again up on the Point, leaning on your seat and thinking of you, with the wind in my face and a storm coming up in the west.

I have been at work all the week, pitching bundles for the man I told you of. Thursday evening I got your letter. It was cold, you remember, and when I came home along in the evening they had a fire in the fireplace and Mary *(Roy's younger sister)* was lying in front of it. Down I dropped by the fire and Mary said low to me, "There's a letter for you. I put it on top of those books." "Where from?" I said. "Eyota." Then I went up to my room and read it. I wanted to be by my lone self, you know, and – oh, my dearie – it did me a great deal of good, that letter of yours. The next day we stacked up with three teams and I pitched 16 loads in a short forenoon – how's that? I read that letter three times that day, for I get *so* hungry for you.

I think I won't work on the farm much more this summer, though I'm glad of the taste of fierce, hard work. The trouble with me is that I go at it too savage. Pa says I try to do a day's work in an hour-and-a-half. This is foolish, of course. I wouldn't like farming all the time. The boy who loaded – about 16 or 17 – would say, "H-O-W?" to everything you said to him before he answered. I don't give this as anything against farming in general, only it was rather monotonous.

I got a nice letter from Miss Peck last night. It's strange how people read in us things we didn't notice, isn't it?

After that rain the other afternoon when I was coming home with the men, we were out on the hills to the east of town, and the sun shone down through a break in the clouds on the blue hills to the west, all covered with mist. I wish you could have seen it.

Mary Allis
(Minimo – Roy's little sister)

I don't know but someway, Anna, everything I see that seems beautiful to me I connect with you now.

I haven't been over in our woods or round on the Point where we read together, for I haven't had time until today, and it is cloudy and dull – I'll save it for another time. This forenoon Louie and I went up toward the rocks and went swimming – it was awful cold. Then we went after chokecherries and "fiercely fed." The dry weather has made the leaves drop off some of the trees, and the wind blows, and things smell and look more like October than the first of August.

I wish we could be together – what comrades we would make! But never mind – there's a good time coming – yes, Anna – I'm sure it will all come out right if we keep on loving each other as we do now. But I must stop, or you will think I'm getting sentimental after all.

Been reading *Witch's Head*. Mr. Hatfield took me to due about reading light literature. Now I like a little taste of it – Haggard just for spice, you know. Hatfield says when he wants imagination he reads *Arabian Nights* or *Grimm's Fairy Tales*. He said you ask the best educators about what to read. I think Hatfield is a trifle conceited – everyone can't have the same kind of spice. What if I do like reading about a good, free fight? If a fellow hasn't enough individuality to keep his thinking powers as he says from being vitiated, I don't think they're worth the saving. Lots of people won't read a thing, even if they like it, until some educator says it's good. This would seem a baby way to me.

Anna, I hadn't ought to trouble you with my crude notions, but you see I write just as I would talk if you were here – just as things come into my stupid head. I'm glad you like my queer letters. They're like no one else's letters at any rate, I guess.

Write to me – a long letter – anything, just so it's from you. This writing is cold comfort, but it's much better than nothing. I love you so much.

AUGUST 12, 1894
Oronoco to Eyota

My Dear Anna:

When I went over on the Point a while ago, there were people over there, sitting a little way from our birch. So I came over to camp here to see you – right where your hammock hung that last night, and the block that you used to fasten it up with ties here by the tree as you left it.

I went to Rochester yesterday afternoon; got my long locks cut and saw Mark and Sisson and Mrs. Titus *(Anna's aunt)* and Mary *(Anna's cousin)*. Mark is going to Northwestern University and Sisson with him, I guess. I wish I could go with them. Mark thinks he can get along there for $300 a year. Mary said she had written you about her plan. I hope we can make it work. I got my class picture and diploma – I'm glad I have that picture. It seems good to see the old faces, and especially the one of my Puritan maiden.

When do you think you will go east?

I read Miss Kinsley's letter – such things are beyond me, I guess. When I reach out and try to think on them, I get beyond my depth – it gets misty and vague. Still I *do* think some on such things, and I try to pray after a fashion, and I believe in you and everything good, I think. Somehow I think with a fellow like me his love and religion are twisted together. Perhaps this is shocking. I wish I were a finer fellow for your sake – physically and every way. I hope I can get to be worthy of you or somewhere near.

The old pond is filling up slowly, and the mud points are ghastly no longer. What is left uncovered by the water is clothed with a bright green growth. They have been catching a fine lot of pickerel the last three days.

I finally wrote to Bowers *(one of their high-school classmates – also in the graduation photo)*. He wrote me inquiring "why in Sam Hill he couldn't establish communications with Oronoco" and rebuking me for my neglect in heartrending words. He wanted to be cheered, he said, by my doctrine of taking life seriously.

So the letter I wrote was spread-eagle in the highest degree. Perhaps it will tickle him, as my nonsense used to when I got on a tear and went to spouting.

I must read Tennyson's *Maud.* I went over in "our woods" the other evening and lay flat on my back – as near where we were as I could, and thought of you, of course. We did more than "speak to each other in passing," didn't we?

I must be going. Hope I'll see you soon. Write.

With the best love I have,

Roy

AUGUST 19, 1894
Oronoco to Eyota

My Dear Anna:

I'm so hungry to see you. Are you going to drive to Rochester as you first planned, or shall I come down to the train? Write and tell me what day you want me, and I shall bide triste.

You see I'm writing in the house like a civilized being. The folks have all gone to church, leaving me and the dog to our own sad thoughts. Did you ever notice that it's lonesomer alone in a house than it is out-of-doors? I have been a little bit sober today myself – doing not much of anything but read a bit and eat peaches and green apples. Perhaps the latter are the cause of said soberness, foreboding evil to come.

Roy's parents, Abraham and Maria, at the family home in Oronoco

I've been working in the mill every day – we've had considerable grinding, but are fixed now so we can handle it.

My eyes have been troubling me a bit for a couple of weeks, ever since I was at work on the farm – that hot weather, when I think my Scottish blood must have got me overheated. I want my eyes to be all right before I go to school.

I'm glad my queer letters have such a soothing effect on your vindictive temper. I have such "spells" too.

Anna, I won't write any more now. I'll see you soon, and then it will be so long when we can do nothing but write.

With my best love,

SEPTEMBER 7, 1894
Oronoco to Eyota

My Dear Anna:

The mood for writing is on so I have come back in the woods to be alone with you.

You have heard from Miss Peck by this time, I presume. I was in Rochester Wednesday – on the rack in the dentist's chair for a couple of hours (you see the folks are preparing me for tough beef), and then went and saw Miss Peck. We had a good talk about school and other matters. She favors my going to Hamline this year, and I don't know but what I shall do it. We are going up early this week, Pa and I, to look the ground over.

You see, Anna – I have lots of rough corners, and Miss Peck thinks for this year I would get the most at Hamline. She said the diamond was there, but it wasn't a polished mind; she thought I would get the most good socially at Hamline, and then I could change next year, if I wished. She said I needed to be centered – like Miss Peck, isn't it? You know how she used to labor with me sometimes, and seemed able to do nothing with me, and I'd get up and say, "Miss Peck, I believe there's *some* good in me *some*where," and that's all she could get out of me. But *you* came and got hold of me, and I think that was the only thing that could reach me – at least it's the strongest.

I hope you won't think I'm egotistical, talking so much about myself. I don't do it to everyone.

Miss Peck's brother Walter is going to Hamline and she would like to have us fellows together – she thinks we would help each other.

Charlie *(Roy's best friend and his sister Blanche's brother-in law)* and I went hunting yesterday – tramped all afternoon and got two prairie chickens. He wanted to "stomp around a little" with me before I went, he said. I can't tell which it will be – Hamline or the U. Even if I do go to Hamline this year, it needn't interfere with our "plan vague" for next, need it?

I rowed up to the rocks this morning. I wanted to see them before I went, and watched them out of sight as you did that day. I remember how you looked – that beautiful way-off look. You didn't imagine how a boy was watching you and thinking, did you?

You will be a great help to me this year, dear little girl. Do you remember the 30th of May under the birch – how I said it seemed that there was so little to work for? It's changed. I wish you were here for a minute. It's hard to tell what you feel in cold writing. When you get your pictures, I must have one. That "miserable" letter of yours I have carried with me ever since I got it – it wasn't miserable at all, and if it *had* been, the ending would have redeemed it. I consider those good endings as "promises to pay," due at the earliest opportunity – and you'll find me a relentless creditor.

I'll write you as soon as I find out where and what. Good-bye, and I love you so much.

Roy

SEPTEMBER 8, 1894
Oronoco to Eyota

Dear Little Sweetheart:

I came over early to write. I feel as if we had buried a dear friend today, for we buried my brown dog Sport this morning. A low-down tough here in town shot him night before last without even speaking to us about it. I saw him yesterday and we had at it for a minute, but he didn't get half what he deserved. It's all right to fight for your friends, isn't it? And that dog was a friend better and truer than lots of folks.

I go to school the middle of this week. Perhaps I can hear from you again before I go, can't I? I'm beginning to feel sort of homesick even now, and your letters do me such good. That doesn't express what I mean, but you understand.

I pretty near got left by the train that morning when I left you. I had to get on by sheer strength and awkwardness. My, how the conductor sweared, and 'lowed that I'd get killed sometime. Say, Anna – it would be worth getting half-killed to stay with you a little longer!

We were in to a concert Friday evening and I saw Frank Zimmerman. He said if I ever was in Minneapolis to drop him a card when I was coming and he'd meet me at the train. Zimmerman is a University man, you know.

I've been at work in the mill this week most of the time. One day they threshed on the Hoyt farm, and Pa was in Winona, so I went to see about the grain, and tied the sacks, and felt very important, of course.

I presume you are getting ready to go. I should like to see you in that red dress. Perhaps it wouldn't be good for me though – my head might be *too* far turned, you know.

When I got back Aunt Minnie and Uncle thought my eyes looked better, and I said, "Anna took superb care of them," and she said, "Little Anna is a good one to have around, isn't she?" I agreed with her. Your mother said to me Monday morning, "We're going to *miss* that girl," and I said, "So will I," and she smiled. I *do* miss you, dearest – every day, so much. My life would seem so poor, now, without my love for you.

It's very dry up here on our Point, but the goldenrod is sprinkled around, and our birch keeps green through it all, just as our love will. There – you will think I'm getting poetical, but a fellow feels a little that way sometimes.

I must be going. Write to me.

SEPTEMBER 15, 1894
Minneapolis to Eyota

My Dear Anna:

We came up to visit, and I decided to try Hamline this year. Dr. Bridgeman said there would be nothing lost if I went to the State University next year. So when you write me, send it to Hamline. I'll be terribly homesick, I'm afraid, before "Yuletide." You go to New York next week, I heard. I hate to have you be so far away from me, but we'll keep near just the same. You must write me about everything – about your brother and old home.

We found Walter the same old chap. He makes a good streetcar conductor, of course. I shall board at the Ladies Hall. Walter wanted to board in a club, but I didn't want to – Miss Peck said not to board at a boys' club if I could possibly help it – that they got to be regular boors in their ways, and I must try to be a "gentle knight," you know, to be worthy of someone I know. I went around to the places that are dear to us and kinda said good-bye before I came.

Write to me, dearest little girl, as often as you can.

CHAPTER 3

A Hungry-Hearted Fellow

SEPTEMBER 23, 1894
1636 Wesley Ave., Hamline University, St. Paul, Minnesota;
to Truthville, New York

Sweetheart:

Well, I hope you are through your journey all right so far. Your letter came to me at noon, and I didn't have time to read or a place to read it until later, but it lighted me up and made a warm place under my coat just to know it was from you.

I found Walter on the streetcar and stayed with him until he stopped work, and then we came over to Hamline. We got registered the next day and took dinner at the Hall, where we board. We room up on the third floor of a house on the northwest corner. It's rather low – I can jump up and touch my head, for I did it the first night we came 'cause Bowers rather thought I couldn't. There are about 255 students enrolled here – 50-odd in the freshman class. Not much like the State U, is it? The boys all try to be friendly, but someway things seem bare and bleak, though I suppose that feeling will wear off. It's some like your feeling when you were first at Rochester and wished you were most dead.

Hamline isn't much of a place – it's bleak and level, and a fellow thinks these soft smoky days about a pond and a Point and woods and the fireplace in the cool evenings back home. Over at the Hall we sit about eight at a table – three or four are ladies. One of them that sits at the head waits on the meat and other fixings. I sit at the foot and pour the water, and haven't fallen down or broken anything yet. There's a young lady sits next me at table who is quite pleasant, but I've nothing to "fess."

While I was writing before supper Walter was lying down. We had been out walking to Como Park, and he said he would sleep while I wrote and to call him when it was supper time. Well, I had your picture before me as I wrote, and bimeby he woke up and said, "What time is it? You blamed scalawag – it's half-past five! Put up that picture and stop writing – we won't get any supper!" We got there in time, though.

Miss Peck wrote and spoke of her "lovely" visit with you. The little book and your picture reached me the 20th. I have read some in it and like it. I'll try to get some good out of it, if only for the "cum amore" and your own dear sake. The picture is good, but it doesn't look as "good as *she* does," as Walter said.

Dearest little girl – I think of you almost all the time. Even when I'm not really thinking of you, it seems as if you were in my thoughts. This sounds foolish, I know. Yes, Anna, I think our great love comes from some great good – it's the best, purest thing in my life.

When I was over at Mrs. Miner's I read some in Riley's *Afterwhiles.* There are one or two little poems in his sonnets that I like – warm little pieces that come right from the heart; that a fellow can feel.

Walter sends his regards and hopes you will have a pleasant visit. I've wondered how you will get along this week in your traveling, but I thought, "Ghaist nor bogle shall na get thee; thou'rt to Heaven and earth sae dear; nothing evil can come near my bonnie dearie" *(from Robert Burns' poem "Hark! The Mavis").*

I hope I shall like it here. You must write and send me a good ending – as often as you think proper, for I'm a hungry-hearted fellow, you know. You will forgive me if my letters are a little warm, remembering my Highland blood and how much I love you.

Roy

In school I'm taking Livy, Algebra and French, alternating with Zoology and Bible Study once a week. The work is not excessively heavy. Livy is easier than Vergil. I think I shall play football some – it's rough and barbarous, and, of course, I like it!

SEPTEMBER 26, 1894
Hamline to Truthville

My Dearest Anna:

It's warm and pleasant today – not like the day when I wrote last – so I came down here where there are some trees. I like to write to you best out in the open air. I've known you most out-of-doors, you know.

That was a good letter of yours that came last. I've very glad that you got there safely. It was intuition that led you to shake those bothersome people – I think you have it if anyone would.

I remember those days I was with you last so well, and our old hammock and the summerhouse. When you got near the familiar places where you grew up, I would have given my right hand to see you. I loved hearing about the mountains and valleys and woods all green. When you said you were so happy it made me restless – not your being happy, but it was bleak and dry and windy here, and the room rather bare, and I was trying to hammer out Livy, and I don't know – I wanted to see you *awful* bad. You won't mind my writing often, will you?

I'm so glad you like everything and are happy. I'm such a queer fellow with my "down" fits that it's good to hear of anyone like you.

I haven't read *The Greatest Thing in the World,* but will do it next, since you are.

We have rhetoricals two weeks from today and I have to have a declamation. Do you think I could speak something of James Whitcomb Riley's?

George Peck and Walter had a little bit of fun with me. The night your picture and little book came, the boys asked me how I was feeling, and I said, "Fair to middlin' – I'm getting a book and letter too." Peck said, "Likely from your father?" Walter said that wan't all – "his father wrote in a very fine, feminine hand," and now they ask me all sorts of things about my "father"!

I went out and played football yesterday. It's a deep game, and I didn't know much about it – only to buck the man in front of me. I got it two or three times in the head, and my nose was bleeding, and I had on Kaign's full outfit (he's the physical director and plays quarterback) and looked quite foot-bally. The fellows 'lowed I'd make "a good little football player after a year or so, if I practiced." I'm most too light for the business, but the fellow I bucked against said I pushed good, and he wishes he had my arm. He was trying to encourage me, I suppose.

I strained my side somewhere under my arm, lifting on the scales when I was home, and the bucking yesterday made it come again. I want to do such things, for I want to be a little something of a man.

Write, dear, and tell me everything about what you do and see. I have the daisies and the lock of your hair with me all the time. You're sure you'll be back next summer, aren't you? I couldn't stand it much longer than that.

Your rather lonesome boy,

Roy

Say, Anna – my letters must be stupid, aren't they? But, dearest, I think more of you and about you than I can write.

SEPTEMBER 29, 1894
Hamline to Truthville

Dearest:

It's about half-past three this Sunday afternoon – just about the time I used to go over on the Point to write and "bide tryste" with you. I wonder if the old birch misses me.

Your letter came last night and had its usual good effect. I had been over to the gymnasium, looking around a little, and up in the library after a book. Heath, a fellow here, came down in the gymnasium and said, "There's a letter for you, Allis, from your girl – it's from Rochester." Then I felt good and gay all the evening. I didn't read it right off though – I kept it like children do their candy. I like to know it's there and I can read it just when I want to.

I didn't hear from home until yesterday, and then came a letter from Mother and one from Aunt Minnie. The folks are all well. I guess they miss me a little, roaring and whistling around. Mother says it's lonesome.

Walter and I went over to Minneapolis yesterday to the U. Frank Zimmerman showed us around. I think I'd rather go there than Hamline. I think I would be happier there, but maybe I wouldn't. It's much pleasanter country over by the U – it's so level at Hamline, and so few trees and no water. I miss those things.

My new friend Douglas is a YMCA man – a good, gentle Christian fellow. He thinks the U is a dangerous place for young fellows right from the country. I would be all right though, dearest, with you so good and true and sweet to think of.

I have read *The Greatest Thing in the World* – it's good. Over in the library the other day I found another book of our "idle fellow" – *Diary of a Pilgrimage*. It's like *Three Men in a Boat*, but with two or three short essays that were very good. I have now *Tales of the Argonauts* by Bret Harte, telling of western life, you know.

It must be very pleasant for you to go around the old places where you grew up. I suppose the tears have come into my little girl's eyes sometimes. It must be a fine country there from your description. How you love beautiful things, don't you?

The last letter I wrote had rather a homesick tone, I guess. I'm glad you said it was a battle to be fought – this homesickness. I'll not get lonely any more than I can help.

Yes, Walter and I are in the same classes. Walter hasn't been working as hard as usual. He is troubled with insomnia – he can't sleep more than 10 or

12 hours a day (!). It don't seem as if I've mixed with people very much here yet, though I may more after a while.

I'm anxious to hear about your brother Frank. If he looks like you and *is* like you, he must be a pretty fine fellow. I wish I could go around with you over your own hills and woods – we two gypsy folk. I'm so glad things are as you expected.

If my time comes, I shall doubtless break my neck at football. But, honest, I'll be careful. I eat at one of the training tables, although I'm not a regular football man. Kaign is a hard trainer, and I can't have no pie, nor fried cakes, nor ketchup, nor tea or coffee. We can't eat warm bread or soft biscuits. I think Kaign would allow me to eat some of your cookies. That one that I put in my coat pocket to keep off bullets stayed there until Mother fixed the coat when I came up here.

Well, it's getting rather late, and I must write to Mother yet. How I love the touch of your soft, gentle hands. Do you remember that time when you put your hand on my head first, over on the old fallen tree in our woods when we were reading?

I'll try and not get downhearted and lonesome and be your good knight. Of course, a fellow will miss the home things, but they'll seem all the better at Yuletide.

I love you dearly, dearly.

Roy

OCTOBER 1, 1894
Hamline to Truthville

My Dearest Anna:

I feel good tonight. I've been over to Minneapolis and to Auntie Nettie's. Oh, it seemed good – almost like a taste of home. When I came in, you ought to have seen Walter. He hugged me like a bear and said, "I'm so overjoyed to see you, dear! Everybody has marked my blue and downcast condition." Then he salaamed and swore eternal friendship. I asked him what was the news, and he brought out your letter with a flourish, whereat I again joyfully shook hands with him and vowed I would do whatever he would have me do, except to saw wood. That was such a good letter!

Friday evening I spoke the old-time "Tam O'Shanter" at the Philomathean Literary Society. They seemed to like it.

I expected Pa this week, but something has detained him. I went to cousin Julius' – it's a nice cozy house with everything good, and plenty of books, for Julius is a lover of books – his wife was an author, you know. It seemed very pleasant to sit around by the open fire and read and talk with the boys. They don't consider me "company," of course. It was more like home than eating over at the hall and then creeping up to my room. I'm a great home fellow, ain't I?

I read a little book that Mark had been reading, written by Elizabeth Stuart Phelps – *Donald Marcy* – a nice little story about New England college life. Did you ever read it? That took up most of my time for reading, except a little of Riley. Uncle Grant came over this afternoon, and I read to him out of *Afterwhiles*. He's a good fellow, is Uncle Grant. Have you read *Afterwhiles*? I like it best of all.

I have been reading some out of *Ardis Claverden* by Frank R. Stockton. Wish you could have the use of a library. Welty and I went to change a book at the Minneapolis Public Library – that will be the place to get books next year if I go to the U. I found books in the catalogue that I've always wanted to read and never could find. We boys went to the Dime Museum after that – it was worth about a dime.

It's beautiful weather here now – cool, but with a gentle warmth in the air too – old Minnesota is trying to redeem herself. Welty and I went to the First Baptist Church and heard a splendid sermon by Hoyt. Welt is a good fellow, I think – we philosophize a little. He is quite a fellow for girls. Well, so am I, but I'm *desperately* centered.

Yes, of course you may *admire* your cousins. Say, Anna – those loves that children have are strong while they last, don't you think? You knew Lulu Holmes *(My grandmother! Another book …)*, didn't you? Well, when I was a little fellow I thought a lot of her. Children are queer folks, aren't they?

Miss Peck expects to come up here in two or three weeks. She'll brace me up some – I need it, for I'm a sad fellow some ways. I wish I *would* dig in more like Walter does.

Uncle Grant said that one night while he was home Mary went away to stay all night with her cousin, and for the first time in almost 40 years, the folks were alone – we children were all away. Uncle and Aunt Minnie went over about 9 o'clock, and my parents were sitting by the fire rather lonesome, I guess. Hey ho! I'll stir things up Christmas! Pa wrote me that he had the brand paved for kindling the Yule log. I'll carry mither on my shoulders in a triumphal procession. All the things and the old woods and pond seem dearer to me because of you, dearest.

I dream of you a lot – waking dreams, mostly. Dreams don't hurt a fellow, do they? I couldn't live without dreaming a little. You get dearer to me all the time, I think. You won't mind me telling you so often, will you? But I'm not half worthy of you, I'm afraid – such a queer fellow. I pray for you, dearest, and that I may get to be more worthy to have you love me. It's no harm to tell you this, I think. I'm a blind sort of fellow in religious things, but I believe in *you* with all my heart. Good-night.

Hello – it's the next morning, and I felt I wanted to speak to you, and tore my sealed letter open. You must take good care of yourself, and I'll be a good boy and study this week. I'm almost ashamed to send this first part – it's written so poorly and with such little care as to literary style. Well, I must carry out my good intentions and get to work.

We're getting to be heavyweight, aren't we? I weighed 162 lbs. with my overcoat on Saturday.

OCTOBER 7, 1894
Hamline to Truthville

My Dear Anna:

We've been bad today – didn't go to church, and I've studied a little. I've raised considerable Cain too – ate up the lemons and sugar and sung and orated to my pard – or rather "my wife" as everybody calls his pard here. Wife sawed the wood day before yesterday, and I carried it up; and I sawed it yesterday and wife carries it up today. We quarrel too, Bowers and I, and when "they's company" tell the darkest stories of each other.

We're getting along fairly well, I guess. I study with my usual patience and determination. I may not be good for spurts, but for steady, persistent work, day in and day out – *that* is where I am strong. Bowers says to tell you that he uses all his influence to try and distract his pard from his arduous toil, but it is all in vain. Bowers says he wishes we had a kitten. We'd put it in the trunk when we went to school. Our room is as bare as a barn, and we get everything scattered around every which way. We think a great deal of your picture – that's the only ornament, if it may be called such, in our room, and I bring it out on state occasions (by state occasions I don't mean company, but when I feel like it). I wonder where we can put it when we get that kitten.

I'm glad you have found your brother and his wife. Of course he's a fine fellow – I presume he's a little like you, with his voice soft and low. Your voice is like Annie Laurie's, you know. Was weighed the other day and I'm 155 pounds. I must get 160 by Christmas time. Won't it seem good to get home for two weeks! I'll write to you from the Point then, if the snow is three feet deep.

There's no one writes such good letters to me as you, dearest. There's no one like you. I compare everyone with you. There is a Miss Benham here that reminds me of you – just a little. She has long dark hair a little bit like yours.

It's been a very dark, cold day with a drizzling rain. The weather has a good deal to do with the way we feel, don't you think? I'm not homesick very much – I think, dearest, you *do* drive it away a good deal. I get hold of so few people that I cling hard to those that I do.

How long will your brother stay in Truthville? Glad he's a tramp. Do you think he would like me?

I like Martin – he's a queer little chap. I think he likes me a little too, and he said when I stopped to see him that he hadn't felt so well in spirit all summer. I might possibly be a little good to somebody, don't you think?

I'll try not to write when I ought to be studying, but, you know – I'm quite a hand to do as I please when you are concerned. Do you remember the time when I ran away from work and went over across the pond in the hammock with you? I've read *Diary of a Pilgrimage*, *Tales of the Argonauts*, and now have *Alton Locke* by Charles Kingsley.

I'll be careful and not get killed in any way. I don't want to die yet. My eyes trouble me some, but I think they will get over it all right. They are not bad at all. They just feel as if there weren't enough tears to moisten them after I have read or studied for some time.

I think of you too so much, dearie. I watched you standing by the gate, all white, as long as I could see, that day I left you. Doesn't it seem longer than five or six weeks to you?

Good night – I'm reaching out for your hands now.

Roy

OCTOBER 16, 1894
Hamline to Truthville

Dearest:

Saturday Walter and I took a long walk. The weather isn't warm here, but it's fresh and clear, and the woods are all red from the oak leaves. Some of the leaves have fallen, but I haven't yet noticed that scent you get when you walk through dead leaves on a still dewy morning in the fall.

Saturday afternoon five or six Hamline fellows and I went to see a football game between the State U and Grinnell College over at Minnehaha Driving Park. We had a great time getting there. We were a little late, and down in Minneapolis the streetcars were full to overflowing – people hanging on everywhere. It was a very exciting game – big fellows on both sides. A football game is a great place for yelling. I went down and saw them close – wild-looking chaps – dusty and sweaty, with great shock heads of hair that they keep brushing back. My hair would be all right for football. I wet it the other night and the next morning you ought to have seen it – it had risen in rebellion! I believe no tyranny could ever keep that down. This football is rather rough, but it's something like fighting, and I suppose that is one reason people like it. I wish I didn't admire physical strength quite so much.

By the way, I found a fellow up here who's loves *Lorna Doone* almost as much as I.

I met Uncle Grant at the Windsor in Minneapolis Sunday. It seemed good to see some of the home folks. We walked around and "did" Central Park and looked over the city a little. Parks are well enough, but I like natural places better, don't you?

We went up to the top of the Northwestern Guaranty Loan Building *(later known as The Metropolitan – arguably the most significant, beautiful Victorian building in Minneapolis)*. We could see over the city all around to the hills all red with the oaks. I like high places. We'll see Mt. Everest someday. I mean to go up there with you some time (Guaranty Loan, not Everest!).

In the afternoon, Uncle and I went to the matinee at the Bijou Theatre. The piece was "The Ship of States" – full of patriotism and love and fighting. It was very good, I thought. After supper we went over to see Julius. He has a very nice little girl – about 2 years old – named Viola. She got acquainted with me the couple of days I was over there, and she remembered me, I guess. We had a great play. She likes to have me hook and bellow, and she pulls and pounds at my hard head. We're great friends.

I'm very glad you like everything so well, but I do desperately hope you won't give up on Minnesota.

Fred went up to Hutchinson on his wheels *(bicycle)* to visit Blanche and Volney *(Roy's older sister and her husband – just married the spring before)* and will stop and see me on his way back. Pa is coming up through this country too this week. A fellow's father thinks more of him than he gives him credit for. I'm getting so I don't feel so lonesome. I would like to get home for Thanksgiving, of course, but think I'll stand it until Christmas.

Something happened the other day that I was sorry for. When I was writing to you Sunday, a page of what I had written didn't suit me, and I crushed it up and threw it down by the stove. When Walter went to build the fire, he unfolded and read part of it without thinking. It was nothing but a sentence – a little bit tender, you know – that wasn't meant for him or anyone else but you.

He told me I ought to be more careful. I didn't know whether to be angry or laugh or what. It seemed a little like sacrilege. It wasn't his fault though. I got very red. It was nothing, I suppose, but still it vexed me. Walter doesn't bother me usually, but once in a while he smiles all over his face, and I have a strong inclination to *kill* him. Anna, you don't care very much, do you? I suppose I make more of this than there is need of – but you know how near some things are to me – sacred, you know.

I told Walter to notify you if I collapsed from studying (!), and he said he would telegraph you immediately.

I wish we had the six-toed kitten you wrote about. Write me as soon as you can. I love you so much. Forgive this scatter-brained letter – it was written in a hurry.

It's a beautiful night still, and warm with soft, bright moonlight. I've just been out walking. I don't believe your eastern evenings can beat this. It would be worth six months of ordinary life to walk with you tonight.

OCTOBER 28, 1894
Hamline to Truthville

My Dear Anna:

I have just been to church and feel somewhat depressed as a result. We have been having beautiful weather here – cool nights and summer days – but yesterday it changed and it is cloudy and rainy today.

We had a welcome visitor at Hamline yesterday – Miss Peck. We were *very* glad to see her. She took me for a little walk and told the boys to give me a "scolding." She asked about you – how you were, and if you wrote me helpful letters. I told her yes, of course. Pa was up Thursday on his way to visit his sister at Osakis. When I came out from dinner, there he stood.

Miss Peck was so sorry that I was disappointed here – or rather, restless and unsatisfied – because the other fellows were carried away by Northwestern. I have no enthusiasm for anything here, someway, but probably it would be much the same anywhere else. I wonder if I shall always be that way – restless and careless and unhappy by spells. No, I don't believe it – I think you will be a great help to me in that way.

I heard Tom Reed in Minneapolis last week. There was a great crowd in the Exposition Building where he spoke. He's a fine speaker – mayhap I'll vote for him for President next bout.

Friday afternoon I walked over to Macalester and saw Alexander Salvini in *Don Caesar de Bazan* in the evening. It was the best thing I've ever seen. It wasn't just acting – it was real. Oh, but Don Caesar was one after my own heart – a brave vagabond, Spanish gentleman – but true as steel at the bottom! I think I'm fitted by nature for a sort of vagabond fellow, don't you? I get terribly tired of talking about good things and duty and the powers a fellow has that he ought to use. I get tired of myself worst of all, though. But I ought to be all right with my health and no real trouble – and you, above all. Miss Peck says I must settle the *one* great question. I don't know how to do that, though. Sometimes I think there isn't any depth to me – that I'm all sham. That isn't so, though, is it?

Write to me, dearest – you're so good and steady and true.

I went down to the State University yesterday afternoon to hear Mott – one of the leading YMCA men in the world. I stayed to tea with Zimmerman and met a lot of State U men. Next year I think I shall be there.

Did you know, Anna, about Frank Jones being so dangerously ill? He has quick consumption *(a widely used term at the time for a disease of gradual wasting away – primarily from pulmonary tuberculosis)*. Miss Peck asked if I had heard about Clara Titus *(another of Anna's cousins)* dropping out of school, and then she said they expected our old friend Jones wouldn't live a month – he has gone home to his mother. This is terrible. I hope it isn't so bad as that. We don't know how to value our health and strength, do we?

Your letter will reach me this noon, I expect. I look forward to that all week. I'm sorry I wrote such a "blue" sort of letter yesterday, but I'll send it along just the same. You must take good care of yourself. I get very hungry for a sight of you.

Roy

I presume I should like that new hat on you. You used to have a broad-rimmed black hat, didn't you? When we went after hepaticas that day last spring, you put it on for me over there on St. Mary's Hill, and you said I looked like a Spaniard – do you remember? Well, I liked you in that hat too. Faith, I don't know what I *don't* like you in.

NOVEMBER 9, 1894
Hamline to Truthville

My Dearest Anna:

I'm still warm from your letter that came tonight. I'm going to just lay myself out and write you a long letter, telling about everything.

Well, you asked what we do at our Literary Society. I haven't been but three times, but they usually have music – vocal and instrumental, recitations, impromptus, and at last they dissolve themselves into a congress – each member being a congressman from some state – and introduce and pass bills, thus getting drill in parliamentary practice. I'm the "gentleman from Arkansas."

I'll tell you about school. There are three buildings – Ladies Hall, Science Hall, and the main University building. My first class is Livy, so you can imagine me going from my room – about 40 rods or two blocks from school – at 8:20. Then I go home and study Algebra until 11:10, and sometimes go to chapel for 20 minutes between Livy and Algebra. After dinner at 1:45 we have Zoology the first three days in the week. Some days we have lectures or work in the laboratory with microscopes and specimens. We have little books in which to make drawings of specimens we examine. I wish I knew a little something of drawing. Thursday and Fridays we have French in place of Zoology. Monday mornings we have Bible study instead of Livy, and Wednesday afternoons we have one period for Zoology, and one for Rhetoricals. I have spoken once in Rhetoricals and have two due. You see – I confess everything to you. Now you can imagine something of the way my time is divided.

After Zoology I have no more recitations and usually don't go to studying right off – often not until evening. I read in this time some and walk. Every day – usually at this time in the afternoon – I take a look at a certain picture and a talisman that I always carry in my old gray coat. I keep that little lock of your soft hair in the same old envelope that you gave me that night in the hammock over at the camp. Dearest, I love you *so* much.

"But to our tale." I look about the same as usual. I'm a bit heavier – 161 lbs. without an overcoat – and wear the same overcoat you know me in, and a brown hat at about the usual angle, I suppose. When Miss Peck was here she wanted me to get my long hair cut, saying she liked it well enough, but it gave me a wild appearance. So straightaway, like Samson, I was shorn of my long locks for a woman. Now do you have an idea "of the way I am" and what I'm doing?

Mother wrote me this week. Every one of us is away, and Mother said the house seemed so strange and still. But the term is half gone, and then we have two weeks' vacation. Oh, it will be good. Mother said when I wrote you to send her love and tell you she hoped you were having a good time. Anna, I ought to be a good fellow, with a mother like mine and a sweetheart like you.

We freshmen folk had a Halloween party, and a good time it was. Walter helped me on with his cuffs and white tie and white shirt and everything, and told me I must pull the cuffs down so "they'd show." I shook hands with everybody, being on the reception committee. They had some music and speaking and the usual Halloween games, and then we went around to the houses of the faculty and to the hall and yelled and sang. There are more boys than girls in the class, but I walked with a Miss Ida Wenger. She's a queer one – full of fun and not very much afraid. She is quite small, and so was elected class giant. Our class yell is: "Rah! Rah! Rah! Rah! We're a wake! Rack-a-fracka booma-lacka – 98!"

I went with a fellow Heath this afternoon and got his gloves. Heath is an athlete – very strong and active – about 5 feet 10" and weighing 175 pounds. His arms measure about the same as mine, but there's such a difference between trained muscle like his and mine. He can box too, and I don't know anything about it, but it's good to work against such a fellow that you know could do you right up. But I don't like him very much – he's very conceited about his strength. When he speaks in prayer meetings, it seems to me that what he says is all put on. He will get on in the world for his brass and good head, but won't be very popular, I believe. I don't believe women would like him – or *ladies*, anyway. I'd rather have less brass and have people like me, even if I didn't get on quite so fast at first.

I'm reading *Felix Holt* – partly because you were reading it, and I want to kinda keep *with* you – and partly to see if Felix Holt was like me, or I was like Felix Holt. I wanted to find out what I was like – "to see myself as ithers see me." I like the book, what little I've read. It seems very good to know that you think of me when you read and think.

I'm glad you spoke to me about going to the theater Sunday. Of course, I won't go there again when you ask me not to. I told you once that you could do more with me than anyone else. I wish I might get up to your high ideal for me. You do me a great deal of good, little girl. I was blue when I wrote before, and ashamed when I got your good, healthy letter.

I'm glad you like your painting. You're an artist by nature, I should think – three times as fine-grained as most people. It would be very pleasant to lie around close to you when you were sketching, and read and talk and watch you.

It seems to me that all my sentences begin with *I* – you must be getting tired of it.

Doesn't it seem strange to be out of high school? How long it seems to think back to our class meeting and picnics and commencement and all, doesn't it? That was a pleasant term. I remember thinking – well, you can see her every day this term anyway, and then she will go east and out of your life. You were very dear to me then, though I didn't realize how dear. And I remember one morning down in the old laboratory when the teacher had shut the blinds – you were standing near me, and I reached out and touched your braided hair. We had been talking, I remember, of Photogen and Nycteris, I think – one of whom was brought up in the light alone, and the other in the dark.

Yes, things do look bright for us. Anna, you must be *careful* of yourself. I don't like to have your hand tremble. You *will*, won't you, for my sake? Good-night, sweetheart, and I'm going to return that last kiss and the one before, first on the forehead and then on the lips. Did you feel them?

Good night.

Roy

I wish I wasn't such a scribbler.

NOVEMBER 11, 1894
Hamline to Truthville

My Dearest Anna:

I went to Minneapolis last night. I dressed up – white tie and everything – because I thought of going to church. By the time I got over to the Hall I was late to supper, and had to stalk clear up to our table in all the imposing panoply of "store clothes." I saw the folks at our table *look*, and it amused and bothered me a trifle. When I sat down, I said they mustn't laugh at my store clothes. That struck them as immensely funny. I heard them say over at other tables, "Hear them laugh at poor Allis." You see my "rough corners" are not seriously abraded yet.

It's been cold here this week – blew hard and snowed quite a little, and is snowing now. I'm sorry that your uncle isn't as well – I think it's partly because of you that he became so much better. If I was sick unto death, I think the sight of you would rouse me for another stand if anything would.

My cousin Julius told me the "latchstring was always out for me." He has a nice library. The books have been carefully selected, and he told me I was welcome to use any of them, and I brought *Over the Teacups* back with me.

Yes, you and I were standing over near the west window that day. How well I remember when we looked down that little green nook in the woods together. I think we were very close together, and were thinking and feeling the same things. It's good to have someone feel the same as you do, isn't it? Bah! I don't like to be with people that you *have* to talk to, and talk silly, too.

I don't see Felix Holt resembles me much, except in having a shock head, big voice, and being rather untidy in dress. I like some things about the fellow – he's big and rugged and strong every way. Do you remember what George Eliot says in the book – that boys who can't do their sums have longings after the infinite? I thought maybe that applied to me sometimes when I don't do my work as I ought to do. Dr. Bridgeman called on us the other night and said he had been looking up our marks, and they were very good, as he expected. You can't tell altogether by marks, though.

It would be *splendid* if we could be together. Perhaps we wouldn't study quite as well, though I don't think I could study much *less*. Perhaps I would do all the better. You know, I never was cut out for a schollard. I don't know what I shall do. Pa thinks of having me read law. Wouldn't I make a fine bloodsucker, though! Well, I'm sure something for the best will come – best for both of us.

I have ups and downs as usual, and sometimes I hate it here, but that is foolish. But I believe in you, dearest, and think I'll be all right sometime. This is a stupid letter without anything much in it, but I can't write tonight someway.

It did trouble me a little to have your hand tremble. I didn't know but you had overdone. You *must* be careful, for you are very, *very* dear to someone else. I'm very well, as usual, though my eyes trouble me a little sometimes – nothing to speak of. I wish I could see you just for a minute.

With my love,

Roy

You will pardon this stupid letter and the way it's written, for I haven't time to write another tonight. It has stopped snowing and is a good deal warmer. It's very lovely in you, dearest, to try and help me, and you *do* help me too. You mustn't think I'm quite as bad as I picture myself about studying.

You don't know what time you will come home next summer, I suppose?

CHAPTER 4

Your Highland Barbarian

NOVEMBER 18, 1894
Hamline to Truthville

My Dearest Anna:

Our spring vacation is from March 15 to March 25. When I read that you thought you would be home by that time, I dropped my letter and shouted! A friend was looking over the letters where the mailman drops them, and he handed me yours and said, "It's from *her*, isn't it?"

I didn't feel like going to church this forenoon, and intended to go and hear Clemens, the chaplain of the second regiment of militia. But Heath came up and stuck around, got out my overcoat and put on my hat, and kept it up until at last I went. I wanted to be with you – you are better than all the sermons that ever were preached.

Oh – I am now an associate member of the Epworth League. I was told that to be an associate member, all that was necessary was to want to be better. I 'lowed I wanted to be better, surely, and that was that.

Douglas and I went for a walk yesterday to Shadow Falls. A little stream runs over a ledge of rocks down into a deep rocky little glen with steep banks. There was only a little water running – mostly frozen into long icicles and columns. It's a very pretty little place, and about 15 rods farther on is the Mississippi. We climbed up a steep point and gathered some cedar branches; put a sprig of green cedar in our caps, like Marion's troopers; cut a shillala apiece, and came home cross-lot through the woods with a splendid appetite.

I am very well – weighed 161 lbs. before dinner without an overcoat. I must take to walking or get some dumbbells or something so I'll get to be "sleek" as Felix Holt says. I've finished the book – I liked it very much. I'm glad you think I'm like Felix Holt – even a little bit. I think I see now how you imagine I am like him, but I'm afraid you are idealizing me, dearest.

Walter and I both received a letter from Homer. He informed me that "Anna had gone to Maine," at which I pretended to be truly surprised. I have often thought of Miss Barnard since commencement and have even gone so far as to contemplate *writing* her (!). As I remember her, faintly, she seemed a very estimable young woman.

We'll have to have another class picnic next summer, and we ought to commemorate Memorial Day in some way. I think it is terrible about Jones. When Miss Peak told us about his sickness, I blurted out something about it's being a pity my being so well and strong and other better folks being sick and dying, but Miss Peck stopped me. You see, I didn't think for the moment, dearest. Life is very much with the living now.

I have read some in *Over the Teacups* – it's good and I like it pretty well. I think it was Dr. Holmes' last book.

Walter has a job as assistant engineer to help run the boilers and pumps over at the college. He will be away evenings and every other Sunday. He wants me to come over there in the engine room evenings and study, and so economize fuel. It's a dizzy sort of a place and I have "my doots aboot it."

Say, I think I have found some sign of a Scottish ancestry. Laurasm – a Canadian preacher here at school – told me he knew several Scottish families in Ontario by the name of Allis.

We had to have essays for Rhetoricals last Wednesday. I was behind two or three weeks, and Walter besought and entreated me, saying that if I didn't write, I was bringing disgrace upon *him*, on Rochester High School, Oronoco, Olmsted County, the class of '94, my father, and Miss Peck. My hard heart was melted. I yielded and wrote a description of the old boat at home. It made them laugh a little, and my professor didn't find any fault – though perhaps that was because of the toothache that was occupying his attention at the time.

I'm afraid this letter bears the impress of the heavy gloom that presses upon my mind. I was very sorry to hear you were sick with a cold. You must be careful of yourself. I'm glad you like *Afterwhiles*. And you think you will be home in March – aoi!

I'm afraid this letter covers a good deal without telling much, but it isn't blue, at least. Do you remember when you decided that you were not going away from Oronoco so soon, and we went over in our woods that day – you asked me why I looked so pleased? I feel about the same as then. I won't bother you anymore with this letter.

Roy

NOVEMBER 26, 1894
Hamline to Truthville

Sweetheart:

When I get your letter, I keep it for a while before I read it – until I get in the best mood for it. Then I think I won't read it all at once – but I always do, in spite of me. I think I had better write Sundays regularly, because I know how disappointed I am when your letter doesn't come, and perhaps you feel the same.

It's bad to say it, but I enjoyed that scolding ever so much. I wish you would scold me some more, dearest. It's a great thing to have you think of me as you do, sweetheart, even when I feel that I'm not worthy of it. Three months and a half and I'll see you again.

I'm very sorry that you have been sick – you must be careful about colds. I have quite a bad one now too, but I can stand considerable colds.

Yesterday afternoon I went for a walk westward clear to the Mississippi, and found a little brook running down through the woods and over the steep banks to the river in little cascades. It must be a very pretty place in summer. Some of the trees were birches – I *like* birches. Saturday evening a few of us saw *Land of the Midnight Sun* at the Bijou. It was pretty good, but nowhere near as good as Salvini in *Don Caesar.*

I went to the Epworth League last night, and toward the last song they asked all the Christians to arise and make a stand. I was the only one sitting around me. I tell you – it takes more sand to sit down sometimes than it does to get up. I hate such things as that. If I hadn't told you I would go, I would cut the whole thing. But that is wrong – they mean it all for my good. Brown – quite a prominent Christian young man here – came up in our room last evening and talked with Walter and me and wanted to pray with us, and he did. He was in dead earnest, this fine fellow – a big six-foot man. The tears were in his eyes, and he was *trying* to do us good. It made me feel sorry to see so much energy wasted. I never saw a man that had much effect on me in such matters. I hate to have them come and work with me that way – I don't believe it does me any good. I seem to get things in another way. Perhaps I'm wrong. I think a great many people lay too much stress upon joining some church. Let's not talk about such things any longer now. I think it will all come right sometime.

We have been having nice weather – cold enough, but not *too* cold. The boys skate over on Lake Como. I haven't been yet. Rube Withrow – the little kid who was always about the mill – wrote me last week. He said he wondered how "I was getting along; that Fred had got a new gun, and they went hunting most every Sunday" and "How many pounds could I lift on the scales?" That he wished I was there – "We would have the most fun." It's good to have the little kids remember you, isn't it? Rube and I used to swim together a good deal. Before I came up here we went and had a farewell swim. It takes so little to make friends with boys and little folks, doesn't it? When I go over to Aunt Nettie's Viola and I have a great play. When I was over there last, she put out her tongue at me, and I made a horrible face. She gravely rebuked me by telling me that it "wasn't nice" and I said I wouldn't do it again.

I'm glad you think your Highland barbarian compares with other fellows. Dear heart, I hope I may get to be more worthy of you. I love you *so* much.

DECEMBER 3, 1894
Hamline to Truthville

Dearest:

I've been home! I didn't hear from home for almost three weeks. As I couldn't get a letter to them much before I would get there, I just thought I'd come and *tell* them. I walked over from the station. It seemed good to get into my "ain countree" again. When I came out of the woods and stepped upon the old pond glistening in the starlight, the bell rang. It was all very still – it sounded like the Angelus, and I pulled off my hat like a Spanish peasant and stood there a minute, and I know I was thankful for my love and home and all.

I stopped at Jim White's to ask him if the ice was all right. He shook hands and said he didn't know when he'd been so glad to see anybody. You see, I was careful about the ice, for I didn't want my time to come until I saw the folks, at least (!).

I came up through the woods, and Duke and Donatello barked, but I spoke to them and they were quiet. Then I went where I could see Mother at work through the kitchen window, and then around front, and I began to whistle then, and tramped up to the kitchen door, flung it open and shouted. Mother was dressing a chicken, but she came at me just the same, and Mary too – Mary knew my whistle. Well, I guess they were glad, but I was as glad as anyone. I went over and saw Aunt Minnie that same evening. She inquired about "Little Anna" as usual, as did the others. My – one wants to be away for a while to appreciate home things, doesn't he?

I had two or three good long skates – all around the places where we have been. Sunday I wrote you quite a long letter from the Point, but when I finished it at home it sounded stupid, and I never mailed it. Our old birch is all right – your name is almost as bright as ever. It looked very different looking off westward from what it did when I took my farewell "look" the last time through the yellow sunlight and blue haze that afternoon in September. The pond is like a lake – fuller than you ever saw it. I could hardly sit upright under the shelf of the "Big Rocks" where the bird's nest is, you know, and the water is to the top of the track where I helped you up last summer.

I was eager to get your letter, but it was very short. It's all right, though – I know you couldn't help it and will make it longer next time. I don't mean to complain, you know. Of course, you had a gay Thanksgiving – we were just our own family and Aunt Minnie.

Pa has been on a visit to his sister at Osakis, and Fay (the one that didn't do a very good job in bringing me up) and her husband made him a present of a fine stag's head. It is in the parlor, high up on the wall. Little Jennie McCray came in and saw it. Mother said she was a little afraid, and her eyes got big, and she said, "Mrs. Allis, is – is the rest of him outdoors?" She thought he had pushed his head through the wall!

I saw Charlie, of course, when I was home. He stayed all night with me once, and we had a good talk like we used to. I think Charlie and I are a good deal alike in some ways.

I have a lot of extra work that I suppose I had ought to do. They asked me to do a Scottish piece at Philomatheans next term. And someone wants me to speak "Tam O'Shanter" at an entertainment in Minnehaha Church, and the freshmen have me on for toastmaster at their banquet. I don't want to be toastmaster. I've got to make a short speech at the beginning, and then am expected to say something "cute" when each of the toasters is introduced. I'm afraid I can't back out of it now. Perhaps I could get through it all right if I had the same little girl sitting beside me that I had last June, who asked, "Where's your sand?" Really, I wish I didn't have to do this.

Walter hasn't got back from the engine room yet. I've decided not to study over there – it's pretty dusty, and the light isn't very good. It's a dingy place all round (a bit of the Donatello in me creeps out) and my eyes aren't quite right yet.

People do seem to guess about you. Douglas made me blush a bit tonight, and said it was suspicious when I looked so happy when I got a letter, when I had been feeling down. Yes, it is suspicious. Dearest, you don't know how I want to see you – it's hard to write what one wants to say.

Well, I must stop now. I'm afraid this letter is stupid too.

With all my love,

I remember how I liked *Ben Hur* when I read it; wish I could take my turn reading with you folks some evening.

DECEMBER 8, 1894
Hamline to Truthville

My Dearest Anna:

I've just finished reading your letter. What were we doing about this time six months ago? I think it was about this time we were getting ready – you were having a little cry.

I told you about the toastmaster trouble I am in. I don't know what to say, and will have to trust to kind fortune to put some ideas into my mind between now and Thursday night.

Quite a party of Hamline students went over to Minnehaha Church to give a little entertainment that I told you of. The exercises consisted of a quartet singing two or three solos, some music by a trio, instrumental music, and two or three readings. After the exercises were over they had refreshments, and we had a very pleasant time. We had a great time in the car coming home – singing and cutting up generally. We didn't get home until the "wee sma hours," and I was so sleepy this morning that Walter and I didn't get up to breakfast.

We are having very warm weather for December here. Thursday when I came out from Zoology the rain was coming down just as it does in the spring in April. It smelled as if the hepaticas would soon be out, and I thought of you – things good and gentle and sweet always remind me of you, dearest.

I have read *Dream Life* this week. Then I found a little book in the library entitled *Essays in Little* by Andrew Lang. Perhaps you have read something of him. He is a critic, and this little book consisted of criticisms on different authors – Scott's poetry, Stevenson, Dumas, Thackeray and Dickens, and one on the *Sagas*. I liked it very much – it cheered me up someway. Don't you like to have someone that likes the same books and authors that you do, and knows so much more than you do about them? Sometimes they tell the things that you couldn't tell and could only feel. He praises H. Rider Haggard, even, and likes good, brave romances, with adventures and love and steel clashing and all. And Dumas and Scott and Stevenson can do that. Did you ever read *The Three Musketeers*? I did once and liked it pretty well. Lang likes Dumas. He doesn't like the realists, like Tolstoi and Zola, with their minute dissections of low-down things and bad thoughts and deeds.

There was a murder over near Lake Calhoun last Monday, and some people seem fairly to gloat over the details. I don't like it – it isn't healthy, is it?

I guess I've tired you by this time with my tirade.

We have our term examinations next week. I don't know how I'll come out; I dread Zoology worse than anything; Livy the least. Probably you will think it strange for me to say this of the Latin – Livy is easier than either Cicero or Vergil. Algebra is pretty tough. Logarithms and choice – my! You may be thankful, Miss Anna, that you don't have to "wrastle" with them.

Anna, I think I had better go to Epworth League. I don't think it will hurt me. You mustn't mind what I said about stopping – you know I'm a little hot-headed and apt to say what I think at the time.

I believe I spoke of my eyes in the last letter, and perhaps you will think they are worse than they really are. I think they're about well now. I don't believe it's granulated lids – I never have anything of that kind trouble me. Perhaps I will see a doctor when I go home for Christmas. Don't trouble about them, dearie – I'll take care of them, but it's very kind and good and like you to remember and speak about them.

I've tried not to do anything to make me unworthy to be your knight. I write more than you do, though not so good quality, of course, in *your* opinion. Perhaps I can manage to get mangled up someway next summer. I'd take a bad cut for the privilege of having you sew it up this minute.

DECEMBER 16, 1894
Hamline to Truthville

My Dear Anna:

I've had a rather lonesome day of it – been right here in the room all day. Walter has been over in the engine room, and it's bleak and blowy outside, and the wind whistles around the corners. Yesterday it was warm and rained hard, but in the night it changed – snowed an inch or so and the wind came up.

I got through the toastmastership all right. I didn't back out, but saw it through, though I dreaded it. We had a fine banquet. Perhaps I will send you the little souvenir we each received. I wish you could have heard the toast – it was killing. It was about the same as at *our* famous banquet. I didn't exactly know what I was going to say until I got up, but I got through well enough.

A few of us walked down to Minncapolis. It was a fine walk – warm and clear – and once when we came over the top of a hill you could look over Minneapolis with the sunset beyond. There are some pretty views from the bridges and down the river.

Oh – I was examined the other day by the physical director – that is, he took my measurements. Kaighn took the width of my chest and shoulders, and said I ought to have been 6 feet high, and my right bicep was 14 ¾. (As you say, I get so few compliments that I must brag a little when I do.) I was surprised that I beat Heath on arms, chest, shoulders, hips, and was about the same below; and he beat me 5/8" on neck, on waist, and weight and height. But Kaighn said my neck was not small for one of my size, so I needn't trouble about that. He said the small of the back was my weak place – not *weak*, but not up with the rest – and said lifting with the knees stiff would be the work to bring me up there. There. I'm through with my vainglorious boasting.

Thursday was the 13th – my folks and Grants' anniversary. It was the first time I have been away. I was suffering in the toastmaster's chair at the time, instead of being with all the clan, but I was doing my duty like a good knight, wasn't I?

Blanche is home. She is going to stay until after the holidays, and Volney is coming for Christmas. All we children will be home again – won't it be fine!

When you write to me next time, send it to Oronoco, for I shall get there next Friday. How I wish I might see you at Christmas time. I had your picture with me this forenoon, and I imagined so hard that I could almost hear your voice. I hope you won't think I'm sentimental, because I'm not, am I?

With my love,

Roy

DECEMBER 23, 1894
Oronoco to Truthville

My Dearest Anna:

Home again! Walter and I left Hamline Friday noon and "out of Babylon" – free and away from the logarithms and all. I got off at the Oronoco switch at 6 o'clock, and dreaded the lonesome walk down the old unused road through the woods with my heavy grip, but Pa and Billy and the horse Fanny were there, and I didn't have to walk at all. The pond wasn't safe to cross, and they were afraid I would try to make it.

It seemed very good to get back, of course, for it seemed an age since Thanksgiving. We boys didn't have anything in the way of heat and such things the last two days because we were going home, you know. When we woke up Friday morning, Bowers said, "We don't need any breakfast – we're going home!" How do you think of a thing that is coming to you, pleasant or unpleasant – something you are dreading or looking forward to? The first thing in the morning, don't you?

Blanche was here when I came, and Volney came last evening. Mother and Aunt Minnie saw Clara Titus the other day when they were shopping in

Rochester. She was clerking in China Hall during holiday time. I walked over to Uncle George's this evening, and saw friends and wiped dishes for Mabel. Louie, her brother, isn't coming home this vacation, and Mabel said she was feeling a little bit "teary round the lashes" today, and I tried to cheer her up a bit.

I can't send that stupid letter, Anna, for it has gone the way of the flesh – I burned it. Never mind, though – this will be stupid enough before I get through. I'm sorry, dearie, if you wanted it.

Aunt Minnie isn't feeling well just now. They both inquired about you as usual, and Uncle wishes he could see you. And I wish *I* could see you, Anna – more than *anyone*. I brought your picture and letters with me. That last letter was such a good one. You must have enjoyed your trip through the mountains. But it wasn't the mountain part I liked best. I liked that part about the kid – that was just like a little kid to think she saw a likeness between you and a hen – what queer things children see! I remember seeing people in the wallpaper; in stains on the ceiling and knots on boards – don't you? I read that part to Mother and showed her the picture. Really, though, my imagination isn't strong enough to see any resemblance between you and a hen!

Pa and Fred and I have been catching doves this evening to send to Chicago. We caught 24.

You wanted to know about the freshmen banquet. I didn't know exactly what to say. If a fellow does something that makes them laugh at first, it's a good thing, for they are good-natured then and don't pity him anymore. When I got up, in my desperation I reached for my mane, and told them how funny and pathetic I was going to be, and to guard against mistakes I was to raise my *right* hand at very funny things I said, and my *left* hand at those calculated to move to tears. I stumbled through it well enough after a fashion, but when the end came and it was time to go, I was signaled to dismiss them. Well, I hadn't counted on that, and they all looked up toward me expectantly, so I arose and said, "Let's yell once and then go," and we all yelled, "Rah! Rah! Rah! Rah! We're a-wake – rack-a-bracka-boom-a-lacka – *98*!" and it was finished.

Say, Anna, I never am guilty of so much egotism in all my life as when I write you – my letters are full of great capital. What do you think of such a fellow?

I wish I could see you, dearest. I love you as I always do, only more.

DECEMBER 30, 1894
Oronoco to Truthville

Dearest:

Your splendid long letter came to me Thursday night. Friday morning I went to Rochester on the stage to have Mayo see my eyes. When I was going down the street, I met Clara. She stopped and talked, but I knew she was in great trouble by her voice and the tears in her eyes. She told me they had just heard of Frank's death that morning. I believe I never felt so sorry for anyone in my life. She tried to be so plucky and brave, but her voice trembled, and she spoke so low – you know how anyone does. I tried to tell her how sorry I was, but I couldn't very well, of course. One feels so helpless. She said he had been better – the doctors were conquering the disease. But she supposed his heart gave out, and that was the cause of his death. It seems cruel. I hate to see anyone feel so bed – especially a woman. It makes one feel as if he would like to get hold of something tangible to do for them.

The shaving case came all right – thank you – and the clover is very natural. I wanted to get something to you, but I was busy at Hamline the last days and didn't get to Minneapolis, and I'm so stupid I can't make anything by my loneself.

Christmas Eve there was a tree at the church, and we all went, of course. It was rather dull, for I guess every kid in the country had a "recitation." Mary read a piece out of *Afterwhiles* that was the only poetry they had. I didn't know she was going to read it, but when she did, I heard "their tresses like the shadows that the shine is woven through," and I knew that was Riley.

We had a beautiful Christmas Day – just cold enough and clear and bright and fresh – regular Minnesota. I wish I could have been there to help you defend Minnesota. You see, I don't know about any other place, and in my dense ignorance I ought to make a good partisan. I heard of the storm down in the Atlantic seaboard, and suppose you are catching it in New York too. Christmas morning Volney and Charlie and I went down the river hunting. We only got three rabbits, but someway we didn't feel very bloodthirsty, and had a good tramp and a superb hunger when we got back. We had a big Christmas dinner. I stayed all night with Charlie, and had a skate up the south branch the next morning before sunrise.

Oh, about my eyes – Dr. Charles Mayo examined them and said the trouble was caused by some strain of the eyes. He took me upstairs and tested them and said there was a slight "stigma," I think he called it. That is when the eyeballs aren't exactly alike – when the distance is right for one eye, but not for the other. It's nothing serious, he said – many people's eyes are that way. He gave me something to put in them to take the inflammation out, and said to come down next Wednesday. It may be possible that I will have to wear glasses while I am studying for a while. That will seem kinda queer if I do.

School commences at Hamline next Thursday. I hate to go back, but I shall, of course. Volney made a proposal to me while we were out hunting – that Charlie and I could come out to Hutchinson, and he could put me pretty well through Blackstone during the summer and give me an idea of the practical part of the business. It was good of him to offer, at least.

Mother sent me down to Mrs. Bates' after the clothes the other day. Mrs. Bates is the one that always talks with her teeth shut. Well, her daughter has been working for us for a week past, and she has twins down at her mother's. I went in and sat down, and the twins were over by the bed. They are awful untidy folks, and can talk an arm off from a slender person. The twins are tow-headed, about 2½ feet high, and look exactly alike. They looked at me a bit, and then you ought to have seen the pitiful look, and then they began to howl and try to hide, but there was no avenue of escape. They both yelled in exactly the same tone. I thought if they were going to do that, I would give them some cause for grievance, and when Mrs. Bates' back was turned, I made up a horrible face, and those poor little chaps thought I was an ogre, I guess. My vanity was considerably hurt, but Mrs. Bates said they were afraid of everyone.

I have strung this letter over considerable surface, but haven't said much. I'm glad you are having such a good time. Thank you for the kind wishes, and know they are returned with all my heart. I seem to want you more than usual today. It does seem very long since I saw you. Know that I love you, my dearest little girl, with all my heart.

Roy

Sunday evening I have read this letter over and it is about as stupid as the one I didn't send. You mustn't lay it up against me, for I didn't mean to do it.

CHAPTER 5

(Anna Speaks!)
Free and Independent

1895

Chinese defeated by Japanese; end of war.

First public film shown in Paris.

H.G. Wells publishes *The Time Machine*.

William Butler Yeats publishes *Poems*.

Art Nouveau style predominates.

First complete performance of Tchaikovsky's ballet "Swan Lake" performed in St. Petersburg.

Wilhelm Roentgen discovers X-rays.

Marconi invents radio telegraphy.

Sigmund Freud publishes "Studien uber Hysterie."

August and Louis Lumiere invent the motion-picture camera.

King C. Gillette invents the safety razor.

First professional football game played in U.S. at Latrobe, PA.

JANUARY 3, 1895
Truthville to Oronoco

My Dearest Roy:

Ever since I received your letter I have been thinking of Clara. It seems terrible for her to bear, but I know she will heroically. She and Mary are both brave, true girls. Life will seem so long and dreary now. I wrote to her last night. Words seem so empty at such a time. My aunt and uncle want me to ask her to come here after a while and go back with me. They thought the change might help her a little. They are tender-hearted people and I think they feel as much sympathy for her as though they knew her. I do hope the girls come.

I'm awfully sorry about your eyes. You must be very, *very* careful, for I hate dreadfully to think that you may be troubled with them all your life. Does Dr. Mayo think it was caused by your working so hard that time last summer?

I have been flying around a little more than usual lately. I went to a party New Year's Eve. We had a nice time – danced a little – and am going to another tonight. Uncle Henry and Aunt Maliza are planning a party for me next Monday evening.

I expect to start for Houlton in a week. It takes about as long to go from here to Houlton as it did to come here from Eyota. I don't like to travel alone.

I had a nice visit with Mrs. Chandler – a Scottish lady – yesterday. She told me about Edinburgh and the castles there. She has been through the castle where Mary, Queen of Scots was living at the time of Rizzio's murder, and she saw on the stone floor of this long gloomy hall what they call the stain of his blood. She has also been through Sir Walter Scott's home. She saw the large oaken chest the bride hid in the poem "The Mistletoe Bough." I never supposed that poem was true, but she says it is. She taught me how to say "michty." I made funny work of it, but at last got it very nearly right.

Have you decided what you will do about Volney's proposition? It would be a good opportunity for you to see how you liked his profession. It would take you quite a distance from Eyota, but our love must make us stronger, not weaker, so I don't mind.

I heard from Nellie. She said, "Roy and Walter seem to be enjoying themselves. I guess Roy gets a little homesick sometimes." I'm glad people keep me posted with regards to you. I think Nellie would be very much surprised if she knew about the way things have gone since school was out!

We have been having very cold weather since the storms, and the sleighing is good. I froze my face going to the last party, so it is a little swollen on one side and red yet – and last night the cat scratched my face, so now I am in fine shape for a party tonight.

Now do take good care of your eyes. Is there a cure for them, or will you need glasses always?

With lots of love,

Anna

JANUARY 6, 1895
Oronoco to Truthville

My Dearest Anna:

It's such a beautiful day – about half-an-inch of snow, and warm and bright. We have had the best winter weather I ever saw.

I went down to Rochester Wednesday to Mr. Titus's in the forenoon, for I had to see the doctor in the afternoon. The folks seemed glad to see me – your aunt said it seemed a year since she saw me. Miss Mary and I had a good visit. Clara was at the bank with her father, but I saw her afterwards. They talked about you. Mrs. Titus said your mother *(actually Anna's stepmother, who married Anna's father six months before he died)* was up there the other day – I guess she wants you pretty bad too. She's a little afraid you might want to stay east once you got there. They said you weren't coming back by March 1st; that your mother thought you ought to have your visit out while you were there, and then you would be better satisfied. I agreed with them, but my heart sank in spite of me. But, dearie, you must never mind me – I'll *keep*, you know. I don't want to be selfish.

Oh, soon after I came, a young man came up to the house with a little lumber that he was going to build some toy of – those monkeys that climb strings, you know. I said to Miss Mary, "That fellow can't throw me over a fence," and how she laughed! She said you're always telling how strong I am (as you think).

Clara seemed cheerful. She told me some about the particulars of Jones' death. He died as if going to sleep, she said – it wasn't painful at all. He had a very pleasant Christmas; Clara sent him the picture "The Soul's Awakening" – you remember it – and she showed me the pocket book that Frank sent her. She seemed to want to talk with me about it. It's hard, isn't it?

Doctor Mayo put some drops in my eyes that dilated my pupils so I couldn't see things nearby. It was to paralyze the muscles that contracted the pupils so he could fit me with glasses. He said my eyes were much better – that I wouldn't need to wear glasses when I studied if they didn't get worse, and I'm sure they won't. He knows what kind I want, and I can get them from him by writing any time. I'm glad I won't have to wear glasses though. I think they are *very becoming* to *some* people (!). You needn't trouble about my eyes anymore, now.

My school reports came the other night thus – Algebra 72, Livy 90, Zoology 90, Bible 92. That Algebra is pretty bad, isn't it? You see it was this way – I had a pretty good daily mark, but Prof. Drew made us copy every example in copy-books to be handed in the last of the term. Well, I hated to do that, and the result was my book was very behind when I handed it in, and the book counted one-third. Then I got a bit rattled in the last examination, and rather went to pieces over the logarithms. They say "an honest confession is good for the soul," and I've made a clean breast of it, as a knight should, to the dearest confessor in the whole world.

This has been the greatest holiday time for eating that I have ever gone through. We have been out to Aunt Minnie's and Reifsniders' and here at home several times to dinner or supper. I weighed 164 lbs. the other morning with gloves and rubbers on. Mercy on us – what heavyweights we are getting to be. You must look superb. Aunt Minnie is coming over here to supper to eat stuffed spare-ribs and bird's-nest pudding that Mother is baking now.

No, I don't think you queer at all – just queer enough. Your last letter came New Year's evening while we were holding high carnival at Uncle Grant's. Ella Wirt was with me at table, and she was bound to see it – where it came from and to see "just the ending." It was such a good letter. We watched old 94 out, so I didn't read your letter until the next year after I got home.

I went for a walk away round where the camp was and over through "our woods" the next day, and I read your letter over again, sitting on the old fallen tree where you put your hand on my head for the first time you ever touched me in that way – do you remember? We were reading and talking, you know. How I want to see you.

I'm more homesick about going away this time than I was last fall. The weeks will go, though, and you and the summer will come.

I'll try and do better work next term. My hair is very long now and quite curly – I must get it cut. I'm just hungry for you, dearest.

Friday evening there was a masked social at the hall here. We had a great roaring fire in the fireplace. I "slicked up" a little and went and had quite a good time, but I wished you had been there.

Oh, I froze an ear the other day, and also sprained my ankle a little lifting on the scales. It's nothing to amount to anything, and is all right now, but I want to hear you scold a little like you did before. I *must* stop.

JANUARY 13, 1895
Hamline to Houlton, Maine

Dearest:

It's about half-past-eight and I have just come home from chapel.

A postal card came yesterday from Charlie Reifsnider, saying Blanche wrote them Volney has typhoid fever. Volney's mother has gone to Hutchinson. I'm very anxious to hear from him. Poor Blanche will be in trouble. Volney wasn't feeling well when they went from Oronoco. The card was typical of Charlie – he told about Volney and then ended with: "I shot eight rabbits yesterday." I hope Volney will get along all right – he is well and strong, and I think he will.

Yesterday afternoon Heath and I went down to the Grand Opera House in Minneapolis to see Eugen Sandow *(known as the "father of modern bodybuilding")*. We were late, but Sandow didn't come until last, and he was what I wanted to see. He was beautiful – I wish you could have seen him. When he appeared first, he was standing in a little alcove on a pedestal, with dark curtains behind, and the light on him. His arms were folded, and he was in the attitude of some statue. Then he posed in different positions, showing the different muscles. It was wonderful to see the great piles of muscle rise all over him under the white skin. He did some wonderful feats with dumbbells. He was a nice-looking fellow – blonde with blue eyes and short yellow hair. He didn't look monstrous either, for he was developed all over and is about 5'8" in height. He looked as I imagine Hercules would, and if I could be a man just as I wanted to be, I should like to be something like that, physically.

I read *Stage-Land* through this morning – you have read that too, you told me? Jerome never wrote anything to equal *Idle Thoughts of an Idle Fellow* that I ever saw.

We have about six inches of snow here at Hamline – there was more to speak of at Oronoco. Two days last week were regular blizzards for wind, and we could feel every gust here in our room.

MONDAY AFTERNOON

I wrote quite a lot more last night, but I didn't like it and burned it up, and thought I'd wait until your letter came today so I would know where to send it. Your letter came this noon and did me good. I told Walter that if I got a letter today I would be a good boy. We've just been having a great time cleaning house. There was quite a lot of patent medicines left by some former lodger, and we took them and threw them into the fire so we could enjoy the odor of the fumes. Walter wondered if it would bring down the wrath of the gods upon us.

Last week I read a little book of Richard Harding Davis's entitled *Gallagher and Other Stories*. I especially liked "Gallagher" and "There Were Ninety and Nine." I have never read *A Window in Thrums* that you told me about. Wish I could get hold of the books I would like to read – a body could do lots of things if he had the money, couldn't he?

When I came up from home it seemed so cold and dreary here that I was the most homesick I have ever been. I feel better now. Today opened beautifully, but it's snowing hard now – warm though, with the wind in the south.

I haven't decided anything about Volney's proposition – I hardly think I can do it. I'm sure our love does make us stronger, dearie – it makes my life *better*, anyway. I'm glad you still think you will come home in March – I get so *hungry* to see you.

So you start for Maine tonight? I'll think of you this evening and try to help you stand the good-byes. I hope you will get through to Houlton all safe and sound. Anna, I think you have the best, tenderest heart in the whole world.

With my love,

Roy

JANUARY 17, 1895
Houlton to Hamline

My Dearest Roy:

I have traveled a good many miles since I wrote you, and now am in the northeastern part of Maine, and can sing "Way Down in Maine" quite truthfully.

I almost lost my luggage! But I found my trunk and got everything attended to, and then I didn't know which train I was to take, so I had to ask a man in the Inquiry Office, and he explained everything very kindly. I should think he would get cross, standing there all day, answering questions.

I had a lower berth, and found that a man weighing about 200 had the upper berth. My! How it cracked and groaned when he climbed in! I put up the curtain and lay looking out of the window for quite a while. It was a beautiful night – clear and bright and frosty outside, but the car was hot and close.

One always feels so faint in the morning after traveling all night, and I had to get up at 4, so you can imagine how I felt when I got off the train at Bangor. About 80 miles of the road to Houlton (which was built only last year) runs through the "Maine woods" – evergreens largely (though there were a great many birches and beeches). Such great, tall tamaracks, spruces, cedars, pines and hemlocks. I never was in a regular *forest* before. Those great evergreens seem to suggest strength and courage and hardiness. We passed a good many lumber camps – regular old-fashioned log houses – and at the stations you would see the lumbermen – rough-looking men, with red or bright-colored coats and moccasins. I supposed they wore the bright colors because they took a fancy to them, but my brother Frank says it's because they can see each other better among the trees and can call to each other if a tree is ready to fall.

A great many of the trees are covered with a gray moss that hangs down from the branches. It grows the thickest on the old trees. I think Longfellow must have been thinking of a forest like that when he wrote:

THIS is the forest primeval. The murmuring pines and the hemlocks,

Bearded with moss, and in garments green, indistinct in the twilight,

Stand like Druids of eld, with voices sad and prophetic,

Stand like harpers hoar, with beards that rest on their bosoms.

This must be a beautiful country in summer – there are a great many lakes and streams. It is a great place for sportsmen. Frank says that last year there were 837 deer, 50 caribou and 30 moose killed and shipped on his railroad during September and October – the first two months of the hunting season. He says there are five kinds of trout in all these streams. He has been wishing so much that it was summer so we could go fishing. I suppose the deer will all be killed in a short time. The only thing that kept people away from the woods before was the difficulty in getting there, but now the railroad has been built, there will be nothing to hinder them. It seems a shame.

So after I arrived, Lou *(her sister-in-law)* and I went downtown to the depot to see Frank. Lou asked me that day if I could make "graham genie." She said Frank was letting on about Aunt Maliza's genie all the time, but she didn't know how to make them. Of course, I was delighted to think I could, but we decided not to let Frank know, in case they shouldn't turn out well. We had them baking when he came home, and he walked straight to the oven door and looked in and smiled all over his face! I was quite anxious for fear they wouldn't taste like his aunt's. He only said "Um" and took another bite – but he ate them as though they were hers, and then ate for breakfast what was left over! He is a great boy. He used to eat 12 every morning when he was in school, and then take 14 in his dinner pail for lunch.

People here travel on snowshoes a good deal. Frank and Lou each have a pair. Frank says I must try it. They used to have snowshoe parties in St. Andrews, and a little company of young people would take long tramps on them on moonlit evenings. We'll have to learn – wouldn't our Minnesota friends think we were wild?! *(Anna did teach Roy to snowshoe, and his snowshoes adorned the parlor wall of my grandparents' house all the years they lived there.)*

When I was in Rutland on my way up here, Cousin Currie and Clarence gave me *The Prince of India*. I commenced it when I was there visiting, but didn't have time to finish it, so they ordered it for me. It seems to me that some of us get more kindness in the world than we deserve.

Lou has kept *The Heavenly Twins* for me, for she thought I would like to read it, so I guess I will, though I haven't a very good opinion of it from what I have heard – Frank doesn't think much of it. Frank has all of Dumas' works, and I shall try to get time to read *The Three Musketeers* while I am here. I guess I never will if I write such long letters, so I *must* stop.

With my love,

Anna

JANUARY 20, 1895
Hamline to Houlton

My Dearest Anna:

Received a letter from Blanche Friday, saying Volney was very, very sick, but was sleeping naturally for the first time in three days, and the doctor thought he would pull through. She said, "He is still delirious, but not so bad as he has been. Think the crisis is over. He is very, very weak, but we trust with the best of care the boy will be all right. Roy, he *must* be! I can have it no other way!" I'm so glad he is better. It would spoil Blanche's life – she is so true and strong, and things take a great hold upon her.

I haven't heard from the folks since I left, but Charlie has written me three postal cards and a letter. I thought perhaps I would get a letter from Mother, as I wrote her more than a week ago, but I didn't – I presume they are all broken up with anxiety about Volney, so I wrote again today.

I didn't do anything Saturday and haven't today, except idle around and read over to Julius's. Reading some in Ella Wheeler Wilcox's *Poems of Passion*. Did you ever read any of the things she wrote? I liked these – some of them. Last week I read *Treasure Island* by Robert Louis Stevenson. It was written for boys, but everyone has read it, and it is a regular pirate yarn. Billy Bones sings a song about, "Fifteen men on the dead man's chest; Yo ho! Yo hoo! And a bottle of rum!"

Friday evening I was on for an impromptu at Literary Society. First I thought I wouldn't go, but Bowers and Douglas yammered at me so much I decided I'd face the music, so I went. You don't know your subject until the president gives it to you after you're on the floor. He gave me the "Senatorial

Election" (Washburn and Knute Nelson are having a great struggle for the senatorial office). I didn't know anything about *that*, and I told them so, but said it reminded me of a ghost story of Jerome K. Jerome's. Then they were bound I should speak "Tam." I didn't want to, for I had spoken it once before, and I didn't want people to think Allis spoke "Tam O'Shanter" every time he got a chance. But they talked me into it, and I've got to do the old thing over again. They say I must have something for an encore. Do you think I could speak something from Riley? Could speak his "A Tale of the Airly Days."

When I wrote Charlie I told him about Sandow. Charlie said he would like to have seen him. You must know Charlie – he and I are more friends than Bowers and I. Charlie can sympathize in some things that I can't with Bowers – he's all right, but I don't believe I would like to live alone with him forever and ever. Bowers don't like me to be lazy and idle like I am a good deal, and he talks at me and makes me worse just to be a contrast to him. *You* can sympathize with a fellow best, I think. Charlie and I are going to South Africa together some day.

Eight weeks and school will be out for spring vacation of 10 days. I hope you'll be home by then. How my heard will pound!

I'm so restless. I wonder if it would have been better to have stayed away from school this year. Perhaps the work at the mill would have done me good – it has been so long that I have been in school, and I don't seem to have got much discipline. I have never studied hard enough. I work well enough at some things. I don't think I'm lazy – that is, very lazy – do you? I can pitch bundles as hard as the next one.

I suppose you're having a fine time with your brother and Lou. How blamed trite that last sentence sounds – anybody could see I had nothing to say when I said that – of course you are.

I wonder what you are doing now – it's about half-past-six. I have your picture here, and am going to think of you *hard* for five minutes – perhaps you can feel it.

With my love,

Roy

I'll try and be more careful after this and write letters you can decipher better. *You* never wuz great shakes at hand-writing – 'member how I used to complain about the Latin you would write on the board for Miss Peck?

JANUARY 25, 1895
Houlton to Hamline

My Dear, Dear Roy:

When you receive this letter you will wonder what has happened, but don't be alarmed. I just feel like talking with you, and that last letter of mine was such a horrible one! Frank and Lou have gone to whist club, and I am alone in my glory and can do whatever pleases me, and it pleases me most to write to you. I like a few hours all to myself once in a while, don't you?

Your letter came last evening, and also ones from Mary and Clara and Mother. I read yours last, as I always do – feeling, I presume, as you do, when you carry mine around in your pocket awhile before reading it. This was the first time I had heard from Clara since Frank died. Clara is a noble girl, Roy. Her letter was beautiful. Did she tell you – her aim in life now is to do the work for Christ that Frank would have done had he lived? She says that although it was for so short a time they were together, he made her a far, far nobler woman than she ever could have been had she not known him.

I dreamed of you and Walter last night. Now don't be cross because I dreamed of Walter too – you know at school I aimed to treat you both alike, so it was force of habit that made me dream of you both. It was also force of habit that made me dream more particularly of *you.*

Wish I could have heard your impromptu on the "Senatorial Election." Yes, I think you could speak "A Tale of the Airly Days." Or what about "Loran Karunteel" – the Irish piece when they are "joompin' there in sacks and … racin wid wheel barrirs"?

I should like very much to get acquainted with Charlie, but I'm afraid I never can if he acts as shy as he did last summer. Were you joking when you asked me if I thought you lazy? Of course I don't!

I do hope Volney is better. It must be so hard for Blanche.

I have read either *Poems of Pleasure* or *Poems of Passion* by Ella Wheeler Wilcox. I can't tell which it was, but I know I liked them.

There is no one like you, dearest, and I love you and *only you* with all my heart.

Your own little girl

CHAPTER 6

The One Who Goes

JANUARY 25, 1895

Volney G. Reifsnider Sr. – Roy's brother-in-law – dies in Hutchinson, Minnesota, of typhoid fever. The local obituary says he "was well-known and highly regarded." Volney and Roy's sister Blanche were married only the spring before. She is pregnant and already a widow.

JANUARY 28, 1895
Hamline to Houlton

Dearest Anna:

Last evening I learned of Volney's death. He died Friday morning at 5 o'clock. I came home this morning with poor Blanche and Volney's parents. Oh, they have had a terrible time. Hutchinson is in mourning for Volney. We are all broken up. It is awful for Blanche especially, but she is wonderfully steady – too steady.

I'll write again, but thought I had better send a little tonight. I'm going to sleep on the lounge tonight for company for Blanche and Mary. The services are at 2 o'clock tomorrow. I'll write you particulars later.

With my love,

Roy

The dear boy is laid out here in the parlor.

*Blanche Allis Reifsnider
(Roy's older sister)*

*Volney Reifsnider
(Blanche's husband)*

JANUARY 31, 1895
Houlton to Hamline

My Dearest Roy: *(Anna, of course, has not received Roy's letter yet.)*

This is a beautiful day – just like spring. I haven't been out this morning, but we're going soon after dinner. Frank and I have been snowshoeing! I wish you could have been with us. We went in the evening. We each wore Indian moccasins made of moose skin. It's hard work to get the snowshoes on. Frank tried to tell me how to do it, but try my best, I couldn't. He fixed the straps right over my foot and said, "Now squirm into it." I wriggled and writhed and squirmed and finally got it right. It is easy enough to do as soon as you know how, but you have to twist into all sorts of shapes to get them on.

It's lots of fun! I know you would like snowshoeing better than skating! You can go where you please, and it isn't hard at all. It isn't graceful – you have to take long steps, and your feet are farther apart than in ordinary walking – but you feel so free and independent, for you can go over the deepest drifts or wherever you please. You ought to see Frank run on snowshoes! Well, we were out about an hour and came home tired, of course – at least *I* was – but feeling *superb*. Frank has great contempt for people who "stay in the house all the time and never know the pleasure and exhilaration of a good tramp." He has often walked 25 or 30 miles in a day on them.

The whist club Frank and Lou belong to meet here tomorrow night. I have been drawing "brownies" on some little cards for them to have in finding their partners for the game, and to carry home afterward as souvenirs. I worked nearly all day at them yesterday.

I am reading *The Three Musketeers* and like it ever so much. It is altogether different from any book I ever read. In some books, you know, you seem to feel and see things as the different characters do and have a sort of sympathy with them, but it isn't so with this book. I suffered when Jean Valjean suffered and was glad when he was glad, but although I am interested in D'Artagnan and his friends, I haven't that sympathy with them – did you?

Something important has happened. Lou and I have been having the loveliest talk, and I told her about you. Mary told me when I came away that I must tell Frank all about you, as Frank and I are the only ones left. I ought to confide in him, but couldn't tell him directly, and the way was open for a good talk with Lou this afternoon, so I told her. She says she knows Frank will be pleased, for he has a great interest in me. I told her that you and I thought a good deal of each other, and that was only growing stronger. She smiled and said she presumed it would always be so. You remember I wondered at first whether our love for each other was love that would last. I don't wonder at all about that *now*.

Last Sunday evening I kept feeling as though something was the matter with you. I suppose I must have been nervous, but I couldn't shake off the feeling.

I will probably get your letter tonight. Friday is my lucky day, you know. I must close and go to work at my brownies.

With my love,

Anna

FEBRUARY 1, 1895
Oronoco to Houlton

Dearest:

Both your letters came to me night before last. I read the "horrible" one first, and then the other – that splendid one after. The first one was good, but if it really had been bad, the other would have antidoted it.

I've heard of *Heavenly Twins* but don't know anything about it. You dislike it so – I've an idea it's a kind of pessimistic book. Don't believe it dear, if it gives you a worse opinion of people than you have. I believe people are better at heart than they seem. When people are in trouble – then is when the goodness and kindness come out.

The Hutchinson people have been so good and generous to poor Blanche in her trouble. She stands it so bravely – she has more strength and nerve than most people. She has stood it *too* well for her own good, perhaps. She has hardly shed a tear, but has looked at times like marble, and her eyes are dry. Mrs. Reifsnider said when they knew Volney was going, Blanche's eyes were so dry it seemed as if she couldn't wink – she only walked and wrung her hands and moaned with such a piteous look in her eyes. His mother stands it bravely too, but his father is pretty much broken. He is a great large man – strong, he used to be – a man of few words, but with a great, warm heart as such men usually have.

I'm glad I came home – you can't comfort people at such a time, but you can be around and near. Someway I can't comfort Blanche and talk with her as I think I could with some. I don't know her as well as I might – I don't know the right thing to do. I must learn and be as good to her as I can. Oh, it will be hard these long years to come – I pity her so. I wished it had been me, but that is wrong, I suppose. He was as fine a fellow as I ever saw. It was good to hear him talk when he would come home from the U – all full of new things, ideas, books – a breath of the outside world pushing up and on – he brought that to me. A true, good, upright gentleman as ever lived.

I can't see how all things are for the best. I hope Blanche will come through all right. Of course, she will never get over it, but she is very sensible and tries to be cheerful and work. It was hard – awful hard – to break up the "little home" she always spoke of. They had only been married nine months and a day, and I hardly ever saw two people that seemed to think so much of each other. They had known each other so long – since they were children.

I've said enough about this – there is no use in talking. Anna, people are better than they seem, oftentimes, and I don't care if *Heavenly Twins* thinks they are not. I don't believe things lots of times because I don't want to. Anna, I hope I will never get so that I cease to believe and trust people – we won't, will we?

The Rev. Trowers – the young minister who came down with the folks – spoke in his little talk at Volney's funeral of something he heard Volney say in a debate – "I must believe this, because it is right." There is a clear watchword, Anna – characteristics of the good brave boy that is gone – to believe things because they are right.

I will go back to Hamline tomorrow. I wrote to you last Sunday a kind of blue letter, I guess, and I was ashamed to send it after I heard from Blanche. I was just lonesome and kinda heart-hungry for you, I guess. It won't be very long until I see you now.

I've scratched this letter off fast – just as the spirit moved.

With my love,

Roy

I never read the poem you spoke of. We will cling together hard, won't we? There is no one like you.

FEBRUARY 4, 1895
Hamline to Houlton

My Dear little Anna:

I ought to be studying, but I feel as if I couldn't just now – not blue, but kinda sad and quiet, you know.

Your letter came, and one from Professor Adams. They were good letters. Professor wrote a good brave letter, and he spoke of you. I told him where you were and what you were doing, along with the rest of the 94's, and he said, "You very modestly left Anna till the last place, but we know that the Good Book says 'that the last shall be first and the first last.'" And then he goes on to say some good things, and gives you the bravest, best compliment you ever had. I will show it to you when you come home.

I'd like to see you snowshoeing. I'd like to go 'long too – reckon I could learn. I never walked on anything but skis, and on them but once for any distance. Of course I would like it.

What does your brother think about me – you must tell me all about it?

It has been terribly cold here – 18-20 below zero in the early morning. I was all right at home, but Bowers must have been cold in our room all alone. When he came here after dinner and found me, he was going to fall on my neck and weep, but I put him into a chair and told him to bear it like a man. He said he was overcome to see me.

I left the good folks at home as well as could be expected. Blanche is very cheerful and brave, but she looks so sad sometimes. When her things came and she was unpacking them – all the little things – it was sad to see her, and she didn't break down at all – she isn't that kind, you know – but it's *there* just the same.

Miss Fishback died the 26th – the day after Volney's death. They graduated in the same class in Rochester High School. We have so many dying – why is that?

I do notice something of the feeling for the characters in *The Three Musketeers* that you speak of. I liked it too – not as I like some books, though – not like *Lorna Doone*. I felt with the characters, in that I was dead in love too.

It was rather strange, Anna, that you should feel something was the matter with me that Sunday evening. It was then that I first heard of Volney's death.

I must get at my Livy. This isn't a regular letter. I just felt lonesome and tired and wanted to talk with you. Good night.

With my love,

Roy

FEBRUARY 4, 1895
Houlton to Oronoco

My Dear, Dear Roy:

Your letter came Friday, and as soon as I saw the Oronoco postmark, I felt sure of the contents. It is terrible for you all. I have been thinking about Blanche – how awful for her. But don't you think, Roy, that those who love each other can never *really* be separated? Nothing can separate us from God's love, and our human love is the nearest like that of anything. If ever we are separated in that way, I believe the one who goes will love the other with a stronger, truer love than ever before – a love more like Christ's.

I have been wondering a little if the feeling I had about you a week ago Sunday was just a coincidence. It probably was, but yet I wonder.

Frank and I went snowshoeing again this morning. It was just about zero. We walked over two miles. We went out in the country, tramped around the river, and climbed a high hill where we could get a fine view of the town and country all around. Just below us were some evergreen woods – spruce mostly. We climbed over fences and ran downhill and had a glorious time. In climbing over a fence you have to climb up to the top rail and then give a jump with both feet. You have to jump as far out as possible, for if you catch the heels of your snowshoes on the fence, it will throw you down, and snowshoes are very long. Mine reach from the floor up to my waist. I do wish you could be here. Never mind – perhaps we will try it together some day.

I am reading *Aurora Leigh*. I have never read any of Mrs. Browning's poems. I read one of Rudyard Kipling's stories in the *Cosmopolitan* the other day. Did you know that Jerome K. is to write a series of articles in *The Ladies Home Journal* addressed to American women? It is to be in the same vein as his *Idle Thoughts*. I do not know how soon the series begins, but we must read them.

My "brownies" took very well at the whist club. The people who are to entertain next time tell me I must think up something for them too. I am glad they liked them. Frank brought your letter just a short time before the people began to come. They didn't imagine where my thoughts were, tho Lou said every time she looked at me she knew what I was thinking of.

Give my love to Blanche when you write her, and lots of love for you, dear.

Anna

CHAPTER 7

Merry and Desperate

FEBRUARY 5, 1895
Houlton to Hamline

My Dearest Roy,

Frank brought your letter Tuesday when he came home to tea. He concluded it would be best for me to wait until after tea before I read it, so he put it on top of the hanging lamp over the dining room table and shoved the lamp up as high as it would go. So I had to eat supper with your letter just out of reach, over my head. After tea Frank took it down and danced around the kitchen with it. Lou and I both tried to take it away from him. He teased me until he had to go back to the office, and at last gave it to me.

I have finished *The Three Musketeers*. I liked it pretty well, but I don't think I care to read any more of Dumas. What do you think about his books? I have been reading some of *Aurora Leigh* this morning.

Yes, we both must learn and be good to Blanche. I cannot see how all things are for the best either, but I am sure that God, who put us – His children – here in the world, and is showing his love for us so constantly, does not let us suffer uselessly. I don't know – I cannot understand *why*, but I am sure God knows what is best for us, and we can trust all to Him.

I have often thought that if my father and mother had lived, and I could have been with my mother constantly, I should be a much better woman. But it may be that I have thought more about spiritual things – about God, because I knew she was *with* God – than I would have had she been with *us*. Perhaps their influence over me for good has been stronger than it could have been had they lived. Perhaps we will understand it all sometime. If there was no sorrow or suffering in the world, we should not be as good as we are.

No, Roy – we must never get to where we cease to believe in the goodness of people. I don't think we ever shall, but perhaps there is danger of being too *optimistic*. I do not believe things are as we *think* they are. We either think right or wrong. We cannot make wrong right by believing it is right. If Dr. Parkhurst and everyone else had believed that everything was right in New York City, I do not know what the end would have been. It seems to me that we must keep our faith in the goodness of humanity, and yet be able to see and judge correctly of its sins, to do the greatest good in the world – don't you think so? The trouble with me is that I cannot see and judge correctly, and I don't believe I ever shall be able to. It is always the blind men and the elephant. Well, as long as it is impossible for me to know the shape of the elephant, I'll believe him beautiful until I prove him ugly, and not depend on what other people say – Sarah Grand or anyone else. Perhaps they have only seen one side of the elephant.

Yes, we will cling together. You grow dearer to me all the time, dearest.

With my love,

Anna

FEBRUARY 10, 1895
Oronoco to Houlton

Dearest Anna:

I am just back from Minneapolis. Walter and I studied Trig some yesterday, then visited the Senate and House for a while. The senators looked very much the same as other people.

Thomas Keene is playing Shakespeare in the Cities. Heath and I saw him last week in *Richard III* at the Metropolitan in St. Paul, and I intend to hear him once or twice more in Minneapolis this week. I would like to see *Hamlet* and *Romeo and Juliet*. I liked Keene very much, but I think I liked Salvini more. Of course, they play altogether different plays – Keene tragedies and Salvini the romantic kind, like *Don Caesar* and *Three Musketeers*. You know what a cruel wretch Richard was – killing the little prince in the Tower and all that. He was somewhat deformed, you know – one leg wasn't right, and an arm a little withered. It made him look sort of devilish – limping around, playing with his dagger. When Richard was born, Shakespeare says he had teeth, which was an omen that he came to bite. But he was brave, this Richard, and when he was killed at Bosworth Field, cut his way clear in to where his enemy Richmond was. In the battle on the stage he fought with Richmond and five or six more. Oh, how he fought, and it made me hot when they came and struck him from behind with a battleax. I almost tried to find a chair to throw at them.

You know the book *Trilby* that is such a rage now – I read about half of it today. I don't know whether I like it or not. I don't believe I *do* like it – it's queer – about the students and artists of the "Latin Quarter" in Paris. Perhaps you have read something else by this author. Why – isn't he the author of *Heavenly Twins*?

I found Jean Ingelow's poems in Julius' library and read the poem "Divided" that you told me was running in your mind one day.

I wish I *were* snowshoeing with you – how deep is the snow? Our snow isn't over 12 inches, but it has been terrible cold for three weeks.

You still think you will start home near the 1st of March? If you do, it's only about five weeks until I see you. Five weeks isn't long. I begin to feel light-hearted already.

With my love,

Roy

FEBRUARY 14, 1895
Houlton to Hamline

My Dearest Roy:

When I woke this morning I opened the window, and although it was snowing, it seemed to me like spring. I have the windows open near me as I write. I think I am beginning to have my "spring fever." The air was soft all day yesterday.

That Sunday evening when I felt so anxious about you, I could not sleep the first part of the night. I kept thinking how much might happen before I could get back to Minnesota. Then I thought perhaps you were in some mental trouble, and wondered what it could be. I would try to go to sleep, and the first I knew the thoughts would all come trooping back, and I would find myself trying to decide just what was the matter with you. I never once thought of Volney. What had been coming to me was that it was some spiritual struggle, and the feelings took so strong a hold of me that I prayed if anything was troubling you that God would bring you safely through it – that you might not lose your faith in Him, but rather feel more sure of His love for you.

I am anxious … what the "bravest, best compliment I ever had" is? You must be sure and bring his letter when you come home, and let me read it, or I shall be more severe than Lorna Doone!

With lots of love,

Anna

FEBRUARY 18, 1895
Hamline to Houlton

My Dearest Anna:

Yesterday felt like spring to me. Walking up from the InterUrban last night, it was dark and snowing a bit, but the wind was strong and March-like. Then I felt the "spring fever," and the wind got into my blood, and I took off my cap so the wind could blow through, and I whistled hard and wanted to shout or fight or *something*! You know how one seems exalted and merry and desperate sometimes? I like the March wind. I wish I could have seen you when you felt the spring. Do you remember a day we had last year – I think it was in February – the day we all wanted to skip Vergil and go find crocuses? I remember you standing at the open south window with the wind flowing in – I remember just how you looked.

I have bummed more than usual this week – three plays in two days – bad boy, ain't I? I saw *Richelieu* Friday, *Hamlet* Saturday matinee, and *Merchant of Venice* Saturday evening. You see, I thought I had rather see the good plays with Keene, and then not go to poorer things. Saturday night the University boys were up in the "University Box" in the theater in full force, and it was lots of fun the way they acted as people came in. There were some ladies up there, who, seeing it was Shakespeare being played, didn't like the noise and shouting, I guess. It's a bad thing to lack a sense of humor, I think – it makes people intolerant sometimes, don't you think?

I heard from home Saturday. All of them are well, and Blanche is getting along bravely.

You asked me how I liked Dumas. Well, I like his books – that is, a certain amount – but they are *French* – and I don't like French books as I do English – they are so hot and feverish, some way. I haven't read many books by French authors, but I never read one that seemed strong and pure and wholesome like some of our English books. Is this what you think of them? Last week I read *Prophet of the Great Smoky Mountains*.

There are only four school days this week. Washington's Birthday the freshmen give the juniors an afternoon reception. I'm on the decoration committee – for my aesthetic skill in driving tacks, I 'spose. Three weeks from next Friday school is out. I begin to feel good that you and spring are coming.

This isn't much of a letter, but I'll send it. I wanted to write you a good letter this time, but I haven't someway – it's stupid. But I *wanted* to. Never mind – I can talk with you soon. Did you ever read "A Scrawl" in *Afterwhiles*?

With my love,

FEBRUARY 20, 1895
Houlton to Oronoco

My Dearest Roy:

Frank and Lou have just gone to whist club, so I have a quiet time to write to you. I have a little pug dog, belonging to a gentleman who lives here, for company. He is lonesome, I guess, for he has been whining. But just now he seems contented, for he is sitting close to my chair, and I am stroking his ears as I write.

Last Friday we all went to a military ball. Frank and Lou danced, but I just looked on – I don't know how well enough to dare try it. The music was fine, and I enjoyed myself even if I did not dance. I like dancing, and I don't care what people say – I don't believe there is any harm in it. The ball was quite a "swell" affair, and the dresses were very pretty. Lou and I exchanged fans – mine matched her dress better than her own. That was the first time mine has been used since commencement. Once I saw Frank fanning Lou with it, and I thought of the way you fanned me the last time it was in use.

The snow is between three and four feet deep and is quite badly drifted. Sunday morning we went to the Congregational Church and heard a fine sermon. He compared the religious beliefs of the Greeks, Romans and Hebrews, and in doing so, told the story of Aeneas' journey through the lower world and the sights he met with there. The sermon is to be continued next Sunday, and I am anxious to hear it, for the religious beliefs of the Romans and Greeks interested me very much last year. You remember some of our discussions last year in Vergil class?

Dearest, *dearest* – can you realize that we shall be together in less than a *month*? I am planning to start from Boston a week from tomorrow, but somehow it doesn't seem as if I'm really going. I shall have to stand the good-byes again. If only Minnesota and Maine were nearer together!

We have been having spring weather for two weeks. Lou is going to have 5 o'clock tea in my honor tomorrow. I don't care much for such things. It seems to me teas are very much like olives – the taste for them has to be acquired. I suppose I would feel differently if these people were friends of mine, but I have only met them once or twice. Frank's Knights of Pythias will give me a banquet and dance next week.

I hope I can hear some good plays when I am in Lowell. I have never heard any noted actor.

I have heard a great deal about *Trilby* – I don't believe I care to read it, though. Sarah Grand is the author of *Heavenly Twins*. The last *Cosmopolitan* speaks of *The Heavenly Twins* as a "thoroughly unwholesome book," and I agree with it. I have an idea *Trilby* is something of that sort, and I don't want to read such books – there are too many really good things in the world to waste my time over doubtful ones, even if a good many people are discussing it. When you finish the book, write me what you think.

Four more weeks. With my love,

Anna

FEBRUARY 25, 1895
Hamline to Lowell, Massachusetts

Sweetheart:

We are having regular spring days and the snow is almost gone.

We had our junior reception Friday. The windows were darkened, the parlors nicely decorated, and we had nice refreshments and a good time, for that kind of thing. The freshmen girls said to us, "You must talk to the junior girls." So Cook and I, clinging to each other for support, went in search of a junior girl, resolved to "talk to her." We found one, but Cook's courage failed him, and I had to go and sit all alone and unprotected in an alcove on a landing and talk with her. We attracted quite a crowd at the head of the stairs, for they wondered at my temerity, and Bowers and Wallace were also very wroth. Miss Dill suggested that we look at them just as silly as we could, and we did. It's difficult to talk through when you have nothing to say.

Enough of the junior banquet. I went over to Julius's yesterday forenoon to see if Viola had got over the croup she had the week before. They were all well. I found "Maurine" and other poems there. Ella Wheeler Wilcox wrote it, you know. I had been feeling not just right, and I read until I was stupid and my head ached in the back, but I took a walk and was all right again. I would like to read something of that woman's life.

Saturday evening I went to the Agricultural Department of the U with Heath, who is physical director there. I took supper with the farmers and watched them while Heath put them through their work. They spent most of the time at basketball, and are a pretty husky lot of fellows. I haven't taken any "gym" work – I don't think I should like it very well anyway. I had rather row or swim or dumbbell it with one or two fellows.

I remember what a time I had fanning you commencement time. I asked you if that was all right, and you said, "Yes, but I can't feel much of it."

We will be together in less than a month! It doesn't seem as if it could be so, but I think of it every hour in the day! I told Walter when you'd be back, and he said, "I don't know if I'll be able to *live* with you these last few days."

I didn't get along very well in Trig today, and I came home and found your letter and read it, and what did I care about stupid old Trig!

I won't try to write how I feel – writing is stupid. Good-bye, dearie. Only *three* more weeks.

With my love,

Roy

FEBRUARY 27, 1895
Houlton to Hamline

My Dear, Dear Roy:

Day after tomorrow I leave! Frank and Lou will go with me as far as Bangor. I have had something of that feeling of being all alone in the world that I told you I had at times, and that used to make me so blue. It isn't so bad *now*, for I know I have *you*. I am so eager at times to get back to you, for it seems as though I could not bear it if we should grow apart. But we *won't* – we *must not*.

I received a good letter from Miss Peck – I will show it to you when I come home. Isn't it lovely to tell you of things I will do when I *come home*, and it is only a little more than two weeks – my!

We had our tea – it wasn't as stupid as I thought it would be. Those 5 o'clock teas are usually the most senseless things. Monday evening we were all invited out, and last evening we went to the Knights of Pythias banquet. They had a toast to "the ladies." Some, of course, had to get off the old jokes about a woman not being able to keep a secret, etc., but Frank just dwelt upon the good in us, as a true knight should.

Isn't it almost time for crocuses and hepaticas, or pussy willows, at least? Oh, I have so many things to ask you about when I see you. We think alike about French books, I guess. After I read your letter I read "A Scrawl" in *Afterwhiles*.

Did I tell you that I have gained 20 pounds since I left home? I have grown to be "moon-faced" just like Tennyson's "Maud."

Only two more weeks! With lots of love,

Anna

MARCH 3, 1895
Lowell to Hamline

My Dear, Dear Roy:

I arrived here last night about 11 o'clock. I left Frank and Lou at Bangor. It was a sad journey. We tried to talk about things, but we were all choking the tears back. I am crying now. I don't know but it is a misfortune to have a heart – it gets torn so. Oh, Roy – these partings are so hard, when you know you cannot meet again for years – perhaps forever. I'm glad Frank has Lou. It seems to me I have more of a heart since I have loved you.

Yesterday was a long, tiresome journey. Frank put me on the train at Bangor, and I had to change cars again at Boston and Lowell junction. I was terribly tired when I got here. The cars were so hot, and my head ached. Mrs. Ingham met me at the station. She had not seen me since I was 12, and, of course, did not know how I looked now. When I got off the car, I saw Mr. Ingham following up another girl who had glasses. I laughed and said, "Here I am!" That seemed to amuse him – I guess he thought I would be more dignified. He has been telling me things I did and said when I was here eight years ago. Mother tried to make me wear kid gloves, he said, but I rebelled. I said they were *tight*, and they bound my hands, and I wasn't going to wear them even if I *was* in the city. They have an elegant house – five horses and carriages, a coachman, etc. – but they have such a cordial way that you feel perfectly at home.

I think it is *time* I came home if you are sitting "alone and unprotected" in a darkened alcove with a junior girl. Why was "Bowers" very wroth? Did *he* want the junior girl too? I'm afraid you and he are as bad as you were last year when you were going to flip pennies to see who should go home with me.

I won't write any more letters if they are going to have such a bad effect on your Trig (!), and I guess I won't write any more now. I'll *tell* you everything – soon!

Lovingly,
Anna

MARCH 5, 1985
Hamline to Lowell

My Dearest Anna:

Yesterday forenoon I finished *Trilby*, and was in a very absent-minded mood part of the day. I like it better than I first thought – in fact, I like it a lot. I don't think it unwholesome. One thing I liked was Trilby's belief. It is a rather fascinating story, and a wee bit gruesome.

Monday I was in kind of a dreamy state. I forgot to latch the door Sunday night. Then Monday forenoon we had a quiz in Trig, and I forgot to take my book to class, and had to run all the way home after it. And at dinner I kept passing the wrong things to the wrong persons at table, so they laughed at me a little about my symptoms.

Your letter came at noon. It seemed such a good letter to me, dear. I was ever *dreamier* after that – and happier. Oh, how these last days will drag! You don't know how I *want* you, dearest. Of course we won't grow apart.

It isn't quite time for crocuses and hepaticas, but walking down toward Macalester yesterday I found on a bush a few brave pussy willows that had struggled out a little. The snow has all gone, but it has been rather cold.

The "Brownings" – our sister literary society – entertained us Saturday night. First they had music and some very pretty tableaux in the chapel. Afterwards we talked, were received, and had ice cream and cake. I don't like such things, but I had as good a time as I could. There weren't enough girls to go round, but I happened to be lucky, and went to supper with Miss Stewart, a senior.

This term I am at a very nice table at the Hall. They are all good people, and try to be entertaining. The fare isn't the best in the world, but it's good and clean, and the butter is nice, and I'm not pining away, I guess.

Twenty pounds – that's a *great* gain. You must be "purtnigh big as me." I weigh about 160 or 162 now.

Oh, I nearly forgot to tell you about Robert Downing. Several of us went to hear him at the Grand. We thought he was going to play *Gladiator*, but were mistaken – it was *Ingomar*. It was a pretty play – Greeks and Barbarians, you known. Downing played Ingomar the barbarian chief, and he looked splendid, for he has immense shoulders, chest and arms (though he was too fleshy). He was a great warrior and, "If he was a god and had the making of the world, he would have not made woman." But when a Greek maiden comes up from Massilia and gives herself as a hostage for her father, he changes someway, and it's funny to see the great fellow, for he doesn't know what's the matter with himself.

Less than two weeks! Oh, but the days they drag. It isn't long.

With my love always,

MARCH 11, 1895
Lowell to Hamline

My dearest Roy:

Last Tuesday we went to the opera *The Mascot,* and on Wednesday we had a "barn party." Gus's carriage house is a regular little hall when it is cleared, and lovely for dancing. They had the carriages rolled out, the floor waxed, and they invited quite a company of young people. We had quite a gay time. The carriage house is heated and lighted with electricity. I'll enclose an item that came out in all the Lowell dailies the next day.

Saturday afternoon we went to the opera again and heard *The Bohemian Girl.* It is in that opera that the girl sings, "I dreamt that I dwelt in marble halls." You have heard this song, I guess – she sang it beautifully.

Yesterday Mr. Ingham and I drove through the city. We saw the manufacturers of Hoods and Ayers Sarsaparilla, and also their private residences. We passed the house of Mr. Hoyt, the manufacturer of Hoyt's German cologne. We saw the home of General Butler, and I saw his granddaughter at the opera Saturday. We went around by the mills, where cotton cloth, prints and boots are manufactured. I never saw so many large mills in my life. Tomorrow we are going to the opera again; Tuesday evening a dance; Wednesday, Boston – look around the city a little; and in the afternoon another play. After the play I take the train home – I am coming by the road that passes through Hoosier Tunnel and crosses Niagara Falls. I think the train stops on the bridge below the falls, so that one can get a glimpse of them. Uncle Gus says I have "spunk" to stop over there and see them, but I feel a little afraid to go alone. They say Niagara is one of the worst places in the United States. Aunt Nan says she wouldn't think of doing such a thing, but I'm going anyway!

I seem to amuse Uncle Gus. He thinks I have a good deal of pluck. He has been teaching me to dance, and thinks I have learned very quickly. He said to some friends: "She's full of ginger – I wish I had such a girl myself!"

I think I shall reach home Friday night. When will you come down? I'll write you as soon as I get home.

Lovingly,

Anna

CHAPTER 8

Hard Straits

MARCH 13, 1895
Hamline to Eyota, Minnesota

My Dearest Anna:

I'm afraid this isn't going to be a very good letter. I'm having a terrible time, and I look so blue that it makes me laugh. I'm in hard straits – I failed Trig. I expected as much, but it bothers just the same, doesn't it? I was intending to take Analytical Geometry, Chemistry, Zoology, and German this term. Well, they won't let me take Zoology as I want to, because there isn't laboratory room for me. And I can't take Analytics until I clear Trig away. I talked to the professor – that I knew I was slow and awkward with mathematics, but if I couldn't take Analytics I might as well go home.

It was a mistake my going to Hamline last year. Now my Chemistry is all wrong. When I went to register this term, they said I would have to take an exam, which I took this morning. The fellow was in a hurry and gave me only five questions – now, you can't test a fellow's knowledge of a subject with five questions, can you? I didn't do well at all. I got a wee bit nervous, and that's not like me in an exam. You see, Anna – it's fatal to miss in this, for I'd have to take this freshman work over. I'll find how I came out this afternoon.

Well, what do you think of me now? I've been kicking myself for a couple of days. I do get to hating myself so, and it doesn't do any good, but how can I help it? I'm no student, because I hate to drudge at mathematics and science. Folks tell me I'm not worthless, but it seems to me I am lots of times.

Well, what's done can't be helped.

Your letter reached me Monday. I went down on the Washington Avenue Bridge to read it. You remember what a beautiful day it was. That was a fine letter – sweet and good and like you. I'm tired of studying and bothering my head.

I'll write you again Sunday, perhaps – I'll try and make it a good one – not full of lamentation.

I wish I could see you now, dearest – oh, so much.

Roy

MARCH 16, 1895
Eyota to Oronoco

My Dearest Roy:

I arrived here this noon. When can you come down? Come any time – whenever you can – for I am so *anxious* to see you, dear – and stay as long as you can.

Lovingly,

Anna

MARCH 17, 1895
Oronoco to Eyota

My Dearest Anna:

I'm main sleepy but want to write you a little bit. Are you there? Your letter from Lowell came to me last night; it had to be forwarded from Hamline. The boys kept me in bed, for I was sick with La Grippe, and when I got up I was so weak and my head felt so light and queer that I knew I would be no good at exams, so I came home Wednesday. The boys took good care of me and got all the grippe out of me, and I've been feeling better right along. Pretty strong now – lifted 750 lbs. on scales as easily as ever Saturday, and put up the big dumbbells. Reckon I ain't so emaciated but what you will know me.

When do you *want* me to come? Of course, I'll come anyway – whether you want me or not. It doesn't seem as if you were so near, Anna – I can't believe you're *there* hardly. My, I want to see you *awfully*.

With my love,

MARCH 26, 1895
Hamline to Eyota

My good Little Queen:

Here I am back again. When I left you at Eyota I saw a handkerchief wave at the window, for I was watching as the stage left. That was the last glimpse I'll have of you for 10 weeks. Saturday I worked in the mill a little – helped Henry unload straw – and in the afternoon I wandered away up the North Branch with the rifle. I didn't kill any ducks or anything, but didn't care much.

Wasn't it nice Sunday morning! Charlie was around the house with me, and he saw some ducks – three of them – over in a little bayou opposite the Point. We could hardly get on to the ice at the edges, but we took the little rifle and found a place to get on near the ferry. Took some poles for safety and got across without danger. We had more fun creeping up through the woods to stalk those ducks! We got near enough at last and fired simultaneously, and one of them flew over in toward the cove and fell on the ice where we found him. It was nice walking through the woods – they seemed springy, and so did the smell of the oak leaves, and warm puffs of wind in your face now and then. I wished you were there. We went over to the place where you and I climbed up to find those yellow daisies Decoration Day *(Memorial Day)*, and where you tore the trimming on your dress, and we had to mend it with pins and thorns.

We got our duck all right – a big mallard drake – and he was beautifully marked. Then we went down the river and tramped around for a while, and then came home, and our family went to Aunt Minnie's and ate turkey. I was glad to get out a little with Charlie before I went away. When you are out with him he is always showing you a place and telling you how he killed some game there. I believe your brother Frank would like him. The white bulldog was with us, and he did something that pleased me, and I said I wished I was just such a fellow as that dog, and Charlie said, "You are pretty near," and I considered that as a compliment coming from him.

We had rather an unpleasant ride in to Rochester Monday, on account of the dust. The train that brought me up to Red Wing was slow and close – not a regular passenger train. I didn't eat any supper, but bought some bananas, and a fellow came in and asked what town it was. I told him, and found out he was "bum" riding on the "blind baggage." I gave him the banana I had left, for I 'lowed he was hungry. He told me a lot of things. He said a car of wheat was a good place to ride in the summertime, but it would freeze a man to death in the winter. A good place to ride in the winter, he said, was a carload of sheep. "Get right in with the sheep, and you can keep warm." Imagine how a fellow would feel and look after riding with the sheep, without anything to eat for a day or two. This young fellow was going to Galesburg, where he said he had a job in view. It was quite interesting to hear him tell.

There was another boy – 18 or 19, I should think – from the pineries. He was rather tough, I guess, but he looked as if no one had ever cared for him. He was going to Main Rock or some such place. He wanted me to go uptown and "have a beer." He said his mother had died three weeks before and every "darned thing had happened" since then. This fellow had bummed some, but only when he couldn't help it. He was a Scandinavian or German, I think. I like to talk with these folks.

I have been a little homesick, as I always am at first, but I remember what you told me last – not to get lonely, and remember I am your knight. I'm so glad I saw you, dear. I feel better and happier. You must write and tell me all you do and think.

With my love,

Roy

MARCH 28, 1895
Eyota to Hamline

My Dear, Dear Roy:

Your letter was waiting for me when I came home tonight, and it seemed so good to get it, dear, for in spite of all my efforts *not* to be lonely, my heart has wanted you very, very much.

I must tell you what has happened during the last 24 hours, though I hardly know where to begin or how to tell it. I'll let you know the worst at once. I have agreed to teach school, and it begins Monday.

I don't know why I ever did such a thing, but yesterday afternoon Mrs. Doty came over and said the Saxton School (six miles out in the country) had not hired a teacher for this spring term, and she and Dr. Dugan had just been talking the matter over, and they thought it would be a fine thing for me to apply for it. It was a good neighborhood, the school was an easy one, etc.

I insisted that I couldn't teach – had never thought of such a thing; had never taken a teacher's exam in my life, and knew I couldn't pass it now if I should try. And even if my education was all right, I didn't think I could govern children. I walked around the room, and we all talked at once, and at last it ended by their carrying me off to apply for it. I protested all the way – that it was the most foolish thing I ever heard of. But I felt very sure they would not hire me anyhow, as I had no certificate and had never taught before, and I thought that by applying and failing I could silence Mrs. Doty and the rest.

Well, I saw the Board. I told them just how it was – no certificate and never taught and never given much thought to teaching, so did not know much about the methods, etc. That evening after I got home I came to realize what I had done, and how awful it would be if I *should* get it. The thought gave me a nervous chill, and I sat and shook just as Negroes do when they are frightened. Then came the reaction and a high fever. Mother grew a little anxious in the night, for she said even when I had been seriously sick, she never knew my temperature to be higher. I was all right by morning, when

Mr. Saxton drove up and said the Board had met, and had given the school to me, provided I would accept at $25 a month.

For a bit I wished I was old and most dead! I don't mind the work – no matter how hard – if I only felt sure I should not wake up a failure of it. Mr. Saxton and his wife encouraged me, and said they were sure I would have no trouble.

We went up to Uncle Henry's and told how things were. Clara asked me if I had ever studied Theory and Practice, and what was I going to be doing the first day. She said Mr. Chapman would have to give me a special examination. There are only two days before school must begin! What am I to do? We went to Dr. Stinchfield's *(Dr. Augustus Stinchfield, one of the founders of the Mayo Clinic)* for dinner. Dr. Dugan was there, and the two doctors, and Mrs. Stinchfield braced me up ever so much. Mr. Chapman was very kind – asked me what preparations I had, and told me if I had any state certificates to send them to him and he would make out a teacher's certificate on my standing. It was all over in two minutes, and a great weight off my mind – though, of course, the worst of the battle is before me yet. I don't know what in the world I shall do?

You will be surprised to find me so weak and cowardly, but just think of my writing and spelling and arithmetic! This is *awful*, Roy. Do you suppose I can ever get through it? My life must not be a useless one. I can't get out of it now, and I *won't* give it up without a *terrible* struggle. I'll hang on like that dog if it kills me.

The school is out just before the Forth of July. Don't let this make you blue, dear. Perhaps I won't have so much trouble as I anticipate. I can't see why they hired me, for they had a good many other applications from experienced teachers, and everyone but myself had a certificate.

You must be tired of this, so I will stop. I'm glad you wrote me about those boys you came across in Red Wing. I suppose we don't know much about how some people get on.

Don't feel anxious about me in my school. I should hate to think you were worrying too. I'll do my best and perhaps I can learn how. Good night, dear.

With lots of love,

Your Little Girl
(who's going to be a school ma'am)

MARCH 31, 1895
Hamline to Eyota

Dearest Little Girl:

Well! You took my breath away, but I had to laugh when I was through reading your letter, and I was *awfully* sorry for you too, dear.

By the time you get this you will be at it. I'll think of you hard, and be with you all I can tomorrow. I'm *sure* you will get along all right – only don't worry about it, Anna. There isn't a school that is worth your making yourself sick or unhappy about. I think you won't have to "govern" much – they are sure to like you. I imagine you won't find it as hard as you think after you get started, and – my sakes – you needn't trouble yourself about "writing and spelling and arithmetic," though I would spell "Forth of July" "Fou*r*th" (!).

What did Miss Peck say to your venture? I guess I can worry a little about you if I want to – though I shan't much, for I'm sure you'll have no trouble, and if they aren't good to you, Walter and I will come down there and make things *reek* – we have sworn it – 'tis changeless as the sea.

Friday my friend Edwin came back to Hamline. He had a terrible headache, and was disgusted with the streetcar business. He was out learning half a day when his head began to ache. He had one line pretty well learned and had been studying the rules. When he stopped work he couldn't sleep or anything, for the streets and rules would keep running through his mind like a nightmare, and altogether he worked up a great dislike for the whole business.

We got some coffee and a good stout lunch. We laughed and talked, and I got him out of his blues a little – got him to stop thinking of streetcars and eat his supper. Then he felt better, but in the morning his headache came back just the same, and he went home yesterday. He doesn't think he is fitted for a conductor, and perhaps he is not – you know what a nervous, high-strung sort of a boy he is. I wouldn't like it either.

I went over to Julius's yesterday. Little Viola was quite sick. Her temperature was 103, and the doctor said she nearly had a convulsion, but it was nothing serious, he said, and she would soon be all right.

I have a little ordeal next Wednesday. I have to take all the exams I missed. We're through with Livy and are taking up Horace – poetry, odes, you know. It's going to be all right – starting into a new author is always a bit harder at first.

I haven't much to write this time. Anna, you won't let this teaching worry and tire you out, will you? I wish I could see you a little while tonight, just for a minute. I'm sure you will be all right. I *know* you're very brave and plucky in time of need, and you are such a conscientious worker that they are sure to like you. Now don't bother yourself and work too hard.

Good night – remember that I love you more than everything else, dearest. Always,

Roy

MARCH 31, 1895
From Walter at Hamline to Eyota

Dear friend:

After Roy's dictation, I now take my pen in hand to let you know by these few lines that we are all well, except myself (Walter E. Bowers), who am ailin', and hope you are enjoying the same blessing. Now, Roy says that's all the suggestions he can make, and I'll have to go on by my loneself.

You know, I ain't much of a correspondent, but I rise to the occasion in this, your hour of trial and anxiety, and will attend to the duties which crowd upon me when I realize, as Roy says, that I am "the pater familias of our class and ought to attend to my flock." Therefore I hasten to condole with you as Roy suggests, and to say I hope your forebodings are utterly groundless. In fact, I know they are, for you'll get along grandly. However, your expression of trepidation has awakened a responsive chord here, and you may be cheered of knowing that our sympathy has constantly followed you since we heard the news, and particularly as you ring the bell at 9 o'clock Monday morn, call the school to order, and lay down the rules to the mischievous urchins. We've been saying it's a pity we haven't that power of mysterious communication with persons at a distance, so that we could make our sympathy felt just where you are, calling the school to order.

If the boys try to break up your school, you can count on us – we've got our plans all laid out to squelch 'em, and it will be done so they'll remember and won't try it again – just send for us. Roy has been in a frenzy of sympathy and excitement. We've hardened our knuckles by splitting each a panel of the door. Roy has drunk a strong solution of ink, and longed for some alcohol and prussic acid. He has been singing: "And I'll buy a big revolver and I'll load it to the muzzle."

And we've laid plans for action in case you have an outbreak in school. We have chosen bicycles as the means of arriving promptly on the scene (I learned to ride one a day or two ago, and will teach Roy as we travel). Everything is arranged – whose bicycles we'll borrow; what weapons to take with us; how we'll force the schoolhouse door; and when we get there, the punishment of the ringleader and all his confederates – what tactics we'll use when it comes to bloodshed – and how Roy can best church those of our enemies who are over 7 feet high! Roy is now exercising with the dumbbells, working up muscle for the fray.

I guess I've said enough in this line. I think teaching will do you good, and I know you'll succeed grandly. Don't get discouraged, and don't get homesick. I wish I could visit your school – probably you *don't*. Good-bye, with my sympathy and encouragement.

W. E. B.

APRIL 8, 1895
Hamline to Eyota

Dearest:

I wish I could write something good to you – something that would seem like touching and looking at you. You don't care so very much what I've been doing this week – that I haven't flunked dead in Analytics so far; that I got 95 for History last term; that I weathered my first oral quiz in Zoology; that I went to see *Faust* last night.

I suppose it has been raining all day with you too. Now if it comes warm we'll have some spring, shortly (sounds like a bloomin' farmer talking).

I've just read your letter over. It seems as if I *never* will see you again. I know you look too harshly at yourself. You know what I believe of you, dear. Perhaps you don't, for I never could tell you just how true and noble and sweet I know you are.

I think sometimes I would like to see the real truth about myself – not what people think, but the real truth. Dearest, if *you're* not spiritual, I wonder what of *me*. I'm such a careless, impulsive mortal, and downright bad in places too. I never got a glimpse of what I was intended to be, I guess. We will try and help each other – I *can* help you, can't I? I wish I could see you oftener, dearest – we'll love all the harder to make up for the distance, won't we?

It was last Sunday when you were feeling discouraged with yourself, wasn't it? The mood has gone by this time, I hope. I'm awful sorry you didn't hear Salvini – he would have antidoted 20 preachers with whining voices and made a body glad he was alive and young and warm-hearted. How I hate preachers with those whining voices. I think always that something like Taillifer's wild, free war song that time at the feast where the old monk was chanting some martyrdom would be so refreshing. That isn't just what I mean, but you understand.

I went down to the library this afternoon and brought back your old *Idle Thoughts* – thought I would kinda like to see it again. I've changed some in these two years, I'm sure. It seems a long time, doesn't it?

So – *Faust*. It was very good, I thought – better than Morrison's Faust that I saw last year. Mephistopheles was better, and so was Marquerite and Faust. Three fellows a couple seats behind me kept whispering and telling all about it until I was hot – anything like that irritates me. Some people haven't any sense of appreciation.

I had a letter from my sister Mary Wednesday. She told me about the dress and hat she was going to wear on the river this summer, and then said, "But what will you care about hearing of such things? I rather forget my brother is 20 years old and in college, but still I know he cares for the home things." I wonder if that was irony – how gracious of me to think of such things; to bend down in my great wisdom. She writes in a slightly melodramatic style sometimes, doesn't she? Just a wee bit – I reckon all girls of 14 with anything dramatic about them do. I'm not making fun of my good little sister, you know. I like to have her write me the way she does.

Say, I've six essays to write in Rhetoricals – I'm behind. Don't you wonder at *that*?! I'm the worst one about writing. I can talk a lot, such as it is, but I hate to *write*. Oh, I'm a bad job. Bowers says I'm a "connoisseur of laziness." Well, he's inclined the same way – only *I'm* in a more advanced stage and can hold myself up to her as a warning – an example of the depths to which people may sink.

Walter came over and we went to church, he stayed to dinner, and we went for a couple hours' walk afterwards. Then we got to talking about a sore subject – myself. I like to talk with Walter – he has a good deal of sense, and he knows me quite a little. If I'm going to amount to anything, it won't do to keep on as I have, will it? I guess I don't count for very much either way – good or bad. And I could if I would – I will yet. I'm dissatisfied with myself, and sort of unhappy a good deal of the time – except when I go in and have fun and a great uproarious time. Perhaps I could drag through life someway in my impromptu way, depending on my wits to carry me through things, but that isn't what I want.

I wonder you don't tire of my letters – stupid and effeminate; worthy of a blind puppy. I'm not blue a bit – I'm not that way much anymore. Please don't feel sorry for me – I don't deserve that. Don't let this trouble you, dear. I can rave a little to *you* if I want to, can't I? I'll be a man yet.

I've read your letter over again. Why do you think it would be more than you could handle – a school in Northfield? Would it be much harder work? Of course it would be if it was a larger school than in smaller towns. You don't want to get a position where the work will be too heavy for you, dear.

I'm glad you're feeling so well. It's good to have someone I can talk to just as I want to – who'll let me rave and hate myself, and who won't believe it, and will love a fellow just the same. You are very gentle and kind, my dearest – there is no one like you.

Good night again, little sweetheart – goodnight in the old way.

APRIL 9, 1895
Saint Charles, Minnesota, to Hamline

My Dear, Dear Roy:

Here I am up in my room at Mr. Saxton's, lying on the lounge, scribbling to you. I get so tired during the day that it's a comfort to stretch out on this lounge and just do nothing.

This has been another blue day. Oh, Roy, I am so unhappy – I am a regular baby, but I can't help it. I'm making wretched work of teaching. There isn't as much to me as my friends think. I don't believe there's anything in the world that I am good for. I don't know what I shall do next year. I don't believe I can ever make a success of teaching. I don't see how I can ever get through this long term. I won't give up yet, though. I don't know one thing about teaching or how to manage a school.

I've read your letter over and over, dear. I'm glad you wrote that last part, for it is such a comfort to know that you *love* me, and I know you will love me even though I fail in everything. I wish I amounted to more.

The bell has rung for supper and I must go. I keep your last letter with me nearly all the time, for it seems a part of you, and it encourages me that you love me and you care whether I do well or not, and I *will* – I will do my best.

With my love,

Anna

I didn't mail this today, and tonight I can add a brighter postscript. This has been a better day than any I have had since I have been at it. I wish they could all be like this – if they were, I think I could like it. One of my girls brought me two crocuses – the first I have seen this spring. I have them in a tin cup on my desk. I'll send the best of the two to you. I must go work.

One of my pupils defined goatee as "a little goat."

I don't know what my life would be these days if it were not for you.

CHAPTER 9

Faith in Each Other

APRIL 11, 1895
Dover, Minnesota, to Hamline

My Dearest Roy:

Well, here I am on the third week of my school and still alive – the week half-gone and nothing done yet!

Tuesday was the worst day last week. I hope this will be the worst for this week, for I don't know what I should do if things were much worse than yesterday. I have a cold and am quite hoarse, and as the children were very noisy, it was hard to talk – that made me feel cross. And one girl had to stay after school – *more* ought to have stayed! They quarrel terribly – worse than you and Bowers. They threw glasses at each other, and one boy got a deep cut in his forehead. I washed it off and tied it up with my handkerchief. Then they fought some more – I stopped that. Then, as I am so unreasonable to forbid them to swear (in English), they swore at each other in German.

But today everything went well, and I am feeling lighthearted tonight. This has been a perfect day, and now, in the early twilight, the air is so soft, and it is so still that it makes me wish, more than usual, that you were here. We would take a walk, and it would all be twice as beautiful.

I guess I wrote you that I board at Mr. Saxton's, three-quarters of a mile from the schoolhouse. I like it here. They are very pleasant and as good to me as they can be. Mr. Saxton is on the Board. They have two children who go to school. It is lovely walking to school in the morning – fresh and nice. I generally start soon after 7 and get back home about 6. As I have 26 recitations, and all ages 6 to 16, it keeps me more than busy.

We have breakfast at 6 – pretty early for me. Living on a farm like this is entirely new to me, but I like it. I like to watch the hired man – a German – eat. He eats five times as much as I do, and he does it in half the time. He goes at it with both hands as though he meant business.

I have commenced reading *Dr. Latimer* by Clara Lenice Berman. I have been reading some of Mary Titus's books, but I'm too tired evenings after I get home to read anything very deep.

I think the worst is over in my school – I hope. Yes, we will try to have faith in ourselves, dear. If we sometimes lose faith in ourselves, we have faith enough in each other to keep up our courage.

With lots of love,

Anna

APRIL 11, 1895
Hamline to Eyota

Sweetheart:

My, I was glad to get your letter, for it seemed long since I heard from you, and I've been anxious to know how you got on with your school. This first week was the worst, of course.

Anna, I believe we're alike in lots of things. I have times when it seems to me that I'm no good at all – I'm not practical, and too dreamy and idle ever to make a success of anything. But we will come out all right. Dearest, I'm glad you said my believing in you helped you.

This is going to be a kind of incoherent letter, but someway I feel as if I loved you more than ever today.

Mary says the ice is all out of the pond and the crocuses are growing on the Point. Tuesday I walked down to the Mississippi – down by Shadow Falls – and hunted for crocuses, but didn't find any.

Monday night was the intercollegiate oratorical contest. The U of M, Carleton, Macalester, and Hamline were represented each by two men. The winner goes to represent Minnesota in the Interstate contest. The contest took place in a church in St. Paul – big delegations from all the schools. There was some yelling, I can tell you! The U yelled as if they were better organized, but we made as much noise. The orations were all good, and our man got first! Most of the Hamline boys had canes decorated with our colors – red and gray – to wave, and the girls had streamers too. When they announced Hamline was first, you ought to have seen us rise up with colors, and we all waved, and then up came the yell of primeval man! Then we crowded together as we marched out and yelled, "Bum-get-a-rat-trap, bigger-than-a-cat-trap! Cannibals! Cannibals! Zip Boom Bah!! Hamline! Hamline! Rah! Rah! Rah!" I wish I knew how many foot-pounds of energy I expended shouting!

Hamline has always beaten the U in oratory. I've worked up quite a little patriotism, haven't I? Probably next year I'll be yelling myself hoarse for the U and rushing Hamline's banner. Renegado!

Last Friday night I saw DeWolf Hopper in the opera *Dr. Syntax*. It was the only good opera I have ever seen. It was light, but very good – oh, it was funny. The singing was fine, and some of the effects were very pretty.

I took my examination in French and got along all right. Most of the boys who had the grippe aren't in school yet. Douglas has had to stop school altogether. I feel nearly as well as before I was sick. I'm sorry about your rheumatism, dear. If you were here now, I believe I could warm it away.

Well, I winna write anymore now. We will try and have faith in ourselves, won't we? Good-bye, sweetheart mine.

With my love,

APRIL 13, 1895
Dover to Hamline

My Dearest, Dearest Roy:

The last two days of school have been awful – I'd give anything if you were here tonight. I've got the ill will of the Germans in my school, and my! they're hateful. They imagine I treat the "Yankees" better than I do them. I kept a little girl after school Friday, and she wrote me a note telling how much she thought of me. It just about broke my heart, but I guess I shall get used to such things. This is all new to me. If there were people in the world who disliked me, I never knew it. But to have some of my own pupils dislike me, and to go to school in the morning knowing it, and to come home at night feeling it – it seems almost unendurable for six weeks more. I must get used to it. Others have to stand it.

Today two of the boys got to fighting. I told them to take their seats. One did as I asked, and the other wouldn't. I told him I'd see him after school. When school was out he said he *wouldn't* stay – started for the door. I caught him by the arm as he passed by me and tried to set him down, but he gave a jerk and was off. I ought not to have touched him. He is only 9 years old. I thought if he *felt* that I was in earnest, he would stop.

I don't know what I shall do about it – not let him come to school, I suppose, until he has been punished some way. If he says he won't go home, I can't make him, and he would like nothing better than to be left out of his classes. Wish I was an Amazon and could pick him up and set him outdoors. If I can't even manage 15 children, I might as well make up my mind never to teach again. There are a few that help me more than they know – just a smile, or the way one will sometimes say, "Good night, Teacher," means a good deal to me.

I must get to work, dear. It seems I have never wanted you more. I can see this fight is doing me good, and perhaps, after all – "Whatever is, is best."

With my love,

Anna

APRIL 15, 1895
Hamline to Eyota

Dearest Little Sweetheart:

Yes, dearest, I do understand it all – I want to *love* you, dear, and comfort you a little if I can. I'm glad we have some faults alike – they help us sympathize with each other. You must write me all about your troubles, my brave little girl, for if it helps you, it helps me just as much.

I liked that last letter better than any I ever had. You mustn't be afraid to tell me everything, for I *can* sympathize, because I've very weak in some things. And, dear, I presume you do better than you think. And you couldn't expect to know all about teaching the first time you tried. You shouldn't worry yourself more than you can help about next year (though *I'm* a great one to preach about *that,* ain't I?). Things generally come around all right when the time comes.

You're making a brave fight, dear – you're not a baby, but the womanliest girl I ever saw. Perhaps this is more of a fight for *you* than others, just as it would be more of a victory for *me* to hold myself down to Mathematics and do it up brown than it would be for Walter. And, Anna, you mustn't worry and work yourself sick – whatever happens, you will be careful for me?

I won't write more – you will understand what I can't say – I want to comfort and pet you a bit, you know. And, my darling – you know I love you not for what you can or might *do*, but because you are *you*.

With my dear love,

APRIL 21, 1895
Hamline to Eyota

My Dearest Anna:

I am just back from Minneapolis. Hasn't it been beautiful weather? This afternoon Welty and I went over near Lake of the Isles; found a warm, sunny place and read. I had *Reveries of a Bachelor* – perhaps you remember the three chapters: Morning, Noon and Evening. It was pleasant there reading. Welty was reading *Dream Life.* I liked Eurica and the English girl, but Bella the most, of course. How the author remembers the sensations that a child has – I think he touches a person and gets his sympathy at once.

If we could only tell what we feel sometimes, so that other people might get the same sensation. Don't the white clouds lying low down in the west in a warm spring, when you look at them against the light blue, give you a vague, beautiful, hopeful sensation sometimes? There are lots of such feelings one can't describe – just little breaths of something beautiful.

This evening we boys went to church, where we heard a young Universalist minister. He talked about books – what ones to read, and how to read them. I liked it. He spoke of *Lorna Doone*, and said he thought it one of the best stories. I like to hear anyone praise a book I like.

I read an article in *The Forum* by Boynson about Romanticists and Realists. He is a realist, I guess, and praised Tolstoy and Howells and Zola, and knocked all a fellow's favorites out. Talked against our romanticists, who write stories with incident and plot – Scott and Stevenson, Conan Doyle, Haggard, DuMaurier, Beatrice Harridan. I felt fierce about it, but looked in another *Forum* and found another article that was a good one by Thayer, saying Realism was on the decline with its "art for art's sake" and analysis; and that the love of humanity for a story – for something with imagination in it – had asserted itself, as is proved by the books now being most written and read. Robert Louis Stevenson has been always popular, even though he has written with Realism at its height. We must read some of Stevenson together sometime.

I saw *Faust* at the Grand in St. Paul Friday. I didn't like the acting someway – Mephistopheles seemed to me to act like the villain dressed in the devil's clothes. Perhaps I haven't the right conception of the devil – it don't seem to me that a fellow would slap him on the shoulder as Faust did. Oh, what a critic we are getting to be (!). Mark Twain said it used to surprise him how much more he knew about playing Shakespeare than did Forrest. I liked Marguerite better – she had two long braids of yellow hair as big as my wrist, and I liked to hear her intonations of how she said "Faust."

Yesterday I walked down south three miles or so to that old wooden tower I told you of – it's about the highest place around.

Well, it's late. This is a poor letter, but you must consider my being sleepy. I think of you so much – wish I could help you. You mustn't work yourself sick, will you? I hope this week will be a good one for you. I'll try and work better too.

With my dear love,

APRIL 21, 1895
Eyota to Hamline

My Dearest Roy:

Your letter – I cannot tell you how good it seemed. You *did* comfort me, dear, and made me feel more brave. I never will be afraid, dearest, to tell you everything – you understand perfectly. I'm glad you think I'm not babyish, for at times I feel as though I was very much a baby, and I wonder if I ever will feel grown up.

I am just getting over the German measles. I came down with them Thursday, but as most of the pupils have had them, I taught Friday. I was quite sick yesterday, but am feeling better today. I shall go back to school Monday morning. The worst part of German measles is the cough that goes with them, but the doctor gave me some medicine, and I shall be all right.

When I discovered I had the measles, I thought of what Prof. Adams said to us once: "If there is anything going on, be there in it." I'm doing my best to follow his teachings.

Don't be afraid that I work too hard – I'm very careful, and I'm not worrying so much now. I know, dearest, that it isn't because of what I *do* that you love me, but you could not help but be disappointed if I make a failure of this.

With my love,

Anna

We must try and not worry about next year. There is some work in the world for us, and we shall find out what it is. (I want to know *right away* though!)

APRIL 28, 1895
Dover to Hamline

My Dearest, Dearest Roy:

Hasn't this been a beautiful day! Mother and I drove out this afternoon. The leaves are coming out on the willow tree, and it's just lovely – I have the window open now as I write, and the air comes in so soft and warm. Everything is still except for some sheep bleating once in a while. It's a perfect Sunday evening. I wish we could be together now.

I have been thinking – it's a little more than a month and I shall see you again. You must come out to my school. Wonder what you'll think of the teacher (!). I'm not so blue now. I got over the German measles all right, and my cold is better. Last Tuesday Mother and Grandma drove out and brought your letter. It's queer, but I keep loving you more and more all the time.

You would have laughed if you could have walked into my school last Friday. It was rainy, and they could not go outdoors, so to keep them quiet

I started them playing some games. I raced and romped with them until my hair came down. I stopped to do it up, when I heard a German girl say she "didn't see how teachers could do up so many hairs"!

I think I sometimes have the same feeling you speak of looking at the sky – the world is full of beauty, isn't it? And this is the most beautiful time of the whole year. I hope we can read some good books together this summer. *Faust* is one of the plays I'm hoping to see sometime.

Last Thursday Mister Saxton and I went after dogtooth violets. We found the ground covered with them in places, and we picked until I was tired. The anemones and cowslips are out. There aren't any hepaticas around here – I'm sorry, for I like those best of all. I wonder why it is that there are some flowers I *love*, and others that I only *like*. I *love* hepaticas – I don't feel the same toward any other flower – I don't know why.

It's late and I must close. Don't worry for fear I'll work too hard – I won't. Last week was a very good one. I wonder how it went with my knight? Good night, and my love for you, dear.

Anna

MAY 1, 1895
Hamline to Eyota

My Dearest Anna:

I hardly ever get any mail at night, and good things seem best when they come unexpectedly. Yesterday the clouds cleared away in the afternoon. I had studied pretty well – was going to hear The Bostonians in *Robin Hood* – and then your letter came too – your good letter. I was happy.

Robin Hood was so fine! The singing was splendid – I have heard The Bostonians have some of the best voices in the country. And it was funny, and the effects were so pretty, and the costumes and dresses of the girls. It was all gay and bright and lively. I am sure you would like it. The great violinist Ysaye has been in the cities, and Thomas's Orchestra – I would've liked to have heard them.

Welty wanted to go to *Faust* again (he had already been twice), and he wanted me to go. I liked it much better this time – I was in better shape for it, and the theater wasn't "barny" like the one in St. Paul. I never read much of Faust, but enough to get the run of it. It's sort of an allegory representing the good and evil influences in a man's life – Mephistopheles the lower, evil part; and Marguerite the good, pure, ennobling influence. Did you ever read it? This is what it means, isn't it?

Wasn't it a beautiful morning last Sunday? Mark and I went to the Church of the Redeemer and heard the Universalist minister Dr. Tuttle. It was a *very* good sermon – his text was "Launch out into the deep." He said people lived too much on the surface – a too superficial life in society, in religion, in love, and in home and friendship – and to "launch out into the deep."

You mustn't think I go to operas and such things very much, because I write you so much about them. There is so little to tell about schoolwork, and it isn't very interesting. We are through with Trig and just commenced Analytical Geometry. I have quite a bit to make up. I don't know whether I will get through Trig or not. Of course, I can if I work on it hard enough. I have neglected it, and ought to be ashamed of myself – I am.

The other studies are all right. Horace is nice – you would like it – and we don't have near as long lessons as we did in Vergil. Meiklejohn's *History of the English Language* I like, and it's easy for me. Do you know, I like things best that have to do with language or literature or criticism? I was reading an article in *The Forum*, and it was very interesting – "The Healthful Tone in American Literature." Did I tell you about the little story I liked by Davis – *The Princess Aline*?

I've just read your letter again, dear, for inspiration. I wonder if you like my letters as I do yours. I haven't been out in the country where the fields are – don't know how things are growing. It has rained a little, and the sun would come out hot and you could almost hear things grow. Yes, I think this is the best, daintiest time of the year.

I wish we could be together. Anna, I'm glad I found you and can love you while I'm a boy. I think it is different than if I had been older. Dear heart, I want to see you so much. Well, it winna be long. Anna, I want to be worthy to have you love me so.

There's a baseball game commencing over on campus between the sophs and juniors, and I must go over and yell for the juniors. A man must love and work and fight, mustn't he?

With my love,

Roy

MAY 8, 1895
Hamline to Eyota
My Dearest Anna:

I'm down by the Mississippi a little way above Shadow Falls. It has been a regular summer day here, and probably has been in southern Minnesota – not a cloud in the sky, and the sun coming down a lot.

Your letter reached me this noon, and as soon as Zoology was over I walked down here so as to answer it out of doors in the woods. I'm sitting on the edge of a high bank – nearly as high as the Point at home – with six birches growing in a clump at my feet. I've just been down to the falls to drink. It is fine to look up and down the river. Both banks are wooded, with different kinds of trees. The leaves are out, and look as though they were fresh varnished. The river is pretty full now too; I'd like to go down there and swim. How quick spring came when it did come – it seems like a new world. I wish – oh, how I wish – you were here with me. There's lots of room in the shade of these little birches.

Last Friday the boys wanted me to go and hear *Robin Hood*. I told them I was "sair tempted," and then, of course, I yielded, and we got all the boys in the house to go. I got more out of it than I did the first time. I should think some of those actors and opera singers would be very interesting people to know. They look so bright and intelligent, and they have been all over, and lots of them educated in Europe in music. I imagine they would be different from most people.

I read *Window in Thrums* this week and liked it pretty well. I got two letters from home. Mother is good – it's the first time she has written me this term. Because she has been so busy and tired, Mary does the writing. A fellow thinks how he wants to get home, and don't think so much that they – the folks back there – want to see *him* too, but I guess they do. Mary is making great plans for the summer when I get back. She's a fine little girl – a *splendid* little girl. A fellow don't make as much of his sisters as he ought to, I believe. I'm going to get acquainted with Mary this summer. I have been away a good deal for four years, and people change. Mary would like to go somewhere to school – she's nearly ready for high school. She said, "Wouldn't it be nice if we could rent a house in Minneapolis, and you go to the University, and I go to high school?"

I don't think I've had my sharp struggle yet, Anna. I am having kind of downhearted times. I wish you were here to talk with now. I suppose I am about the age when a fellow is unsettled, and don't know what he can or will do. I know I have *you*, though – the best of all.

This isn't much of a letter.

With my dear love,

MAY 17, 1895

Hamline to Eyota

My Sweetheart:

Your letter came this noon and I'm sorry for you, dear. You mustn't let it hurt you, dear, because a bloomin' passel of Germans don't like you – what do you care? Everyone that knows anything likes you. You mustn't let it "pretty near break your heart" because some of those children don't like you – *I* do *immensely.* I hope it hasn't been so hard this week. I'll go on and write you what I have been doing just as I always do. I wish I could help you, but I don't know as anything I can say would do any good. I know you are a brave little girl.

I was over at Auntie's last Sunday for a while. Welty and I heard Doctor Hoyt give a fine sermon about how one gets by giving, and how we must die to certain things to reach our aim. Went with Welty to see *Captain Swift*. It was given by the Giffeweill Stock Company, and we thought it a nice little play – a tragedy – good all through.

We Philos have to entertain our sister literary society this spring. The Amphics have to entertain their sisters too, and we are going to charter a boat and go for a trip down the river toward Hastings. I guess it will be a nice little trip.

We have considerable fun at our table – now we have a feud with the table next to us. The others got wind that we were going to have a spread in the bookroom because we were secreting off sugar, bread, spoons, etc. I'm afraid we got into a bit of a to-do that involved canes and the mingled sound of wailing and rejoicing. I have been in a few other scraps – I don't know but what I might possibly get called up for my escapades, but I haven't – yet. I'm developing a good propensity for carrying on – a fellow has to have a little fun.

I have been reading parts of *For Faith and Freedom* by Walter Besant. It's a historical novel about things that happened at the time of Monmouth's attempt for the throne of England. That was the rebellion that Tom Faggus in *Lorna Doone* joined, and he was wounded at Sedgemoor, you remember.

I will be so glad to get home – it seems like a long time. I'm in some doubt whether I shall be in school next year – whether it's the best thing for me. Of course, I should be doing something.

I wish we could see each other once in a while. I think we need each other, dear. I know you are keeping up good courage, and that your soul is good. And don't you mind what the Germans think about you – don't let it hurt you more than you can help.

With my dear love,

Roy

MAY 19, 1895
Dover to Hamline

My Dearest Roy:

Nothing very dreadful has happened since I wrote you. "Johnnie" has behaved himself very well. I have been *awfully* blue though. Saturday I went to Rochester and saw Miss Peck and had a good talk with her. She thinks I haven't any reason to be so discouraged over my school. She pointed out one thing I hadn't thought of before – that in being so blue, the children have seen only the *gloomy* side of my nature. She says that if I could only bring out my *sunny* side, she is sure they would like me.

The sunny side seems to have deserted me entirely, and fun is an effort now. If this first pull discourages me so, I wonder how I'll ever get through the world? I wish I could know what work is best for me. Miss Peck thinks I would make a good primary teacher. There's something in the world for us to do, and we will find it. I think I'll not be so blue this week. I'll try and look at things as she says I must.

I heard something yesterday that encouraged me. It was nothing much – but one of the Board said something pleasant about me! I have been reading some of *The Faith that Makes Faithful* today. I thought it would help me, and it does.

You must be tired of these letters of mine – all just alike, continually harping on school and my troubles.

I got a new hat and new silk waist in Rochester. They're not very "stunning," but I like them. Clara is as full of life as ever. I'm glad I have two such girls for my friends – but more than all, I'm glad I have *you*, dear. You must get acquainted with your sister Mary this summer. If you become close friends *now*, I think you will always be so. But you will find that she has grown five years older in six months – girls of her age grow old in jumps without knowing it themselves.

We have each other and good health, so we must not get down-hearted, and I believe we shall find the work that God intends for us.

With my love,

Anna

MAY 24, 1895
Volney G. Reifsnider (Jr.) is born in Oronoco – son of Roy's sister Blanche and her deceased husband Volney.

MAY 29, 1895
Hamline to Eyota

Dearest:

It seems like such a long time since I heard from you. I missed writing last Thursday on account of the excursion down the river.

Oh, the good news from home! Saturday morning the telegram came from Charlie: "The boy has arrived and everything is OK." I was glad for that, I can tell you. I'm so glad for Blanche. In our dining room, one of the fellows said, "What are we going to do to Allis, 'cause he's 'Uncle' now?!" And they said, "Bounce him!" Feeling greatly honored, I submitted without a struggle. The third time they sent me up, my forehead and toes broke into the plaster of the ceiling. Allis will leave *some* mark behind him at Hamline, anyway.

It's dreadfully close and hard to work, and these big beetles keep coming in – they don't seem to have any sense, going blundering along. Walter went home Saturday. We divvied up the spoils and he "split" – I miss him.

Blanche and Baby Volney

We had quite a fine trip down the river Thursday. The boat started from St. Paul. There were about 200 of us, and we went down 20 or 25 miles. Stopped in a nice place while people went ashore in the woods, and then had our refreshments. We had a great time eating salad, sandwiches, lemonade, cake, and strawberries and cream. Most of the boys had someone with them – I was one that didn't. I hadn't ought to have gone that way – a fellow doesn't have so good a time.

When I came up to my room yesterday afternoon, I found it "stacked." Stacked is a technical term, I suppose, so I will explain. The bed was pushed down through on the floor springs, and on this were piled table, chairs, clothes, Bowers' trunk, my grip, books – everything. I will get back at those fellows, I reckon, before I leave. I lugged the 16-lb. shot over from the campus (don't you tell it was me!) and put it in one of their beds. I think it is *very wrong* and ungentlemanly to stack my room. I'll get even wi' those kids.

I received an invitation to the alumni banquet in Rochester. I *hope* you will go. We had a great inter-society ballgame, but it's always the unexpected that happens, and the score stood 11 to 4 against us. When I got home there was no letter from you, and my cup of bitterness was full.

I hope I can see you soon. You have had a hard time, dear, this spring. The fun will come back, won't it? Don't you think you can come out to Oronoco for a while this summer? Dearest sweetheart – I would give so much to see you just now.

JUNE 6, 1895
Hamline to Eyota
My Dearest:

This is probably my last night in Hamline. I feel I must write you a little.

I'm going out to Osakis Saturday to make my cousin Fay a short visit. I'm very glad to go, but I want to get home more than anything to see *you*, sweetheart.

I heard two baccalaureate sermons Sunday – ours and the State U's. I was here all day yesterday, but didn't go to commencement today – I was oppressed with many speeches and went over to Minneapolis. This afternoon I have been learning to ride Wells' wheel.

I liked that early-morning letter. Good-night, now, dearest. You will forgive this letter – so short and ill-written – for it comes from your sleepy boy tonight, with such a lot of love.

I hope I get your letter soon, for the day when my sweetheart's letter comes is marked in white, you know.

JUNE 18, 1895
Dover to Oronoco
My Dearest Roy:

It is 11 o'clock, so this must be short. I have been correcting examination papers and making out report cards all evening.

These are busy days for me. I am at my wit's end to keep the little ones busy and quiet while the older ones take their examinations. Oh – a member of the Board visited my school Friday. He says my classes are well-conducted, but that I must be more *firm*. Oh, I *hate* to be exacting – I suppose I can be firm and not be cross about it, but I haven't learned how yet. When I see you I must tell you how I punished a little boy today.

Can't you come to Eyota a week from today? Don't let anything keep you away.

Good-night, dearest,

Anna

CHAPTER 10

Free Again!

JUNE 23, 1895
Eyota to Oronoco
My Dearest Roy:

School is out, and I'm free again! My, it seems good! I thought I would have to make out report cards Friday night, but I got everything done Thursday, and then Saturday was *such* a long day. It seems to me I did more things that day just to kill time than I ever did before. I was up before 6, and while it was fresh and nice in the morning, took a walk through a grove nearby. I couldn't find any flowers except flax and white cornel. In the afternoon I tramped through a grain field and found a pretty purple flower – something new – so I carefully pulled it up root and all and took it home and analyzed it. It wasn't the rare treasure I supposed it to be – it was corn cockle. They laughed at me to think I didn't know what it was. I don't suppose you could persuade a farmer that cockle is pretty.

We were going to have a picnic the last day, but it rained and we had to eat our picnic dinner in the schoolhouse. Some people from Eyota brought me your letter while we were eating our picnic dinner. I had to wait until everyone had gone before I could read it. Then I picked up my things and swept out the old schoolhouse for the last time. I was happy at first, but somehow when everything was done, I almost hated to leave. The three months here have been good for me. I have learned more of myself than I ever knew before. I have had more confidence in myself during the last month's time than I had before, and that seems so good to me. It's awful if you haven't confidence in yourself, isn't it?

Wasn't the sunset last night beautiful? I sat out on the porch and watched the sky after the sun had gone down. It was a deep orange color next to the horizon, but grew lighter higher up. It was streaked across with black cloud. The trees and buildings stood out so black and distinct against the bright yellow.

Ella Kinsley and I are going to paint some this summer. Oh, there's so much I want to do – just little things that don't amount to much.

I was disappointed when I found you couldn't come Tuesday, but never mind – it won't be long. It's a comfort to know you're not as far away as you were when I was downcast.

With love for you, dear.

Anna

Has the baby got curly hair?

JULY 14, 1895
Oronoco to Eyota

Dearest Little Girl:

I won't write much of a letter tonight, but I want to talk a little with you. I wish it were a year ago tonight – 'twas a Saturday night a year ago when you came. I've been living it over these days. Mary came home yesterday and brought with her *Ships That Pass in the Night*. I have a tender feeling for that little book – a different feeling toward it than any other, and if I had read it alone, perhaps I wouldn't have cared for it.

Last Monday I called at Mr. Titus's for a few minutes and saw Mrs. Titus and Mary. I saw that Miss Mary was busy – a person can tell, if they observe at all, when people want to be at their work, even if they talk with you just the same. She said if you visit them, they would be very glad to have me come and see them while you were there. 'Twas nice of her to ask me, wasn't it?

Some folks are coming out camping this week. *(In addition to their milling business, Roy's family ran the "Lake Shady Camping and Picnic Grounds" – renting out boats and tents and scheduling picnics, boating outings and other summer festivities.)* I've been doing all the grinding, for Fred has been to La-Crosse and is dressing stone. Have had a good deal of fun this week with the boys – swimming and rowing and cutting up.

I must see you again soon. Write me, dearie – I think of you so much. We are so near now – we must see each other as often as we can. Good-night, sweetheart.

With my love always,

JULY 17, 1895
Eyota to Oronoco

My Dear, Dear Roy:

This is one of the evenings when I am lonely just a little, and I have been wanting you so, dear.

I have been out on the porch watching the bright colors fade in the west. What were you doing, I wonder, a year ago tonight?

I have just taken my *Ships That Pass in the Night* from the bookcase and read a little in it. It brings those days back again so clearly – like a perfume or an old song that brings back not only the things that happened, but something one can't name.

Mary has written me twice since you were here. She says she has something "important" to talk with me about – wonder what it is.

I just finished *Over the Teacups*. Number Five in that book seems to me very much like Mary, except that Number Five is older. My, I want to see the girl – the first thing I know that new minister will be walking off with her, and then I don't know when I ever shall see her.

A history class has been organized in town. Someone from the Northwestern University Association has been working up the subject in several towns in this part of the state. Mother belongs, and I am working with the class while I am here. We study Egyptian history first. All ages belong, and nearly all are women or girls – there's only one young man in the class.

A bunch of us girls went to a party a week ago. We drove the carriage and the horse Roxy, and coming home we more than raised Cain. It was a beautiful moonlight night. Lottie has a very sweet voice, and we sang quite sensibly for a while, but we had not gone far when we caught up with some other folks. They were driving dreadfully slow. We followed them for a while, and then finding a place where the road was wide, we drove as close as we could and commenced to sing "Under the Willows" (you remember it). When we got to "He told her he loved her," they couldn't stand it and tried to get away from us, but Roxy – silly old horse – had become interested too, and wouldn't let them get far from us. They would make sudden turns and try to get away, but we kept close and kept singing, "And now my dear friends, they are taking a ride." We had to give it up at last.

The next morning the minister's wife told Aunt Matt that she heard queer noises in the night. It alarmed her, for she thought it was someone crying. Aunt Matt says she doesn't know what we're coming to when three girls that are said to be as well-behaved as Lottie, Alice and I, act like that. Well, we thought it was *fun*!

With my love,

Anna

JULY 24, 1895
Oronoco to Eyota

Sweetheart:

Fred and Charlie and I were up the pond all day Sunday. Charlie had been wanting to get out and cook our dinner. Monday and Tuesday I shocked in the oats for the German farmer. I pitched a lot, and burnt my neck to a blister, and got my hands full of rose-thorns, so you mustn't mind if I write but a little, for I feel a *lot*!! Oh, but it will be great to have you here just as you were last summer.

Charlie Reifsnider
(Roy's best friend)

After supper tonight I went back through the woods toward the pond and lay down and watched things – wasn't it a beautiful evening? I thought perhaps you were out enjoying it all. I always think of you more at such times. That last letter you wrote me was *very* good, dearest – splendid – you don't know how good it was for me. It will be a thousand times better to see you, though.

It's getting late and I must be up in the morning to go and shock rye. Can't you write me again, Anna, before Sunday? I want to hear about things, and that note mustn't count for a letter. Good-night, sweetheart.

With my dear love,

I saw our harvest moon tonight.

JULY 27, 1895
Eyota to Oronoco

My Dearest Roy:

I'm taking time by the window again this morning to write to you. What do you think of a young woman who stops in the midst of her Saturday morning's work to write to her – what *shall* I call you, dear – lover? I wouldn't like to have Grandma give her opinion of her.

I have been reading *Helen's Babies* aloud to Aunt Matt. There is a little boy in it whose mother thinks he has an artistic temperament. "He is so fond of the beautiful," she says, "but the stories he delights in having people tell him are stories of fights, where everything is 'aw bluggy'"! You must read it if you have not already.

What a glorious time we will have in a week.

With my love,

Anna

JULY 31, 1895
Eyota to Oronoco

My Dearest:

I can't help being anxious about you, dearest. I'm so afraid you have worked too hard. You know how your eyes troubled you last summer after that hard work. I won't be able to stand it until Monday – to know if you are better. You will be very, very careful, won't you, dear, for you know how I love you? I don't know what I should do if you should be seriously sick.

Mother and I drove to Rochester yesterday morning. We did some shopping in the afternoon, and I made an appointment with Dr. Bucher to have my teeth attended to. I intended to have four filled and one wisdom tooth pulled, but after he filled two, he decided that that was all I could stand for one day, so I have got to have another siege. I wish I could have seen you while I was in Rochester.

I only asked for your opinion, you know, and even if you are blinded, your opinion is better than anything else. Good-night, dear.

Your Anna

JULY 31, 1895
The Birch Tree
Oronoco to Eyota

My Dearest Anna:

The last of July, isn't it? I've been laying off repairs and thought I would write a little as I was lying around the mills.

I've been kinda sick – don't know what is the trouble – pain in my side. Saturday I stacked for a fellow. We did a pretty good day's work, and I was pretty tired – drank lots of water and ached all through. I was feverish in the night. Monday I went pitching in the field. I hitched 14 big loads on the forenoon, but it was hard. I felt so exhausted and tired that every shock seemed like the last one. I stopped at noon, for I was afraid I would be sick if I stuck it through. I slept last night, and I'm better today, but not in shape hardly to go at it again. I think perhaps it was a touch of fever hanging about me, for I was hot and cold in the same breath. I'll be all right now. I hope I won't be busy so much when you are here.

Wish you were here right now – it's breezy and shady up here under our birch. Your name written here is almost worn off by the wind and the weather. The water is up pretty well now – about as it was a year ago Decoration Day.

What do you suppose is my opinion of such a girl as you speak of, who stops in the midst of her work to write to her … she's in doubt what she shall call him. Well, I'm blinded you say, and perhaps my opinion won't hold.

I want to see you, dearest. With my love,

CHAPTER 11

Farewell, Farewell

AUGUST 25, 1895
Oronoco to Eyota

Dearest:

It almost seems strange to write you – it has been so long I hardly know how to begin.

I have been miller all the week. My father went to Waseca after the sail-boat and just came back last night, so there was a little more to see to.

It seems quite a long while since we took our walk a week ago and said good-bye – does it to you? That Monday morning when I wakened, it was a little later than usual, and I sprang right out, and as soon as I got to my feet, it came over me with that kind of a pang one has – that we had said *good-bye*, and I wouldn't see you until Christmas. How such things do come over you first in the morning.

I had a glimpse of you when you went up to the house, and thought I saw you start to come down the hill once. Dearest, I felt so sorry for you when you went. I wanted to take hold of you and try and comfort you. I wondered if you knew that. I knew something of the way you felt – a combination of things. I felt restless and kind of lost all afternoon for you, dearest. I so hated to lose you. Well, perhaps you are tired of this and think I'm a foolish boy.

Tuesday I ground in the forenoon. In the afternoon I went over to Char-lie's, where he was at work. You remember how hot it was, and after a while we went down below their house to the old swimming hole shaded by the willows. We put on some old shoes to keep us off the stones, and went stalking down the middle of the river. It seemed good – walking through the cool water up above the knees with your clothes off, and as free as an animal, with nothing to hamper, for no one ever goes down the river. We did just as we pleased, like a couple of kids. We built a dam across a "riffle" and ran the water to one side. Then we dug the stones out and piled them up the side so that we made a nar-row channel for it to run in like a "race," and the water ran very fast.

We went down there again today and dug a pool below the little falls, and partly blocked the stream below, and had a superb bath. It felt so good to feel the swift, cold water go over your chest and shoulders. But we stayed in the sun a little too long and I burned my shoulder. I'm feeling better – have gained three or four pounds and feel first-rate – good as ever – honest, for you can't see me.

All the campers are gone, and the boats are all in – probably there won't be more until after the fair.

I suppose you will be in Winona a week from tomorrow. I don't know what is to become of me yet. Mark Miner wrote me, saying he might go to the U this year, and we could room together – "have the room fixed up with things from home, you know," he said.

I'm afraid I can't come and see you, dear, before you go. I wanted to. I have to be here this week. I want a letter from you. I'm so thankful that we could have this two weeks together. I've fallen in love with you all over again – deeper than ever, little girl.

With my love,

Roy

AUGUST 27, 1895
Eyota to Oronoco

My Dear Roy:

It does seem a long time since the afternoon we left Oronoco. Oh, that was a dreadful time for me – almost as bad as commencement. If I could only have gotten away from everyone! I had been down by the boats, thinking they must be nearly ready to start. I came up the bank, and just as I came up, they commenced to sing that old song: "How can I bear to leave thee." They were all standing in a group where the tents had been, and the tents and hammocks and *everything* were gone, and it all looked so desolate! Then the music! It was beautiful – Mrs. Knapp's voice so full and sweet, and the girls and Harold and all singing. I kept on up the bank, thinking I *wouldn't* cry, until they came to the "Farewell, farewell." Then such a rush of tears came that I turned and ran down the hill and up to the Point. I thought I had control of myself when I went over by the mill, but Mrs. Knapp undid it all, with her lovely words and the hug that went with it.

I have been very busy since I came home. Mother said today, "Perhaps you had better go to the U." I'm not, though – it wouldn't help me with primary teaching. I'm going to Winona. Mrs. Lane – an acquaintance of Mother's – has found a nice boarding place for me, and she will meet me at the station and take me there, so I won't have any trouble. Now that I am getting ready to go, a good deal of enthusiasm has arisen.

I have been hoping that you could spend next Sunday here. Can't you get away? I know you'll come if you can, so I'll just "'bide." I'm glad you're feeling better, dear. A gain of three or four pounds in a week after I left! Wonder how much you lost while I was there.

It would be nice if you and Mark could have a room together. I hope things won't seem so cheerless as they did last year.

Your letter was just lovely, dearest – especially the last three lines. Oh, Roy – I can't find that little curl of your hair. I always kept it in my writing desk, and now it's gone. I've looked and looked for it. I could never think as much of another one as I did of that, for it was the first one, you know, and I had it so long.

I must close, for it is very late. With love, from your tired little girl,

Anna

CHAPTER 12

Hard Work

SEPTEMBER 2, 1895
512 Main St. Winona, Minnesota; to Oronoco

My Dear Roy:

It's just 8 o'clock. What were we doing yesterday morning at this time? I must have been packing my trunk, I guess.

When I got here yesterday Mrs. Lane and Mrs. Blair were at the station. They brought me here and introduced me to the Van Anders. Mrs. Van Anders is a sprightly old lady, and Mr. Van is tall and straight and slim – at a little distance you would take him for a young man, he is so straight.

I am the only roomer, but six other girls take their meals here. I shall probably have a girl with me by tomorrow. I am delighted with the place – my room is small, but it's just as cozy and nice as it can be. There is a bay window on the south side, and from the windows I can look out toward the bluffs. The room is heated by a furnace. I have hot and cold water, and they are going to put in gas soon.

Everything is so dainty and pretty in my room – muslin curtains and pictures and all the little things that make a room seem homelike. So often in a bedroom the pictures are not good enough for any other part of the house, but these are not that kind. Two of them – a picture of choir boys (you have probably seen it) and a girl asleep – I like particularly.

After dinner I went to The Normal. I was there until 6. I went through the process of being classified, which consists of:

Filling out blanks telling where your parents were born and other interesting things.

Waiting.

Presenting state certificates and having standings copied.

Waiting.

Being measured by physical-culture woman, and filling out a blank telling your age, weight, measurements, etc.

Waiting.

Filling out a blank telling what you know about music, and singing the scale.

Waiting.

Seeing President Shepard and talking things over with him and finding out what you had better study, etc.

Then you are passed through the hands of a lot of teachers and a librarian, and at last you are free!

The Normal seems large compared with our high school. We won't have another Miss Peck or a Mr. Adams to help us. Since I starting writing, a girl has come who will be here with me. She seems nice – I like her looks. I'm so glad I didn't go to the Normal Home. We drove past it yesterday – it's a dingy brick building and looks like an orphan asylum, and Mrs. Lane says the food is very poor. The board here is only 25 cents a week more than at the Home. I wonder why girls go there.

Work does not begin until tomorrow. I asked one of the teachers if there was any work for today, and she said, "No – just have a good time and go off on the bluffs!" I'm having the good time first by writing to you!

Write me soon, dearest. It's a long time until Sunday.

With my love,

Anna

I like our house. The street is quite a pretty one. The porch is covered with beautiful vines. Mr. Van A. has a black horse and has promised to take me around the city soon. They have a nice soft cat too!

SEPTEMBER 9, 1895
1409 Sixth St. S.E., Minneapolis; to Winona

My Dearest Anna:

I have just carried my grip into my room – Zimmerman's and mine. Pa and I came up on the train from Pine Island. The room is much better than what I had last year at Hamline. I went around some with Pa until supper time; had my overcoat on and carried my heavy grip – 50 or 60 pounds – a half mile, I guess. It's very close and warm tonight. Our room isn't far from the University. I'll register tomorrow morning – it will be a busy day for me. I'm sure I'll like it better this year – much better than Hamline.

Now write me as soon as you can, dearest, for a letter will seem so good from you!

With my dear love,

SEPTEMBER 13, 1895
Winona to Minneapolis

My Dearest Roy:

I'm so glad you're at the U! I think this will work out much better for you.

We're getting to hard work. School begins at 8:15 and closes at 12:30. I have four subjects each day, and they and chorus practice take up all that time. I have Psychology and Methods, which teaches us how to put what we learn in Psychology into practice. Then comes Reviews and Methods in Geography. Mr. Freeman teaches that. He's fine – he thinks of ever so many queer questions! We have to reason, and then he'll act as though he doesn't believe you when you answer him, and tries to make you back out! He does this just as often when you are right as when you are wrong.

Then we have Reviews and Methods in Reading. Miss Harris is the teacher – I like her *so* much. She is so full of animation – wholesome and fresh and good – so unlike most teachers. There's something about her, and it didn't come through some grinding process that took off the freshness. Miss Sprague is my Geometry teacher. My, she knows Geometry! The girls say, "Even Pres. Shepard is afraid of Miss Sprague." I like Mr. Shepard. He's a little man, but very pleasant.

I haven't told you about my church experience. Mrs. Blair asked me last Sunday to the Episcopal Church, and Mrs. Lane claimed me for the next Sunday at the Methodist. Then Luva Cady invited me to go with *her* to Congregational Christian Endeavor. I agreed to go to all of them, and Friday the teachers passed around blanks, asking us what church we expected to attend. I wrote Congregational on mine. Well, Saturday, two ladies called on me, and said they heard my mother was a *Methodist*, so on those grounds they claimed me (!). And then the bell rang, and I wish you had seen the faces of the Mrs. Methodists when Mrs. Congregationalist came in! In a laughing way, they accused her of trespassing. Mrs. Cong. said, "Oh, no, you're mistaken – Miss Anna has expressed her preference for the *Congregational* Church." Then they all looked at me, and I flushed as though I had committed some crime, but I told them why I had decided as I did.

(I hope they won't find out I'm a Baptist through heredity; a Presbyterian by education; a United Brethren by association; that my brother is inclined to be a Unitarian; and my second cousin's wife is the granddaughter of Miller, the leader of the Millerites!)

I have been reading *Main-Travelled Roads*, and I like it. I'm reading *Figs and Thistles* now. We won't have much time for reading.

I like everything and everybody – and *you*, of course, above all! Must go to work.

Anna

SEPTEMBER 16, 1895
Minneapolis to Winona

Sweetheart:

Well, I will try to tell you events somewhat as they happened. I had a terrible time – it was hard getting everything straightened out, and changing from Hamline to the U complicated it all the more. You know I hadn't known I was coming – it was kind of a last-minute thing – and I hadn't any catalogue to look courses up, no one to advise me, and things were all new, of course.

Registering here is quite a job. You have to go round the circle four times, just like you did. When I came around the second time, the registrar said what I had would only admit me as a freshman! (I thought – this is going to be a long day.) They sent me to a committee to see about such things, and I bided my turn. My fall term's markings had been lost, so I had to go over to Hamline and face Dr. Bridgeman. He had hay fever, and looked sober and kinda "down his nose" to have anyone leave Hamline. He said, "I hope you're doing what's for the best, Allis, but I don't believe it." I saw Will, and we walked down to the InterUrban, and it kinda cheered me up to see someone I knew was glad to see me, for I was getting disheartened a little.

I couldn't finish registering until the next forenoon, so that evening I came over to Auntie's to meet Pa. I was hot and worried and kinda wearied. Minnie had me come out on the steps in the moonlight with her and Mark, and we talked, and I felt better, and stayed all night. I went down on the same car with Pa till I changed to the InterUrban. I never felt quite so sorry to leave him before – I so hated to do it. It didn't seem right to be an extra burden to him – a worn, resolute old man. He has fought his life through against such long odds, always.

I got registered that day. The hot weather and change of weather made me feel kinda off, I guess. Anyway, Anna – I got so homesick and discouraged as I think I never was before. I'm ashamed to say so, but you know you said, dear, that I could tell you anything. It seemed as if it would have been better if I hadn't come to school – that what I must take would do me no good. Well, I thought lots of things, lying alone in my room in the dark. Then I took a walk. I would have given anything to see you, Anna. I know you believe in me, and 'twas cowardly to feel down so.

I felt better next day, but it has been a rather lonely week, although I found Heath and one or two others I knew. Mark can't go to school – I'm sorry for him – he has to work the streetcars, and doesn't like it at all. I feel much better, now that I've got started – probably being sick had something to do with it, and then I'm always so lonesome when I'm first away. I'll get over that, probably. I'm going to try and get some good out of this year.

I'm a sophomore Scientific with freshman Drawing and Rhetoricals. I'm taking History, German, Psychology, Drill and Drawing, and Chemistry. We drill three or four times a week. I think I shall like drill, though I won't own it quite like the others.

Your letter came Saturday, and I was wondrously glad to get it. I felt better to have anything that came from you.

Minnie asked me to come over Saturday evening. There was a fireman's parade downtown, and they held the streetcars back 'till it was over; and when they did come, we had to stop often, so when I got back to Auntie's it was nearly 11 and the folks gone to bed. I rang the bell a little and called at Mark's window – not very loud. I didn't want to waken the whole household. I couldn't get back to my room at the U so late, so I went out in the shed where they keep the wood, found an old rubber coat, and slept there through the night. I laughed at myself to think what a crazy mortal I am – always having such escapades. I had to keep turning so the ground wouldn't feel hard. When the hired girl Bertha found me (she's a Norwegian girl), she said, "You hadn't ought to do that – it will hurt your back. But you're young then – I used to sleep that way."

The folks in the house were horrified that I didn't waken them, but forgave me if I'd promise never to do so again. Lulu Holmes was over Sunday, and we went to Shutter's Church and heard such fine music and a grand sermon. Last evening Minnie and I had a walk around by Lake Calhoun. I wished it was *you* with me though.

I shouldn't wonder if Mother and Mary would be up here next year, rent a house, and Mary and I go to school – wouldn't it be great?

I have so much I want to say to you that I could write on all afternoon, but I must write Mother and go home and study German. That's going to be pretty stiff, but we have a fine teacher.

Anna, I hope you won't think I'm *very* faint-hearted. I'm queer about being lonesome, you know, dearest, and this summer has been such a *good* summer, and then all these changes – you'll understand, I'm sure? I'm going to try and do well even if I don't like things, and I guess I will like everything after a bit.

I'm glad you like everything so well there – what an *even* little girl you are.

Julia Marlowe plays in *Romeo and Juliet* at the Met in St. Paul next Friday night, and I hope I can hear her. Joe Jefferson and O'Neil and Salvini are coming to Minneapolis this winter.

SEPTEMBER 19, 1895
Winona to Minneapolis

My Dear Roy:

I was glad to get such a long letter, and I'm glad you told me about your homesick and discouraged time, for I *can* understand, and I *do* understand. And, dear, always remember that I do *believe* in you – I wish I could tell you how fully. Do you remember what Boag Woodley tells Markham in *Figs and Thistles*? It's this: "A woman may and frequently does know a man's capacity better than he himself." And you know I'm not the only woman who has faith in you. Tomorrow you will be 21. I expect my knight to do better things this year than ever before!

I must stop and go to work. I wish I could say something good – because it's your birthday – but you know I wish *lots* of good things for you this year.

With my love,

Anna

SEPTEMBER 23, 1895
Minneapolis to Winona

My Dearest Anna:

Here I am in the same place and with the same circumstances as last week. This is the last week the folks will be here, and there is no knowing when I'll see them again. The last week went off all right – I feel a great deal better. People are apt to have a fit of nostalgia when they change all their habits from home to strangers, from work to study, aren't they?

Your letter came Friday. 'Twas good, too, although short, and I thank you for the "lots" of good wishes. You see, Anna – your wishes count more than most people's. The day before my birthday I thought, with sort of a queer feeling, that this was the last day I would be a *boy*. But really, you don't notice so much difference as you would think at first.

Friday I went to St. Paul and saw *Romeo and Juliet* as I intended. I enjoyed it greatly – a lot. I liked the chamber scene best, where the morning broke, and Romeo left for the last time. Juliet made a beautiful picture there – all white, with the red morning shining on her. I wish you could have seen it – I thought of you, as I do at such times. It was very beautiful.

Tell me all about yourself and what you're doing. I've been reading some in *Mill on the Floss*. I never read *Figs and Thistles*.

Good-bye.

Roy

It seems a long time since I saw you.

SEPTEMBER 28, 1895
Winona to Minneapolis

My Dearest Roy:

Guess what – I heard Julia Marlowe! I think she's fine. I've been wanting to hear her ever since I knew she was coming here, but didn't know exactly how I could manage it. I enjoyed it every bit! How graceful and beautiful she is – and her voice! I liked the chamber scene too. How beautiful she looked, sitting on the steps of the balcony after Romeo had gone, with the beautiful red light shining in? And her voice and the expression in it in the balcony scene – oh! I am so glad I went.

We girls raised Cain at dinner today. Two of the girls who take their meals here are dreadfully blue and homesick, so the rest of us tried to cheer them up. Miss Taylor and I generally act the worst. One of the girls said today that she hadn't laughed for so long, it seemed as if she had forgotten how.

I *am* happy and I didn't expect to be, and sometimes I'm just overjoyed to think I can be so *very* happy. I like the work, and I feel so full of vim and enthusiasm. People are so kind, and everything works to make me happy. No – things work just the same when I'm *unhappy* – it's all in *myself*. I'm afraid I'm *not* an even little girl. Since I've been here, I've been wildly happy sometimes – but I dread the thought of another time like last spring.

I'm so glad you're feeling better. Do you like the U better than Hamline? I have just been reading some of James Whitcomb Riley's prose stories – they are as good as his poems.

Last Tuesday evening they had receptions for Normal students at several of the churches. I went to the Congregational. A Mr. Parker from St. Paul (he is in our class) invited me to go with him. I suppose my face showed how I felt, for he said he knew it was a great favor for him – almost a stranger – to ask, but he hated to go alone. There are only two boys in our class, and they are as great chums as you and Walter used to be.

I have been reading some of Helen Hunt Jackson's poems, and I like them. One of them – "The Way to Sing" – I liked so well that I copied it.

You mustn't use such big words in your letters – one of them went beyond any of us and the dictionary! If you use such big words, I'll have to take your letters to someone to interpret!

How do you like German and Psychology? I like our Psychology very much, but ours is more child study than regular psychology – it deals particularly with a child's mind.

I hope you are going to like your work and not get blue, dearest. I believe I could drive the blues away if I were only there. You must write me a long letter next time.

With love,

Your Little Girl

I woke up early this morning with a horrible cold on my lungs. You feel such a weight on your lungs. I *hate* a cold. I'm not going to church today. I'm sitting in the southeast corner of our little alcove, and the sun is shining on me, trying to warm me up. I have on my red wrapper and that white shawl you like. I'm such a frozen child when cold weather comes.

I'm going to draw a plan of our room so you can imagine me here, and I'm going to read some in *Lalla-Rookh* today.

Anna

SEPTEMBER 30, 1895
Minneapolis to Winona

My Dearest:

I'm glad I waited until today to write you – it's easier to write after your latest letter. I haven't had so good a one for a long time – 'twas so like you. I'm *anxious* about that cold – tell me as soon as you can, Anna, how you are. I wish I could be there whenever you're sick.

This has been a pretty good week. I have been boarding here at Mrs. Stevens' where the club is to be. The food is first-rate, for she is a good cook and very nice and pleasant too, and the people boarding here are good folks that I like. We have lots of fun at mealtime. Zimmerman and I are getting notorious for telling stories. Some people doubt the *veracity* of some of my stories (explanation: veracity means *truth*; be careful not to confound with *voracity*, which has a different shade of meaning!).

Nostalgia is the scientific term for homesickness. Sometimes I forget to put my thoughts into simple language that may be comprehended by a normal freshman – pray excuse me (!).

I'm glad you heard Julia Marlowe and liked her so much. Didn't you like Mercutio, too, and what did you think of Romeo? 'Twas all very *southern*, wasn't it – warm and demonstrative.

Joseph Jefferson is to be in Mpls. this winter, and Salvini and O'Neil and Helena Modjeska. I mean to see a few of them; 'twill help a fellow to grow.

Cousin Mark is pretty lonesome with the rest of the folks gone. I went over last evening and stayed all night and kinda talked with him – tried to keep him cheerful, you know. It's hard on him – guess it's the first time he's been away from his mother. He was a little sick this week – it's not a very pleasant job being an extra on the streetcars – and Mark is kind of a reserved, gentle, sensitive fellow, I think.

After breakfast I walked around Lake Calhoun and Lake Harriet – been doing considerable walking. Zimmerman and I are going to work up a system – time for studying; time to go to bed; time to get up; time for exercise, etc. If we can stick to it, we can do much more, and the time will pass quicker too. Can you imagine me doing that? I'll tell you how it turns out.

Oh, yes – I like it here *much* better than at Hamline. I'm going to try and do something this year – I'm trying now. It's hard, for I haven't been used to holding myself down and working. One reason I am at times discouraged and dissatisfied – restless – is because I never do anything *very* well. I never have *excelled* in anything. I like too many things to get on well in one. Then I get to doubting myself, and get down, and the work suffers. I imagine so much what I would *like* to be, and never get there – I lose enthusiasm. But, Anna, I'm trying to subdue myself a bit. I intend to do the things I hate, no matter how I feel about it – exercise when I don't want to, take cold baths, and be hanged to them all.

Well, there's a tirade! But I'm going to send this letter just the same. Yes – I'm going to like things here very much, I think. I've played baby enough.

Night before last we had a jolly time over at the YMCA. "A bushel of apples and a bushel of fun," the notice said. The boys sang first – college songs and the like. Then a young man – a freshman, and great on dialect, I should think – gave an imitation of some speech of a Norwegian Populist politician. It was killing – you should have heard Zimmerman's laugh. It was all informal, you know. After a bit, they brought in apples in a box, and Zimmerman said, "One, two, three – make a grab." Straightaway, each one got as many as he could – I got four. Then while we were eating we told stories – some pretty good ones, too. I didn't tell any, for I felt a wee bit shy.

I'm getting tired and must go to studying. This is the last day of September, isn't it? It won't be long until Christmas – I'm *living* for that time. I hope I'll be satisfied with the term's work. You must take care of yourself, little sweetheart. I'm thankful for that good letter, and glad you're happy and contented.

With my love,

Roy

OCTOBER 4, 1895
Winona to Minneapolis

My Dearest Roy:

That letters of yours was a lovely one – I like *long* letters.

I am alone tonight. Miss Taylor has gone to a reception given by faculty to Normal students. I don't feel well enough to go. I saw Dr. Lane yesterday, and he gave me two kinds of medicine and said to see him in a couple of days if my cough is not considerably better. It's regular old-times bronchitis I have. You remember how I used to laugh and then cough so hard in Vergil class? I'm hoarse as a frog. The teachers take pity on me and don't call on me for long recitations. You mustn't be anxious, dear – Dr. Lane doctored me for a good many colds when I was little. He was my father's doctor too (Doctor says I look very much like my father).

I'll have you understand, Mr. Allis, that I'm not a Normal Freshman! And if you don't stop being so saucy, I'll smile at Mr. Parker (!). Mr. Parker prefers the Normal to the State U 'cause they're so rough and barbarian there (!).

Yes, I liked Romeo and Mercutio. When you looked at Romeo through opera glasses, you could see how wonderful his facial expression was – his face expressed everything much better than his voice, I thought – did you? I think Mercutio was fine. I liked him in the dream speech and in the fights – and in his fun. If any more good plays come here this winter, I should like to hear some of them. I shall probably be in some little town next year, and won't have a chance to hear anything good.

Good for your new plans! It *is* a little hard to imagine you doing it, but I'm glad you are. We have regular hours for study too, and I think I accomplish a great deal more than letting things go until I feel like it. You must tell me how it works. I'm so glad you like the U and your boarding place so well. Send me some more "tirades!" Oh – I must have your *picture* – I really *must*.

I had a letter from your sister Mary. She seems full of enthusiasm and plans. She's the kind of a girl I like – I want to know her better.

I must stop writing – it's 10 o'clock – time for sick people to go to sleep. Good night, dearest.

With my love,

Anna

OCTOBER 4, 1895
Minneapolis to Winona

Sweetheart:

It's just after supper. I usually take a walk after supper – past the east side of campus, down to the InterUrban line, and then across the Washington Street bridge, where I can see the lights and the river. Ever since the first or second year I was in Rochester I have walked alone in the night that way. I wonder if it's a good thing to do – perhaps it leads to introspection. I think about myself and get to thinking I'm not much good, and it isn't the way to do. What makes me the kind of fellow I am, I wonder?

Never mind – I'm writing to you. You don't know how I wait for your letters. Yes, words seem empty – I understand, dearest. I try to write something to you, and sometimes it seems queer-written – not what I want – and I tear it up and stop trying, when I know I could *tell* it to you.

The folks are all so sorry for you, Anna – about you're being sick. I meant to write sooner, but I don't have much time during the week. I have to have lots of time to waste – you know me a little that way. I have 28 hours a week in lecture, recitations, lab work; and three hours' drill. My afternoons, except Saturday, are solid until after 5 o'clock. I draw two hours or one hundred minutes every afternoon. I'm getting along fairly well, I guess. As Miss Peck said – I waste lots of energy. Will I never learn?

We saw a football game Saturday between the U and Ames. We won 24 to 0! When it was through it was just getting dark; the lights were lit. We all dashed across the athletic field. The band was out there – *our* band – and oh! we felt good, and began to form behind the band to dance the "serpentine." It's an institution, that serpentine, for venting enthusiasm. I guess it's distinctively a Minnesota custom – I never heard of it anywhere else. This is the way it's done – first comes the band; then five or six hold hands and string out pretty well across the street. Three or four feet behind is another line, and so on indefinitely. Then the band marches on and plays, and the lines wave back and forth across the street in opposite directions, keeping time in a kind of hippity-hop. They zigzag, you know – when one line is going to the right, the one behind it is going toward the left, and it looks like a snake – and we *yell*, man! I tell you – three or four blocks that way is a queer, wild sight.

People would come running out of the stores and to the windows and look and laugh and hold their sides. It was lots of fun while it lasted – a jolly good time – one of those that come once in a while when you feel bubbling over and just glad because you're warm and well and feel strong. I forgot the things that bother me – or, rather, the things I bother myself with.

My letters are written so haphazard. You mustn't mind – I'm your barbarian, you know. I'm trying not to be barbarian, though. Anna – I want to *be* something – to be *worthy* of you. Life wouldn't be anything to me but for you, dearest. I think of you and love you all the time.

OCTOBER 11, 1895
Minneapolis to Winona

Sweetheart:

I suppose I ought to be at work, but I want to write you just now, someway. I didn't want the week to go by without speaking to you.

I've got along pretty well this week. Wrote an essay and took a quiz in History and Rhetoricals. The Fraulein put me through a course of sprouts in German this morning, but I didn't flunk. Z has been having a terrible time with ringworm on his face. For the last two weeks, he couldn't go to class for several days, but he's getting nearly cured now.

This is going to be a stupid letter, I'm afraid – all full of statistics. Z and I have been taking a trot before we go to bed. We think it's a pretty good thing. We haven't been following our plan of work very closely, but I've exercised quite a bit, at least, and feel first-rate. Only I have a bad cold coming on that makes me feel stupid, as you see.

Our club is getting along fine. There are 19 of us – six of them girls. We have two tables, and have good jolly times at meals. There is a young lady – Miss Sperry – that I kinda like. She is rather enthusiastic, and a little inclined to gush, and she bothers quite easily. Talks considerable, and so it's easy for the boys to bother her. She's bright – a sophomore. Likes Rider Haggard (a good point) and the kind of books I like.

I have got sort of a reputation for being a funny fellow, for some reason. They've been teasing me to speak "Tam O'Shanter." We have fun, Z and I – we generally cut up the first thing in the morning and sing. Did you ever hear Zim laugh? He has the heartiest laugh in the world. He always reads a chapter out of his Bible at night – aloud, when I'm here – and sometimes I take a turn. I just told him a yarn, and we've been laughing fit.

We have two pictures in our room from *Munsey's Magazine.* I like the one of "St. Cecelia at the Organ" and one of the Farnese Hercules *(Ironically, in 1901, when Roy won a national intercollegiate Strongman Contest, defeating entrants from across the country, newspaper articles called him the "new Hercules of the colleges.").* I have the St. Cecelia over our table – I like the face. After a day or so, Z said, "Do you know who that looks like?" I looked, but I couldn't think, and he said, "Anna." Then I saw the throat and chin *did* look a bit like you, and I knew why I liked it then.

I had such a good letter from Mary this week. I hope you may get to know her better. She said in her last letter, "Next summer, when you come home, I'm not going to play croquet, but *see* and *be* with you. Really, I don't feel as if I really *know* you – do you?" She's such a good little sister.

We have about a week at Thanksgiving time, though part of it is taken up by exams, and about 16 days at Christmas – won't that be great?

Well, Anna – I'll give you a picture when I get some, if you want one. Those down home are not like me, and I don't want you to have one of *them*. Don't see what you want of me anyway.

Last Sunday I finished *Mill on the Floss*. I think it's one of the finest and saddest stories I ever read. Did you like it? I wish I could have you to talk to and think with, dearest.

With my love always,

CHAPTER 13

The Only One Left

OCTOBER 12, 1895
Winona to Minneapolis

My Dearest, Dearest Roy:

I have just received awful, awful news – my brother Frank is dead. Shot himself accidentally yesterday – I can't make it seem possible. It will almost kill his wife. If I could only go there. Oh, I'm so glad I saw him last winter. He was so strong and full of fun – and he and his wife loved each other so. And of all awful things – to shoot himself. I wish you could be here, dearest. I thought of you when the telegram came, for I have been anxious not having heard from you – but I never thought of Frank. Oh, how I wish I could be there. My father, mother, Frank, all, all gone – oh, it's too awful.

Darling – I think of you through it all, and it's such a comfort.

Anna

OCTOBER 14, 1895
Minneapolis to Winona

My Own Dearest Anna:

I'm trying and trying to say something to you that seems good and comforting, and I cannot. But, dearest, I'm very close to you and trying to bear a part of it. I wish I were with you – you don't know how my heart goes out toward you. Your letter just reached me this noon. 'Tis terrible – I cannot see why things are so. It seems as if the finest, gentlest people have the most to bear. It will be hardest for Frank's wife. Oh, things are cruel! Yes, I'm glad you were there last year.

I don't know what to tell you, Anna – I want to help you. You must read through the poor, commonplace words what I *would* say. Try to think, my own *dearest* little girl, not of the words, but of the *boy* who is sorrowing with and loving you with all his heart and strength – more than ever, now.

I'll write again very soon, dearest. Forgive the happy, gay letter that reached you just when you were in trouble. I want to do all I can to help you – I'm so sorry, sorry for you and Lou and all.

All my love,

OCTOBER 15, 1895
Winona to Minneapolis

My Dearest Roy:

I just came home from school and found your letter waiting for me, and it was full of comfort, dear. No matter what happens, I can never feel alone while I have you. I have not heard anything more, except the telegram. There has not been time. Mother came down yesterday – I was surprised to see her. We couldn't talk about Frank, though. I can't talk with Mother about things I feel.

I wrote Lou, poor girl – it will be *so hard* for her. It's hard to know of it and be so far away, and I his only sister too. Our people are all so far away that I doubt any of them can go. Things do seem cruel sometimes, but we know so little. We can't tell how things will work out – we can only leave it all in God's hands and trust Him fully.

Write me soon. You don't know how much your letters help.

With my love,

Anna

I was glad of that gay letter – it didn't jar, as you thought, but was a comfort to me. It was good of you to think of coming down – dearest, you are such a comfort. I can't write, but I feel it all.

OCTOBER 18, 1895
Minneapolis to Winona

My Dearest Anna:

Your letter came yesterday, and I was so *glad* to get it, for I was restless and anxious and wanted to hear about you. I would have come to Eyota, but I was afraid you wouldn't be home, and I was out of money. When it was too late, I bothered myself – regretting that I hadn't gone and tried to help you. I wish we could have a talk – just for half an hour.

Mother wrote me this week, and the folks are well, and the baby boy has on shoes and short clothes and has grown immensely. I don't know whether I can go home Thanksgiving or not – we have a week, but part of it is taken up by exams. I suppose you will be home – hope I can see you then – you don't know how I want to, Anna. We have about 16 days for Christmas.

School has been dragging along about as usual – nothing particular occurring. School life is so regular, isn't it? Last Sunday I went to Hamline and saw Walter and some of the other people, and Walter and I took a long walk. He bought some peanuts, as he always does on any special occasion, you know, and we sat on the rail of the transfer bridge and ate and talked, so it seemed like old times. I shouldn't wonder if Walter would be here at the U next year. He intends to teach this winter.

Sunday, if it's nice, I'm going to take a walk down the river. In this town you get so you don't notice the clouds and hills so much – the sky seems farther away – doesn't it seem so to you?

I wrote this not because I had anything to say, but just to keep near. I mean to write often, if you don't mind. You needn't answer them all if you don't want to.

With my love,

Roy

OCTOBER 20, 1895
Winona to Minneapolis

My Dearest Roy:

Thursday the news came that I have been looking for for so long – a letter from the Presbyterian minister's wife in Houlton, talking about Frank's death.

He and Lou had gone off to the woods on an outing. Frank had not had a vacation during the summer, so they took a car and went off, 40 miles from Houlton, to spend a week or so there. At about half past 4 Friday they started out for a hunt. Lou stepped out of the car first, and stood by the car waiting for Frank, while he locked the car door. He had his rifle under his arm, and somehow – in locking the door – it slipped and fell in a slanting position, and as it fell it went off, and the bullet went through his heart and lung.

Lou was beside him in an instant, but aside from this terrible "Oh!" he did not make a sound. She could not tell that he even breathed after she got to his side. She was all alone – they were there in the woods, four miles from any station. Apparently at half-past 6, someone came for Lou – wondering where she was – and quite a number from Houlton went down. They did not get there until between 10 and 11 at night. The minister's wife said she never saw anyone in such distress as Lou. They had put Frank on the bed in the car. Think of Lou being there all that time – either alone or with strangers – oh, it's awful.

The next day they took his body to Lou's home in Passamaquoddy Bay, where Frank and Lou have had so many good times, and he was buried there Monday. Mrs. McKay said it was pitiful to hear Lou's appeals to those around her – "How can I live without him?" Poor little girl – if I could only have been there. I couldn't have comforted her, I know, but it would have been something to have his sister there. I have told you how they were always together – I'm glad they were together even when he died. I was afraid Frank might have been off alone, and perhaps suffered a long time.

I can never be thankful enough that I was there last year. This will be an awful blow to my uncle and aunt. They thought so much of Frank – as though he was their own son – and they were so *proud* of him – we were *all* proud of him.

Write often, dearest – I wish we could be together right now.

With my love,

Anna

Words never seemed so empty as they do now – I feel so much, and can say so little. This has made my heart very tender; and, dearest, I *love* you – love you so. You have all my heart now.

When Volney died, Lou was so sorry for Blanche – she seemed to have as much sympathy for her as though she knew her, and now Blanche is thinking of Lou in the same way.

OCTOBER 27, 1895
Winona to Minneapolis

My Dearest Roy:

Your letter came yesterday, along with many letters from so many, telling how much they thought of Frank. I know it's all true – I could see it when I was there. People didn't wait until he was dead to show they liked him. He might not have seen it, but I could see it in people's eyes as they talked with him – not just the people of his own society, but every ragged Irishman or Frenchman he ever knew seemed just as happy to see him. I am glad I was there as long as I was. I knew then that this *man* was as fine a fellow as the *boy* I used to know.

My aunt and uncle say Lou is half-crazed with grief, and bereft of reason. There was insurance – $12,000 – all payable to Lou – and the president of the company Frank worked for said they had intended to make him superintendent of a new road – the youngest man they knew to hold that position. But that is no comfort to her. My aunt says by spells, Lou will talk about it. But then she will go almost wild – says when she shuts her eyes for sleep, that awful sight comes before her. It is one comfort to know that there was not even an instant's suffering.

I can hardly realize I am now the only one left of our family.

Do you have Mechanical Drawing? I'm supposed to work two hours each afternoon at free-hand drawing. I need more than two hours for Geometry. I have a dreadful time – I'm the worst one in class – I guess I never will get through it.

I'm going to think of you about the time you are walking evenings. It's probably between half past six and seven, isn't it? Twice this week Miss Taylor and I have taken a walk after supper – the evenings have been so warm and nice.

You must try to think of pleasant things on those walks – you must have the confidence in yourself that I have in you. I can't help but know this, dearest – that you will do more for my sake than you would for yourself – not because I deserve it, but just because you love me. And I don't believe your ideal of what you want your life to be is the "wild African." I'm sure of this, dear – knowing as well as I do how much there is to you, and what you want your life to be for my sake as well as your own – I shall have more reason to be proud of you every year.

With my love,

Anna

OCTOBER 31, 1895
Minneapolis to Winona

Dearest:

I'm so very sleepy. We have a quiz in History tomorrow, so I'm just going to say goodnight to you now, and write a long letter Sunday. I've been getting along all right this week; heard from home yesterday, and got a picture of Blanche and the boy. I was glad to get it. Your letter came Tuesday – your good letter. There is no one like you.

You must think of me from about 7 to half-past – that's when I take my walk. Write me about yourself, Anna – your trouble and sorrow and all. We two must keep as close as we can.

With my love,

NOVEMBER 3, 1895
Minneapolis to Winona

Dearest Anna:

I hope this will be a good letter and atone for the last one. I wish I could see you.

I love the picture of Blanche and little Volney. Showed the folks, and they were pleased too. Mary spoke of you and said, "We all feel so much for Anna, and speak of her every day." She said when I wrote you to give her "true sympathy."

What a beautiful day it was yesterday. In the afternoon I went down to St. Paul, getting back about sunset. I wondered if you saw it, and after I left the streetcar, I walked west until it faded, and thought perhaps you would be out in the moonlight too.

The week has gone about as usual. I didn't do so very well in the quiz I told you of. I draw freehand – I don't like it, but I stick to it, for I wouldn't want to take it again next term. I got a glance at my instructor's book, and after my name it said "improving." I never had any drawing at all before. I think I'm doing better. Next Thursday is Rhetoric. We have to hand in a character sketch of someone – I wonder who I had better take?

There's a girl medical student – Miss Stahl – lives across the hall and boards in the club. She's nice and sensible and a great worker. I'm going to tell you about some of the people – perhaps you'd like to hear about them. I like Miss Sperry as well as any of the girls. She is quite large; tall and strong; looks bright and is *very* enthusiastic. It's fun to get her started about something she's excited about. She likes queer books (for a girl) – the kind boys usually like, such as Haggard, Stevenson's *Treasure Island, Tom Brown at Oxford*, Scott, etc. I guess she's very good in rhetoricals and debates.

The younger Miss Stevens is a queer little body – when you tell her anything that pleases her, she jumps right up and down like a little kid. She has never had any brothers, and Jim says she doesn't know how to appreciate boys. She is apt to treat you as if you were another girl – a little fresh. The other Miss Stevens is different, and I like her better. She's rather small; a senior; a terrible worker – great in sciences and mathematics. She has a very resolute look on her face, from wrasslin' with mathematics, I s'pose – may I never get that look on *that* account.

Olson – a medical student – has been in talking. I don't like medics as a rule – I wonder what it is about their work that makes them the kind of men they are? I don't think it necessary.

I have my whole uniform now. Some of the boys wear their uniform a good deal, but I feel sort of out of place in it, except when I'm drilling. I like drill pretty well, and we get some fun out of it.

I presume you are better in Geometry than you think. I'll have Trig next term after Thanksgiving, and Analytical Geometry spring term. What a time we poor unpractical children have!

I wish I could have seen your brother Frank. Of course he was a fine fellow. It's terrible for his wife. I want to be good to you, little girl. I'm sorry for you, and I love you so much, so much. It is less than two months now until I see you again. I get so *hungry* for you. Your faith in me helps a lot, dearest, and your letters are good. Don't you tire of mine? They seem so much alike to me.

Good-night, sweetheart – my dear little queen.

Roy

NOVEMBER 9, 1895
Winona to Minneapolis

My Dearest Roy:

The mailman just brought me *The Princess Aline*. We were talking about Richard Harding Davis last evening, and one of the girls told me I must read this book – thank you for it! I shall read it tomorrow.

What kind of work do you have in drawing? We have been studying how and what to teach little folks – free-hand paper cutting and clay modeling. I was surprised to find how valuable they are. All sorts of things can be done with paper-cutting – Columbus and his ships, Priscilla and John Alden, different natural objects – and it teaches the children to observe color and see beauty in the colors of nature as well as in form.

Here I am writing a regular essay on paper-cutting and clay modeling. I modeled a round turtle the other day. The children can do better than we can!

We finished Methods in Reading. I got my class standing – 95, exam 88½, making an average of 92. We have to do a great deal of library work in everything except Geometry. Miss Taylor and I each have to prepare a topic for recitation taken from Herbart and the Herbartians. We divide up on it – she prepares half and I prepare half. I have everything done except Geometry – I usually do that the first thing Saturday morning, but I felt like writing you instead.

We have had visitors at the Normal nearly all week – presidents from Mankato, St. Cloud and Moorhead normal schools. Yesterday they talked to the school after opening exercises. The one from St. Cloud came from California this year. He said he first heard of the Winona Normal 20 years ago from a former president of this school – very glowing reports – and soon after, married a graduate of Winona Normal, and she sang its praises night and day. He told us a good deal about the schools of California.

Why don't you tell me more about the rest of the people who board in your club? I'm going to write you about the people at our table. If you're tired, you can stop and rest here.

First there's Miss Larruze – she's the *queerest* girl. The girls don't like her very well. She always acts so languid, and doesn't seem to have any interest in anything. I came very near having her for a roommate, but I'm thankful I didn't. She is careless and disorderly. She soaks up all the time talking, and puts her elbows on the table if she feels tired.

Next comes Miss McCormick from Montana. We all like her, but she has been *so* homesick and discouraged. She's older than the rest of us, and has just been at home and had an easy time all her life. She grew tired of doing nothing and came here to school, but she had been out of school so long she did not stand well in exams, and had to go into the lowest class. She's very sensitive and conscientious. She works hard, and when the teachers scold, she takes the scolding all to herself. Studying comes hard for her, but she is plucky, and I like her.

Next are two girls from Red Wing – Miss Wise and Miss Walters. They are nice, pleasant girls. Then there is Miss Ingalls – I like her too – she is altogether different from the rest of us, though. She has been to boarding school all her life, and has a boarding-school girl's ways. She has been in society a good deal, and thinks more about it than the rest of us do. Some of her family died during the last year, so she dresses in black. She's tall and straight, and with her black dress and dark hair, she's almost beautiful. Some of the girls don't like her, but she doesn't care whether people like her or not – she will only be gracious to those she likes. I like her.

I haven't said much of anything, although I've written so much. Oh, I must have one of your pictures. We had our pictures taken some time ago – I'll send you one if you give me one of yours?

With lots of love,

Anna

NOVEMBER 11, 1895
Winona to Minneapolis

Dearest Roy:

I'm going to finish telling you about the girls at our table (I think you've had a sufficient rest!). Miss Lantry has red hair, is an only child and just a little spoiled, but we all like her – she's so friendly and good-hearted. She pouts when things don't suit her, but laughs at the same time. She goes home to Minneapolis every week. Her father is an engineer. She and another girl are taking the kindergarten course.

Next comes Miss Taylor. She is a jolly, good girl – bright and full of fun. We get on famously. It must be disagreeable to have a girl for a roommate that one doesn't like – you have to be together so much.

Last is Miss Alder. She has been very homesick and unsettled ever since she has been here. You know people who always speak with a weak whine in their voice? Miss Alder is like that. She went home to her sister's wedding this week, and we all thought she would feel better when she came back, but she had hardly seated herself when she said, "I feel worse than ever." We all burst out laughing. I'm *sorry* for her – I couldn't shake off the blues when I was teaching last spring, and I tried my very best. Perhaps she tries just as hard.

As a rule the girls aren't happy here. I find it all much better than I expected, for I was afraid I would have to go through another time like last spring. That last year at our high school was a good year. I heard some of the seniors translating Vergil the other day, and it brought back those good times when we translated – how you struggled against it! Well, you were driven by the Fates. I'm glad we went to school together.

Who did you take for your character sketch? How did you come to decide upon the scientific course, with all its mathematics?

Are you going home Thanksgiving? We have several days then, and I'm going home. I hope I can see you then – it seems such a long time since I saw you.

I received a letter from Lou. She's trying so hard to be brave, and to bear it in the right way. She wishes I could be closer – she says I seem nearer to her now than ever before. I feel as though I should leave everything and go to her. Lou says she thinks Frank knew a second after the gun discharged that he was dying.

I'm glad if my faith in you helps you, dear. How could I *help* having faith in you? No, I don't tire of your letters – I read them over and over. We must keep near each other – we have, and I think we will. If I see you at Thanksgiving, it will be only about three weeks more. My birthday is the 11th, you know.

I think *The Princess Aline* is good. I'm sleepy, so good-night.

With my dearest love,

Anna

SUNDAY MORNING

Isn't this a beautiful day? There's a mist between us and the bluff – as though it was behind a veil. I think I'll try to sketch Sugar Loaf. I wonder if I could sketch from nature. I had to make up a little scene one day of a road and an old stone wall and trees and hills. Perhaps I could do it better if I were drawing the real thing. Let's try it together next summer. Wouldn't it be lovely if we could sketch some of the places around Oronoco and make them look right?

Mrs. Van Anders just came in – she asked if I was writing to "some of the dear ones?" Well, I *am* – to the *dearest* one.

This is the last day I will be 20. When I was 18, it seemed so strange to think that I was of age – that the law said I was old enough to think and plan and decide for myself – for I didn't feel so. I somehow want to take things into my own hands now. No one but myself knows what is best for me – I must do things in my own way, and just be myself.

CHAPTER 14

Long, Lonesome Days

NOVEMBER 15, 1895
Minneapolis to Winona

My Dearest, Dearest Anna:

It is the middle of the forenoon – time for work – but I'm going to write you just the same.

I was so glad to get those last letters. Sunday and Monday were kind of long, lonesome days – I had a dull headache that kept right at it all the time. It was a fine day, though, so I tried to walk it away. Then Monday I couldn't study much – I felt so out of sorts, and for a while before supper I lay down in the room and fell asleep. When I awakened and went down to supper I found your letter, unexpectedly. Things seem peculiarly good sometimes just on waking, don't they?

Well, I'll answer some of your questions. I draw cats, figures of leaves and fruit and things. Yesterday I started shading with charcoal. Yes, I'll enter into your plan for drawing. I'll go 'long with you and hold your things, if there isn't any feed to grind. I hope we can do it.

I chose Charlie for my character sketch. It wasn't much of a masterpiece, I reckon. The subject was all right, but the treatment – not so much. The criticism on another paper I wrote ("Why I came to the U") was "Shows too little care." That is one of my faults, isn't it? In everything.

I would send you a picture, of course, if I had any, Anna, but I haven't – and I'm strapped and a little more, so I'll have to go without yours until I have money to buy mine. I would like one *awful* much, though.

There is a great deal of anxiety about the Wisconsin football game tomorrow. We're not full of confidence, but I guess we'll win – if we do, the town won't hold us!

I'm glad you wrote me about the people you live with. There are 22 of us here now. Kotlaba is a very fleshy fellow – a freshman – from Winona. He's a good fellow, and plays the piano. Harry Smith is a little bit of a fellow – a junior – and the most effeminate fellow you ever saw. He uses the same expression girls use – Oh my! etc. It isn't what he says so much, as the feminine or girlish way he says them. He laughs and covers his face with his handkerchief, and is overcome and sinks down over a big lesson or story just as girls do. He's a very good boy, I guess.

Miss Webster is from Owatonna. She sat next me for two weeks, and I like her – she's pleasant and sensible and likes fun. I like to hear her laugh. Roy Stone is a freshman and a nice fellow. He's a miller like me; he's a sharp, witty kind of a chap. He and Miss Sperry quarrel quite a bit – mostly in fun, of course. Moody is a dental student with a great opinion of himself. I don't like him – he's a medic. He's a great "Christian" – defends going to church; says he wouldn't marry a girl that didn't belong to his church, etc. I don't like him. Olson is another medic, but isn't so disagreeable as Moody. F.S. Anderson is a senior and a minister and a good strong man, I think. He's a Swede with light hair and a big strong face and chin. I should imagine him to be very set in his ways. Well, enough – I don't want to tire you.

I won't go home Thanksgiving, I'm quite sure, but there are only about four weeks after that until Christmas. I want to see you so.

Anna, if a fellow does something wrong and mean and unmanly, and feels very much humbled and sorry – don't his being sorry help? Did you ever – no, I don't suppose you have – have the bad seem to come uppermost, and – just for a minute – you forget the good? Perhaps it wouldn't bother *everyone* quite the way it does me. But I worry that by being so, I couldn't come quite so close to you as I did when we seemed to be living and feeling together. I'm going to try not to be so hard on other people.

It won't be long until I see you, dearest.

With my love,

Roy

NOVEMBER 16, 1895
Minneapolis to Oronoco

To: My Dear Little Sister Mary:

I got your letter, and a good one came this noon from Mother. I've just finished writing to her, so you only have the dregs of me. If you read Mother's, you'll get the same things over again – cute expressions and all.

I'm hoarse as a frog from the Wisconsin game this afternoon. There was a great crowd and a hard-fighting game. We're all satisfied – beaten though we are – for our team was just as good as the great Wisconsin's, if not better – with the exception of the famous kicker O'Dea. I wish you could see a big game like that – the enthusiasm and all.

There's a fine course of lectures this winter at the Lyceum Theatre – William Dean Howells, Julia Ward Howe, Charlotte Perkins Stetson, James Whitcomb Riley. If I have the cash I'll hear Riley. Howells spoke the other night. I didn't go on account of funds, but he was in chapel here at the U next day, and I got a good look at him, and he made a little speech. Howells is the leading American realist in fiction, you know. He's no orator – seemed almost troubled and embarrassed in giving us that little speech. He struck me as very unassuming, quiet and sincere. He looks like his pictures – gray-haired – looks like a student – heavy body and square shoulders.

If I can get away from the restaurant, and the roads straighten up so they can be ridden on, I may come home Thanksgiving. I want so to come before the folks go. I haven't the cash to come any other way.

I have to get a book review in by Wednesday. It's to be at least 600 words – a critique of Edwin Markham's new collection of poems entitled *The Man with the Hoe*. I'd like to do pretty well on this – it's hard, and I don't know how to tackle it – the poems. Most of them don't appeal to me especially.

Miss Wilder told me the other day that I had talent and originality when I write, and use forceful, expressive words. She said my sentences aren't well-formed. You see I put things off, and then hammer them out in an hour.

I love you very much, always.

NOVEMBER 16, 1895
Winona to Minneapolis

My Dear, Dear Roy:

Your letter came this morning. I have been sick for several days, and was sitting half-asleep in a big rocking chair in my room. I guess your letter seemed as good to me as mine did to you. I was wishing I were home, only I know Mother would insist on my staying there until I am perfectly well, and I can't miss so much school.

Monday – my birthday – I commenced to cough hard again (I had not got entirely over the other cold), and my lungs felt congested, so I went to Dr. Lane. He said my heart was causing all the trouble – sending too much blood to my lungs, and so congested them. I stayed out of school Wednesday and Thursday. Friday I went, but had to come home – I felt so cold and faint. I'm a great deal better now. Doctor says I had considerable fever, and now that it's going down it makes me feel weak and horrid. I think I'll be all right by Monday.

I'm glad Dr. Lane is here. I'd hate to have a doctor I didn't know – he was my father's doctor when he was first taken sick, and he has cured me of a good many colds. You don't know, Roy, how I wish I were stronger – for your sake, more than anything else.

I'm afraid this letter will remind you of the "medics" whom you dislike so. Perhaps medical students are horrid, but when they are old men like Dr. Stinchfield and Dr. Lane, they are about as fine men as you find, I think.

Dearest, I wish I could see you for a few minutes. I can't write what I know I could make you understand if you were here. No matter what has happened, it can't separate us a particle. Don't you know how human I am? How often I do things that are wrong? We must love each other all the more, dear, for we can understand each other better.

I love you, love you with all my heart.

Anna

NOVEMBER 18, 1895
Minneapolis to Winona

My Darling:

Your letter just came, and I must write you. Dearest, won't you write me *soon* if you're feeling better? I'm troubled. Oh, I wish you were here now! Your picture and letter have made me want to see you so – I can't tell you how! Dearest, I love you much more than ever. I wish you had my brute health – you who try and do so much and are so plucky and brave. Words *are* weak, little sweetheart.

Haven't you been doing too much? Anna, there has been so much other trouble for you. Dearest, you won't do too much, will you, for my sake? Write me soon. It won't be long until I see you.

With my dearest love,

NOVEMBER 18, 1895
Winona to Minneapolis

My Dearest Roy:

I'm feeling ever so much better. Doctor says it makes him "happy" to find how well my heart is behaving, and I don't cough quite so hard. I'm in school again and feel like working.

You'll have to take back what you said about "medics." Doctor said he was going to ask Pres. Shepard to see that the teachers gave me an easy time for a while, but I didn't want him to. But it was good of him to plan to do so. He's as good as he can be.

We have five days' vacation Thanksgiving, so I will have quite a rest. It will be a short time from then until Christmas, and then you'll be home. No – I don't think I'm overworked. I guess Doctor didn't think so either, but as I am not quite strong yet, he wants me to have it easy for a while. I want to keep as strong as I can, for your sake, so I'll be careful not to do too much.

Your letter was such a good one, and I wasn't looking for it, so it seemed better than ever.

With love,

Anna

Roy – you're just the *dearest* boy, but you mustn't worry about me.

NOVEMBER 24, 1895
Minneapolis to Winona

My Dearest Anna:

Tomorrow are examinations in History and German, and I've got to work tonight. I dread the German. I am through with exams Wednesday, and we have no school until a week from Tuesday.

Joseph Jefferson is going to play *Rip Van Winkle* tomorrow night. I guess Zim and Buck and I will go. He's to play three nights this week.

I'll write a long letter this week – you'll forgive me, I hope. I was so very glad to get your last letter – I *was* troubled. When I write next, I suppose I shall direct it to Eyota.

With my dear love,

Roy

NOVEMBER 27, 1895
Eyota to Minneapolis

My Dearest Roy:

I finished my exams Tuesday and came home on the evening train. I never saw happier girls than those at Miss Van Anders'! All but two were going home, and they were planning how they would surprise their people.

I think the cats knew me. Coming home doesn't seem what it *should* be without you here. I don't see why I should miss you so, for you have been here so few times. And I didn't expect you to be home at Thanksgiving, so I didn't have my mind made up to see you. But I go around feeling as one does who has been to the train to meet someone and they didn't come. Never mind – I'll see you at Christmas, and that will be soon. Why weren't Oronoco and Eyota put nearer together – then I would have you during your whole vacation?

Tomorrow we're to have our Thanksgiving dinner at Aunt Matt's. It seems good to be back, and no Geometry to worry me – I failed the exam, I know. I hate to face Miss Sprague when I go back. Oh, I can't bear Geometry People, who are good at mathematics, and think that one who *isn't* doesn't know *anything*! I used to feel badly because I couldn't understand those old problems, but now I don't *care*. I wouldn't be like Miss Sprague for the world, even if she is one of the best instructors in the state.

You asked about rules at the Normal. They're rather severe with the girls, though they don't trouble me much. The thing I dislike most is to have to go to Miss Sprague after being absent and get an excuse. She asks so many questions, and looks at you as though she thought there was no need of your being sick. She asked me how I took cold. I don't like Pres. Shepard as well as I used to either – he seems to be a policy man, and treats us like children sometimes. We're not supposed to communicate to each other after going into the assembly room in the morning, even though it's before school opens, and yesterday he made each girl hand in a slip of paper telling whether or not she'd communicated, and if she had, what it was about. That seems to me so *little*.

I have told you the *bad* side of the school because you asked me, but there's a *good* side too. Some of the teachers are fine. Miss Speckman – the drawing teacher – is lovely. She likes the East, too – we had a nice long talk one day about the East, and about girls – two very interesting topics. And I like our Psychology teacher, Mr. Kirkpatrick – he's one of the most perfect gentlemen I ever saw.

This isn't a good letter for Thanksgiving – I've been grumbling too much. I shall think of you tomorrow – I wonder if you will be homesick and lonesome. Good-night, dear. We'll be thankful tomorrow that Christmas is coming.

Your little girl

NOVEMBER 28, 1895
Minneapolis to Eyota

My Dearest Anna:

It's about 8 o'clock, and I'm alone and just a wee bit lonesome. This is the first time I was ever away from home on Thanksgiving, you know.

Sunday evening I studied until midnight, got up at 4, took a cold bath to waken me, and studied until 9. The History exam came first, and that was all right; but in the afternoon came German, and I didn't do well at all. It was hard and queer and what I hadn't studied much. I guess a great many didn't do very well.

Monday night we went to hear Jefferson in *Rip Van Winkle*. I wish you could hear him – oh, I do – you would like him immensely. He was so natural.

Last night Buck and Stone and I went to hear Jefferson again. He played *Cricket on the Hearth* and *Lend Me Five Shillings*. It was very fine, but I liked *Rip Van Winkle* much better. Jefferson played Caleb Plummer in *Cricket on the Hearth*. I guess you have read the story. I think Jefferson has such a fine, good-natured laugh – everything is so natural, and you laugh and feel kinda like crying all at once. I would like to be such a man.

Melba sings Saturday evening at the Exposition Building, but I can't afford to hear her. I suppose she's the greatest living singer. Prices were doubled for Jefferson, but I wanted to hear him more than once. Probably I could appreciate him better than I could Melba.

I got a letter from Mother and another from Mary – such good letters. I believe the folks do like me a bit. Mary has been sick, but is better and back in school; the doctor thought she was threatened with typhoid fever. She has been reading *Daniel Deronda* and liked it and wanted to know if I did. I never read it. I guess my little sister is growing into a woman – she wants to go to school. She said in this last letter, "Oh, Roy – I hardly know what I want, but I feel as if I wanted more life, more knowledge, more books, and more room. Did you ever feel so?"

Walter has been with me since 10 o'clock this morning. We went to church, and he took dinner with me, and this afternoon we walked down to the public library, but couldn't get a book today. I'm going to get something to read this short vacation. I didn't have any card, so one of the girls offered me hers – the folks here are really good to me.

I'm sleepy – have been up nights lately and have a cold. And this is a stupid letter. Anna, I want to see you so – you can't imagine.

With my love,

Sweetheart – I'm glad you're not the mathematical kind. There's a girl here – Miss Stevens – who's a regular "shark" at math and science, and I think the work is sort of souring to her. I wish I were more of that kind, though.

DECEMBER 1, 1895
Eyota to Minneapolis

My Dearest Roy:

Yesterday I went to Rochester, and when I came home, I saw your letter first thing. I was glad to get it, for it seemed so long since I heard from you. I suppose one is waiting for me in Winona. It seemed like going home to go to Rochester. Mary is full of plans for her wedding, and we spent most of our time talking about it and the pretty, dainty things she can make for herself or the house, out of so little.

I surprised them when I came. The girls didn't know who it was, so I hurried out to the kitchen. Mary was frying doughnuts, and Clara paring potatoes. Just as it was growing dark, Mary played and sang, and it seemed like old times. Then Clara came home from the bank (she works there afternoons) and sang a Scottish song – you must get her to sing it for you sometime. Then Uncle Henry came home, we ate supper, and he walked down to the station with me. I got a new dress and some fancy work for Christmas presents.

I wrote to your sister Mary – she's just the kind of girl a girl ought to be. I wish I could see more of her. You must get better acquainted with her, Roy – you don't know how much I want you two to be close friends. She's reaching out to you now – perhaps more than she will when she's older – and you must be quick to respond. Tell her what you think and feel, and confide in her. She will understand – perhaps better than you think. I don't know why I have written this, unless it's because I remember so well how I felt at her age, and I want you to just *love* that little sister of yours – and let her know that you do.

I never read *Cricket on the Hearth*. I think Mary heard Jefferson in *Rip Van Winkle*. I wish I could hear him. I read several short stories by Jerome since I've been home – "John Sugarfield" and "The Woman of the Saeter" and others. "Silhouettes" was queer – I don't exactly understand it. They have some very good books in the public library in Winona, but it's hard to get recent writers – they're out all the time. I've tried ever so many times to get *The Raiders*.

I go back to Winona tomorrow. Then it will be only 18 days until I'm home again, and then – oh, there's so much to talk and *think* about. I *do* want to see you, dear.

With my dear love,

Anna

DECEMBER 5, 1895
Minneapolis to Winona

Dearest:

It's getting late, and I can write but a little. I started to write you this afternoon, but it was so discouraged and faint-hearted I was ashamed to finish it. Oh, the work I have – listen – History, Old English, Trig, German, Chemistry, Philosophy, Sanitary Science, and Rhetoricals.

Trig is terrible – it's extremely uphill – I've been so discouraged. I flunked this morning. Someway I can't see how I'm getting much good out of school. I have to take so many things I don't want.

There – it's a shame to wreak all my grumbling and laziness on you. I guess I'm a bit of a coward – I'm sick of things.

You are very good, dearest. I'm just living for Christmas to come – you don't know how I want to see you. Someway I can't write tonight – forgive me this letter, won't you?

With my love always,

Roy

DECEMBER 8, 1895
Winona to Minneapolis

My Dearest Roy:

This is just a perfect day – I wonder if you're out enjoying it. I believe I'll take a walk after I write you. I wish we could take a walk together today – over the lake and out toward the bluffs. Things have looked more beautiful this week – perhaps because it's warmer, or I feel so well. Sometimes the sunset lights up Sugar Loaf and makes the rock a beautiful rose color.

I've been thinking about you, dear – a great deal, since your last letter came – and have wished that I could drive away your blues. I'm glad you wrote me how you felt. I think of you and care. Does everyone have that much work? You won't have to take what you don't want except for this year, will you?

I got my standings – they were very good in everything except Geometry – I fell below grade in that. I've been reading *Birds and Poets* by Burroughs. I like it – it's about birds and the things that poets have said of them.

When do you come home? How long do you stay, and when are you coming to Eyota? Oh, Roy – it seems as though two weeks is an age.

With love – *so* much love,

Anna

When you come to Eyota, bring the baby's picture for me to see.

DECEMBER 8, 1895
Minneapolis to Winona

My dearest Anna:

I've just finished *The Raiders* – got it yesterday. I like it better than anything I've read for a very long time. I wish we could read it together – it's as good as *Lorna Doone* nearly, and reminds one of Stevenson just a wee bit. I showed it to Miss Sperry and told her scraps to get her interested. It's fun to see her – she gets so interested. I think you would like a good many things about Miss Sperry. I hadn't read aloud to amount to anything since we finished *Kidnapped* up in the hammock on the hill that last Sunday.

I've just been lazy all day; hardly been for a walk; just laid right still and read myself full as I haven't for a long time. And I want to see you, Sweetheart – perhaps I will three weeks from tonight. Think of it – just a few days until we go home. These last days will crawl.

Frank has been sick and kinda blue the last few days, but he's feeling better now. He's been in bed for quite a while. He acts up and snores horribly – makes remarks in his sleep – and I get his sword, and look like Caliban, and yell and gloat over him, and prick him until I wake him up. He's really asleep now, I guess, but here I sit with the naked sword before me on the table. We have wild times! Frank can imitate cats, dogs, pigs, etc. This evening a cat was in the hall, and Frank mewed like the mother cat, and the poor little kitten thought it had found its folks sure, and you should have heard it yell. We had to stop that, and I went out and brought him in – a little Maltese fellow. I took him down to Miss Jessie. It wasn't her cat, but she said, "It's just a little kitten," and said she had a father feeling for all kittens and would take him in (I knew she would). Do you suppose your cats will remember me?

Tomorrow I must work. Tuesday we have our first lesson in real trig. We've through with logarithms, and I guess things will get better – faith, we can sympathize with each other about math, can't we?

I registered for new studies. Old English is going to be rather dry and useless, but it can't be helped and is good "training." The teacher has very light hair like a saint's aura, and a precise way of speaking – so good and precise you feel like shocking her a little – you know how?

I wish we were where we could say good night the old way – I want to see you so much. You will get tired of that, I'm afraid – the same old song every time. Good night, dearest – I love you as I always do, and more.

DECEMBER 16, 1895
Minneapolis to Winona

Dearest:

I've just been out for a walk – down along the river for a couple of miles. What a change in the weather – hasn't it been fine?

Anna, you mustn't let my blues trouble you. The faculty made me drop Old English. I was glad to do that, though I'll have to make it up next year or sometime. Old English seems so stupid with its "tham, thon, thos" – I dinna like it.

Saturday I went to the library and got the *The Black Arrow* by R. L. Stevenson and read the most of it yesterday. It's not as good as *Kidnapped.*

Last week Buck and I went and heard the Bostonians in *Prince Anamias*, and again Saturday night in *Robin Hood*, which I liked as well or better than ever – it's the gayest, prettiest thing I ever saw, and it does a person good. They have such a lot of pretty people in the troupe. The girl who plays Maid Marian – oh, but she is pretty.

Perhaps you think I have been going to theaters too much. You see, the boy who carries a jug of water for the club each day from the University spring ceased in the performance of his duties; and I – true to my aristocratic ideas, and burning to crush out the middle class – took his place and now carry water for 25 cents a week. That's enough for a theatre a week, to say nothing of the fiendish pleasure I take in thus breaking down our independent peasantry.

It had been nearly two months since I had been over to Uncle Julius's, so I went last evening. I took lunch with them and played a little with Viola. I am going over oftener after this – they were very good to me last year.

I'm going home next Friday. I'll have about 17 days, you see. I'll come to Eyota soon after Xmas – the sooner the better. I try not to think about it and anticipate more than I can help. I'm so glad you're feeling well. It *has* been beautiful weather, and knowing I shall see you soon keeps me kind of warm and merry.

With my dear love,

I'll bring the baby's picture, of course.

DECEMBER 22, 1895
Oronoco to Eyota

My Dearest Anna:

The folks have all gone to bed. Someway I want to write a little to you tonight.

I came home Friday as expected – I guess the folks were glad to see me, and wasn't I glad to see them! Oh, you should see little Volney now. He was asleep when I came, and when he woke up he didn't know me at first – was kind of afraid of such a long-haired fellow, I suppose. He said my face was familiar, but he couldn't place me. He felt my face all over with his soft hand, and knows me now (I'm talking like an old grandmother).

We built a fire on the ice at the foot of our Point and skated. There was no one on the pond, and everything was perfectly still all over the country. I like to skate along that way – the motion and the loneliness make your blood kinda tingle, and you want to sing and shout – and I did too.

Be careful and don't take a cold or anything. When can I come and see you? When do you want me? How long are you going to stay? Good-night, dearest little girl. I love you so much.

DECEMBER 22, 1895
Eyota to Oronoco

My Dearest Roy:

Here we are back home. I can just think what a happy time you're having today – being at home, with your father and mother and Mary, Blanche and the little boy – all so glad to have you there. Only a few days and *someone else* will be gladder than all of them to have you *here* (!).

During vacation we have to make observations – preferably of one special child – and report in Child Study when we go back to school. You must help me when you come down. I wish there was some child nearby I could have around a good deal. This is the most interesting part of Psychology.

How have you got on in your water carrier business? I think your wages are too high – if the boy who had experience did it for $.25, they ought to have commenced lower with you, and then raised your salary (wage sounds too commonplace) as you gained experience in the business (!).

I'll see you soon. I'll keep everything to tell you.

With my love,

Anna

DECEMBER 24, 1895
Eyota to Oronoco

My Dear Roy:

I spent yesterday in Rochester. Mary is to have a little reception at the house after the wedding. She hopes you can come. She was in a great hurry, and will be until after the wedding, so I offered to invite you for her. Come down anytime and stay over Sunday. I have to go to Rochester Monday to stay until after the wedding, so come early – as soon as you can.

I've been busy with a dressmaker here since I came home, but she will be through tonight. What a snowstorm we're having. I wish I could see the baby.

Mother has lost her needle and accused me – I must go and hunt for it, so good-bye and "Merry Xmas." Perhaps we will be together when the New Year comes in and I can say Happy New Year to you!

With lots of love,

Anna

CHAPTER 15

Two of the Best Comrades That Ever Lived

1896

    William McKinley elected 25th President of the U.S.

    Puccini performs *La Bohème* in Turin.

    French physicist A.H. Becquerel discovers radioactivity.

    First modern Olympics held in Athens.

    Beginning of Klondike gold rush in Bonanza Creek, Canada.

    Modern Woodmen of America receive a charter. Through this organization, Oronoco has its heyday of campers.

    May 6: Groundbreaking for Minnesota Capitol.

JANUARY 3, 1896
Oronoco to Eyota

My Dearest Anna:

Oh, I wish it were two weeks ago tonight, and I was just home and going to see you. This vacation has seemed very short. I saw you such a little time – almost like a dream – and I had intended to tell you so much that someway I didn't.

I hated to leave you, Anna – more than you think. No, I guess you know how much. As soon as I had gone a little way, I felt as if I had lost my last friend, and I wanted to come back and just be with you again. Something was warm back of my eyes in spite of me.

I missed the stage and thought I would walk. Dearest, my heart was way despairing at leaving you. I'm such a queer boy – sort of a barbarian and woman, I guess. As I was walking along – and 'twas dim and dark by that time, so I couldn't see but a little – I happened to glance down, and something glinted in the road. I looked, and 'twas a great horseshoe, with the toe toward me. I took it along with me, and it cheered me up. I'm sure it meant good for us – aren't you sure too? Or why would it come right out of the night that way, when I was thinking of you with my heart pretty full? You remember the horseshoe you found me long ago?

Perhaps I shall see you again before this weary five months passes – we'll hope for something, won't we?

Fred and Charlie and Hector and I went out for a little while in the afternoon, but 'twas cold, and the rabbits lay close, and we only got four. The folks were glad to see me. The baby had a great cold – about like mine. They wanted to know all about the wedding, and asked about you. I was over to Aunt Minnie's today and talked quite a bit about you – told her a little about how you looked at the wedding, with your hair like a queen.

I won't write more this evening. I'm sure I will be better and gentler and work better, dearest, just from the little time I saw you. Can you write me Sunday, so I'll get it soon?

With my dear love,

Roy

JANUARY 3, 1896
Rochester to Oronoco

My Dearest Roy:

I'm feeling gloomy, and nothing is interesting anymore. I have been thinking of you this morning, and wondering if you're feeling the same. After you went yesterday someone proposed that we make New Year's calls, and I didn't feel a bit like it and made some excuse. But Uncle Henry said, "Oh, you must go," so I went with the others. At one house an orchestra was playing softly, and I felt dreamy and a bit "teary," and I didn't care to make any more calls, so I left.

After I came home I got Mary and Clara to play and sing some of the old songs. We all felt a little sad. Clara says to tell you that you made your *mark* yesterday, telling stories – you *did* too.

They left this morning. We didn't decorate their trunks. We took rice down to the station, but didn't use it – we didn't feel in the mood.

I'm going home tonight. I'm thankful for the good time we had, aren't you? I wish that plan of coming to Minneapolis as soon as the Normal closes may work. When does the U close? I'm afraid my interest isn't wholly in the primary school. I want you to take me around Minneapolis. How long, long it is until then ....

With love,

Anna

JANUARY 4, 1896
Winona to Oronoco

My Dearest:

Your letter has just come, and I am *so* glad to get it. I can hardly think I go back to work day after tomorrow, and the happy time together which we thought about for so long is past, and it will be so long before there is another one. Dearest, can you write me what you had planned to tell me? I'll close my eyes and imagine you beside me telling it.

We must keep close to each other through our letters, for it will be so many years when there are *only* letters, with just a few days together once in a great while. Try to tell me just what you think and feel, dearest – tell me about things that trouble you, and about your success, and I will too. We will be two of the best comrades that ever lived.

Roy, I've read your last letter over and over. I think I never left you when it seemed so hard as it does this time, but I won't be blue – I'll go to work soon and stop thinking. I was going to write something cheerful, for I'm afraid you will be blue when this letter reaches you, and I'd like to cheer you up – but I can't write quite as I feel.

I have kept the horseshoe I found that first summer at Oronoco, and I'm going to keep it always. This ought to be a good year for us. It's the first one we ever commenced together. We'll take the horseshoes as a good omen.

I finished *The Raiders* Friday – it's *fine*. Do you remember a Scottish story in *The Youth's Companion* about a troop of soldiers who were hunting for a man? It told how they rode and talked in the moonlight; how they were overheard by the daughter of the man for whom they were searching; and then how they hid him from the "troopers." Parts of *The Raiders* reminds me of that. I must have been 9 or 10 when I read it.

I'm sorry you missed the stage. I'm afraid we were at fault, but I wanted to keep you until the very last minute. Here's a kiss – can you feel my arms, dearest?

Dearest, you're *not* a "sort of barbarian and woman" – you're the finest, truest, noblest, *dearest* man in all the world, and I don't half deserve the love you give me!

Your own little girl

JANUARY 7, 1896
Minneapolis to Winona

Dearest, Dearest Anna:

Your letter came this noon. Anna, that was the *best* letter that ever was written. I'm going to carry it close to me all the year. The letter that comes first after I have seen you always has a peculiar *dearness*, but this was the best of any.

I wonder why it was so much harder for us to leave each other this time. Dearest, you understand me better than most people – better than *anyone*. As I went down the street toward home I felt oh so lonesome – I can't tell you how. I think you felt the same way. Yes, Anna, we must write and keep close as close as now. What a dear little comrade you are – there is no one like you.

You won't mind if I write rambling, will you? I'll try and write you about whatever troubles me, be it silly or not.

I left home Monday. Said good-bye to Aunt Minnie and Uncle and Charlie, my old pard. I believe Charlie was sorry to have me go – his voice sounded a little that way when he said good-bye and shook hands. The little boy and Blanche weren't up when I came away, but I went in and spoke to them. He waked up and cried when I came in, but quieted down when I stooped over and felt his soft hands and face. I hope nothing ever happens to the boy. I hated to leave my mother and Mary – worse than usual somehow.

Over toward the station, when I looked back, the sun shone out over Oronoco and the pond and the points. When we go back it will be warm and June – raining a little, perhaps. Wouldn't it sound good to hear the warm rain drip through the green June woods? Yes, it seems a long, weary time without seeing you – dearest, I love you so.

Zimmerman was on the same train as I, as were a lot of U folks. I got here in time for dinner. Part of the club were back, and in the afternoon I went out and bought some provender for supper, for Miss Webster wasn't back yet, and I – being President – was next in command.

I *was* heavy-hearted – just as you thought I would be. It's kinda cowardly for me to get that way, I suppose, but I will *think*, you know. If I had been with you and talked with you *longer*, thoughts that all the year I had meant to say would have come back. I wish I could write you something that would be as good to *you* as that letter of yours is to *me*. I want you to write me as you feel – I like those letters best. I hope that scheme about coming to Minneapolis will work. Summer vacation June 5. I'll try and keep from being homesick for you all I can.

I talked with Mary Sunday in the way you wanted me to. It was just for a few minutes, but I think perhaps she will speak and write to me more about what she wants to tell me.

I brought the horseshoe with me and hung it over our door. Yes, little comrade – we will try and make this a good year. And you really believe all that about me – my dear, blinded little girl? Anyway, sweetheart – I love you as if I were what you think me. Dearest, you help make me better than everything else.

I don't know as there was any special thing I wanted to tell you. I can almost feel your warm arms, my own dearest, and now I touch your hair and forehead and lips. Good-night.

With my dear love,

Roy

You must take good care of yourself, Anna, won't you? I would give anything to see you just now.

JANUARY 12, 1896
Winona to Minneapolis

My Dearest Roy:

Wednesday I worked at the Normal until almost dark, and as I came home in the twilight, I was thinking of you, and wishing in a dreamy kind of way that there would be a letter. I thought it was too soon to expect one – and wasn't I glad when I came in and saw one lying on the stairs! And, dear, that was one of the *best* letters, and the *best* part – the part I shall think of very often – is that you think I understand you better than anyone. We will be two of the dearest friends that ever lived!

I have got settled again at my work, but that first day was hard – I couldn't settle down. Miss Taylor didn't come that night, and I felt rather lonely, and got out my class pictures for company. I ended the day by getting a high fever and felt weak the next day, but I was all right as soon as I commenced work.

I've been reading Hawthorne's *A Blithedale Romance*. It's a strange, mysterious story, but I like it. I liked *Marble Faun* best of any of his I ever read – how much alike all his stories are.

We've had interesting work in Nature Study this week. We've been tracing birds – some of our common songsters. I have been reading a wonderfully interesting little book – *Birds Through an Opera Glass*. Did I ever tell you how a little bird used to sing in the woods by my schoolhouse? Such a sweet, pure little song – I didn't know what it was, but it seemed to say pe-wee – and I have found that it really *is* the wood pewee. I'm going to show it to you next summer, if we can find one. Its song – compared with the bobolink and meadowlark – is like lilies of the valley compared with roses.

I've found out the name of a flower I tried and tried to analyze and couldn't. I asked everyone about it, but no one knew – until I described it to Mr. Holzinger. I had hardly commenced with my description when his eyes grew bright, and he told me the name of it, and all about the family. He said, "Miss Barnard – you deserve to know about that plant." So he took me into a room where he keeps specimens collected from everywhere – some of them from Germany – and showed us some beautiful plants. I'll spare you the name of the plant – it would cover a line or two – but I'm going to study it next summer. I've had some of the loveliest talks with Mr. Holzinger, He has such a big warm heart – it does one good to be with him. "There's nothing so kingly as kindness," after all. Some of the students don't like him – I can't see why. I suppose they haven't seen the best side of him.

I'm writing by the window. The sky is beautiful tonight – I wish you were here. Perhaps the reason it was harder for us to leave each other this time is that – do you think it possible? – we have grown a little dearer to each other?

With a heart full of love,
Your little girl

JANUARY 14, 1896
Minneapolis to Winona

Sweetheart:

I've just finished reading your letter. The week has dragged by, and it seems an age since I left home – how very long that first week always seems.

I have a great cold on my lungs and all over. Downstairs after dinner, I sit on the register and play I am a sick Eskimo. Saturday I was hoarse and coughing, and Frank put me in hot water about half an hour. I was singing and making remarks all the time, and there was great hilarity. Frank is the greatest hand to get tickled. The hot bath didn't do much good, though. It's just a cold, you know – you mustn't trouble yourself about it any. It does make one feel disagreeable, though.

I got an "incomplete" in History. I didn't like that – didn't expect it in *History*. But then I remembered I didn't hand in a map of Charlemagne's Empire, and lost some of my first lectures. I must make it up and hand it in. "Incomplete" work must be made up within one term or it becomes a "condition." Conditions not made up before the subject is again offered become "failures." Failures must be taken over again.

How is your Geometry? I don't like the old "trig." I'm becoming a little bit better now, I guess. Oh, I'm the *laziest* mortal – Anna, I wish you could study my case! I was talking with Bowers about my studying, and I said, "I think I'm a good reader – anything I can get by *reading* I can do easily and all right." And Bowers said, "Yes, you're a *very* good reader – you're an expert at *skimming* – but you haven't really learned to *study* yet." Yet poor old Bowers thinks I can do almost anything if "I feel in the mood." I must get on top of myself yet.

You spoke of a story you read long ago in *The Youth's Companion*. I remember it too – it was "The Covenanter's Daughter," I think. I remember something about the "flash of the trooper's steel in the moonlight."

Saturday I went down to the library and got *Barrack-room Ballads* by Rudyard Kipling. I rather like them – they're rough and strong, some of them; sometimes with a realism that shows Kipling must have been there and seen it. 'Twas in India, you know – telling about a scrimmage: "And the brown flesh blued, where the bayonet kissed, as the steel shot back with a wrench and a twist." And again where Captain "Crook" O'Neil, in his peaceful home, thinks back among other things: "The stench of the marshes – the raw, piercing smell when the overhand stabbing-cut silenced the yell. The oaths of his Irish that surged when they stood where the black crosses hung o'er the Kuttamow flood." That reaches my taste for the horrible – isn't it nice?

Last Sunday Walter and I went to Gethsemane Episcopal Church. The service is rather pretty, but it tries me – doesn't it you? Probably because I don't understand it and am not used to it.

I like Mr. Holzinger because he's *good* to you. I presume he wouldn't like *me*, though, if I were in his classes. Yes, we will find that bird with the clear little song, if the summer ever comes. I wish we could be together all the springtime – from the last of March to the first of June – and do just as we wanted to. What a dreamer!

You didn't sing to me this last time I saw you – you will next time, won't you? You know I like to hear you sing "Close by."

I guess I shall have to get some pictures taken – I don't want the whole class of '94 keeping you from being lonesome (!).

I'm so dull and stupid today – I won't write more. Take good care of yourself, won't you? I wonder what it was that was *best* in that letter of mine. I know what *I* liked best in that one of *yours*.

Good-bye, dearest.

JANUARY 19, 1896
Winona to Minneapolis

My Dearest Roy:

Several of us girls went to the Episcopal Church this morning. I don't like their service very well – it seems so superficial. I presume if I understood it all I could feel it – parts of it *are* beautiful. The church is dim, and when, during the prayer, we all sat with bowed heads, and the choir boys sang softly, "Keep us this day without sin," a worshipful feeling came over me.

What a perfect day this is. I am sitting by the open window. Miss Ingalls is downstairs playing the piano, and the world seems peaceful and beautiful just now. Miss Ingalls has come here to room, so now there are three of us girls here. You remember I told you about her – the boarding-school girl? I like her, though I can't admire or even approve of a great many things about her. I sometimes wonder why I like her?

I'm anxious about your cold. You mustn't go to taking hard colds – you hadn't got over your other cold, had you? It takes so long to get over such a cold, and you are so careless. You *must* button up your overcoat, and don't stand outdoors without your hat on. You want *me* to be careful, but if *I* must be careful, *you* must too.

I received a letter from your sister Mary this week. She is thinking and planning about going to school next year in Rochester. She said she enjoyed having you at home so much. and how you hated to go back, and said, "It seems to me as if I could not go away from home and stay so long at a time." She will be homesick, as you were, if she does go. She's a lovely girl – her letters are natural, and she writes about what interests her. I'm afraid you didn't give her a good impression of the Normal, for she said she didn't think she would like it.

When I went to get my hat for church this morning, I found that a *mouse* had eaten part of it! It was all chewed up, and the scraps scattered all over the rest of the hat. I'm thankful he didn't eat the hat *itself* – how I would have looked going to church with a hole in my hat?! Miss Taylor found him in the wastebasket one night eating peanut shucks.

We have interesting work in psychology now in Child Study. Mr. Kirk-patrick gave us special topics to work up – mine is "The Development of Language in the Child." I brought home some books on the subject and read a little yesterday. One of the books – *The First Three Years of a Child* – is wonderfully interesting. There is so much in it that I never thought of – what a wonderful, wonderful thing a little child is! The author Vereg says a child is blind until it's a week old. The girls say that can't be so, for they have seen little babies look at them and smile. Vereg says a smile at that age is reflex – that a child can't distinguish objects until it's about a month old. Well, they're wonderful little people anyway. You must study little Volney next summer.

We have only one week more with Mr. Holzinger. One day he said some things that made some of the girls think he didn't believe in the Bible or God, so they asked him about it. He gave us a good little talk – I liked what he said. He doesn't care much for creed or doctrine. He says the highest and best thing we have is our intellect, and that whatever tells us what is true and good and right, we should hold to. He said, "Science can't prove there is a God." I said, "Science can't prove that there is such a thing as courage or sympathy either." Then he spoke of how surely we know those things, and said he believed in some great and loving power that puts life into everything.

One of the girls said after he had gone, "I guess he's pretty near an infidel," and I said that whether he was an infidel or not, I wished more people were like him.

I think your taste for such horrible poetry must be development of the "brutal instinct," which they tell us is in every child (especially boys), and that we must be careful not to rouse it. I confess I don't find it "nice." Mr. Holzinger *would* like you – you're just the kind of person he likes! I don't think much of the boys here – there isn't one in the whole school that I like. I wish you could just *see* the boys here – I feel like *shaking* them sometimes.

I wish we might be together this spring – from when the first pussy willows come until, well, like you said, the first of June. You dear boy – yes, I'll sing "Close by" next time I see you, though I can't see why you like it – no one else does. You must be sure to have your picture taken, else I'll have the whole class of '94 out every time I'm feeling lonely, and you can't be sure which one I look at oftenest (!).

With love,
Anna

JANUARY 22, 1896
Minneapolis to Winona

Dearest Anna:

This has been rather a busy day. I was up late last night reading my notes and getting ready for a History quiz this morning. I hadn't done as much reading as I ought to, but I did the best I could.

I didn't get along well in Trig this morning. Professor Downey is good in mathematics, but hasn't much sympathy for poor, awkward, unmathematical folk like me. I didn't write my logarithms in the way by which you save chalk. Then I made a bit of a mistake, but the answer came *nearly* right. Downey said to me, "You remember what the answer was, didn't you?" I didn't remember, of course – I never had worked it before – but I got red and looked confused. Sometimes one gets kind of "rattled" working at the board – do you ever? We don't like math, do we? We'll do as well as we can though – shake?

I'm covered up with things I hate to do. There's an essay in Rhetoricals for last term and two for this – one of them an oration on "The Voice of the People." Then I have to make up that incomplete in History, and do about 600 pages of reading and take notes on it all. I should write a lot of letters too. I've felt kind of sick of it all for the last few days. I'm telling you everything, though don't like to have you feel ashamed of me either.

Saturday night Buck and I went to *Wang* – a comic opera set in Siam! It was very funny. When I was downtown Saturday I got *Prairie Folks* – short sketches or stories by Hamlin Garland. I liked it – liked it very much – as well, yes, better – than *Main-Travelled Roads*. When you come up next summer to visit the primary schools, I'm going to read you a little of it, if you can spare the time.

I guess you didn't like that last letter of mine – my nice poetry shocked and disgusted you. Well, maybe I don't *like* it exactly, but I always laugh when I read it aloud to Zim – just for fun, you know. Yes, I presume it *is* the remains of the brute.

Do you ever get to hating to go to some class, whether you have your lesson done or not? I feel that way about Trig. How do you like everything this term about your work – are you happy? Maybe that's a queer question to ask.

It gets serious, this living, doesn't it? I wish we could do as we want to about things – that is one trouble with me. We got to talking the other day after dinner about whether life would be worth living – whether we would want to live if there was nothing else beyond this life; if it simply stopped here. They didn't think so, but I said *I* thought I would – that there is down-heartedness and unhappiness – longer stretches of it – but there are times that even it up. Miss Sperry didn't believe I thought that – "You – the most discontented person I ever saw?" she said. There *is* something else though, I hope.

I had a good letter from Mary. I believe she and I will get acquainted. I might as well try and be good to my little sister, seeing as I don't seem to be much good at anything else.

We went over and got weighed today, and I lost two or three pounds. I have just had my hair cut, and the folks at the club laid it to that!

My cold is about well now – being careful doesn't seem to make any difference with me – guess it's fate. You mustn't let fate have any chance with *you* though.

I must go to work now. Write me soon, dear.

Roy

JANUARY 24, 1896
Winona to Minneapolis

My Dear, Dear Roy:

Your letter came this morning – I'm sorry, dear, that you're feeling blue. I'm glad you wrote me just as you felt. I want you to always, and, dear, no matter how discouraged and downhearted you get, that could never make me ashamed of you. You know how much faith I have in you – and, no, I don't believe you do or can know it all. I get discouraged sometimes too, when things hardly seem worth working for, but never mind – there's a good deal for us to look forward to, and things *are* worth working for – even Geometry for me, and Trig for you. Yes, we'll shake over our mathematics and go at them again.

Miss Sprague said yesterday she had more faith in me than I had in myself. It seems to me the teachers have all been kinder lately. They stop and speak to me when I'm passing through the halls or library.

Dear, that last letter of mine – I only said that in fun about "brutal instincts." I knew you didn't expect me to think that poetry *nice*, and I knew *you* didn't think so either. It didn't shock or disgust me a bit, and I did like your letter – I always do.

As it's Friday night, we girls have been having a jolly time singing and dancing. I don't know how to dance very well, but I like to try it with the girls once in a while. I have lots of work tomorrow – an examination in Nature Study, and I haven't reviewed a bit yet. Then there are all my other lessons, and a sleigh ride tomorrow evening. The much-despised Normal boys have gotten it up. We are to drive to Homer – a little place six miles from here – go coasting, have supper, and home again.

This afternoon was our last day with Mr. Holzinger. He told us something about his life. He studied for the ministry at Yale, but before he graduated he had the chance to come here, so he gave up his plans, for he said he thought he wouldn't have made a good minister. I told him how cheery and good it had seemed in his class.

Yes, I am quite happy now. I think sometimes I'm never quite happy except when I'm with you – but it makes me happy just to *feel* well and be able to work.

Yes, this life would be worth living, even if it ended here – but it doesn't. I think sometimes that I wouldn't want to live if it weren't for you. You mustn't think you're not good for much, Roy – I wish you could know what you really are.

Take good care of yourself. I'm afraid you have never *tried* being careful – to see whether or not it makes any difference. Remember that I love you and have great faith in you, and we'll stand by each other, always, as comrades should.

With my love,

Anna

JANUARY 27, 1896
Winona to Minneapolis

My Dear Roy:

Here I am in my place at school, writing to you, and right in the midst of study hour too. I have been practicing the vertical hand *(a new trend in writing – writing vertically rather than traditionally slanted to the right)* for about half an hour. Miss Taylor is working at the desk across the aisle. She saw me take out this notepaper, and looked very wicked, with her big black eyes, and said she'd "tell." This room has to be kept as still as can be all day so that any who want to study here can do so.

The examination wasn't hard – I guess I will stand quite well. We have methods in Elementary Science, Chemistry, Physics and Astronomy for the next six months. My Geometry *does* bother me – I'm always sure I won't pass in it. I've said to myself that I wouldn't care anyhow, but that isn't really true, of course. I dread to go to Geometry, always – I have a perfect *horror* of it.

This term is half out. Oh, I *hope* you will come home during your spring vacation, even if it's only a few days.

Lovingly,

Anna

JANUARY 28, 1896
Minneapolis to Winona

Dearest Little Girl:

I just went to the spring after water, and there were so many waiting that I thought I would come home and do something instead of waiting my turn.

It's been springy today, almost, hasn't it? I did all right in Trig this morning, and as I came out of doors and felt the air and sun and saw the light looking softer than usual, I felt, well – you know how I felt. I'm so much of an animal about such things.

I haven't been to Carnival yet. Perhaps I'll go Thursday night. There's a University Carnival Club – they wear uniforms and belts and maroon-and-gold toques and are the escorts of the Fire King. I haven't had time before, but think I'll put on my uniform and go with the gang. There will be a great time – the last big night. The boys were telling how the St. Paul High School fellows were out in their football suits; then there was the club of Devils, and our boys got to rushing with the Highs and the Devils and tossing 'em. It will be a lot of fun and a big scrap (brutal instinct). Say, dearest – I didn't mind what you said about my brutal instincts – don't you think I can tell when you are in fun? Besides, perhaps it *is* a little bit that way.

Last Friday Miss Sperry and Miss Webster asked Frank and me over to a little gathering where they stay. The lady there has "Friday nights" for those living in the house. We had a very pleasant time. There was an old gentleman who could tell a story as well as any I ever heard. I told one or two modest little yarns too. I didn't feel out of place or shy, and Jim said he was proud of me (Jim's foolish!).

Wednesday is University night at the Metropolitan, and Palmer Cox's Brownies are there – if I can find time I should like to see that. You see, I'm two theaters ahead for carrying water (faith, that's a queer way to say it!). Saturday I went to the Ski U Mah concert at the chapel for the benefit of the YMCA – I had to be patriotic, you know.

I'll go and get some water now before supper. I ought to write better – it must be a job to forge through my letters. I'm afraid I won't be home in the spring. It seems so long, long without you, dear heart. I love you all the time.

Roy

JANUARY 31, 1896
Minneapolis to Winona

Sweetheart:

I'm just back from my walk. It's after 8, but I'm going to write you tonight anyhow. How is that cold? I hope so much that it didn't get hold of you hard.

Last Tuesday evening Sousa's band gave a concert in the Lyceum Theatre – I thought that was a good thing I hadn't ought to miss. It was grand. There was some classical music – *Tannhauser* by Wagner; a "Hungarian Rhapsody" by Liszt, etc.; but in great part it was popular music. We kept encoring them, and got Sousa's old-time marches – "Washington Post," "High School Cadets,"

"Manhattan Beach," "King Cotton March," and a new Humoresque – "The Band Came Back." I liked the classical music, but I'm afraid I liked Sousa's music best. There was one piece – I liked the music, but I also liked the *name* someway: "And I, Too, Was Born in Arcadia." Strange, isn't it – how a name like that will strike you and run in your head? It calls up imaginings to me.

Sunday I read some in a little book of Stevenson's: *The Merry Men and Other Tales and Fables.* There was one short story – "Thrawn Janet" – that was splendid in its way. It was so well-written and very uncanny. I didn't dare go to bed, almost. Miss Sperry says Andrew Lang thinks it is the best written short story in the English language. What a hideous word "Thing," spelled with a capital, is. Another one – "Olalla" – was different, but I liked it – wish you could read it.

I'm not going to theaters for a long time unless something very fine comes. I went to hear Sousa, and they said that Henry Irving and Ellen Terry are coming sometime this year. *Remenji* comes the seventh of March, and I hear Paderewski is coming too. What I mean is – that I'm not going to ordinary things. I've just counted up, and I've been to 14 theaters this year – there's a confession! That's too many, I think – don't you? Almost always it has been Saturday nights. I've gone so it hasn't taken time from my work.

I gave my special topic in History. I dreaded it, but got through all right, and the instructor didn't find any fault. I have a terrible time in Trig – I'll never get through it in the world, but I'm going to try and hope for the best. I'm getting along all right in Chemistry, though I worked four days – two hours a day on one problem – last week and got a little behind, but I've caught up.

I got a letter from Mother that made me homesick. She's been sick two weeks with grippe, and is weak and "slim," as she always says when she's sick. It was such a good letter. She was sitting in the chimney corner, and said: "If you could take a look into the old home this morning, you would see your little slim mother looking out that west window. That always reminds me of you, and gives me that homesick feeling, as I look through the woods and down to the water." Mither thinks of a fellow, I guess. I wish I were going home in March.

Last year at this time I was looking forward to seeing you when you came back from the east – how good and sweet it was to think of. You were glad to see me that time, weren't you? I remember how you looked in that soft red wrapper.

Well, it's getting late, and I must study. I'm sorry I haven't done better work. The folks at home believe in me so – I've had the fairest chance of any of us children, and have done so little. This is a poor letter, but I'll send it. Don't think I'm blue, for I'm not the least bit. Dearest, you won't lose faith in me, will you?

CHAPTER 16

Desperate

FEBRUARY 2, 1896
Winona to Minneapolis

My Dear Roy:

I didn't go to church today – I've taken cold again, and I'm trying to keep it from settling on my lungs. I dread to think of another long siege.

I've been reading poet Maurine Hathaway – "poetess of the Pines." I didn't like her as well as I thought I should. Her poems seem sort of half-finished – as though she had put the thought, the life, the fire, into them, but hadn't stopped to make them beautiful. I wonder what sort of woman she is – strong and passionate, I imagine, but not spiritual. Do you know anything about her? I remember you wrote me last winter about reading her.

Last night I went to a lecture on "Social Reform in Fiction," based on Kingsley's *Alton Locke*. This was one of a series of lectures on social reform by Mr. Zueblein – a University Extension professor from Chicago University. Did you ever read *Alton Locke*? A number of the Normal teachers were there; they asked a good many questions, and it made it very interesting.

Our class in Nature Study (chemistry and physics) visited the electric light works. Mr. Freeman found that some of the girls had never talked through the telephone, so he called up a young man at the YMCA, and five or six of us talked to him. (Mr. Freeman said the young man would have it in for him next time he saw him!) The poor fellow didn't know what to say, and the girls shouted, "Talk louder – I can't hear what you say!" and "There's another girl coming to the phone – talk some more!" After the girls had finished, Mr. Freeman asked the young man if he had had a good time. We didn't hear the answer, but Mr. F. seemed very much amused.

I didn't write you much about the sleigh ride, did I? We had a good time. The boys responded to toasts after supper. Some of them were very good – Mr. Parker toasted "Our Girls." I never dreamed of his getting a joke on me until he said, "We have all often wondered why Miss Barnard's heart is so closely wedged from the outside world."

How much like spring these last few days have been – isn't it almost time for hepaticas? There will be lovely flowers on the bluffs in the spring – it's just the place for ferns and hepaticas and violets and bloodroot, and all the flowers and green things that come out then. I have some pussy willows opening in the window – you know, if you put branches in water in a sunny place they will come out. I have hard work keeping these – Tommy the cat comes up every evening and tries to chew them!

I wish you *could* come home in the spring, dearest. I haven't answered your sister Mary's letter yet. I'm glad you had that little talk with her – I don't believe you know how much you can be to her. I think I understand girls better than boys. I don't know how a *boy* of 14 thinks and feels, but I think I do understand *girls* a little.

Aren't you ever going to send me your picture? Good-bye, you dear, dear boy.

Much love,

Anna

FEBRUARY 9, 1896
Winona to Minneapolis

Dearest Roy:

I have been hungry for a letter from you, dear – more than usual – and this last was such a good one. I was glad to get that picture of the camp. I hope we'll be there again next summer.

When I heard that Sousa was in Minneapolis, I thought you wouldn't miss hearing him. It's strange how music will strike one sometimes as that piece did you. Fourteen theaters in '96? Yes, I *do* think that's too many, and I'm glad you think so too.

Don't laugh at me for this, but when I read about you working on that problem, it gave me a queer little thrill, and I felt like saying *good* for you! I'm afraid I never would have stuck to it like that.

My cold is getting better, I guess. Monday I was quite sick, with considerable fever and pains shooting through my chest. But Dr. Lane gave me some medicine, and I stayed out of school the next day, and I feel quite well now. I'm hoarse yet, and cough considerably, but that will soon wear off. Miss Harris asked me to give a topic on China in Christian Endeavor meeting tonight. Being hoarse bothered me some, but I'd do a good deal for her. I worked most of the afternoon getting it ready. I was warm and tired when I came home, so I took off my stiff, rustling dress, and put on the old red wrapper.

Miss Taylor is reading. I wish you could see her now – she's interested in her book, and she looks unusually pretty.

I wrote Mary this morning. I would like to have heard the rest of what your mother said. I could almost see her sitting there, with her beautiful white hair and sweet face. I like your mother more than I do most people. I'll take good care of her boy – his heart, anyway.

I think you have done a good deal – and Roy, dear – I shall always, *always* have faith in you.

Your little girl

FEBRUARY 10, 1896
Minneapolis to Winona

Dear Little Girl:

Your letter came tonight – Frank brought it up to me, where I was study-ing by the stove, and sleepy. I've been wondering just what you were doing. Yes, I would have liked to see Miss Taylor, but there's *someone else* I'd rather see (!). I'd give quite a piece of life for a kiss, it seems to me.

Saturday evening Zim couldn't study, and he wanted to go over and see Thad and Mary. We found the place, but they were out somewhere for a call. We waited, and made the acquaintance of the cat, and bimeby they came. It seemed good to see them – their place is very nice and cozy. Thad said, "You don't know how nice it is being *married*." We had quite a bit of fun – cut up a little. Thad showed me around, and he'd strut and point and say, "That's *my* stove over there; that's *my* wife," etc. Mary asked me about the theaters I had been to. Thad would look sanctified and tell her every once in a while, "Remember – you're a *preacher's* wife."

Miss Sperry took an interest when there was a to-do here, and we boys were yelling. She said to me, "O, I *wish* I was a boy – I wouldn't have to be so *dignified*." She's in the last preliminary contest to decide who shall represent Minnesota in the debate with Wisconsin. She was in mortal fear she'd forget her piece.

I didn't go to church yesterday – went over to cousin Julius's to dinner. I'm sorry for him – he's lonesome. He seems to want me to come over often – he's alone there with the children. I think Julius likes me. I *must* go over more – a fellow ought to be kind to people when he can.

This letter is getting *intolerably* stupid ….

I read a book Sunday that I liked a whole lot – read until my eyes were red and tired, but I finished it. When you go to the library try and get *The Light that*

Failed by Rudyard Kipling and tell me how you like it. I don't know whether you will or not – yes, I know you will. Never mind the *roughness* (it's not *bad* roughness). I'm thankful I'm not blind – how it would be. I like Kipling – his people aren't namby-pamby, and they're not perfect either.

Anna, were you in fun when you asked me if I had gone to 14 theaters in '96? Didn't I say I had gone on Saturday nights almost entirely? Well, there have been five weeks of school since Xmas, consequently five Saturdays – oh, I forgot – your *mathematics* – pardon me (!). What a monster of a theater fiend you must have thought me – no, I meant I've seen that many from the 20th of last September.

Anna, my dearest little girl – I wish I could see you now.

FEBRUARY 15, 1896
Winona to Minneapolis

My Dearest Roy:

I ought to be studying Geometry, but I feel like writing to you. The decree has gone forth that we must write the vertical hand in the next examination. It looks so awful and takes so long and, O dear, I can't bear it. If it was any place except the Normal, I wouldn't write it and take the risk, but I know too well what would happen here if I didn't.

The lady with whom Miss Lantry boards was going away last evening, and the girls invited some boys up. On coming home from the literary meeting, as we passed the house, we saw their overshoes on the porch. Someone proposed that we hide them, and without stopping to think, Miss Taylor and I ran up the steps, took the rubbers and dropped them in the shadow of the porch. Of course, the boys had to go home without their rubbers! Oh dear – why did I ever do such a foolish thing? I'll never, never play any more pranks of that kind – I'm going to behave after this. What do you think of me anyway? I guess you've heard enough of this.

Hasn't this been a beautiful day? There's been something springy in the air and sunshine all day.

As soon as I woke this morning I told the girls it was spring. They were shivering around and thought me "considerably off." It was cold, but spring was definitely in the air – I wonder if you have felt it too. This has been a good day.

The Light that Failed is in the library here, but has been checked out. I got *Bog-Myrtle and Peat* by Crockett, and have read several of the short sketches – some of them I like.

I guess I wrote you that I have been working for some time on my special topic in Child Study – "The Development of Language." I didn't realize I had collected so much on it – covered nine pages of Normal tablet paper. We were limited to 10. If I could only give my time to things I like. I don't suppose that will ever be possible. I enjoy work like Child Study.

I didn't think you quite such a theater fiend, and I *did* figure that all out – that you would have had to go to two theaters every Saturday, which I didn't think reasonable. See how Geometry has developed my reasoning powers?

It's late, and I must practice the vertical hand some tonight. How will I *ever* get through an examination writing that? Good-night, dear.

Anna

FEBRUARY 21, 1896
Minneapolis to Winona

My Dearest:

Somehow it seems a long time since I wrote or heard from you. I'm a desperate fellow these days. Exams come week after next and, of course, I'm behind with my work as usual, with about a thousand pages of history to read up. Trig has been pretty stiff. I've no time for me.

Valentine's evening I went to a little party. There were about 20 there. I had a very fine time – the people were all so nice, and it was good for a fellow to be there. I felt comfortable, and wasn't afraid of breaking the cook-stove or something (!).

When do you go home, Anna? What time was it that you came back last year? I wish I was going to see you. Doesn't it seem pretty long to you too?

Try again to get *The Light That Failed*. I lent the one I had from the library to Miss Sperry, and she liked it immensely.

I'm not going to write you any more tonight – it's late, and someway I have nothing to say – nothing that seems worth the telling. We've no school tomorrow, and I intend to read and take notes out of Taylor's *Origin and Growth of the English Constitution*. Constitutional history is rather dry.

Forgive me, and write me just as if I had written a *good* letter. Dearest, I wish I could see you once in a while – I think it would be a good thing for me.

With my dearest love,

FEBRUARY 23, 1896
Winona to Minneapolis

My Dearest Roy:

I've just read your letter. I've been looking for it for several days. Somehow, I'm feeling a little bit lonely, dear, tonight. I wish we weren't so far away from each other, but I love you just as much as though you were here – and will always. We won't let distance make any difference.

Our exams come week after next too – I have five. Geometry will settle the question of graduation for me – I hardly hope to pass. Mr. Holzinger said something that made me feel good – that my paper in Nature Study was "splendid." I don't know yet what he marked me. I go home March 5th, if I go. I won't go if I don't pass Geometry – I will stay and study up and try again.

I'm sorry you've been sick, dear. Don't get blue – I'm afraid you are. We can sympathize with each other about our work. Here's a good-night, my dearest, in the old way.

Anna

FEBRUARY 29, 1896
Minneapolis to Winona

My Dearest:

I'm oh, so sleepy; but I want to speak to you tonight. I've been working pretty well – for me – the last few days. We handed in our notes in History this morning, and I've been reading desperately and taking notes. Miss Ransome, a medic, said yesterday there were dark rings under my eyes from lack of sleep, and thereat I was exceedingly encouraged – perhaps I can get nervous prostration – wouldn't that be nice!

No, I'm not blue at all – you would be though, if you were as desperate about your work as I am. I feel relieved at getting those History notes in. Today I've been in school nearly the whole day solid – had the exam in Rhetoric. But I'm not blue. I wish I had done better work and wasn't so desperate, of course, but a body can't be blue with such weather as we've been having. I wonder if you had your "spring fever" any of those warm days.

Next term I'm going to work seven hours in the chemical laboratory every Monday, and do my chemistry up for the whole week on that one day. That will be pretty tough on me when the warm weather comes, won't it? And I'm going to take Zoology next term. I wish I had Botany instead, because *you* like Botany. That was fine to have Dr. Holzinger say that – I'm proud of you.

Faith, it's been so long since a prof or teacher has said any such thing about *my* work that it would seem queer.

In the desperate reading I've done during the last few days I got interested in old constitutional history. Now if I "water this spark," maybe I can get to be a scholar yet. I've got to study Trig yet and draw a map showing the "Division of Verdun" and it's late, and I'm sleepy, sleepy.

I liked your last letter. I wish I could have been with you when you were lonely. No, we won't let distance make any difference, though it's hard not to see each other but once in so long. I'm going to write longer letters to you – I mean to be a good lad now. Good-night, Anna – I want to see you so much, and I love you with all my heart.

You mustn't work too hard and not eat, and take walks and take care of yourself generally. You must do these even if the "accursed" Geometry does suffer. You're like a fine race horse that has to be held in. I am too, ain't I – bah!

MARCH 3, 1896
Winona to Minneapolis

Dearest:

I'm tired too tonight. I have taken two exams today, but I'm going to write you just a little. That last letter of yours was a lovely one, even if it was short.

I have finished all my exams except Geometry – that comes Thursday morning. I shouldn't think you could work seven hours at anything, giving close attention all the time. I don't like to have you work so hard as you have been doing lately, dear. I'm glad it won't last long. You don't want to have nervous prostration next summer when I'm in Oronoco.

After supper I lay down on the couch in the dark for a while. I was thinking of you, dearest – I wish you were here now. I'm so tired, and that Geometry just haunts me tonight. I'm not working so very hard – I am "taking plenty of sleep and exercise," as Pres. Shepard tells us.

Good-night, dearest, and here's a kiss.

Anna

MARCH 4, 1896
Minneapolis to Winona

Dear Anna:

I want to address you differently tonight, but Frank sits at the other end of the table, and if he should get up and glance my way, he couldn't help seeing the greeting. I ought to know the Gaelic – you remember what Flora Campbell said to Marget Howe in *Beside the Bonnie Brier Bush*: "It is a pity you hef not the Gaelic; it iss the best of all languages for loving."

I liked your letter, oh, very much – I was waiting for it. It isn't the length that makes letters good, is it?

I have taken two exams today – History and Trig. I guess I might hae done waur in History, and I did better than I expected in the other, but not well enough. Those History notes I handed in and read so hard (for me) came back marked "good," so my desperate reading counted some. Tomorrow afternoon comes German. Don't let the Geometry bother you more than you can help – I'm not going to care about the bloomin' Trig.

Night before last I saw *Trilby*, played by the Palmer Company. It was very good, I thought. I wanted to see it partly because you told me about it last spring – do you remember – when we were riding? Svengali was fine. I liked him – that means, of course, I hated him – 'twas his playing I liked. Trilby sang "Ben Bolt" so we could hear her but couldn't see her. The lady who sang it had a beautiful voice – not like Svengali's, but a strong sweet voice.

Salvini comes next week – *Don Caesar*, *Three Guardsmen*, and *Hamlet*. I think I can take in all three. I'm glad I lay off for something good to come. *Hamlet* – that's a departure for Salvini – I'm curious to see what he will do wi' it. Someway I can hardly imagine him playing such a part.

I had a letter from Mother yesterday. I like to have her write me. I didn't write home until Saturday, so my letter didn't reach them – Mother said they were so disappointed. I suppose a fellow's letters mean more to the folks at home than he thinks. Perhaps it's kind of an event for Mither. I must write regularly. I haven't missed a week yet, though.

If you go home tomorrow probably you won't get this, right off. I hope you get through that Geometry all right, but don't let it break your heart if you don't. We know more of some things than these mathematical people.

I read another book of Rudyard Kipling Sunday – *Mine Own People* – short stories – some of them more or less connected. Two or three of them are good and gruesome. *The End of the Passage* was great that way. I read it aloud to Zim Saturday night – Zim never has read much, and he thought it terrible. It fascinated him, and he said he didn't think it healthy – said it didn't uplift him. I laughed. I mustn't develop my love for the gruesome too much – my imagination is strong enough anyway. I'm going to take *The Light That Failed* over to Mrs. Creswell sometime; I want to see how she would like it – I like to see how things strike different people.

My head aches a wee bit, and I'm going to sleep. I was in fun about the nervous prostration, of course. I rather enjoy the idea of overworking – the novelty, you know.

Take care of yourself. I wish I could have been with you, little sweetheart, when you wanted me.

With my dear love,

Roy

MARCH 17, 1896
Minneapolis to Winona

My Dearest Anna:

I feel kinda lonesome tonight, and I'm going to write you a little. I wish I could see you now. Your letter came Monday – it was good of you to write me so soon. I'm so glad you got through that exam all right – it was fine – I'm proud of you.

I knew you wouldn't care less for a fellow just because he failed an exam. If a person works as they should, they usually come out all right – unless they're stupid, and it isn't very consoling to know that. I got through Chemistry all right. I went up the next morning, and one of the assistants saw me coming and said, "I suppose you've come to learn your fate. What would you say if I told you you fell through?" I thought that would be pretty hard luck, and thought that was what I had done, but he said I got through all right.

I found out this afternoon that I could take Zoology too. I won't like the stuff, I'm afraid – I hate to fuss with a microscope and scratch around with little dead fishes and things. I never will be a scholar – all I'm good for is to amuse people and make some friends, perhaps.

What rumors of war there are. An English expedition is going up the Sudan, I hear, to support the Italians in Abyssinia *(a reference to the Italo-Ethiopian War)*. I'd like to go along – it would be better than school. It's foolish to let some little school work bother me, isn't it?

Oh, but Anna! I had something worth living for last week. Friday I heard Salvini in *Hamlet* and Saturday *Three Guardsmen*. He was a good Hamlet – better than Keene – but as D'Artagnan, he was the best thing I ever saw.

Salvini is a dearie from the ground up. I can gush if I want to – I had rather be Salvini than *anyone*. I wish you could hear him in that. If I hate things so, I like others harder still, don't I?

That was a good, kind letter to me, dearest – you *are* the dearest, truest, sweetest one in the world. I wish this term was ended. I'm getting tired of things, and want to stop studying – or pretending and trying to study. I wish so I could see you. Dearest, I love you anyway, even if I haven't amounted to much yet.

With my love,

Roy

Anna, I'm afraid you're taking too much work – don't you do it – remember, dearie, won't you? You are of more account than anything else. You won't try and do too much?

MARCH 22, 1896
Winona to Minneapolis

My Dearest Roy:

I wonder what you're doing today. I feel restless and unhappy – sort of discouraged over myself. I've been hoping this mood would wear off, so that I could write differently, but it won't go, and besides – we promised to write as we felt.

It's probably partly because I was so restless last night. I had all sorts of dreams. I was washing dishes, and you were wiping them, and I spilled dishwater on you, and you were cross about it. Then I was hunting for something I couldn't find. It was in the night and dark, and the grass was wet with dew, and I had on a white dress and slippers. They were getting soaked with dew, but I couldn't find what I was looking for. Then I was traveling with my father – the train went so fast and made so much noise that I couldn't talk much, but it seemed comfortable and good to have him there beside me and taking care of me, just as it was so long ago. It doesn't seem 10 years ago, Roy, that he died. I don't believe there's a day goes by that I don't think of him. These dreams went on all night, it seemed.

I went to church this morning, and heard a man with a long face and a whiney voice talk about the need of Sunday schools in the west. It was kind of tiresome.

I've been giving myself an overhauling today – just as you sort out an old drawer once in a while. I was surprised at the rubbish – so much that's superficial and trifling, and so little that's spiritual. I wonder if I ever shall be what I want to be – that is, what I want to be at my *best* moments. The trouble is I don't want to be *hard* enough all the time, but, dearest – I *do* want to be what God *intended* I should be. We must help each other in this.

I'm so glad you passed that examination! My – I hope war will never come any nearer us than it is – I wouldn't like to be worrying for fear you'd go.

Salvini was here – he played *Don Caesar*. I would have gone, but I didn't know anyone who was going. You must write or tell me about *Three Guardsmen*. I'm glad you do like things so hard.

I had a letter from your sister Mary this week. She spoke of liking the spring winds blowing in her face (just as you do). She said she thought it pleasanter in summer than in winter, and then added, "Maybe it's because Roy isn't here in winter." She spoke of how much she wanted to see you, but said she didn't dare say much to you about it because she was afraid of making you homesick. I'm not so careful, I guess. But, dearest – I think it does one good to know they are missed, and I don't believe we can be told it too often.

I like my little class in Model Teaching. Something happened the other day that does me good when I think of it. Miss Levitt told us one of the children – Jussie – is not very bright. She was hurt when a baby, and cannot remember as other children do. She can't control herself very well either, and she wanted us to know this and so be considerate of her. The next day when I took the class, I somehow felt a big wave of sympathy come over me for Jussie. I called on her for the lesson of the day, and she gave it beautifully. She stood near me – looking into my eyes as she gave it – and I felt proud of her. Miss Levitt said in criticisms that afternoon that she never knew Jussie to do so well. I believe she felt my interest in her. I know *I* am at my best with teachers who have sympathy for us – like Mr. Holzinger. I wish I could get nearer the children – I believe there's a great deal in loving the good out of children, don't you?

I don't know yet where I'm going to teach. One of the girls in my class applied for a school in Northfield. I hardly dare apply for fear I would be "biting off more than I could chew."

I'm not working too hard. Did I tell you that everyone spoke of how well I was looking when I was home? I'm going to try to take a walk every day after dinner. I'll remember, dear, and be careful. I wonder if you know how good it seems to have you care.

With my love,

Anna

MARCH 27, 1896
Minneapolis to Winona

Dearest Anna:

That last letter, little girl, I liked so well – there's no use trying to tell how much. And I felt very unworthy too. I got up and walked around and thought lots of things, sweetheart. I ought to be a man if anyone is. I know you think of me much better than I am – very much – but I don't believe it hurts me. I wish I could see you – you're my good angel.

Now I'll tell you about things and be *friendly*. I went to Analytics with my usual dread this morning – a little greater than usual – but I pulled 10, I think. Bad stuff, Analytics – may none of it ever fall your way. I'm not arranged right for studying mathematics. Bowers says I have very good mathematical ability; only he says my math is in about the condition his Latin was when he commenced Cicero, and it will take training similar to what he took to bring my math up. I'll never take the training – I'm trying to get along in it, though someway I hate dreadfully to flunk.

I wonder what you would think of Miss Sperry – she's a queer girl. She's just such a fellow as me in some ways. She's very impulsive and hates herself too. She likes the same kind of books and characters that I do. I like to talk with her – she's very enthusiastic, and borders on gushing, but she doesn't get enthusiastic over foolish things. She would have made a great *boy*. She got cross at me a night or two ago for some unknown reason – I guess I ran against her humor some way. She said she "hated Mr. Allis," and I came along just then, and she said, "Speak of the devil." She said she didn't exactly *hate* me, but had no *time* for me. Since then I've been very careful around her – she'll get over it in a day or so. She does it partly for fun, I think. I like her – she's so generous and good-hearted.

Wasn't that a great storm, and doesn't it seem good today, when the sky looks spring-like? Only two months more – it seems so long since I saw you, dear. Do you think you will come to Minneapolis to visit the folks and see the schools?

Next Sunday is Easter, isn't it? Walter and I will go down to the big Episcopal Church Gethsemane and hear the music. I'll be thinking of you then. Take good care of yourself – remember that I love you *all* the time, and it's the *best* part of me that loves you best.

Roy

APRIL 9, 1896
Minneapolis to Winona

My Dearest Anna:

Frank has gone to class; I like best to write to you when I'm alone.

We had quite a snowstorm last night, and today everything is dazzling white, but it's going fast. I've had lots of mishaps today. First – while we were having some fun snowballing before and after drill, a fellow threw at my head, and I ducked suddenly, and the bayonet around my waist tore a great three-cornered hole in my uniform trousers. Then tonight I tipped my plate full of dinner all over into my lap, and 'twas greasy too. I had lots of fun out of it, for the boys laughed until they cried to see my expression and what I remarked under my breath.

You must be warmer down south there in Winona than we are. I haven't heard of any flowers except pussy willows being out yet. Yesterday was a gray, raw day, but in the afternoon I didn't feel like work (as usual), and I went for a walk – way down the river to St. Thomas Seminary and back – nine or 10 miles, I think. Had a superb appetite for supper. I sat at the head and waited on folks, and set them a fine example, and talked and made merry so that they ate nearly everything up. When I make my fortune, I'm going to keep open house!

Won't we be glad when school is out? Analytics is pretty stiff – I don't know how I'll come out. I haven't been to Rhetoricals this term, and I'm about seven or eight articles behind. I hate to write essays so. You know you're my confessor, and I must tell you my bad things.

I'm glad you saw Sol Smith Russell. No, I never saw him, but I'm going to this week. Tomorrow night is the intercollegiate oratorical contest, and I ought to go and shout for the State as I did for Hamline last year, but I'd rather hear another play.

I'm sorry you didn't hear my hero Salvini. He is altogether different in his kind of plays and acting from Russell, of course. But I like Salvini's kind best of any I ever saw – where there's love and war and adventure, and firm "wrists of steel," broad Spanish hats, and swords ringing in vaulted passages – you know the kind I mean. You don't like that style so well, I know, but you would have liked Salvini immensely, I'm sure.

I hope you will get a good school – one you'll like. Miss Levitt is right – the children would like to hear your voice. You see, I'm not the only one that likes it (!). I like to hear you sing, and your voice – I don't know – it has a tone about it that seems like yourself and reaches me.

Oh, someone likes to hear *me* sing – Mrs. Childs in our club. I was singing a verse of "Ben Bolt" in the hall one day, and she was there. A few days after she wanted me to sing it for a lady who was taking dinner with her. She said she thought I had a sweet voice and it brought tears to her eyes. There – she was in earnest too. Miss Sperry said she "didn't see anything so remarkably sweet about it – there was a good *deal* of it." I guess Miss Sperry was right. (You'll laugh when you read this and say something wicked next time you write me.)

When is your school out, Anna? Oh, I want to see you. It's been so long – probably I'll be a little bashful at first. You always do your duty, or as near as anyone, I think, Anna. I don't do as well as I ought – but, dearest, I want to be a man for *your* sake – I will too, yet. I love you – every fiber of me.

CHAPTER 17

Spring Spirit

APRIL 12, 1896
Winona to Minneapolis

My Dearest Roy:

Isn't this a beautiful morning! I'm just up, have taken a cool bath and feel as fresh and good as Mother Nature herself. The grass is beginning to look quite green, and the birds have been singing with all their might. A robin comes and eats the berries on a vine just below my open window, and there's a springy smell that makes me feel like going to the woods – if you were here, we'd go. The hepaticas will soon be out, I think – that warm rain last night will help bring them.

Perhaps it *is* warmer here – the flowers come out early in this sandy soil on the sunny side of the bluffs. Miss Taylor feels good this morning – she's singing away as she buttons her shoes. Even the sound of the horses' feet as they strike the soft, muddy road sounds spring-like.

I agree with Mrs. Childs – I always knew you could sing, and I'm not going to say anything wicked!. I think you could sing "Ben Bolt" equal to Trilby when I heard her. I wonder what it is in my voice that you like. Miss Smith calls it a "little wizard voice," and says I bring tears to her eyes when I sing.

I worked nearly all day yesterday. I wrote three papers on Child Study – one on Attention, another on Will, and a third on Discipline. I've learned considerable during my five weeks of teaching.

We have to change classes next Thursday – I don't know where I'll be put. I hate to leave my class. I taught them "Wynken, Blynken and Nod" the other day. I never taught a child a poem before – it's fun – more fun than it is to hold the attention of a large audience, for children give themselves to you completely. Their lips shaped the words as I spoke them, and when I paused they would give it back again beautifully.

I'm not going to apply for that Chatfield school. The 2nd grade – the only one without a teacher – has 61 children. My cousin John, who is on the School Board, advised me not to apply, for it's said to be very hard. *(Anna would later teach in Chatfield – 30 miles south of Rochester – in the fall of 1898.)*

I want my teaching this time to be different from last spring. How discouraged and heavy-hearted I used to get, and I would try with all my might to throw it off. No wonder I couldn't teach – a person can't be very bright and enthusiastic feeling that way, and isn't much use trying to teach children.

I heard the frogs sing tonight. I thought perhaps they would be – it's been very warm today – so I was listening for them. It sounded so good – I heard the first faint little "tr-r-r" just as it was growing dark. The soft wind blew in my face, and I thought about hammocks and camping, and that night the wind blew so very soft – the first year I was in Oronoco with you. I'll be glad when camping time comes again.

Good night, dearest, dearest.

With my love,

Anna

APRIL 19, 1896
Oronoco to Minneapolis

My dear Brother Roy:

Your letter was received in due time, and I was so glad to hear from you again, as I always am, and so glad of the little poem of Riley's. I don't know what there is about that little piece that gives me such a sorrowful, tender, and yet pleasant feeling. I like it better than any other of his, don't you? Thank you for copying it for me.

I'm sure spring has come, and I'm so glad. The crocuses have come, and a few of those little blue flowers that grow in Aunt Minnie's yard and along the path by the bluff – wood anemones, aren't they? The dear flowers seem like a message to me from a land far better than ours – how I love them. I'm going out this afternoon to gather some, and will send you a few in hopes they will keep their springy fragrance until they reach you.

Today is Fred's 38th birthday, and a beautiful day it is – bright and sunny – and the only thing to mar the beauty is quite a wind blowing, but we can't expect to have it perfectly perfect. This morning they launched boat No. 18, and if the wind goes down a little, I'm going for a row. Uncle has a stern wheel on his old boat, and they say it works nicely, but I would rather have a good pair of oars than sit in the stern and turn a crank. What do you think – or don't you ever think, as the slang phrase goes?

Cousin Julius was down Wednesday and stayed all night. I like Julius – I think him a good man. He can tell you better about the Baby than I can write, but I will say that little one is the most muscular boy I ever saw – he creeps and can stand alone for a minute. But as the floors have been so cold all winter, we could not give him liberty enough so he can walk yet, although he can take hold of his little rocker and push it along.

That horrid Analytics – I wish you didn't have to study it. But don't let it bother you so that you can't enjoy the other term work. What is it the study of, anyway?

I must close now. There isn't much in this letter, but it is from your ever true and loving little sister.

Mary

APRIL 19, 1896
Minneapolis to Winona

My Dearest Anna:

There – I've run overtime again – I was going to write you yesterday, but I was coming home from drill and Heath stopped me, and he sat with me whilst I ate my dinner. Then Heath and Zim and I and some others got to jumping and all kinds of crazy things people always do around Heath. I had never jumped to amount to anything, and it lamed me. Then four of us started down the river "to walk 400 miles." We only did 10 or 11 – but we found a few hepaticas! I never see hepaticas but what I think of you and how you like them.

Some of us took a little walk this morning to get some crocuses. I wanted to go down the Mississippi where the water and bluffs were, and so did Miss Sperry. She seemed to enjoy it a lot – I guess it's the first time this year she had taken a tramp where she could do as she pleased, and she's a regular country girl. It was hard walking up and down, over streams, climbing banks and everything, and we had to go over some boggy ground. But she went wherever I did and didn't want any help. I'm afraid she'll be lame, though, for we walked at least 10 miles. We had a good time, for the river is up and very fine – so broad and still and strong.

It's been a beautiful day anyhow. I wish you could have gone along – rather, I wish it could have been *you*, dearest. How good it seems to have it spring. You think you can come and visit the schools along the first of June, don't you?

I've worked pretty hard on Analytics – well, no, not very hard – but I've tried. It's the worst stuff I ever struck. A body can see through it, but there are so many formulas and things to remember. I'm afraid I'll never get through it, but I'm going to keep at it to the finish just the same.

The ice will be all out of the pond by this time, and the boats in, likely. I wonder if our birch tree is all right.

I haven't talked to you about Sol Smith Russell yet – isn't he *fine*, though? Salvini, Joe Jefferson and Russell are my three best actors now. I saw Russell at the Saturday matinee in *The Rivals*. I wonder if he played that in Winona. It's an old play of Sheridan's, you know. I liked it immensely. Then in the evening I saw him play *Mr. Valentine's Christmas* and *An Everyday Man*, and I liked those better still. That last play – there's more good everyday life in this existence of ours than swaggering romance, of course. It was so sweet and wholesome and not overdone. I wish you could have seen that – it was only a little one-act play with two characters, but it was so beautifully done. I will tell you what I can about it when I see you.

Just back from going with Wells – a medic in the club – to the Methodist Church. The service was pretty good, but I was tired and didn't enjoy it as much as I might. My conscience bothered me a little because I didn't stay home and work after bumming all day. I don't care – it was better outdoors this forenoon than at church.

I heard the frogs last night for the first time. Have you had your old spring feeling this year? You didn't have the real article last year when school was worrying you. I hope you haven't lost it.

My, I'm tired and lame tonight – that jumping, and then I didn't sleep very well, and then quite a little walk again today. Good-night, dearest. I'm so sleepy. Perhaps I'll write twice this week to make up for not writing sooner. I wish I could see you.

With my dear love,

Roy

APRIL 22, 1896
Winona to Minneapolis
My Dearest Roy:

Miss McCormick and I went after hepaticas Saturday just after breakfast, and it was almost noon when we got home. It was a glorious day – fresh and clear. We climbed almost to the top of the bluffs before we found any. I fairly shouted when we saw them – they are the *dearest* flowers. I believe the last I gathered them was with you and Clara two years ago. I thought of that time when I saw them.

It's just beautiful on the bluffs now. I wanted to lie down among the hepaticas and stay there all day. In one place the water trickled down the side of the rocks and made the moss so soft and green. The hepaticas were growing close by, the air was clear, and the sky blue as blue can be. I was almost to the top of the bluff, and I could see away off – oh, ever so far – and the wind was blowing. I felt all the life of spring, and it seemed beautiful to be alive. Yes, I've had the spring feeling – I'm just feeling glorious! I haven't felt so well for – I hardly know how long – not since I have been in Winona. I don't know any reason for it, except that it's spring, and I'm not working as hard. It's only this week that I have been so wild.

Wish I could have "gone along" with you and Miss Sperry. I want to meet her when I come to Minneapolis – I'm sure I should like her.

Sol Smith Russell was here only one night, so he didn't play *The Rivals* – he played *Mr. Valentine's Christmas*. I liked it. You can't tell what you like in a play like that – might as well try to tell why I like hepaticas – but it was beautiful.

I have a new class in Model Teaching (that should not begin with capitals – am I growing egotistical about model teaching?). It's a class of 12 – bad boys and good girls, Mr. Galbraith says – in the fifth grade. I teach history. They are brimful of mischief – it's called the worst class to manage in all the model schools. I guess they put me there to give me much-needed discipline in governing power.

There are eight boys in the class – about 12 years old. I'm going to make a special study of boys, and try my best to learn how to get at them. I told them a story the other day – they like that, and are as still as mice and listen, as good as they can be. But as soon as I stop – slam! goes a book on the floor, or they all want to talk at once.

I got marks today for my first six weeks of teaching. It was better in most ways than I expected, though it's all so very, very far from what it ought to be.

Plans & methods	B
Preparation	A
Skill in questioning	B
Languages & manner	B
Discipline	B
Power of holding attention through interest	B
Care & manners in mechanical work	A-
Observation & criticism	A
Results	B

This is what Miss Levitt writes: "Miss B. has made marked improvement while with me. She is an ambitious teacher, and one that will be successful in her work. She holds her children well, and her voice is quite firm, but lacks a little in enthusiasm and brightness. Miss B. is interested in teaching, but does not make the children feel her interest as she should. She is conscientious, faithful, spends much time in preparing her work, and presents it well and thoroughly. With experience, I think she will make a very good teacher."

You see – I'm only *medium*, but I believe I *can* be, *sometime*, a little *more* than medium. I'm going to work for it.

I'm almost counting the days, dear, until school is out. We will have so much to talk about!

With my love,

Anna

APRIL 26, 1896
Minneapolis to Winona
Sweetheart:

A day like this makes up for a lot of winter, doesn't it? What have you been doing? I've been doing as I wanted to all day. I hadn't read anything for quite a while, so I went down to the library and got Crockett's *The Men of the Moss Hags* and read it last evening and today. It's a good deal like *Raiders* – same style and kind of book. This one was about the Covenanters, of course, as you see by the name. I liked it pretty well.

This forenoon I walked down under the bridges to St. Anthony Falls. The river's up and comes over thick and strong. I climbed out where the spray flew over me and enjoyed the strength of it. The water beaten and churned up by the logs and rocks was all shades of brown and yellow. The maples are coming out, aren't they, and the willows along the river are fringed with light green. I'm glad the winter is gone – I don't like it.

I was out on the front porch reading comfortably and looking at things as I wanted to, when it came over me, as things do, that it would be but a little over a month until I saw you. These months seem a long time to me. You will be glad to see me, won't you – perhaps as glad as when you came home from the east?

I wish I were as honest and conscientious a worker as you are. Those marks are all right – perhaps if we worked together you could hold me down to do better work than anyone. I'm hammering away in Analytics – more time on that than everything else. I'll never get through.

What a stupid letter! Brace up, Allis ….

Well, there are other things. We had inspections drill yesterday, and did our first firing with blank cartridges. It was quite fun. There were a lot of people out to see it – we usually have a good many spectators Saturday. I like the drill best that day, for we have the band out and battalion drill. I told the folks at the club a great yarn about what Lieutenant Leonhauser said about me at inspection – how he spoke of my figure – said that "a man with a figure like that needn't do anything else." Is it wicked to lie so?

Zim wanted me to go to church with him this evening; said Dr. Egbert – one of the brainiest men of the state – was going to talk, but someway I didn't care to hear anyone "brainy" or otherwise.

Things will be fine with another week of good weather. I should have liked to have seen and been with you up there on the bluff when you found your flowers and felt the strength of the spring. I'm so glad, my dearest, that you're feeling so well.

I can't think of much tonight to write, and this is a dull letter. If you were here, though, we'd take a walk, and I think I wouldn't be so stupid. It will seem so good to see you. My dear little girl – good-night.

APRIL 30, 1896
Oronoco to Minneapolis

My dear Roy:

Your letter was duly received, and I thought I would write you a few lines so you would hear from home this week. We're house-cleaning, and you can imagine what a fine fix we're in! Fred painted the kitchen today and yesterday, and we're living in the dining room. You know tomorrow is the first day of May – the first day we can fish.

It's rained nearly every day for a couple of weeks, and the river is up quite high – within two feet of the platform – but it's going down slowly. I guess we'll be full all summer this year – several companies have engaged the grounds for camping, including the Episcopal Choir Boys and the YMCA. They're going to camp on the other side of the river. I was over there the other day – it's beautiful – so level, grassy and wild. Let's go camping this summer – what do you say?

The Boy can almost walk! I will be so glad when he does.

Joining with the others in sending love, I am yours,

Your loving sister

Mary

Pa wants to know how much money you need to finish this term and come home? Answer soon.

MAY 1, 1896
Winona to Minneapolis

My Dear Roy:

How do you like my notepaper? It's our regular Normal paper – everything we hand in must be written on this kind of paper, including application for excuses.

Have you wondered why I didn't write? I've been nearly buried with work all week. Tuesday it was announced that the examination to make up conditions would be this afternoon. I didn't suppose it was coming so soon, and I wasn't ready for it.

I've not been doing much Geometry lately – too full of spring spirit. I couldn't possibly neglect my teaching, and an exam in Review & Methods in Arithmetic came this week, so it gave me very little time to study. I took the Geometry exam this afternoon. I haven't much hope of passing. I hope your Analytics will be all right. This was our last chance on Geometry – if we don't pass, we can't graduate. I don't like to be *beaten*, I declare. I'd try it again if they let me.

Oh, last Sunday I had the loveliest time I've had for so long! Miss McCormick's uncle took some of us out driving. We had some beautiful black horses that liked to go, and a comfortable carriage. He took us out across the river bridge, and we wound around among the bluffs in Wisconsin. Sunday was a perfect day – the river was beautiful, and the air so fresh and good. We girls all got out and gathered anemones and bloodroot – the hillside was thick with them. How we did enjoy it! I like Winona better than any place except Oronoco – there are so many wildflowers here. They've come out thick and fast now – the bellworts, prairie and wood violets, cowslips, dandelions, and the shooting star that grows here – did you ever see it? It's a small purple flower – something like the cyclamen in shape – and very fragrant. Elmer Shepard brought some – I'd never seen any before. I like Elmer – he's a regular boy. He likes flowers, and he knows when they will grow. I guess he's as much of a tramp as we are.

We came back about 6, but none of us wanted to go to supper, so we drove along between the lake and the bluffs. The frogs were just beginning to sing. We drove toward the west, and it was all gold and red, and so was the water, only softened. The air blew cool and damp in our faces, and by and by the moon came out and shone on the water, just as it used to last summer at Oronoco. I thought of you so many times, dear. "I wish and I wish that the spring would go faster, nor long summer bide so late." Some things *are* "ill to wait."

I liked your letter. It wasn't "stupid" a bit.

This is May Day. You ought to carry Prof. Downey a basket of flowers tonight – maybe he'll improve your grade! Grandma sent me a box of flowers yesterday – pansies, periwinkle, Jacob's ladder and iris. They were as fresh as though they'd just been picked. She and Mother have both been quite sick with grippe, but are better now.

I've gone back to my old handwriting – aren't you glad? I'm not going to torture my friends anymore with the vertical hand. My! It seems like putting on a pair of old shoes after having had on tight ones, to go back to my normal handwriting. I went to see Miss Smith, and she said, "Now, my dear girl, tell me what your trouble is." I told her how I rebel against that vertical hand. She says she feels the same way, and I needn't do it anymore. She says it's a regular child's hand, and there isn't any style or individuality about it. It makes it so much easier for me to do my work, for I can write 10 times faster now!

Just think, dearest – a month from tonight! But oh, a month is an age – especially a month in the spring. The apple and plum blossoms are out too. I guess I can't write sensibly – I haven't felt so much like a little girl since – I hardly know when – I guess not since the days they used to say they'd put stones on my head to hold me down.

With my love,
Anna

MAY 5, 1896
Minneapolis to Winona
Dearest Anna:

I was glad to get your letter – I was beginning to be afraid you weren't well. It looked good to see your old handwriting – like an old friend.

I'm sitting out on the back porch. It's awful hot, and the hot summer wind comes sweeping around the house in gusts, so you mustn't mind the staggery writing. I enjoy the heat – I'm so glad it's spring. Things have come out so fast that everything looks new and strange – it's like a miracle. I wish I were home – it's too bad to miss all this spring weather there.

I'm afraid I'm lost in Analytics – bad boy. Today we are to have our weekly quiz in Zoology on sauropsida (birds and reptiles), and I hammered away at it hard all last evening and reckon I was better prepared than usual. I kept working away while I slept; had to wake up and reason with myself – "just go to sleep now – you needn't work at that anymore" – you know how one does.

Write me another letter that isn't sensible – I *like* you that way. I *love* you *any*way. Oh, a month is long in the springtime, but it's less than a month now. When is your school out and when will you come to Minneapolis? Oh, how I want to see you.

I went to see Warde play *Julius Caesar* last Saturday. He was good, and the man who played Cassius, and they had some supernumeraries to make the mob who were funny. I had to stop listening to Mark Antony to laugh at the "supes." I'm not going to have any such in my troupe. Oh, I haven't told you that I'm thinking of going on the stage, have I? Yes – I'm going to play melodramatic pieces and be another Salvini. I suppose I had ought to have talked with you about this before (!).

I wish I knew something nice enough to say to you, dear – I *don't* though.

With my dear love,

CHAPTER 18

Change

MAY 14, 1896
Winona to Minneapolis

My Dearest Roy:

I've just got great news! Pres. Shepard called me into the office this morning and told me I had been elected at Cloquet for 1st Primary! I'm delighted! It's about 20 miles southwest of Duluth. I haven't accepted yet. What do you think, dearest? Do you want me to go?

I haven't heard from Mother yet. Pres. S. says it's a nice place, with a splendid superintendent. I don't know what they pay their primary teachers. *(In fact, women teachers were paid much less than men in the Cloquet school system – Anna and other female teachers were paid around $40 a month, and male teachers around $130.)* Pres. Shepard asked if I would want to go so far from home, provided I could get $5 a month more. Well, it's a primary – what I want – and have been so much afraid I couldn't get. Two other girls from my class are going – Miss Roth and Miss DeGraff. Miss R has a first primary too, and Miss DeGraff a second primary, so I won't feel quite like a stranger in a strange place. Miss DeGraff is one of the most sensible, sympathetic, dearest girls that ever was. I'm glad she will be there.

I will probably go to Minneapolis at Christmas time. I won't be so very far from Cloquet. The only trouble is that it's so *cold* there. But everyone thought I wouldn't be able to stand it in Maine, and you know how well I did there. Perhaps the change will be all right. I think I'll try it.

Lovingly,
Anna

MAY 17, 1896
Minneapolis to Winona

Dearest:

Your letter came last night. I'm delighted – if you are too. I think it would be all right, if it wasn't for the cold. You can tell better than I, though. Perhaps a grade the wrong age would bother you more than winds from the lake. You

Dearest Anna
a love story

"Before my grandmother, there was Anna."

So begins the true story of a family secret, a trunkful of hidden letters, and a love story buried away for almost a century.

In 1894 Roy and Anna graduated from high school and began writing hundreds of love letters to each other until 1898, when Anna died, suddenly and tragically. Roy was devastated. Even after he married, he grieved every year on the anniversary of Anna's death. The letters lay hidden for decades, until his granddaughter brought them out of the shadows.

Who was Anna — the woman Roy loved so deeply that he mourned her even after his 63-year marriage to someone else?

This is Anna and Roy's story — a snapshot in time in the waning days of the Gilded Age; a love story for the ages. In Anna's words: "We will write as often as we must, for we are never going to be tired of each other, if we live a thousand years."

Carol Allis

authorcarolallis.com

know what's best, sweetheart – "the queen can do no wrong." It's fortunate getting an answer from a school so soon, I should think. Walter is going to teach next year. He has two or three places he hopes for.

That was fine – your getting through your Geometry. I'm proud of you and ashamed of myself, for I won't get through Analytics, I'm sure. I'm wanting a good big talk with you, dearest, when I see you.

Nine of us went to Minneapolis and walked over to Fort Snelling the same afternoon you folks had your jaunt. We had a little picnic – lots of fun and adventures.

I think I will be out of exams and free a week from next Thursday. And you – when are you coming to Minneapolis? It's been so long – I'll hardly know you. I'm not going to write but little scraps to you – it will be so much better to say it to you when I can *look* at you. I'm wanting to see you so, dearest.

With my dear love,

Roy

If the cold up there was going to hurt you, sweetheart, I wouldn't have you go for the world. You can judge better than I.

Anna and schoolmates, Miss McCormick and Miss Taylor, at Winona Normal

Anna's Winona Normal graduation photo (21 years old). The unusual black ribbons on her dress are Victorian mourning ribbons – in memory, of course, of her dear brother Frank.

MAY 19, 1896
Winona to Minneapolis

My Dearest Roy:

I can't study or do anything these days – time never dragged so. I'm just about wild to get away! The days are beautiful, and I'm so strong and happy and careless. I'm coming to Minneapolis a week from Thursday on the Milwaukee Road. I get

Winona State Normal School Class of 1896 (Find Anna!)

into Mpls. about 11 a.m. Will you be busy then? Do you want to meet me?

Isn't it glorious that I will see you so soon? I have lots to say too, but I'm going to save it all.

With love,

Anna

MAY 23, 1896
Minneapolis to Winona

My Dearest Anna:

I can't study much either, and the time drags. Yes, I'll meet you – there's nothing I'd like so well! I have an exam in Zoology that afternoon, but I can get back in time. Oh Anna, I *want* to see you – do you understand?

I'm not going to come out well in my work – you'll be ashamed of your boy, I'm afraid. I will be glad to see you, dear.

JUNE 11, 1896
Oronoco to Eyota

My Dearest Anna:

I'm home, you see, but had quite a time getting here. I packed up my traps Saturday and shook hands with folks. I was kinda sorry to leave them. I commenced shaking hands around the table from right to left, but before I got to Zim, he got up, and I noticed I mustn't shake hands with him then – Jim is rather easily affected, and the tears were in the old boy's eyes.

When we got out of St. Paul a little way, it began to rain pitchforks and piano stools, and over those high bluffs the other side of Hastings came torrents of thick mud, and we were stopped for an hour, I guess. Then after we passed over a bridge, it washed out, and we couldn't get back to St. Paul, and between Hastings and Red Wing the track was undermined and covered with sand in lots of places. There we stayed all night in the train – we darsn't leave it, for there was no telling when it would go. I was almost strapped for money, and didn't have anything to eat from Saturday noon until Sunday forenoon.

It was awful stupid there in the train – couldn't lie down in a car seat without hanging over somewhere, and feeling oh, so stretchy and cramped if you did fall asleep. I lay in all kinds of shapes, and went out and walked every little while. There were the usual folks on the train – a heavy gentleman who snored, a lady with a voice that kept you awake, and right in front of me, some folks newly wedded, I think, and they were spooney a great deal.

But I got home all right Sunday – left my grip and walked straight down through the woods. It's an old road that people use only in the winter, and, dearie, I wished you were with me. It was just after the rain, you know – warm, and the green woods so close – you could just smell and feel the sweet, warm June. I went down on the Point, and after a while I saw Pa down with his boats, and called, and he came and got me – rowed fast, too. Mary was up in her room and heard me the first time I shouted. They seemed glad to see me – all of them – and I was so glad too.

Little Volney is the finest little fellow you ever saw, and Mary is taller and rounder. You must come up sometime and see us – you will when you come camping. Everything is looking fine. The pond is like a lake – so big and full – and everything strong and green. The banks up the south branch are lined with wild roses.

Last evening after supper, when I was through work, I rowed around the Point just before sunset, and climbed up to the birch and sat in your seat and wished *so* you were with me. I *want* you, my dearest. Then I rowed on up and passed Uncle and Aunt Minnie – they were picking daisies on that point that reaches out as you turn to go to the rocks. They were beauties, and Auntie handed me a great bunch, saying she wished Anna had them just as they were then. I took them and said they were yours and would send them to you.

I've been helping on Will Mayo's *(Dr. William James Mayo – one of the famous Mayo brothers)* house – shingling part of the time – and I will work there all the week, probably.

Answer me soon, dearest, and try to come on that picnic you spoke of. I'm so glad for our gypsy week together.

With my dear love,

JUNE 15, 1896
Eyota to Oronoco
My Dearest Roy:

The folks have gone to church and I'm here alone. I don't feel very well, so I didn't go – my cold has been growing worse instead of better. I'm hoarse yet, and cough considerable. Doctor was down and says I must wear a suit of woolen underwear all summer. Can I ever stand it? He's spoken of trying cold baths as soon as I get over this cold. It has been so long since I've had a hard cold, and I have been so well that I thought I didn't need to be careful.

Tuesday we were in Minneapolis, and Helen and I went up to the top of the Guaranty Loan Building. Oh, it is magnificent! And Friday Uncle Lib from Dover drove up with his pretty team and lovely carriage, looking for someone to take a ride and praise up his horses. I had rather ride after a team like that than eat breakfast any day, so I went to Dover with him. They have the most beautiful, rare rose garden I ever saw, and while Aunt Mary showed me the roses and gathering some for me, Uncle Lib picked strawberries. When we came in, he had them all ready for me – wet with dew they were, and so big and fresh. And the *cream*! I just had time to eat them and catch the train home. The roses are beauties – about a dozen different kinds, and such a lot of them.

I wish Miss Taylor could have come home with me and enjoyed it all. She never was in the country, and she loves flowers so, and riding, and grass and trees, and everything that we have so much of here. I'm going to send her a box of pansies tomorrow. I told her how the roses look – she said she never had enough roses in her life. The country is better than the city, even around the lakes and Minnehaha, isn't it? It seems so good to get on the top of a hill, and see the wide, wide stretches of fields and patches of woods. How beautiful the clover fields are – all pink and so sweet.

Eva and Mother and I took a drive yesterday morning. I'm going to be a regular "gadabout" all summer, and do just as I please. I wish I might have taken that tramp through the woods with you, dear. We will someday.

I have been reading a story in the *Cosmopolitan* by Beatrice Harraden. It isn't like her *Ships That Pass in the Night*.

I've been uncomfortable this afternoon – so warm. Those flannels will make a regular Xanthippe (is it spelled right?) of me. I feel like scolding – I don't believe doctors know it all. I've a good mind to take them off! I'm afraid they will make me tender – oh, how I *hate* flannels. I don't care if I do scold – if my temper is ruined it will be because of the flannels, and the doctor will be to blame for it. I can't stand it! This is worse than vertical writing – I'm more rebellious, I mean!

Dearest, I love you so.

Anna

JUNE 16, 1896
Oronoco to Eyota

My Dearest Anna:

Aw – take 'um off! My, I'm pitying you. I never could wear flannel next to me – they tried it on me when I was little, but I suffered so they gave it up. It wasn't the scratch of the thing exactly – it was an awful feeling that nearly sent one out of the top of the house. I'm so sorry you're not as well as you were, dearie. You'll be all right pretty soon, I hope, if those things don't kill you.

Did you *really* love me when you were writing and feeling that way? I was glad to get your letter – very glad. Anna, I *so* want to see you.

I've been working all day mixing mortar and lugging brick for building the fireplace and chimney in the Mayo's cottage. It was new work and terribly hot on the roof. Mary gave me some lemonade along in the afternoon – I drank three glasses, one after another. If she had given me the whole pitcher, I think it would have gone at a pull.

I was a bit tired tonight, and just at supper came an old gentleman, his wife and daughter, and a boy. They belonged to the YMCA gang. He had written Pa two weeks ago for a tent, but I think Pa never got the letter. Fred was tired, the chickens had to be caught out of the trees, and the clothes had to be taken for washing. But I piloted the old gentleman over into the grove. They had determined to stay there all night – no tent, and a thunderstorm coming. I told them I'd do the best I could for them, so I rowed back a second time, got some canvas and fixed them up some. They had forgotten their lantern, and I let them take ours. Now I'm waiting for my papa.

I had a good time yesterday. I fixed up so I looked decent and clean – then a body feels more like a gentleman, right? Charlie and I went up to the cemetery and took up some roses for Blanche. It was a regular summer day, wasn't it? We made ice cream – 'twas so fine! We must have some when you come.

A queer letter, this, don't you think so? I just felt like talking a wee bit with you. Good-night, dearest – my poor, tortured little girl. I'm awful sorry!

With my dear love,

Roy

JUNE 18, 1896
Eyota to Oronoco

My Dearest Roy:

I was glad to get your letter so soon, and it was a good one – seemed like talking with you for a minute, dear.

I *have* taken "um" off! I kept them on for three days, but I couldn't stand it any longer. I scolded and fretted for two days – you'll laugh, but I couldn't help it. It made me so nervous and horrid – I cried, at last, and declared I'd be comfortable no matter what. Doctor doesn't know – he won't like it – he likes to have people do as he tells them. My cold is better – I don't cough as hard and am not very hoarse.

We took a drive this morning out where I used to teach. It seemed so good as we went over the old road to think I wasn't going back to that school. How I used to dread it.

I've just read *Mill on the Floss* again. I like it better than ever – I think it's one of the best books I ever read. We'll try to have lots of sympathy for folks, won't we?

This is a scrappy kind of a letter. Here's a good-night kiss – close your eyes – do you feel it?

With my love,

Anna

JUNE 24, 1896
Oronoco to Eyota

My Dearest Anna:

I meant to write earlier, but Charles came and called me to look at the moon behind the clouds – the clouds were standing out big and white and so soft. It must be raining down in Eyota.

Yesterday Charles and I went to the circus – took it all in and got home about 10 o'clock; weren't drunk or nothing. A body always feels kinda 'shamed, coming home from a circus someway.

I worked on Mayo's cottage until Saturday. Wasn't it a fine day last Sunday? There were a lot of people here – all 20 boats were out, and I rustled up a couple more. It was hot, but I was clean and cool and dressed light, with my big Cuban hat, and things were so bright and sunny. I felt good and wanted you.

The folks have been to town today, and just at evening Mary and I went out on the pond. I've been feeling dissatisfied with myself all day and guess I wasn't a very good comrade – I wanted to keep still and row.

I liked your letter so, sweetheart. I had just finished when someone shouted, "Why, hullo, Roy!" and 'twas Clara. I was awful glad to see her – she was coming up through the brush looking for her mother. I helped her through the fence – she caught her dress – and she went up to the house and saw the folks. She was "up with the Methodists" in an Epworth League picnic.

Tell me when you're coming, if you can. I must see you soon. I closed my eyes as you told me, dearest, and lay back on the grass, and remembered as hard as I could. You're a sweetheart.

With my love,

Roy

JUNE 26, 1896
Eyota to Oronoco

Dearest Roy:

I have just got home from a horseback ride. Eva has never ridden horseback since she was a little girl, so I saddled Roxy for her and put a bridle and blanket on the old horse for me. The boys were firing firecrackers, and the old horse is dreadfully afraid of them and the smell of powder, so Mother wouldn't let me ride one and lead the other for fear they'd jump and throw me off, so she said *she* would ride Roxy. Mother has never rode horseback before in her life! She finally got into the saddle, and then she was afraid – it was too loose and wobbled, and she hung to it. We discovered when we were nearly up there that she hadn't put her foot in the stirrup for fear she would fall off.

My coal-black charger was a beauty – did you ever see the old horse? He's nearly 30 years old – tall, raw-boned, with a big head; has the heaves dreadfully. He has been in the pasture all summer and is never used, except for light work on the farm. Imagine an old faded-out blanket folded over his back, and on this steed so beautifully caparisoned – myself seated. Imagine me in my old blue gown and Eaton jacket and a white sailor hat on my head – my face very red from my efforts at catching and saddling my horses (and from laughing), and my hair sticking every which way. We rode up a back street and some children saw us, and how they did laugh, and I laughed too. We had lots of fun. Don't you want to ride the old horse when you come down? He jumped and trembled at the firecrackers and acted quite coltish.

Did you look for us this week? We couldn't come, for I have had a dressmaker longer than I expected. Perhaps we'll come next week – I'll let you know when. When can *you* come down? What are you doing the Fourth? Come as soon as you can, because I *want* you!

I'm all over my cold now. I've been reading *Rob Roy* and some of Bret Harte's stories. I have done more sewing than anything else. What is a Cuban hat like? When I come to Oronoco, I'm going to see how you look in it!

This isn't much of a letter, but "Simply take what the scrawl is worth; knowing, think the rest."

With love,

Anna

JULY 5, 1896
Oronoco to Eyota

Sweetheart:

There's such a beautiful sunset – if you were only here. I came up on the Point and sit in your seat just now. It's beginning to darken a little. There's such a cool, soft little breeze come along, such a one as you like, my dearest, and as it sweeps along from the north I can smell the barley a mile away so plainly.

I want to come and see you at the end of the week if I can – may I? That afternoon we had was so short, and it wasn't like seeing you *regular*. I wonder what you're doing. I want to see you so just now – can't help it – such an evening as this. I wonder if you aren't a little nearer than usual.

Yesterday I didn't do much – sailed over to the grounds and watched the ballgame. Today I've watched boats a little, but been doing just nothing at all a good share of the time except read. I think one ought to have their Sundays. I got a book out of the library – one of Dumas' – *The Man in the Iron Mask*. It's like the rest of them, and I rather like it.

I won't try to write more – it's getting a wee bit dim. I'm going to lie down here until it gets dark. I wish you were here, dearie. Close your eyes too and imagine.

If you were here now, I think you would like me.

Roy

JULY 8, 1896
Eyota to Oronoco

My Dearest Roy:

I'm here alone. Grandma has gone to a Women's Christian Leadership meeting and Mother is in Rochester. A friend of hers sent for her – her daughter is not expected to live, and she wanted Mother there. Mother knows how to take care of sick people – she is always so cool and quick, and does things quickly and easily without seeming to hurry.

I'm so glad you're coming soon, dear – I'll look for you Friday, and you must stay over Sunday. I was watching that sunset Sunday evening too. After Christian Endeavor was out, I sat on the porch and read until it grew too dark, and then I watched the sky. I was thinking of you, too – I wonder if we *were* nearer than usual.

Eva and I have been reading one of Frank R. Stockton's stories, "Mrs. Cliff's Yacht." It's in the *Cosmopolitan*. Have you read it? If you haven't, I must tell it to you when you come down. We translated some Vergil together and read *Othello*. I'm still reading *Rob Roy*.

I received proofs of the pictures I had taken at Winona. Don't know whether they are like me or not – I guess I'll see what you think. One of the proofs makes me think of what Tammas says in *A Window in Thrums*: "The genteel thing is no to laugh, but just to put on a bit of a smirk."

Eva did enjoy the boat ride and the whole trip. She said when we were driving along, "I feel as though I had been to church." I asked how that was? "O, kind of uplifted and good," she said. It was beautiful going home that night – the cool air felt so good after the hot day. The blue sky and the yellow sunshine were so you could almost touch them. I can't imagine anything more beautiful than this world.

I used to read Revelations when I was little – about the streets paved with gold; the precious stones and crystal (I took it all literally). And I thought I shouldn't like it in Heaven unless there was a brook and deep, thick grass beside it, with white violets hidden down in the grass, such as there was in our orchard. I decided that there probably was such a place, but they didn't think to speak about it in the Bible – queer child fancies!

I'll see you soon. Good-night, dear, dear Roy.

Anna

JULY 9, 1896
Oronoco to Eyota

My Dearest Anna:

Don't expect me tomorrow night – I can't come this week. Fred isn't back yet, and we're going to repair the flume, so I'll be busy. I *want* to come and I'll *try* to; I *must* see you soon. I thought if you were expecting me and I didn't come, it might disappoint you a little bit, so I write this.

With my dear love,

JULY 13, 1896
Eyota to Oronoco

My Dearest Roy:

Your letter reached me Friday. I looked for you on the train that brought your letter, and then Saturday evening I watched the train just to see if you came, but said to myself that you wouldn't, so that I wouldn't care, you see. I'm trying to "possess my soul in patience."

I've been lying in this hammock in the summer house all afternoon. I didn't do much this morning either. What a comfort to be able to lie around when you don't feel well and know you don't have to go to work! I wouldn't have thought of stopping if I had been teaching, but here I have been babied all day! I've been reading *A Singular Life* by Elizabeth Stuart Phelps Ward.

Mother is home now. Alice Brannon died. The funeral was here in Eyota and I had to go. They wanted all the girls she used to go with to go together. I dread to have to go to funerals. I think it's sort of a heathenish custom, with all the ceremony and fuss; and the people, when their hearts are almost broken, must drag themselves out before folks and be preached at and sung at and stared at, when what they want most is to be left alone. Oh, it's horrible. I've been through it, and I hope someday our friends can be buried without funerals.

Vacation is half over. I dread to go to Cloquet. Perhaps I won't dread it when the time comes. I guess I'm bound to be gloomy today, but I'm not usually – I'm as happy as one of those sparrows out there. Oh, bother – they've gone to fighting now! They are the most quarrelsome birds.

Come down when you can.

With my dearest love,

Anna

JULY 14, 1896
Oronoco to Eyota

My Dearest Anna:

For two nights I've tried to write you, and someone came here both times. It's nearly after 11, but I won't fail this time.

I wanted to catch the train and come to Eyota Saturday evening. I spoke about it that afternoon, and Pa said he thought he would need me Sunday. I was disappointed, but didn't say so, of course. Perhaps if he understood how much I wanted to see you, he could have got along without me. We're putting in a new flume – the old one is leaking water out of the pond, and we couldn't have the boating spoiled. It's a big job – I feel sorry for Pa.

Henry and I have been getting hay all day. I've been pitching in the field – first I've done for a long, long time. Oh, but hasn't it been hot? It was almost worth standing the heat, though, to get the water afterward.

I'm going to talk wi' you when I come, Anna – wouldn't I make a good doctor? I've been thinking about it considerable lately. I'll have to work pretty hard tomorrow, and you won't mind, will you, dearest, if I write only this little scrap tonight? It's so warm I guess I'll sleep in the tent. I think of you lots. Good-night now.

With my love,

Roy

JULY 16, 1896
Eyota to Oronoco

Dearest, dearest, dearest:

A doctor is what I *want* you to be more than *anything* else! I've often thought of it. It seems to me your big, broad sympathy and your "humaneness" make you especially fitted for it. Everyone likes you, and you can come so close to people and do them so much good. Oh, Roy – I *do* want you to be a doctor! It's better than the ministry or missionaries or *anything*. It seems to me the noblest work in all the world, and I think you would be a good deal like Dr. Stinchfield – you know he has always been my ideal. Wish you could see him and talk with him about it.

But a doctor never has any time to stay at home, and, dearest – I don't like that. We must have a good talk when you come. I hope you can come this week, but you know I can "bide" until you are not needed so much.

I thought of you that hot Tuesday, and wondered if you were grinding. I thought it wouldn't be so very hot in the mill – that there would be a cool breeze coming in those west windows. My, it must have been hot in the hay field! It was so hot that it seemed as though I couldn't dress up that afternoon, so I kept on my old loose morning wrapper, hoping no one would call. I watched the sky when the storm came up. Wasn't it glorious? I think I never saw the whole sky so troubled – clouds all over, and such beautiful colors!

I won't write anymore now. I wanted to tell you tonight what I thought about you being a doctor.

You wouldn't be like the "medics" – you would be like the man I've loved. Isn't this a crazy letter?

Lovingly,
Anna

JULY 17, 1896
Eyota to Oronoco

My Dearest Roy:

I have a headache this morning – something I seldom have – and I feel as stupid as can be. I'm glad you liked my queer letter. I hope you can come this week. We are coming to Oronoco the first of August. I wish I might have been with you and had a share in your thoughts of important things – that is, if you would let me – would you?

I'm glad things came about just as they did two years ago. Nothing can take these two years from us. I've very glad you didn't take my advice to not fall in love until your second year at the U (!).

With my love,

Anna

JULY 20, 1896
Oronoco to Eyota

My Dearest:

You're enthusiastic about my becoming a doctor, aren't you? Well, I'm real glad you are. We'll see. I've been thinking about things, and if I do that – study medicine – if I can do it – I think I ought to get at it. Yes, we will have a "big talk" when I come down.

Here at home my work is queer. Some days I work hard, and some I don't do much, but I'm expecting to all the time, and that's about as bad. Folks are always coming, saying, "Where's Roy? Tell him to do this." I'm the man of all works, you see. Henry and I had a tough job Friday – dragging old planks and timbers from the flume they are tearing down. We dragged them out with a horse – I drew them together, and Henry managed the nag. I was in the water all day, and when I stopped – oh, I was cold.

All this forenoon I helped over on the campgrounds – burning brush and other things – and this afternoon we set up and fixed four tents for campers who come this week. Oh, we're going to have a summer resort. The water is fine now – almost as clean and clear as in spring.

Oh, I want you with me, dearest. I was out on the pond a little while ago – what a grand old moon it is. I lay down on my back in a pasture where I landed and watched things and thought of you, of course, and other important things. Two years ago this time you were in Oronoco camping that first time, weren't you? That was a good summer, wasn't it? All new then, wasn't it? It will always be new.

Perhaps I'll come and see you at the end of the week, only don't expect me. I liked your letter, little girl, and I love you so much – with all my heart.

Roy

I write miserable letters to you lately, Anna, but all the time I'm expecting to see you.

AUGUST 28, 1896
Eyota to Oronoco

My Dear Roy:

I hardly know how to write to you – it has been so long since I have written, and today a letter seems to me a cold, lifeless thing. I almost hate to begin to write again, for it makes me think of the long time when letters will be all there is for us. We have had such a good time together. No word from my school yet.

I got up a little after five Monday morning. There was a thick mist over the river, and it was dreadfully chilly. Aunt Hattie and Clara got us a good warm breakfast, and we ate it in the kitchen tent by the fire. I felt warm and good after that. We started at half-past six, and it was beautiful driving. Do you remember Hamlin Garland's description of an early fall morning and how the men started for work – in *Main Traveled Roads*, I think?

I wonder what you will all do tonight – a campfire, and you will all sit close to it, with pillows and rugs and shawls. Thad will read aloud – some story that is very thrilling, perhaps. I can imagine him reading it very dramatically, and can see you all with the firelight in your faces.

Hasn't it been like fall today? The wind and the smoke in the air, and once in a while a breath – an odor or something – it goes so quickly you can't tell what it is – that tells you it's fall.

Everyone tells me how well I look. They tell me I'm dreadfully sunburned and freckled and tanned, and then ask me if I had a good time.

Roy, dearest, you don't know how I miss you. I can't put what I feel into words – I'm not going to try. I think you're feeling something the same, and I know you understand. This isn't a good letter – I'm sorry, dear. Perhaps I can write something better soon – brighter and more cheerful. I'm a little bit heavy-hearted tonight, and lonely, and I want my comrade – my friend.

With my love,

Anna

AUGUST 28, 1896
Oronoco to Eyota

Dearest Anna:

Don't think because your letter was not wonderfully cheerful that I would like it less – I think I liked it much better as it was. One likes to have a little sympathy, sweetheart – better than a cheering-up, sometimes. Dost understand, maiden – I was very lonely and heavy-hearted too? I saw the carriage when you went away – caught a glimpse of it straight down from the house, and again on the bridge, and – Anna gone, I thought.

How the wind blew the next day – yes, it was like fall. That day you went, as I climbed the bank at noon, the wind swept down from the pond, and I felt that feeling so faint and sad and sweet that comes on the first fall winds. It seemed as if my summer, in every sense, dearie, was gone. I miss you so.

We finished the tube Monday, and we've been rodding and planking. It hangs on awfully – for some reason I'm tireder than usual tonight – caught a little cold, perhaps. Tuesday night I rowed over to camp. 'Twas so windy we couldn't have a bonfire, but went into the tent and read. They were eating supper when I came, and I sat down and talked with them, and they fed me peaches and crackers. We read out of Sir Walter Scott's *Weird Tales* – I read "Wandering Willie's Tale" and Thad "The Lady in the Sacque."

I went over again last evening – they seemed glad to see me. The campfire was a splendid one, and we were about as you imagined us. Thad was on his high-heeled shoes – he got to telling us of a hazing scrape in college. Someone rowed up into the cove and sang, and we cheered them. The girls sang "Oronoco," and we gave the yell – the last for a long time, likely. The fire died down to bright embers. Thad finished his story, and I shook hands with the folks and came home.

I hope my letter won't be depressing. What times we will have some day, won't we? I wish the someday was here, though. I'm kinda weary and won't write more. How lifeless the writing does seem – well, it's a great deal better than nothing.

Write me as soon as you hear when you're going, if it's only a little bit. Good-night dear, dear little girl. I love you as I always do, and miss you and want you so much.

Roy

CHAPTER 19

Little Girl Alone in a Far Country

AUGUST 30, 1896
Eyota to Oronoco
My Dear Roy:

I have received word to be in Cloquet to take an examination Sept. 4th, attend a teacher's meeting Sept. 5th, and open school Sept. 7th. I find I cannot get there in a day – I reach Carlton at 6 p.m. and there is no train from there to Cloquet that night, so I shall have to go Wednesday the 2nd. Miss Roth is in St. Paul, and we can go together. She writes me that most of the teachers board at the hotel in Cloquet. I'm not sure I can stand to live in a hotel for nine months. Miss Roth has first grade – the same as I – and I hope we can board together.

I dread that examination – I haven't reviewed much. I dread the first week awfully – I wonder if I *ever* shall feel grown up and confident "like a man." I got your letter this morning – you write the *best* letter. I shall be happy whatever comes, if you love me so.

We were invited up to Aunt Matt's to dinner Tuesday. Florence put an aster at each one's plate. In Thursday's *Bulletin* there was an item about an aster party in honor of the return of Miss Wheeler's niece Anna Barnard – all in wonderfully high florin style. The idea – "my return" – after being away only two weeks!

I lead Christian Endeavor tonight – they wanted me to lead again before I go. The subject was "The Happiness of Heaven" and the chapter was Revelations 21. I've been thinking – I should like if we could both read the same Bible passage every day. How about St. John?

Next time I write I shall be in Cloquet. I'm anxious to begin. I have such a dread of it's being a failure, and now that the time is so near I can't bear to wait, and have such a cold, anxious feeling whenever I think of it.

With my love,
Anna

SEPTEMBER 3, 1896
Oronoco to Cloquet, Minnesota

Sweetheart:

Thought I would write a little this evening to the little girl alone in a far country. You're there in Cloquet probably now, worrying about something – perhaps that examination tomorrow. Don't trouble yourself any more than you can help, dearie. I haven't much to say tonight, but I remember how good your letters look to me when I get them after going away.

It's been a beautiful September day – the leaves are turning on the birches and poplars already. The work on the flume drags on, but I think we'll get done this week. John smacked me on the left arm just above the elbow with a sledge yesterday. It didn't break it (my arm – not the sledge), though folks say it was a wonder it didn't – just bruised and lamed it; 'tis all right. I didn't think he had come so near. I can sympathize with the John Ridd in *Lorna Doone*, struck up in the hay there: "And I heard the bone snap like a twig" – remember?

There – I guess I've complained enough – you'll think I'm a grandmother.

I was in the boat this afternoon when someone up in the woods on the south side said, "Boom-get-a-rat-trap," and I said, "Bigger than a cat-trap," and, of course, it was Clara. She shouted hello, and how was my arm, and we talked a minute.

I'm afraid this is prosy, this letter.

I hope you'll write and tell me how things are; I know when school commences you'll be busy. Of course I love you, darling – how could I help it – I love you more than everything. Now good-night, and take things as easy as you can.

With my dear love,

SEPTEMBER 5, 1896
Cloquet to Oronoco

My Dear Roy:

I have a little time before teachers' meeting, so I'll write to you. It's going to be a long letter, so take a good deep breath, and I'll begin at the beginning!

I left home Wednesday. I saw a good many Rochester people on the train, including Walter, who said he would come to my assistance if they aren't good to me here! We met Dr. Stinchfield on the street, and he said, "Well, what are you doing so far away from home this time of night?" And I said, "I'm going to my school!"

It was after 12 when we got to St. Paul. We were tired and sat down in the parlor. The light came in, very dim, and Florence opened her heart to me, and told me some of the aches there, and I comforted her the best I could. You have taught me how, dear – you have warmed my heart by loving me, and so it seemed the easiest and most natural thing to take Florence in my arms and tell her that I could understand.

I met Miss DeGraff, and when we reached White Bear Miss Roth got on the train. We talked for a while about the summer and good times and our schools and Cloquet. Someone behind us commenced to play the mandolin – music "like the wind blowing through a sliver on the rail fences down East." It was so faint and fine, and I fell to dreaming of everything pleasant. After a while the music stopped, and I grew industrious and studied some for that exam. We were then going through the burnt region around Hinckley. My, it's dismal – as far as you can see, a forest of dead, charred trees, and nothing green except the grass, and here and there some little trees that have started up. *(The Great Hinckley Fire, two years before, destroyed the town, burned some 200,000 acres, and killed at least 418 people.)*

When we reached Cloquet we found Mr. Cloyd, the superintendent, and one of the Board at the train to meet us. They brought us here to Mr. Thompson's – it's a hotel, though they don't take everyone. All the teachers except one board here. Mr. Cloyd says it's very difficult to find good boarding anywhere else, so I think we shall stay.

The teachers have a large table at the end of the dining room, and we have jolly times at meals. We three girls and Mr. Lewis from the U are the only new teachers, and the others are bright and lively. We're all teachers, except one – Mr. Bolton, assistant cashier, who's said to be "the nicest boy in town." They will have a furnace here soon. The schoolhouse is just across the street.

I like Mr. Cloyd very much. He called on us the first evening and told us we must not judge Cloquet from the part we could see. Miss Roth was quite homesick when she got here.

All along the railroad track are piles and piles of lumber. The buildings look dingy and it's untidy about them – I think we have not seen the best part of town yet.

Mr. Johnson, the Presbyterian minister, is very cordial and good – I liked his sermon. The people here seem very nice. I think I'll take a walk this afternoon and see if I can find where these nice people live – what part of town, I mean. I think I shall like it here.

We went to the school building to take the exam. We talked about how we dreaded it, and I said the first thing I thought of when I woke Friday morning were the words of Esther before she went before the king – "Fast ye and pray for me." The exam commenced at 9 o'clock; seven subjects – four written and three oral. They weren't hard, but during the arithmetic exam, two of the Board were there, and they talked every minute – about teachers who had failed; the foolish things they said in their exams; "that girl who had to leave because she didn't pass, when she was so highly recommended too;" and they were sorry for her – very sorry – but she had to go, of course, etc. I was almost wild – couldn't think at all. My head throbbed and my eyes blurred, and I wanted to cry. I knew such a thing could never be excused in a teacher, and whatever I did, I *must not* do that. It came to an end at last, and it was quiet in the afternoon, except that I had a high fever from the morning's experience.

Yesterday at teachers' meeting my work was given me – the "A" division of the first primary. Miss Roth has the "B." My children have been to school about three months. Miss DeGraff has 2nd primary, and we three girls are the only teachers in the building. The rooms are on the first floor of the Odd Fellows Building – sort of an overflow school, next to the central building. The rooms are pleasant, the work is well planned out and arranged for us, and Mr. Cloyd seems very kind. He said to feel free to come see him any time. He makes me think of my brother Frank a little – his voice and the shape of his eyes and the way he moves them and looks at you.

As Monday is Labor Day, we don't keep the children but an hour – just to get their names and give them their books. We have a teachers' meeting Monday, have to get our registers in shape, plan the work for Tuesday, and I want to fix up my room – put up some pictures and decorate the board – so I shall be busy all day. Tuesday we begin regular work. Miss Roth and I are going to think of this verse often: "Be strong and of good courage; dread not, nor be dismayed."

I heard about my exam – they said I did very well. When I came over from the schoolhouse I got your letter, and it seemed so good to get it! It seems such a long time since I was camping and saw you. After supper one of the teachers played the piano and we all sang, "There is sunshine in my soul today." The last time I sang it I was home, and the time before, in Oronoco. Mr. and Mrs. Thompson are very nice; she plays and he has a good bass voice.

I read some after that, and went to bed early, and had the worst dreams ever – that I fooled around at school and didn't get through with the children when the time came to dismiss; that there were worms crawling about on the floor; some horrible-looking people came and looked at me through the windows and scared me; that I had flowers – among them, lilies of the valley – but they were all deformed. Then I thought my father was sick and outdoors, and it was raining, and I couldn't get him in. So I woke tired – do you wonder?

I'm awfully glad you didn't break your arm, dearie, but it must hurt about as badly. What a gypsy Clara is – calling to one out from the woods somewhere, and usually out of sight.

You dear, *dear* boy – you must write to me often. I'm going to do my very best, and I usually come out pretty well in the end – perhaps I shall in this too. I will be careful – I can't teach well unless I'm feeling well, and I would be careful for *your* sake anyway. You *do* help me, dear, by loving me, and by being who you are.

Here's a kiss – you said you'd remember.

With my love,

Anna

SEPTEMBER 10, 1896
Oronoco to Cloquet

My Dear Anna:

I've just read your letter – your good, long letter – over again. That last kiss is so fresh in my memory – oh, I *do* remember.

I'll tell you what I've been doing – it seems tame to tell, but in the midst of your other tortures, you won't mind much. It seems good to me to be out of school. I wake up partway sometimes and kinda think of school work that ought to be done that there isn't time for now. And then comes the thought – man, there *ain't* any studying to do.

Sunday I went over to Reifsniders and Charlie and I walked down the river. It was a fine day, and things look beautiful now when the sun shines. I like the woods – not gorgeous so much yet, but changing. The leaves have turned enough to be soft and mellow, with patches of color here and there. I like them when they're full color too. Charlie had his long rifle, and we shot a few times at a mark. We looked up places where we're going to gather grapes.

When I came home about 2 o'clock Walter was here. He came up on his brother's wheel and stayed with me until Monday. He intends to work hard this year and graduate. He was sorry I wasn't going back. I believe old Bowers likes me, 'spite of all. The rest of the time I worked. I've walked around in the woods some. I always do that – better notice sunsets than ash-heaps. I walked over to camp this noon – it was raining a little; leaves were falling. One tent still stands.

I hope you will like it in Cloquet – you will if anyone can. How those oak-worms must have impressed themselves on your nervous system? It sounds queer to say – that those hideous things would make me think of you – but I *do* remember how you *jumped* every time we saw one. When you have your bad dreams, dream me in, and I'll take you over into an ideal dreamland – woods without oaks; just maples and hickories, tall and straight – and read to you.

I must change my time of writing so you'll get my letter Saturday and you can write me Sunday, when might perhaps be easier for you. I'll write often – I never write very long letters, somehow. Write and tell me everything, Anna, dearest – you know I care so much.

With my dear love,

SEPTEMBER 13, 1896
Cloquet to Oronoco

My Dearest Roy:

I'm not going to write much tonight. I commenced a letter to you, then tore it up. Somehow I'm lonely and tired, and Miss Roth is gone, so I had a cry. I don't know what is the matter – I just keep crying. Not half an hour ago I told Mr. Cloyd I hadn't been homesick or lonely at all today. I thought I hadn't, but, dear, I dread the thought of work tomorrow, and I seem so far from you. You must write to me often – that was such a good letter you wrote last. I intended to write a good one in reply, but somehow I can't.

My work seems to tire me so – it does all of us new girls. Next week will be easier, I think. Mr. Cloyd is just as good to us as he can be – so is everyone. I like the children, and I think I shall like the work. I'm not used to standing, and I can't sit down a minute during the day, except at noon. I shall be all right – as soon as I get used to it. Mr. Cloyd thinks we look tired and tells us we must take more exercise. He sends one of the teachers to take us out walking when we're so tired, and he posted us all off to a free lecture "to get our minds off schoolwork."

I have 36 children – they're from the best families, mostly. One of them – Alfred – is the dearest, sweetest little boy. He has large blue eyes with long dark lashes and dark hair. I think of him as my little King Alfred. I have some who have been to school before; Miss Roth has the beginners.

The children bring us all sorts of things – flowers, "a string of beads to wear on your wrist," apples, slate pencils, colored pictures of actresses, an enormous poster of some political meeting "to put on the wall," six caterpillars, and candy – including some strong-smelling ones the girls call "whisky killers." I have also been promised a puppy and a parrot!

Good-night, you dear, dear, boy. I want to put my head down in the old place and be petted a little tonight. I love you so and think of you often.

With my love,

Anna

SEPTEMBER 16, 1896
Oronoco to Cloquet

Dearest Anna:

Lots of times I like your "poor" letters best. I wish I could take "the tired" for you, dear – I'm never with you when you need me, am I? I'll write often – oftener than I ever have before.

First a little of what I've been doing. The other morning Charles and I went hunting pretty early. We had seen a few ducks the night before, though it's a bit early yet for them to be lighting in the pond – on their way south, I suppose. It was misty and pretty cool. I like such a morning – you know it's going to be warm when the sun gets up. Charlie, like the sun, *wasn't* up yet, and thought we'd better eat breakfast. Mrs. Reifsnider had good coffee, and the wheat cakes were oh so good – just the right thickness – and the syrup neither too thin nor too thick – just perfection.

Then we took a boat and went way up the north branch. Got me a duck up there – don't know what he was doing all by his lone. 'Twas a fine morning – perfectly still, and so cool, and the woods and water and sky all so beautiful. We went away up to the "riffles" on the south branch and shot 11 snipe coming back. Charlie's planning how we'll hunt this winter. He's such a close observer of things – he sees game and signs I don't – always taking notice of everything. That afternoon we went graping. It was about the first day I'd been off duty for quite a while.

Sunday I stayed around – the way a body does. Walked around through the woods and over where the camps were with Charlie. Sailed a bit and had quite a time tacking up against the wind. It was my second time out, and I haven't it down fine yet. After supper we walked over to Trout Brook to look for a place to camp for a week – either there or down the river by the "oxbow bend." We want to go when the leaves are off and you can see the partridges.

We got back late. The moon was shut out by clouds partly, and it was fine walking. We could see the lights come out in the little groves where the farmers' houses are, and as we came out on cemetery hill, it was good to catch the fresh breeze from the west and see the hills way off – dim and looking larger for the mist. I thought of you and how I wanted you – oh, I want you *many* times, dearest. If I could have spent the evening with you when you were so tired and lonesome, dear little girl, I couldna have stopped with only a *little* petting.

I'm exercising besides work, taking care of myself, cushioning the place for your head – your dear, queenly head with the beautiful hair. Remember I'm with you, dearest – I think of you and love you always. Be careful of yourself.

With my dear love,

SEPTEMBER 20, 1896
Oronoco to Cloquet

My Dearest Anna:

I've been so restless all day – I'm a restless mortal, anyhow. It's been a beautiful September day – clear and cold, with a wind. This morning I went sailing for a couple hours. The day ended with a glorious sunset. I was over at Aunt Minnie's with Mary for a few minutes, and I got restless and came out on the Point and thought about us.

Of course, you don't read much now – I haven't either. I've been reading some of Tennyson. One short poem I ran across I rather liked, though perhaps other people wouldn't – "The Voyage of Maeldune," founded on an Irish legend. I'm always liking pieces and poems that you never hear of. Perhaps I haven't the best taste ....

I've been watching my cousin George's little girl Clara – I feel awful sorry for her. She's a nice little girl – about 12 years old – and she lives under a despotism. What makes it more hopeless is that her mother thinks they're doing the best thing for the girl, and there's no other way. They won't let the poor child do anything she wants, and there isn't the least particle of sympathy – they don't put themselves in Clara's place at all. Some of the things they won't let her do would be comical if it didn't seem pitiful. I intended to roast them about it – 'twouldn't do any good, you know, but would make me feel better. I hate tyranny, and it seems cowardly to rule a child as if it were a convict, just because you are stronger.

Of course, you don't know these people, but I thought how you would be sorry for her – you're so gentle and considerate, dear.

Yesterday we pulled up all the tents and camp equipage and brought them home and stowed them away. I have to keep going at something or I'd get so restless elsewise.

I hadn't ought to send such an untidy letter, but I'm sleepy. I'll do better next time. I want to see you, darling – it seems such a long time.

SEPTEMBER 20, 1896
Cloquet to Oronoco

My Dearest Roy:

This is your birthday, dear. I've been so busy I lost all track of time, and never thought of it until today. I have thought of you so much today.

After dinner some of us went for a long walk. We followed the river down for about two miles. The woods are beautiful now – almost as beautiful as the woods in my "east country." We had such a good time. Everything that I thought beautiful I wanted to show to you – oh, the pines, and hemlocks, the moss and vines and bright leaves, the grey rocks with hairbells on them and red vines climbing over them. And the river – the St. Louis – flowing swift in places; then still and quiet when it reflects the trees and blends the colors so beautifully – oranges, reds and soft greenish yellows. Then an opening in the trees, where you could see away off through the trees where the colors looked soft and faint and dim.

I brought home all I could carry of vines and leaves and flowers. My hand ached with the load (I had to carry my skirt with the other). We found everlasting and wintergreen and ground pine that I have never seen except in the east, and some violets and one wild rose – I'll send them to you. I don't think I shall never pick violets again on your birthday. I wonder what the little things were thinking about – to come out in this cold weather. It's been cold enough for November some mornings this week, but it warms up during the day.

Friday evening we teachers were invited to Mrs. White's. We had a lovely time! We danced and sang and played. Then Mrs. W. brought in slips of paper marked "A Floral Tale of Love." She read questions, which were to be answered by the name of a flower. The first – "The girl's name and color of her hair" – was answered with Mary Gold (marigold). "The Father's name and position in church" was Elderberry, etc. There was a prize for the one who answered the most. Another girl and I got the largest number – 22 – so we drew lots for the prize – a beautiful bunch of roses. She got it. After refreshments some ladies played on the mandolin and guitar – they knew how to play, and I enjoyed it so. Last evening some of the young men who take their meals here came up to the parlor and sang. They sang most of us to sleep!

I have taken a science class. I didn't intend to, but Mr. Bolton – a young man who eats at our table – asked me to take his class. The children like him, I could see, and hated to have him stop. I like Mr. Bolton – he's the nicest young man I have met here.

We had a fire nearby Thursday night. I was wakened in the night by the most horrible noise I ever heard. I heard it in my sleep first, and thought all the children were crying. Then I thought they were all coming down the street screaming. Then I realized 'twas something that groaned and wailed in a horrible half-human way. We thought 'twas in the lumberyards at first, but then we found out it was a livery stable afire, and seven horses were burned – terrible.

They're putting in a furnace now, so we won't have to build a fire any longer. Did I tell you we have two rooms – a bedroom with a sitting room opening off from it. We're very cozy and nice, and I feel contented and happy. If only my work goes all right, I shall like it. I don't mind being in a hotel as much as I thought I should.

We're over the post office, and the men's lounge is on the corner under our window, so we get a good deal of noise. But you can shut your eyes and ears to most anything if you really have to – I don't mind it a bit now. I think it's a good thing for one to have to fit one's self to different conditions. I'm glad of the opportunity – it will make me so much the stronger, I think.

There are a good many French here, as well as Swedes. The luggage men thought I was French, for I heard them say as they brought up my trunk, "Anna Barnard – must be French!"

I have 35 children now. I had to give up my little king – we found he belonged in Miss Roth's room. I hated to let him go. Perhaps I shall have him again after Xmas. The time flies up here – it doesn't seem two weeks that I have been teaching, though it seems an age since I left Oronoco.

I've just read the last chapter of John. Should we read Corinthians next? Write me as often as you can. And you will be careful, dear, when you go hunting? I worry about you so. Roy, you're the *dearest* boy. Your letters are *so* good. You don't know how this helps your little "school marm."

With my love,
Anna

SEPTEMBER 24, 1896
Oronoco to Cloquet

My Dearest Anna:

I've just read your letter over again. What a philosopher you are – you make the best of things, don't you? I'm so glad you're contented. You must write me about these people you tell me of – how they look, etc. – especially what they mean to you. I'm sorry you're going to work Sundays too – I hate to have you tire yourself all out, but I s'pose you can tell best. "A willfur man, mann have his way."

I'm living kind of an uneventful life. I stay outdoors most of the time when I'm not in the mill. I am exercising and feel first-rate – not heavy yet – about 151, with light clothes. I've been running some each evening – I think it's good for me. I'm trying to get into good shape this year so I'll be a little bit more satisfied with myself (though that I'll never be). Probably I won't hunt very much. Charles talks more about it than we'll ever carry out, and I'll be careful, my dearest – don't worry, Anna.

I haven't been reading any to speak of. After I get through things after supper, I lie down and watch the fire. When I get restless, I go outdoors. How I'd liked to have gone down the river with you Sunday – reckon I wouldn't have been restless then. The wind has been blowing a gale all day. Wouldn't it be wild out sailing tonight in the moonlight? Charlie Mayo ran on a sandbar and capsized last Sunday.

Yes, let's read Corinthians together. I read the third chapter tonight. I'm going to write short letters to you often. I wonder how a kind of diary letter would do? I'm afraid it wouldn't work. Strange that you like my letters so, when I write in such a haphazard way. Your letters are the *very* best shot in the week for me. I must try and keep as near you as I can this year, Anna – we must be as near as we can to one another.

You must take good care of yourself, dearie. I know things will go all right.

Roy

SEPTEMBER 27, 1896
Cloquet to Oronoco

My Dearest Roy:

I've been to church and had my dinner, and now I can write to you. You're good to write so often – your letters are just right – don't you worry.

This has been kind of a rough week. The children act up considerably – nothing very bad – just mischief. I felt pretty blue Wednesday – I came home at noon, and I felt so tired and discouraged that I had to cry. I couldn't get over it all afternoon, and had to leave the schoolroom once to choke it down. I couldn't even go to teachers' meeting that afternoon. The teachers all thought I was sick, and came trooping to my room here at the hotel to see me. The children knew something was wrong too. I have felt more courageous since then. Mr. Cloyd visited my room for about 10 minutes, and he said he liked what he saw of my work.

We had a great time yesterday. Mr. Batson – a man who boards here – took some of us for a long ride. We were gone until after 5. We drove about 20 miles – first to Carlton, then Chub Lake, and then to Thompson. We had a fine time. This is a great country – it's beautiful. The trees are gorgeous. We drove through woods of pine and maple, oak and birch. The leaves are more brilliant here than they are at home, and the evergreens make the other trees seem more beautiful.

I thought of you so often, and wish you could see it. The country is rocky and wild down around Thompson – rough, bare, grey rocks, with a few pines growing on the sides and tops, and some little trees that seem to find a place to live and grow and turn beautiful in spite of the rocks. The St. Louis has worn a deep chasm through the rock. From the bridges we could see the falls above us. There's a mill there, and below the dam the water rushes against the rocks and is thrown up white and beautiful. Then it winds around through this deep gorge. Away up on the sides of the gorge we saw logs that Mr. Batson said were left by the water last spring. My – I'd would've liked to see it then! We saw only a few farms – they're so different from those at home. The fields are covered with stumps – a potato patch was thick with them. The potatoes couldn't be planted in rows, and a man was digging them with a hoe. Mr. Batson says the soil is good, but men don't want to have to clear the land of stumps as long as there is so much prairie land unsettled. They were burning stumps as they stand in the ground in a good many places. We passed through some country that looked as it did around Hinckley – the trees were burned and dead, but standing – pines so tall and straight they seemed like old warriors, and you felt like cheering them.

Chub Lake is very pretty – much prettier than its name. It's considerably larger than Lake Calhoun. We drove through the most beautiful woods to get to it, where it seemed as if you were riding into a flood of sunlight. The trees were so yellow, and the lake perfectly still. There were woods on all sides, and not a house in sight, except an empty summer cottage and a couple of boat houses. Some people from Cloquet own a little steam launch there, and they often have gay times in summer. We grew quite cold before we got home, though we all wore winter coats. It was like a day in early November – bright, but cold. They say that it is often 50 below zero here.

Now I must tell you about some of the people. There are two tables of teachers. Mr. Cloyd is the superintendent – unmarried; about 35. He's a great tease – says he can always tell when one of us gets a letter by the absent-minded air we put on; says he has asked the postmaster to put all square envelopes that come to the teachers in his box! I like him, but he says unkind things of people a good deal – I wish he didn't do that. He's just a bit impatient too. He never has been anything but kind and good to me, but I can see how he speaks out and might hurt pretty badly.

Then there is Mr. Lewis – the high-school science teacher. He has very frank blue eyes, is a good singer – a great YMCA man. He works hard, comes late to his meals, but always seems friendly and sort of sunshiny. Miss Archibald is about Mother's age, I should think – has faded-out blue eyes and light hair. She's quite large – wears her shoes several sizes too large. Her dresses are nice enough, but never look pretty. She's jolly and good and sort of motherly. She would never be shocked at anything we girls would do. The first thing I ever heard her say was, "Well, girls – can we *lick* this year?"

Miss Lynch is engaged, and everyone teases her (except us new ones). She's nice and I like her, but I like them all. She's more dignified than most. Mr. Bolton is assistant cashier. He's small and slender – only a little taller than I (we measured). He has light hair and blue eyes. He's said to be the best boy in Cloquet. I think I told you I have taken his science class. He thinks October the best month of the year, and I took down Helen Hunt Jackson's "October Bright Blue Weather" for him to read – he thinks it very beautiful.

The sixth seat at the table has no regular occupant – sometimes Mrs. Thompson sits there – the landlord. I don't like her very well. She plays nicely for us to dance. You wouldn't like her very well either. She has very thick hair and small, pretty hands, but she's just a bit rough. I sit next, and then Miss Roth. Have I told you about her? She's smaller than I – dark hair and grey eyes. She's so quiet – has a low voice, and speaks rather slowly. She's sensible, and we get on beautifully together.

Miss Mumpy is small and thin and demure and ladylike. Mr. Thompson is next – proprietor of the hotel and member of the School Board. He's large, full of fun, not a bit dignified, and he says things you wouldn't say, dear – mostly swearing. Last Monday evening we all danced and I waltzed with him – he thought I was an "old hand" at it.

Then there's Miss Gelstan – she's the nicest little teacher of all – about the age of us new ones, and the prettiest. She's very small, has a pleasant voice, and has such a winning manner you fall in love with her at once. Miss Hayes is Miss Gelstan's chum. She calls Miss G. sweetheart and all sorts of names when we are alone together. Miss Hayes is the greatest cutup of all.

Miss Ferguson has the jolliest laugh. Her room is next to ours. She goes into everything heart and soul. She can dance like a boy (I mean she can take a boy's part in a waltz or two-step). Then there are people who board here, and I see them occasionally: Mr. Mackey – editor of the *Pine Knot*; Mr. Watts – a clerk; Rev. M. Allen – Episcopal minister; Mr. Batson – don't know *what* he is – about 40; belongs to glee club. Danced with us Monday evening, and always smells of tobacco.

Well – what do you think of the people and the country? It's new to me, but I'm interested in them – you would be too.

I'm afraid you're going to be restless and unhappy this winter – you must try not to be. I wish you *would* write a diary letter. I don't think it would work for me, for my head is so full of school work, and I'm *not* going to talk school all the time to you. I shake it off some (not my head – the school) over Sunday.

Tomorrow is school again – I'm kind of tired, and I wish you were here. Oh, I hope things will go well next week. I'm so anxious to have this a success.

Had the funniest dream about you – you had grown very broad-shouldered, owing to your exercise. Then we went to a football game between *cats* – they were on a side hill and 'twas *covered* with them! You explained the game to me (!).

Miss Roth tells me to stop writing and go with her for a walk. I guess you will be tired by this time. I love you always, dear.

Anna

CHAPTER 20

Lonesome

OCTOBER 1, 1896
Oronoco to Cloquet

My Dearest Anna:

I sleep over at Aunt Minnie's now, so that's where I'm writing from. I've been working on the road today, and probably will the rest of this week and into the next. Henry and a team have been at it four or five days – we have so much land that it takes lots of road work. It's been a grand day – all hazy like Indian summer – and the sunlight so warm and yellow. September took such a gentle farewell wi' us. I went by the pond last evening and watched the last September sun go down – red as a ball of fire. The water in the old pond is fine and clear now – higher than it was, and slowly coming up.

Anna, you always say when you're away somewhere in the fall that the leaves are brighter or softer than they are here – do you do that just to make me dissatisfied?! They aren't much better, are they? The oaks are all red now, and I like to see them set down so bright in the woods where the leaves are either off or yellow. I guess I'm a Celt in my liking for so much color.

Auntie went to Minneapolis Monday. I wish I could have gone too – I'd liked to have gone over to the U, seen everybody, and gone to a theater. I get lonesome, Anna. You see, I've been used to having someone to talk with – I mean, people who are kind of interested in the same things I am – and, of course, I miss it. I'll do something different next year.

It seems an endless time since I saw you, and it's been but a little over a month. It's too bad, isn't it, that we can't change some of those we have around us that we don't care for at all, for those we *do*? I was in a "mood," I guess, the other evening when I read your letter – half-angry that other people could see and touch you, and I couldn't. I didn't thank you for the flowers you sent me, did I? I do it now, then. You're the greatest case to find flowers away out of their time.

I hope you've got through the week all right. You must try and have all the fun you can, so that omnipresent thought of school won't tire you out. Take care and don't work too hard, dearest. I've been thinking of you many times today – the way you were that Sunday evening when I was at Eyota the last time. You had on that white dress and we'd forgotten to get anything to eat.

I'll try and not get lonesome. Write to me – everything. I'm trying to be as I told you I would. I love you dearly, dearly.

OCTOBER 4, 1896
Cloquet to Oronoco

My Dearest Roy:

The girls have all gone to church, but I thought I'd stay home and write to you. I've been studying my lesson since breakfast. I like my little class – I have two girls and two boys about 13 years old. One girl said, "We liked Mr. Bolton, but I think we shall like *you* just as well."

I've taught a month – it doesn't seem as long. We drew our money out – never earned as much before, so we felt very big and important. There was a fire very near us Friday night. We all ran around the halls carrying our watches and pocketbooks. There was about $500 among us, I guess, and we didn't intend to lose that. It's dreadful the number of fires they have here – they think some of the men who've been discharged from the mills are doing it. People all act wild in a fire – it's strange. The buildings are mostly wooden, and there are such piles of lumber – Mr. Cloyd said the whole town could burn up in a couple of hours *(a portent of things to come – in 1918 a disastrous fire destroyed most of Cloquet).*

They have splendid water power – each of the four large mills keeps an engine ready night and day. As soon as they yell fire, the whistles scream and the engines begin to pump. Every man runs out and pulls and pushes the hose cart, and they all scream, "Turn on the water!" When it's turned on, it comes from two or three different directions. My, how it hisses and shoots through the flames – a white stream. Then the flames fall down, down, and the smoke rolls up yellow and thick. Then there isn't a spark to be seen, and you can only see the men by the light of the moon or a window or street lamp. They splash through the water, their rubber coats all shining wet, and go out on the street. We go back to bed and it's all still again.

We are at the end of a long hall, and we thought that if this hotel should burn, the stairs might go first, so we've buckled our trunk straps together around the bedpost. If we have a fire, all we'll have to do is throw the straps out the window and go down it. I wish I could try it – we would some night, but we're afraid someone would see us, take us for a burglar and we'd get shot at!

We danced for about an hour one evening last week – all the teachers, and Mr. Cutliff, who is a tailor. He is a very fine dancer. He's tall and acts as though he wants to be "elegant," but doesn't know just how. He has a heavy moustache and curls the ends of it. He sort of looks like his fashion plates – expression and all.

Mr. Cloyd proposed that several of us take a boat ride up the river. We had a fine row – the air was smoky, owing to the forest fires, and the sun set like a ball of fire. The leaves are growing brown and dull now and falling. The spruce and pines are pretty, though. We rowed up in sight of the Indian reservation and came home.

There are a good many logs in the river – old, green, water-soaked fellows, with their heads just out of the water. The river is divided into four "pockets" for the logs. They reach up for about two miles. There the logs are sorted and each sent into its own "pocket," where they float to the right mill. The divisions are made by chaining logs together. Probably you know how this is done, but it was new to me. The river isn't as beautiful up here as it is in Oronoco – it's so filled with piles of logs, to break the ice and prevent them from going the wrong way.

Cloquet is wild and unfinished looking – a bit rough, too. But the scenery is beautiful, and the leaves *are* brighter than they are in the southern part of the state – Mr. Cloyd says so too. You dear, *dear* boy – the idea of your thinking I say things just to make you dissatisfied! I have to look for beautiful things and talk about them to keep from getting dissatisfied myself.

Try not to get lonely or dissatisfied or restless, dear. You can get in good trim physically this year, and being at home will make you want to work with all your might next year if you go back to school. You can do so much for others too this year, like Mary and Blanche.

I think I'm doing all right – Mr. Cloyd seems satisfied with my work. Miss DeGraff had some trouble governing her room, so Mr. Cloyd asked her to exchange with Miss Roth. I hope the bluest days in my teaching were back there in my country school. I learned so much then.

I wish you could be here in place of some of these folks (Mr. Cutliff, for instance!). These people know that I'm Miss B, a school teacher – that's as far as they care or even think. *You* have my heart, my thoughts, my dearest, truest love. All that is best in me reaches out to you and up to God. Aren't you satisfied?

Three little girls have just been in to see us – they asked for our pictures. I gave them one of my old graduation pictures, and Gracie looked at it and said, "Oh, isn't it pretty!" I didn't dare look at Miss Roth – I knew she'd laugh out loud. Gracie said, "We used to have a pump in our cellar, but now we have a furnace instead." The children talk of these things all the time.

Write as often as you can. I think I understand how you feel, dearest. I write about the good times, but it's hard most of the time. I'm interested in the work, though, and can begin to see results.

Do you ever get tired of my long letters? You are the *greatest* boy.

With my love,

Anna

I've just read the 13th chapter of First Corinthians – the one I like best. I think of the way Drummond explained it in *The Greatest Thing in the World*. It seems to me you would like it too, for you have more charity – more love for everyone – than anyone I ever knew.

OCTOBER 7, 1896
Oronoco to Cloquet

My Dearest Anna:

I intended to come over early and write you a good letter, but Charlie came, and I had to stay, and it's late, and it willna be a good letter at all.

I wish you could know, Anna, how much you do for me. That last letter helped me a great deal. I wish things people say sometimes didn't hurt so. Pa said something this morning that seemed altogether uncalled for – that stung and made me sore and angry all day. He didn't mean to do it, I think – of course, he didn't. He was sort of hurried, I suppose. It's foolish to let things take me so, but a fellow has to have something to distinguish him from animals.

Things don't bother me as much when I think of you. Everything would be gone without you. You don't mind me telling you when I'm bothered, do you? If you could only have on your glasses and *see* me when I say some things, you wouldn't take so much stock in them. That's one great difficulty of writing, dearest – sometimes it's only a *mood* that passes right away.

Sunday Charlie and I went away off down the river – gone from noon until dark. We went where I had never been before – to the "Oxbow-bend" and the "Hogback." It's the wildest looking country around here anywhere – great bluffs and ravines, so you couldn't see a man 10 rods. There's where I'm going when I'm in hiding from the arm of the law. It was a great day to be out in the woods. From the bluffs you could see away off west, and it was hazy a little, and all you could see of the hills was the golden shimmer from the yellow leaves. I was hungry as Loki when I got back, but wasn't much tired. I intend to tramp around and go on expeditions Sundays, for it's the only day I have without work. It isn't wrong for me to think so, is it, dear?

I took your last letter down to the mill to read. It was closing time, so no one would come to interrupt. I carry that letter with me all the time. Anna – I *love* you so – I don't know how to tell you – I'll do more than *tell*. It's kind of you to say such things of me, and good to know that you think them, even if I can't. I *ought* to be a gentleman of the right kind. You asked if I ever got tired of your letters. They are a thousand times better than anything else the week brings.

I'm glad your school is all right. You face unpleasant things in the bravest, best way, dearie. There's no one like you.

This is an awful stupid letter. I ought to tear it up, but I won't. I'll write again. Good-night.

Faith – what was it I was going to say – oh, yes – why don't you girls buy a *rope* for a fire-escape? Put knots in it.

OCTOBER 11, 1896
Cloquet to Oronoco

My Dearest Roy:

I wonder if it's rainy in Oronoco today. It rained here all day Friday and Saturday.

Miss Roth and I put our rooms together at recess and taught the children songs – that is, *I* taught them, for Miss R can't sing as much as I. One of her children asked if "Mrs. Barnum" couldn't come in again and teach them new songs. (The children call me Mrs. Barnum all the time – I've tried to break it up, but they *will* call me that.) The people here at the hotel have taken it up, and now I'm either Mrs. Barnum or Mrs. P.T. My school isn't a circus anyhow (!).

At breakfast we were talking of nationality, and each one told what they were. There were Scot, English, Irish, German and Yankee among us. Mr. Cloyd is part Scot.

School went pretty well this week. Yesterday I read a good deal about children and teaching, and get a good deal of inspiration from it. I hope it won't evaporate the first thing on Monday. Do you remember William Hawley Smith, who spoke to us once in high school on choosing an occupation and then working toward that? It was sort of heresy, and some of us went to Mr. Adams to see if we could drop Math or Latin or something else, because those studies wouldn't help us in what we were going to do. I've been reading some of Smith's articles in *The Public School Journal*. He has more sympathy for the bad boy than anyone I know of, unless it's you, dear. I'm going to see if I can't get at some of my restless inattentive little ones – find the things they like, if possible, and lead them over to like the right things.

Mr. Cloyd hasn't as much tact and patience as he might. He saw that three of my boys were troubling me, and said right before them, "These three are bad boys. If they bother you, send them to me, for I'm death on bad boys."

Miss Gelstan told us something funny that happened in her room. Mr. Cloyd came in to hear her mental arithmetic class. He told the children to sit in position (arms folded). He was about to begin work when one boy punched his neighbor with his elbow. Mr. C. jerked him up and shook him. The other boy was so pleased that boy No. 1 boy got a shaking, that he giggled. Mr. C. promptly shook the *other* boy. Then that tickled a *third* boy, and *he* giggled. Mr. C. grew angry and said it was a sad time if a man couldn't come into a room without being laughed at. I like Mr. Cloyd very much, and feel I could go to him about anything and he would help me.

I got your letter yesterday. I had started for school, so I took it over there and read it. You thought it stupid, but I thought it was one of the *best* letters you ever wrote. I want you to tell me all about the things that bother you, for I *do* understand. I'm so glad, dearest, if I help you some. You must write me as you would talk to me – I'll put my glasses on to read, and think of your face, and imagine hard.

I sometimes wonder if I really help the children any – not simply teaching them to read and write, but to see and love beautiful things, and to help them into something higher. There's need enough for it. As I find out more about the families my children come from, I have the more sympathy for them. Some are so very, very poor – I hardly see how they can live through the winter. The mills have not been running for so long that they have used up all they have. Most of my children are from the best families, but there are some who have so little.

I read *Patsy* by Kate Douglas Wiggin. It's a touching little story – if you ever come across it, read it. I have *The Idiot* by Bangs to read today.

The teachers have organized a literary society. We meet in our sitting room every Tuesday night. I am secretary. I'm glad we have it – it will be good for us, and I'm getting tired of dancing and singing. We don't dance oftener than once or twice a week anyhow, and I don't like dancing always with Mr. Batson or Cutliff, and I feel have to, of course. And I step on Mr. Bolton's toes when I try to waltz with him. Seems to me I feel the need of fun – or something that I can throw myself into with all my might, that isn't school or anything like it. If I keep quiet or read, I'm sure to think of the day's work and the things I've failed in.

Bryan is to speak in Carlton from the train platform on Sunday. My teachers are all going down to hear him. I'm glad of the chance – I'd rather hear and see him than McKinley. I've wished I might ever since I read about him. *(Democratic presidential candidate William Jennings Bryan was defeated by Republican William McKinley a month later in a presidential campaign considered by many historians as one of the most significant and complex in American history.)*

There's no service in the Presbyterian Church this morning, so I'm going to stay at home. Perhaps you are taking a long tramp today. We have had white frost several times. It seems like the last of October at home.

They tell me I'm getting fat and look lots better than when I came – Miss Roth tells me my face looks like a full moon.

This letter is mostly school, and won't be interesting to you, perhaps, but I think you would want me to write about what I care for.

Lovingly,
Anna

OCTOBER 14, 1896
Oronoco to Cloquet

My Dearest Anna:

Your letter just came tonight. I waited for my friend Lou to come and run with me, but he didn't show up, so I ran alone. I've run out across the country a couple of times. The folks in town don't know what to make of it – seeing a fellow running bareheaded and coatless through the darkness. One night as I went staving along, a man picketing out his cow by the side of the road said in an anxious tone, "Is anybody *sick?*" I ought to've told 'im I was a trifle touched my*self.*

A couple of nights ago it was misty – almost raining and dark as Egypt – and I ran out south. I passed a couple fellows with a lantern shined out into the ditch. One of them – queer kind of chap – said to me afterward, "If I'd been alone, you bet I'd've *run* when I seen you." These things tickle Mother immensely – she was telling Aunt Minnie about it, and got herself to laughing that contagious way she does sometimes.

We're having beautiful Indian summer weather – frosty nights, but soft, beautiful, sunny days.

This evening is different – it seems like spring, just before things begin to get green. It's warm; there's a beautiful low moon that makes a long silver path way up the pond, and the wind comes blowing gently and fitfully. Sounds rainy, like April. I hate to have these days go – a body feels as if they wanted to stay out and get all of the last warm sunshine.

We have a very uneventful life here. I haven't been away since I saw you at Eyota. Charlie says we live like mud turtles. I've been grinding some and pulling nails out of old planks. Oh, how I hate it – a regular old woman's job. I've been working at it a good share of three days, and my hair turned grey, almost. Charles knows how I hate it and would come and bring me metheglin. Wonder why I hate a puttering, anchor-scouring job so – part of my makeup, I suppose. I do it just the same. I get sort of tired of things sometimes, and want a little variety, but it's what everyone has, I guess. Things will come out all right. If I get to studying medicine next year, probably there'll be lots of nail-pulling in one form or another.

I've been reading very little. I got Thackeray's *Memoirs of Barry Lyndon* out of the library, but I don't like it. I rather think it was written to slash at some Irish traits. I like *Henry Esmond* best of any of Thackeray's. I'm afraid we don't put ourselves in other folks' places enough, or we wouldn't be surprised at some things they do. If I do sympathize with bad boys, as you say, it's because I would be bad myself under some circumstances, I know. In his preface to *Henry Esmond*, Thackeray speaks of watching with the crowd the spectacle of the Lord Mayor driving out in state to a state dinner, and Jack Newgate going, guarded, up Tyburn Hill to execution; and he says, "But I look into my heart and think – I'm as good as the Lord Mayor, and know I'm as bad as poor Jack, if educated up to love gin and dice and pleasure and placed on Hornslow Heath with a purse before me."

Yes, I remember Hawley Smith so well – he's the man who turned my attention to the dangerous fact that life for me was too serious an affair. Du-Maurier is dead, isn't he? He was quite young, too. And yesterday I spoke of Salvini, and someone said he was on his death-bed. I hope it's not true – do you know – have you read anything of it? It affected me to hear such – Salvini was my hero, someway.

You can't tell how much you help the children – I'm sure you do, dear, though they wouldn't realize it. I'm glad you have a good superintendent – a harsh, conceited one might be a bother. I never could teach school – I'd be ashamed to bluff and bully little kids. It's all right, I suppose – has to be done, mayhaps. I believe you make a fine teacher – I bet I would like you – that is, as the child way back. Don't ever think, dearie, that I'm not interested in your schoolwork. You don't tell me too much – on my word of honor, if you "talk school" too much I'll tell you.

I had a letter from Walter a while ago – he's rooming alone and working hard. He said, "You must write me – we must be together a little if we are so far apart." I thought that rather a sentimental way of putting it, for Bowers.

I will love you always, sweetheart. I straightened out your letters a little Sunday; looked through some of them. I could trace everything that has happened to us. It's good to have a friend like you, Anna.

Write to me, dearest, about everything – your letters seem so good. I love you always.

OCTOBER 18, 1896
Cloquet to Oronoco
My Dearest Roy:

I don't feel very well today – I've taken cold, and it makes me cross, for I know it's the beginning of colds, colds, colds all winter long.

We had a hard snowstorm Thursday night. The snow hasn't gone yet, and it's so cold and wintry. It was beautiful here Wednesday – Miss Johnson, Miss De-Graff and I went walking after supper, and it seemed positively spring-like. When we came downstairs the moonlight shone in the hall. The door stood wide open, and we stayed out quite a while – it was so warm.

Last night there was a Presbyterian social and dance. We were invited to the dance, but didn't go. The young men have a dancing club – they call it very select, but it isn't so very. Mr. Batson is in it, and others like him. I have to dance with Batson when they dance here, but I won't go *there* and dance with him or anyone else I don't want to. I can't bear him – he's a rough, horrid old codger. I'd be ashamed to be seen with him in Rochester or Eyota. The boys here were a trifle cross because the teachers won't go. They'll get over it.

Bryan was in Carlton Tuesday. We all went down to see him. He spoke from the platform of his car for 15 minutes. I was quite near, and had a good chance to see him and his wife. I was disappointed – he looks older than his pictures, and has a dark-skinned, hard, unrefined face. He looked particularly disagreeable when he smiled, for it was all put on, and his eyes never looked anything but cold and determined. He made a few supposed-to-be-funny sarcastic remarks. Mrs. Bryan seems a gracious, ladylike little woman with no thought of self – even when the people cheer her and give her flowers and make a great fuss.

I got *Days of Auld Lang Syne* from the library and have read a little. Yes, duMaurier is dead and cremated, and his ashes in Westminster Abbey, I think. And, yes – I heard Salvini was not expected to live.

Oh, I wish I were home today. I felt restless yesterday – went from one thing to another and couldn't get centered with anything. Tried to make our plans for next week's work, but nothing seemed satisfactory. I want something – I don't know what.

I think I'd better not write anymore if I can't "be good." I feel blue for some reason – my cold, of course – so I can't write.

With my love,
Anna

OCTOBER 22, 1896
Oronoco to Cloquet

Sweetheart:

That letter of yours sounded blue. I hope you feel better, dearie – wish I could "divvy" up on colds with you.

It's been pretty sharp weather here too. Bah – what do you care about the weather – I must try and say something to get you over being *cross*. It frightened me the way you killed, cremated and put poor duMaurier in Westminster Abbey, as if he were naughty and sent to bed (!).

I haven't been doing anything very interesting or blood-curdling – grinding feed and straightening nails. This last is nearly completed, and my locks are working back to their normal shade. By the way – I had my hair cut about a month ago – pretty short for me. It isn't long as it usually is, and I don't feel very Byronesque and natural.

I read the last book in the series by Dumas – *Son of Porthos*. I liked it too – as well as *The Three Musketeers* or even better. I think you would like it better too. He was a fine fellow – that young countryman from "Belle Isle in the Sea" – who went up to Paris to find out who his father Porthos has been and the three he had spoken of – all dead now, except that old unprincipled arch-plotter Aramis, who was worse than ever now he was old. He was tall and strong and straightforward and pure and loyal and could fence like the archangel Gabriel. Wouldn't it be *grand* to be such a great Herculean fellow? I would give half my life to be such – I *hate* myself sometimes. That is the first book I've read through and enjoyed real well for a long time.

I had a letter from Miss Sperry this week. She said she supposed I would be shocked and grieved at her violation of Ruth Ashmore's laws (I wasn't!). *(Ruth Ashmore's Laws was a column in* Ladies Home Journal *that offered "motherly" advice to young girls.)* I think it real gentlemanly of her to write first, don't you? She's teaching First Primary in Madison, Minnesota – I dinna ken where that is. I guess she doesn't like teaching very well. I think she's pretty good in some things, but wouldn't think she would make a good First Primary.

I'm so sorry you're not feeling well, Anna. I wish I could see you – I'm sure I could drive away the blueness, at least.

Oh, Mary had *The Birds' Christmas Carol*, and I picked it up and read some. Do you remember when we read it that time? It brought memories back, and I saw you again. Dear little sweetheart – I *love* you so.

I've been reading straight on in Corinthians. What now?

OCTOBER 24, 1896
Cloquet to Oronoco

My Dearest Roy:

I have recovered from my blueness, if not my cold. I had a fine ride this afternoon with some of the others to Carlton. The air was clear but cold. We wrapped up well; I wore overshoes and took my muff. The little pools beside the road are all frozen. There is skating on the pond, and the river is frozen over. Things look bleak – everything is covered with a white frost each morning.

I've been talking with the children about Helen Hunt Jackson's poem "Down to Sleep" – do you remember it? I wasn't sure whether they would like it or not. It was beautiful the way they entered into it. I read a little, and they asked for more. Even my little Indian could tell some of the "low tones as through the forest creep." They imitated the wind in the pine trees, and the noise of the squirrel and robin, and the call of the wood pee-wee. They were interested in naming flowers that have laid "down to sleep," the "sweet eyes shut tight;" how Jack Frost covers them every night with his velvet coverlet, and how Mother Nature will soon send the snow – an even thicker coverlet for them.

Next week I'm going to talk with them about the part of *The Vision of Sir Launfal* that tells how the little brook "built a roof 'neath which he could house him, winter-proof." I'm sure they will like that. We have talked about Giant Gravitation, who lives in the center of the earth and draws everything toward him. Some of them saw a picture of a giant in a book and called it Giant Gravitation.

The next morning after our talk about "Down to Sleep" one of the children said, "Jack Frost and his sister were out last night and covered our pansy bed." "Who is Jack Frost's sister?" I asked. "I don't remember her name." Up went several hands! "Who do you think, Susie?" "Mother Nature!" Some seemed to agree, but one hand was still up. "Who is she, Frank?" "She's ... she's that women you told us about yesterday – Helen Hunt Jackson!"

I've been reading *The Days of Auld Lang Syne*. It's fine – better than *Bonnie Brier Bush*. You must read it if you can get it. You'll like Jamie – he was called the Cynic of the Glen. They said he had a "nippy tongue," but he was true blue, like his eyes – "Not the soft azure of the south, but the steely color of a Scottish loch in the sunshine, with a northeast wind blowing – a keen, merciless, penetrating blue. Cant, false sentiment and every form of unreality shriveled up before that gaze."

SUNDAY MORNING

It is perfectly still this morning. The flags across the street hang motionless, and no one is stirring on the street. It's still in the quarters below us, and the only sound I can hear is a cowbell away off, and Mr. Thompson getting wood for the furnace. Now the canary below is beginning to sing. It's going to be bright today – I'm glad.

I couldn't finish this last night because some of the teachers came in and talked. It's hard work to accomplish anything on Saturday – there are so many of us, and we go running in and out. I took back *Auld Lang Syne* and got *Henry Esmond*. We'll try to keep together in what we read.

I guess I have the "school marm" way of putting things so bluntly, if my remarks about duMaurier struck you in that way!

Mr. Cloyd called me in Saturday – asked how I thought I was doing – how I felt about my work. I told him, and asked how it seemed to him. He said, "You're doing splendidly." Wasn't I glad? I may get called down tomorrow for something, but I'm glad he thinks my work is all right today. It makes me have more confidence in myself – more brave to go on.

I sent to Dr. Lane for the medicine that helped me so much before, and the prescription came yesterday. I hate to take it when I teach, for it has chloroform in it, and it makes me so sleepy. Even when I move around and talk, it seems as though my mind was half asleep.

Miss Roth and I had an invitation to a party yesterday. We're not going. Some of the people are nice, but some are tough, and the old teachers advise us not to go on account of what people will think. This is a queer place. There are not enough *nice* young people, so the nice ones and the rough ones all go together, and people think nothing of it, except that the teachers are not expected to do so. We form a little class of ourselves. If anyone invites one, they invite all, and it is just us – no outsiders. I suppose Miss R and I were asked this time because we're younger than the other teachers. Miss Roth misses young people – she says she feels about 45, and people call us "old maids" – she doesn't like that!

I get on all right. If I have one or two friends, books, and am all right in my work, I can be satisfied. And I *like* Cloquet. I don't care if people are tough – they are *people*, just the same. I've seen good ones, and those like myself, and I want to know those people – not go to parties and be one of them, but to see why they are who they are. You ought to go to a political meeting here to see some of the sorts of men. The hall is always packed with men – most of them rough-looking and roughly dressed, but looking as if they wanted to get at the *truth*.

We have had the brightest moonlight nights – they are glorious. Yes, I remember *A Birds' Christmas Carol*. I can see the parlor, the shades drawn low, and the breeze coming in and moving the lace curtains.

Can't you come to Minneapolis Christmas? Nine months is so long, dear.

With my love,

Anna

Shall we read Ephesians next? Then Philippians?

OCTOBER 30, 1896
Oronoco to Cloquet

My Dearest Anna:

It's a good night to read – it ought to be to write, but there's no telling.

It rained last night and has been quite warm and raining all day. I'm in my room at Auntie's, where I always write now, and I can hear the water running over the dam. It's been a long time since I heard that sound last – you hear it so plain from here, and it sounds so soothing and pleasant as you drop off to sleep. The flume, dam and tube are all tight. That was a hard job; everything has been easy in comparison since – except pulling nails. That's the beauty of hard things, isn't it, philosopher?

Uncle Grant came home yesterday – wanted to be here for the election. The campaign waxeth hot, doesn't it? I'll exercise the right of a freeman for the first time next Tuesday. I haven't talked politics so far, for I don't like to talk and argufy about any such thing unless I know about it real thoroughly. But I've listened and read a bit and made up my mind. It doesn't seem as hard for me to decide this year. I think the democratic platform – the Chicago plat-form – has some things in it – some principles – worse than free silver. I must learn more about these things. *(Bryan crusaded for the common man against the rich, who he believed impoverished America by limiting the money supply, based on gold. Bryan wanted the money supply based on silver.)*

Uncle Grant saw the football game our boys played with Purdue in Minneapolis – 18 to 6 in favor of U of M. I would liked to have seen it so much! Oh, I'd like to see a game – go wild, and get back and have a big time at supper, and eat up all the baked apples, and then go to the theater with the boys – sit in the front row on my old overcoat and watch folks; eat peanuts and dream dreams while the orchestra played.

I'm not very sorry that I didn't dig harder the last two years in school. Of course, I'll have to dig in the future, but I'm not going to regret my past "badness" more than necessary. Isn't it good – that as a rule we remember the pleasant things, and the others fade away? I thinkna on the Allis who got conned in math and went blue and despised himself – because he was idle, and didn't do what he intended to. But a body never does quite as well as he intends, does he?

You should see little Volney – he talks some now. He thinks so much of Fred, and Fred does of him too. It's funny how Fred goes into a drugstore inquiring about baby foods and such. I tell Fred – why doesn't he use his accumulated knowledge and hire out as a nurse? He's a good bloke.

I'm glad the school and your work is coming so finely. A little honest praise helps a lot. If there could be such a person – who could come at each one of us in just the right way – we would do *anything* for them, wouldn't we?

I wish I could come to Minneapolis Christmas time, but I don't think I can. You know how I want to see you, dearest. The time does seem so *very* long.

With my dear love,

CHAPTER 21

Hard-hearted and Ruthless

NOVEMBER 1, 1896
Cloquet to Oronoco

My Dearest Roy:

We went to Duluth yesterday. It was a horrid day – cold and sleety. Most of us got new hats. Mine is large, black, with some red velvet that comes down to my hair in the back; has some wings on it, and it tips a little to one side when I have it on. Now you know just how it looks!

It was the first time I saw Duluth. The sidewalks are very slushy. You run into everyone with your umbrella, and you're out of breath and have to cough. And between holding your umbrella and skirt and a half-dozen parcels and a big hatbox with four hats in it, and looking for a shoe store, and realizing you have just three hours to do everything and get back to your train – you don't see much of Duluth.

I saw the lake through the fog – a long pier running out into it, and one or two vessels by the side. We passed through more lumber yards and piles of bark, and then we were out of Duluth. I hope I can go sometime when I can see what the city really is. I'm not as disagreeable as you would think from that description of our trip.

I got a *McClure's Magazine* the other day. It has an article about Ian Maclaren and pictures of Drumtochty *(a castellated mansion built in 1812 in Scotland – still there)* and places spoken of in *Bonnie Brier Bush* and *Auld Lang Syne*. Watson was not a hard "digger" at his university. The article says: "Life-long friendships are among the choicest gains of the academic years." I have been reading *Henry Esmond* – I like it – I'm glad I got it. I was prejudiced against Thackeray after reading *Vanity Fair* – I thought I *never* wanted to read anything more of his.

You will get this letter the day you vote. Mr. Johnson's sermon this morning was to those who were going to vote. I almost wish I *could*. I'm going to – for county superintendent. All the teachers are interested in that. I wish all good men were as much interested in politics as they ought to be. It seems to me some who are brave in everything else are cowards in that. They are interested enough in which side will win, but don't try hard enough to know the truth and do their part in making things right.

The gold men had a great parade last night. I wondered where all the men and horses came from. It seemed as if I was looking at all the men in Cloquet packed into the hall at a political speech. And the horses! There were ponies, carriage horses and great strong mill horses. Some had saddles; some had blankets; some nothing at all. The band went first, then men on horse-back – a long line of them; the horses going two by two. Some of the horses were frightened and trembled and shied. Then four sensible old mill horses came stalking along, looking as if they wondered what such a fuss was all about. Then came a long line of men – some with torches; some with lanterns hung on the end of a pole; some with lamp chimneys fixed with pasteboard in the ends and candles. There were a good many lumbermen, with their bright coats and boots that lace up outside their trousers – they reach nearly to the knee. Some of them had on red leggings, and their trousers turned up halfway to the knee. There was an old, old man with a silk hat and a long white beard who walked with a cane. He took long steps, and seemed to look around for a place to step each time, for the streets were very muddy. Next to him was a lumberman who seemed to be looking after him.

It was fun looking down on them all from my window. Everyone had a tin horn – you couldn't hear yourself think while they were passing. That's the way they share their enthusiasm up here! The tin horns fell to the small boys, and they had to toot up during the sermon this morning.

Let's read a book together. You would finish it before I, for I have so little time to read. Shall we? Thanksgiving week is coming on now. We make so much of that in primary grades.

Time to close. I miss you terribly.

With my love,

Anna

NOVEMBER 6, 1896
Oronoco to Cloquet

My Dearest Anna:

What black nights we're having – regular November nights. I believe they're the darkest in the year. Faith, I was afraid, almost, back in the woods – I believe our old mill is *haunted*. When I've been there alone in the afternoons, time and again I hear the door click and open, and I turn and the door is *shut*. And there in the backroom, sometimes I have the feeling someone stands beside me, and when I look – lo! Thin air. Do you suppose it's some troubled water sprite that comes up through the flume? I'm a-talking through my chapeau ….

Speaking of chapeaus – oh, I'd like to see you in that new hat! The broad and black one, trimmed with red velvet, that comes down to your hair behind, and sits a bit to one side. I'd like that one, I guess. Why don't people wear soft white hats anymore?

Well, I exercised the right of a freeman Tuesday. Oronoco went 61 majority for McKinley and sound money, and as Oronoco goes, so goes the world. I'm tired of campaign eloquence and literature. Sometimes when they spread it on so thick, it's enough to make one vote for the wrong side – if you knew which one that was. It's all right, though, to stir people up and get them to thinking – though I'm opposed to thinking generally, ain't I?

Tell me I'm all right next time you write, please. It seems an age since I saw you. Perhaps you wouldn't know me – shall I tell you how I look? Well, about the same size as usual, and the features not altered so much as one would think. As to attire – gray trousers (a trifle dusty and ragged, just at present) and an old tan sweater (which is boss for grinding feed – fits snug and keeps the dust out), and to crown all in this magnificent figure – a blue cap.

(What a goose of a letter this is going to be. Forgive me, for auld lang syne.)

All kinds of folks come to the mill. George Nye – the old raven I told you of once, who always goes to funerals and likes to be around lifeless humanity – came yesterday. He said to me, "You ain't quite so fat as you were in the summer, are you?" I told him I was a little *fatter*. I suppose he thought what a beautiful corpse I'd make. Fred says he always says the same thing to *him*. If I die first and George Nye comes to my funeral, Charlie is going to shoot him; and if Charlie dies first and George comes to his funeral, *I'm* going to shoot him – we've agreed.

Mary has Victor Hugo's *Ninety Three* out of the library, and I've been reading some of that again – have you? I like Victor Hugo – what short sentences he uses. They're very effective too – sometimes pounding away like blows. Mary hardly knows whether she likes it or not. I think, as a rule, she and I don't like the same books. She never read *Lorna Doone*; had it out and started, but didn't finish. She doesn't like *Three Musketeers* or anything like them. She likes *Little Women*, *End of the World*, *Lena Rivers*, etc. She doesn't read Scott, but liked *David Copperfield* and *Daniel Deronda*.

Yes, I'd like very much to read something I knew you were reading. What can we? I'm glad we like the same sort of things as much as we do. Mary's best friend Mable likes Dumas – the duels and adventure. Miss Sperry was the queerest girl about being fond of battles and kindred things.

It's been a little over two months since I saw you. Take care of yourself, dear. This isn't much of a letter, but I'm going to let it go. I love you dearly.

NOVEMBER 8, 1896
Cloquet to Oronoco
My Dearest Roy:

This is another gloomy day. We've had rain and snow and sleet all week. People are out in sleighs today. The icicles hang in a deep fringe from the store across the street, and the sun wouldn't shine for anything. I asked the children one cloudy day last week where the sun was, and one of them said, "It's gone to China." I guess it has – it might as well be there for anything we've seen of it lately.

Things went pretty well this week. I'm getting severe – I think my voice and face and eyes must be growing hard, for I have to be hard-hearted and ruthless all the time. If Johnny whispers, he *has* to stay after school, no matter how he wails. I had to punish a child Thursday – she's a regular little tiger when she's angry. Mr. Cloyd said, "If a child sets his will against yours, stop it immediately, and tell the school to pray while you work, and roll up your sleeves and go at it." I didn't do that exactly – I kept her after school, locked my door, and told her I must punish her. She shook her fists at me and said, "Well, I've got my hands!" She used them too – she stuck a pin into me. I have the marks of her nails on my hand yet.

Well, it didn't last long. I took her in my arms and talked with her after it was over, and we left good friends. I hope I'll never have another such struggle with a child – it makes me hate myself. I guess I wrote you how a month or two ago I talked to a little girl until it seemed to me she must be good – just because I was so anxious to have her so. And right when I thought she must surely see how she had done wrong, she said, "Miss Barnard, have you got a pocket down there for your watch?" Hadn't heard a word I said. There is encouragement too, in seeing for myself that they are learning – even more – in having some of the mothers tell me their children were interested and doing well.

I never read *Ninety Three*. I want to read it sometime. Oh, I wish you were here today – we would read *Henry Esmond* together and talk. You decide what book we shall read together next.

Perhaps *I* haunt the old mill – my thoughts do sometimes. Why can't people haunt places *before* they die, as well as *after*?

I voted too last Tuesday – for a woman! I'm glad my first vote was for a woman. I'm not a "women's rights" woman, but I think it's nice to be a woman and to stand by other women.

I'd forgive you anything, almost, for auld lang syne, but I've nothing to forgive – it wasn't a "goose of a letter." You dear boy – if you were here I could tell you you're all right, and you would know I meant it. But I'm getting to be such a reserved old school marm – I declare, I'm almost afraid to tell you how I love you.

I'll try not to get hard-hearted and cross for your sake, dear, but I know I'm not half so tender-hearted as I was when I commenced last fall. It doesn't trouble me much now to make a child cry. You'd be ashamed of me, but I can't help it.

I must close. Good-night dear, dear Roy.

Anna

We may have only one week for Christmas. If we do, I think I'll stay here and not come home.

I'm inclined to get homesick Sunday evening. Well – not exactly homesick, but lonely. I think about you and miss you so. I think of that night last August, when we were at camp. It's still and beautiful; the crickets are singing for us down at the foot of a tree nearby. My eyes are closed, and I'm trying to feel myself away from you – here in Cloquet, writing to you. You are saying, "You're tired and a bit lonely, perhaps." Then it comes over me with a rush how I will feel, how I *do* feel tonight, and – we must remember, dearest.

NOVEMBER 10, 1896
Oronoco to Cloquet

Dearest Little Girl:

I won't send this after it's written, but I want to speak to you so. Your picture and letter came tonight. I've just been reading it – and your picture, dearest, is so like you – my gentle, sweet little queen. Your picture, when I haven't seen you for so long, touches me deeply. I do remember August, darling – oh, so well.

You didn't mean it, dear, did you – I know you didn't – that your voice and eyes were getting severe and hard, and you were getting so you weren't so tender-hearted. Your eyes wouldn't get that way – I won't let them. You never could get that way, Anna – you *never* could. You're my ideal for gentleness. I would rather lose my right arm and be a coward than have my ideal lessened a bit.

I'm glad for that letter. You mustn't get afraid of me and reserved. I do miss you and think of you – yes – and whisper to you sometimes, though you can't hear. And all the time I love you deep and fierce and strong, with a better, gentler feeling than any other thought brings to me.

Perhaps you won't like this letter. It isn't a letter, but you'll forgive me. Perhaps it sounds like a woman's – I am a woman and a Cossack, I guess.

I love you dearly.

NOVEMBER 12, 1896
Oronoco to Cloquet
My Dearest Anna:

'Tis my night for writing, and I thought I would get at it early and write quite a bit.

We've been bothering Mary a little, telling her great horrible things – for example, how if a man should have his funeral sermon preached and should die in the winter, they could freeze him and sharpen him and drive him like a post and put a flat stone on his head. I got to scuffling with Mary earlier – I vexed her a bit someway, and then told her if she wouldn't accept my 'pologies, I'd bite her; that she wasn't a young lady for me – just my sister – and I had an inalienable right to bite my own sister, while I would never bite ordinary ladies. I did bite her then (well, not hard), and she fought – pulled my hair. Mary is strong and heavy, but I scrapped easy and tired her out. You never can scuffle hard with a girl – you're afraid of breaking them someway.

I also got to scuffling with Val Shay – a general rough chap – yesterday in the mill. When we crashed down to the floor, he struck his face on the hopper and cut it. I didn't mean it to happen, but he came in and started scrapping when I was busy grinding. I was sorry, but 'twasn't my fault – he's such a rough creature.

Well, you don't care about this ….

It's kinda cold here. I don't like cold weather. We have about a foot of snow. Tuesday it was some comfort to see the sun, which we have not seen for a long time. I like spring and fall, but summer best of all. Maybe we should live where it's warm? And I have a huge cold, and yesterday worked sort of mechanically, and felt that big, dazed feeling one has with a cold. I did a lot of grinding yesterday, and today the stone was up being dressed. I had other tasks as well – like Caesar, "had all things to do at one time." Today, all day, I felt merry and good.

After the snow was over, the woods were like a dreamland, for the snow clung thick on everything. In the night it had cleared, and the sky was bright pale blue – winter sky – and it was good to see the sun again.

I wish I could see you. I know you're there, just the same, but it isn't like having you right before me. I like that last picture – it was taken in Winona, when you came down from the car when I was waiting for you.

If I'm tiresome in my letters, please tell me, and I'll try and be careful. I hate to do stupid things.

Lately, I've been out with the boys after rabbits. I'm not used to shooting with a shotgun and at things running, and the first day I shot a good many times, but didn't *get* anything. I was ashamed – I had "missed my kill," as Mowgli says (Kipling's *Jungle Stories*, you know), and I was angry. The next time I did better. We slew – the four of us – 15 those two hunts.

There – I shouldn't tell you about rabbit-shooting. I don't like it especially myself, though I wasn't very murderous – Charles and Fred did most of it.

Sleep is in my eyes. Take care of yourself, dearie, and don't worry. There's no one like you in the world.

With my love,

Wait – I'll try and think what we shall read together. I wonder what there is good we both haven't read and can both get it?

Yesterday was your birthday – I thought of it all day. I wanted to send a remembrance to show I thought of it, but could think of nothing but my bowie knife, and I didn't know as you would care for that (!).

NOVEMBER 15, 1896
Cloquet to Oronoco
My Dearest Roy:

Your letter that "isn't a letter" is one of the best you ever wrote! I didn't know you cared so much.

I've watched myself this week – tried to see if I really am severe and hard-hearted. My voice *is* harsh and sharp sometimes. When Johnny isn't minding, I can't call him to a halt, and at the same time keep my class interested and see that every child in the room is at work, unless I speak that way. Some of them don't need it; some are hurt worse by a *look*. I'm surprised and ashamed – there ought to be some other way of getting at everyone than by being *severe*. I believe there is, but when a child must be stopped *right there*, and there isn't time or chance to attend to him individually, I *have* to be severe. I believe there are teachers who always speak gently, and I do the best I can, but I *can't* always make them mind by being gentle.

If you could step into my school room someday and spend an hour or two there, you would go out with your ideal of me shattered. I almost wish you could, for you ought not to go on thinking of me as I'm not – I would much rather you found it out now. I think I have a deeper sympathy with children, and understand them better, and really care more for them than I used to. I'll try to be as gentle as I can, dear – for your sake.

Three of us had birthdays Wednesday – Mr. Cloyd was 32, Miss Lynch 25, and I 22. Mrs. Thompson invited some folks over, and made birthday cakes for each of us. We had quite a bright table – the other tables were envious! We each had a birthday letter from the Episcopal minister who boards here. Two of the cakes had rings in them – Miss Lynch and Mr. Thompson found them. After supper we came up to the parlor and told stories.

Last night Mr. Thompson took all the teachers sleigh-riding except me. I have taken more cold and am about laid up. They all packed into a big sleigh. Mr. Cloyd was feeling gay, and they had a splendid time. I watched them get started, and then did as I used to when I was little and had a cold and couldn't go sliding – came to my room and cried because I couldn't go too. I'm 22 and not yet grown up. I didn't go down to dinner today. Miss Roth brought me some tea. Mr. Cloyd scolded me because I don't take care of myself. He thinks because I have a cold and don't get over it that it's carelessness.

I'm going to California next year – what's the use of staying here and only half living half the year? I feel 60 years old all the time, and have for the last month. When you graduate a full-fledged "medic" you may come to California too, if you want to. I'm no good to myself or anyone else half the time in this cold country.

My dearest, dearest Roy. I ought to be ashamed to answer your good letters in this way. My cold makes me savage. I do love you, dear, and I want so much to be all that you think me.

With my love,

Anna

Things have been pulling me a hundred different ways. I'm not kidding about that California plan, although I'm not sure it would be better for me. You know how I used to cough in high school? It seems to be worse instead of better each winter, except the one winter I spent east. But how could I go there away from you for so long? Oh, I should like to see you so tonight. I'm glad you like my picture. Good-night, dearest, dearest Roy.

NOVEMBER 17, 1896
Oronoco to Cloquet

Madchen:

I'm afraid my letter bothered you, dear – I didn't mean it so. You must remember I'm not very practical in some things, and you mustn't take too much stock in what I say. There – isn't that frank? I know very well one must be firm and resolute to lead people, and I know that my ideal wouldn't be shattered, as you say, should I come into your schoolroom. I wish I had your dear head in my arms, and then I think I could make you understand. You are all right, I'm sure – of course you're human and get cross sometimes. It doesn't matter, Anna – I love you anyway.

I'm so sorry about your cold. If I could only eat and breathe and pump blood for two. And, dearie, you must never think you must write "good" letters to me – dinna, *dinna* do it ever, unless you feel like it. We are comrades and will share things all we can, shan't we? Think of the blue, morose doses I've inflicted on you, when nothing real and tangible was the matter with me, and you're half-sick and tired and perhaps blue and discouraged for the time.

Please, dearie – write to me as you feel. I think California would be *good* for you. Of course, to be away from you so long – well, it would be like a foretaste of death, but the right kind of love will reach across heaven, they say. It's a good plan. We'll talk about it.

Good-night – yes, in the old way.

Roy

You felt blue when you were writing me, didn't you? I won't try to cheer you up – how a body hates to be told everything is all "skittles and beer" when it doesn't seem so at all. Now don't try to write me a good letter; I'm no fair-weather folk, I hope.

NOVEMBER 22, 1896
Cloquet to Oronoco

My Dearest:

I've been reading some of your letters this afternoon. We are the *best* comrades – the best that ever lived, I believe. I know you didn't mean your letter to bother me, and it didn't – only that I realized more how you cared if I grew cross and hard-hearted.

My cold is some better. Mr. Cloyd asked the other teachers to take charge of my children in the halls, and to attend to my lines when they go home, so I don't have to step out of the school room, except when I go to school and come home.

I have to lead Christian Endeavor tonight. There is to be a convention here next Friday and Saturday, so only three days of school next week! We have extra work, examinations and reports to make, so I'm glad for the break.

Mr. Bolton came home this week from a hunting trip – six deer. Sometimes I see them brought into town – I saw a man with one on his shoulders. It's such a pity to kill the beautiful things.

I had a letter from Mother yesterday. She thinks I'd better go somewhere else next year too; that I may be able to get a school there in California, even if Pres. Shepard can't help me.

I'm going to do as you say and not write a good letter. It seems to me I can't think of anything to say to you, but I've been thinking of you all day – from the time I first awakened this morning.

With my dearest love.

Anna

Did my last letter have any little finger marks on it? I sent it to the office with one of my boys.

NOVEMBER 25, 1896
Oronoco to Cloquet

Dearest Anna:

I'm so glad that cold of yours is even a little better. It's been bothering me to think how you were feeling. You don't feel more than 59½ years old now, do you?

Won't the spring seem good? We're having beastly weather just now. Yesterday it rained and sleeted, and the rain froze as it fell, so this morning a body's life was in danger – everything had a coat of mail. Today it's rained all day with a thick fog – London weather, I guess.

Last week we had some fine skating – evenings, mostly. I wonder if the motion and sensation of skating is anything like waltzing? I've gotten better at it. Thursday evening it began to snow, and there was moonlight bright enough to see well. Charles and I skated quite a ways that evening – several hours after supper – and we felt we had our "sea legs" by the time we finished. And oh, what a flood tide of hunger I had! Auntie was still sitting up when we came home, and she got me bread and butter and peach preserves and beans and a baked apple – 'twas a lunch to remember. Are you hungry nowadays? I should think it would be hungry work if you weren't feeling well.

Tomorrow is Thanksgiving Day. The turkey is stuffed. Wonder what you will be doing. We're just going to have a good dinner and not grind feed.

Did you ever read *Daniel Deronda*? I never did – Mary liked it. She has *Lorna Doone* out of the library, and I'm reading it again. I've read on past the time when Tom Faggus came, and a bit farther where the Doones robbed "Uncle Ben" and tied him on the pony. I still believe *Lorna Doone* is the sweetest, most wholesome story in the world – what is it I like about it so? Perhaps because it came across me just at the right age and in the right time o' year.

Last Sunday I read "The Minister of St. Bede's" in *Ladies Home Journal* – probably you read it – Ian Maclaren's. I liked it too. That magazine has other good things in it besides "Side-Talks" *(a popular column that attracted thousands of letters from young women and girls)*, hasn't it?

Walter Bowers' mother died Sunday morning, and, of course, Walter is home. She has been getting worse all fall – it was paralysis, you know. I'm sorry for them.

Guess I've nothing more to tell you – only to take care of yourself, Maisie, and don't worry yourself more than you want to. I've had a cold for a month. It got on top of my lungs and made me cough, and I have the tag end of it yet. It didn't knock me out at all, of course.

I liked your last letter, even if it was short – I can't tell you exactly why, but I did. It seemed as if you really had been thinking of me, and touched my hand, and told me so kindly.

Dear heart, I love you.

NOVEMBER 26, 1898
Cloquet to Oronoco

Dearest Roy:

The girls have all gone to church except me. I'm staying in, trying to keep from taking cold. It's a stormy day. It rained last night and now it's turned into sleet. It's the kind of a day one likes to stay in and read and write.

I went to a Masonic dance last night. Most of the teachers went. We had a good time, and I danced some. The people here go into everything with might and main. You would like to watch them dance – they all talk and laugh and skip around. They're as different as can be from the dances I went to in the east – they're more dignified there.

The members of the School Board and the teachers made up a dance together. Some of the Board had not danced for years, and most of the teachers didn't know how very well. Mr. Cox and I were always dancing when we ought *not* to, or wondering what to do next when we *ought* to be. Then we'd get switched off somewhere where we didn't belong, and throw the whole thing out of place, and the rest would yell at us and gesticulate, and the music would twiddle-do-twiddle-de, and we would take hold of hands and skip back.

I haven't read much. I wish it didn't storm so – I would go down to the library for a book. My cold is better, I think – I feel better, anyhow. I don't seem to be in letter-writing mood, but I could *talk* to you, dear, if you were here.

With my love,
Anna

DECEMBER 3, 1896
Oronoco to Cloquet

My Dearest Anna:

What shall I say that you care about? Glad to the heart am I, damsel, that thou recoverest thy wanted health and spirits, though I marvel but little in good sooth that Boreas so clingeth about thee. Wast not courtly said?

It seems longer than usual since I wrote you. Thanksgiving Day was like April – it rained and rained and wasn't at all like November. I ate two dinners – one at Reifsniders at noon, and another at 4 with my own kin. That night it turned cold, and the roads froze hard as iron, and in all shapes, and they are that way now.

I went to Rochester to see Walter the next day on the stage. It was awful cold, and the roads were a fright. We had a balky, kicking team, and there were five of us – any one of whom would weigh no more than a partridge. Going down the hill about halfway to town the front wheel on my side went all to pieces, and down dropped the blooming old covered stage. It caught my left foot under the whole business and held it there, and there we lay next to the kicky old nags' heels. But they didn't *run*, else I would have no left foot to write to you about. It pounded and lamed me, but not enough that I couldn't skate. No one was hurt. My hat blew off, too – over seven or eight miles of prairie. The bad luck all came from going back after a buffalo coat, but that's another story.

On the street I saw Mrs. Titus a minute. It seemed so good to see her – she looked hale and hearty. She inquired for news from the north, and I told her how things were all well with you, except the colds accursed. I came up on the train with Walter Saturday – as far as the Oronoco switch. I was kinda glad I wasn't going away to live in a room on campus again.

Sunday I had a good skate, and an hour or so of it again yesterday. Anna – you don't care a bit about all this, do you now, really? I'm going to stagger on through it all, however, and tell you how poor Rube fell on the ice and hurt his head terribly – nearly cracked his skull; how I've been grinding feed; and all what the weather is. No, I won't do it – I'll be a good lad and tell you good-night. It's plain to see I canna write just now.

With my dear love,

Roy

DECEMBER 6, 1896
Cloquet to Oronoco

My Dear, Dear Roy:

This is a beautiful morning, and I feel oh so good and strong and well. I'm almost over the cough – just a little once in a while is all that's left.

I thought of the beginning of a hymn I heard in Houlton when I woke this morning:

> "Still, still with Thee, when purple morning breaketh
> When the bird waketh and the shadows flee
> Fairer than morning, lovelier than the daylight
> Dawns the sweet consciousness
> I am with thee
> Alone with Thee, and the mystic shadows

The solemn hush of Nature newly born
Alone with Thee in breathless adoration,
In the calm dew and freshness of the morn."

(The hymn is by Harriet Beecher Stowe, author of Uncle Tom's
Cabin.*)*

I'm beginning Christmas work in school this week (the children are full
of it already). I'm thankful I can sing again and teach them some Christmas
songs. Oh, I like teaching better than ever before! I never did anything I like
so well as my work this year. I'm going to read *The Birds' Christmas Carol* to
them. It's such a beautiful time to teach the thought of unselfishness and love.
I'm glad of these lessons for myself – I need them more than the children do
– I get cross and unkind sometimes.

I made some sewing cards yesterday. It's a bell with Merry Christmas
across it. Mr. Cloyd sent for sewing cards for us so we wouldn't have to make
them. Most of the children believe in Santa Claus, but some declare, "There
ain't no Santa Claus, but just your father and mother." We ignore all such
remarks. One little fellow came to me – his face fairly shining, he was so eager
to tell me – and said, "Santa Claus isn't coming to Cloquet this year, they say,
so I'm going to Duluth, where he *is* coming, and then he'll find me!" They
have a Santa Claus in the bakery, and they give the children a peep of him.
You ought to hear the discussion as to whether he's a "truly" Santa Claus or
not.

Mr. Cloyd and some of the people in town are doing a great deal for the
poor. Mr. Cloyd keeps close track of the children – he has provided shoes for
ever so many. I received a note from the mother of one of my children, telling
me that if I found that any child lacked warm clothing, to send them to her
husband's clothing store. The people are so ready to help, and they say they
depend on the teachers and doctors to know where to give. You know the
mills were closed most of the summer.

I got *Daniel Deronda* from the library yesterday. I commenced it last
summer when we were camping. I read to you the part where Gwendolen has
hopes of being an actress, and tells Klesmer about it, and how Klesmer talks
to her and discourages her so. Suppose we read this together? I have finished
Henry Esmond – I liked it. Thackeray is all right, in spite of *Vanity Fair*. I'm
not reading "The Minister of St. Bedes." I didn't get the beginning of it, but I
read the rest of the last *Home Journal*.

We have lots of fun among ourselves here. Miss Ferguson has been taken
sleigh riding and skating with Mr. Batson a good many times. Mr. Cloyd says

she's a disgrace, but we just tease her some. When they came home, we stood in our doors all down the hall and sang, "Blest be the Tie that Binds."

There! I'll stop now. I wrote all this as punishment to you for not telling me more of your tales!

Lovingly,
Anna

DECEMBER 10, 1896
Oronoco to Cloquet

My Dearest Anna:

It's quite early in the evening. I've read your letter again, and been sitting comfortably and thinking moderately. Don't be frightened – I shan't wreak all my thoughts on your helpless head. Imagine how *glad* I am, dear, to know you're feeling so well and good.

We've had three beautiful spring-like days – wind in the north, thawing, a fresh smell, and warm skies at sunset. It seems unusually good because we've had so very little sunlight all fall. It's lovely in the morning to look down from the top story of the mill and see the hills up the river all red with the light.

How little Volney likes his mom! He always has Fred draw him pictures of the moon, and every night when there is one, he stands and watches it. The first night he took me by the finger – we were alone in the dark – and pulled me where we could see. "Stars," he said, "many – my, my!" and then made that noise people make with their tongues when they're filled with amazement. He's a great little boy – talks a good deal. I ask him, "Where's the king?" and he points to himself; and then, "Where's the king's ox?" and he points to me! (This idea is from *King Solomon's Mines*.)

I remember so well when you read me some from *Daniel Deronda*. Yes, we'll read it – I have the first volume here now – perhaps I can read a bit after I'm through writing.

Mary's feeling kind of sad. Mabel Clapp – her *very* great friend – is going away to school in Painesville, Ohio. Her rich uncle and aunt came out to Minnesota on a visit, and Mabel is going to be sent away to school. How excited the girl is! Her Uncle Kip isn't inclined to do things by halves, and very likely she will see Wellesley or somewhere 'fore she's through, and "Aunt Ada says she'll see to my wardrobe." Mabel and Mary came to the mill to break the news to me, and I am mightily pleased – Mabel is smart as steel. I wish Mary could go too. Well, Mary is downcast, of course, because her friend goeth from her, albeit glad to have her go.

Don't girls generally get to be *very much* friends with some other girl and can't live without them? Wouldn't it be brutal to tell them they would get over it eventually? Mary is a great deal nicer girl, I think. I must try and console her a little.

It's good you like your work and are so pleased with this year. I'm better pleased with this year too than I have been with the last two. I'm doing my work every day and not dragging on anyone, and I'm well and getting stronger. I want to be in good form for next year and the years to come. I hope things will come right for next fall.

Are you coming to Minneapolis for Xmas? When does your school close for the summer? First of June, likely. Six months, oh – it's not nearly so long as nine. Can you imagine how much I want to see you?

With my love,

I saw in the paper that Alexander Salvini's wife said he was "on the road to recovery." He has been at his father's villa in Italy. Twice the doctors gave him up, and it seemed as if one couldn't be so ill and live. But they took him to Florence, where he got better after a change of weather and an operation, and he's getting well. I knew he wouldn't die easily – I'm so glad! We'll see him again sometime. *(In fact, Salvini died Dec. 15 – right after Roy saw his performance.)*

CHAPTER 22

Jekyll and Hyde

DECEMBER 13, 1896
Cloquet to Oronoco
My Dear Roy:

I've just come home from church. We had a good sermon this morning. We have had beautiful spring-like weather all week. I feel spring-like too – I will be so glad when spring *really* comes.

Yesterday morning I opened the window and watched the sun rise. Oh, the sky – such beautiful shades of pink and gold! The air was frosty, and the smoke from the mills seemed to form a hazy cloud. But then Mr. Cutliff appeared in the street below, fired a snowball at me, and the enchantment was gone. I went down to breakfast of "oatmeal cakes and coffee please."

Saturday was a good day. We went calling in the afternoon. I used to dislike making calls, but now that the people I call on are the mothers of the children, I like to meet them. After dinner we went into the parlor and had a little sing and read part of *A Houseboat on the Styx* by John Kendrick Bangs.

Our lesson in church was about temperance, and the superintendent asked those who were "abstainers" to raise hands. I couldn't raise my hand – I've taken whiskey and glycerin for my cough for the last month. I've drunk cider too. Some of the students in my class all looked at me. Mr. Bolton said he couldn't raise his hand either. He had just been talking about truthfulness – the children had promised to try to be absolutely truthful in every way. In some ways I don't like Mr. Cloyd at all. He's hard on people – he thinks his judgment is right, and if someone isn't what he thinks they ought to be, he hasn't any sympathy or patience with them. He doesn't approve of dancing, and he uses every opportunity to say mean things of those who do. He never seems to think it's wrong to say mean, cutting things. He never has said anything to hurt my feelings, except when he took me to due about "letting my cold go." But he's always stepping on someone's toes.

I'm reading *Daniel Deronda*. One side of Deronda makes me think of you: "His early-wakened sensibility and reflectiveness had developed into a many-sided sympathy, which threatened to hinder any persistent cause of actions," and "His imagination had so wrought itself to the habit of seeing things as they appeared to others, that a strong partisanship – unless against immediate oppression – was an insincerity for him." I wonder if I'm wrong in thinking that side of him is a bit like you – do I understand you or not?

I know my last letter was so filled with enthusiasm for my work, and how I like everyone and everything so well – I hope it wasn't too much. I'm glad you're happy too, this year. School closes the last of May. I shall be home by June first. June, June, June!! It will always be the best, the sweetest month in the year for us, won't it?

I have just read what I wrote about Deronda. I don't mean, dear, that I think you're unable to "persist" in any "cause of action." I think you'll understand what I mean when you read that part of the book, but I wanted to try to explain.

Miss Roth has been reading *Days of Auld Lang Syne*, and we talked it over some. Have you read it? Mother is reading *Dale Carnegie* and likes it.

Oh, dear – must close now. With my dearest love,

Your Little Girl

DECEMBER 17, 1896
Oronoco to Cloquet

My Dearest Anna:

I like your last letter – it's just a dear one. I'll send this to Minneapolis. I'm glad you're going to spend Xmas there with your folks.

I'm reading pretty deep into the first volume of *Daniel Deronda*. I like him – what I've seen of him – very much. I don't know, dearie, whether I'm like him in the way you spoke of. It would be a pretty easy way to explain away my shortcomings, wouldn't it? I've read enough about the man to see the truth of it. Perhaps there's a little resemblance (don't think me conceited!).

I never read *Days of Auld Lang Syne*. I've read *Beside the Bonnie Briar Bush*, and that's about all. I'll read it sometime. Let's see – Ian Maclaren is a realist, isn't he? I rather like him even if he is. I like "romanticists," you know.

It has been snowing almost all day, and there wasn't much to do in the mill. You don't know what's coming, or how much – I like that about it – to have hard runs and then calms. Father had rather have it moderate all the time.

One afternoon last week I went hunting with Charlie after jack-rabbits. They're working into this country from the west – big, white fellows that weigh 10, 15, even 20 pounds. It was warm – the snow was all off, except in the woods (you hunt jacks on the prairie, you know). The fields were three or four inches deep with mud, and we tramped around quite a distance to the north, but found no trace of jacks. We were resting on a pile of rocks on a hill when we saw two little lone white spots on the black ground 'bout half a mile off. One ran before we got near, and we banged away with the rifles, but didn't get him. The other I shot right through the eyes. It didn't hurt him any – you're not sorry I shot him right, are you? I was glad to get one the first time out, for Fred had been hunting several times and only got one.

Honest, I won't tell you any more hunting stories until I kill a mastodon in Alaska, if you don't want me to.

I don't believe much in having people stand up – I don't like it. I presume if they asked all those who were not *excessively* addicted to the cocaine habit to stand up, I should sit right there. I should think with children who care more for what you thought of them, and hated to be different from others and had a keen sense of shame, it would tend to make them stagger out of the line of truth a little, don't you think so? It would be a temptation. (Am I talking like a *good* book? I guess not a bit, now that I think of it.)

Yes, June is good and sweet. This one that is coming will be best of all – nine months is *so* long. Dear heart, I will be *so* glad to see you. I liked your letter – you are the *dearest* little girl.

Roy

DECEMBER 20, 1896
Cloquet to Oronoco

My Dearest Roy:

I've just been reading *Deronda* – he *does* make me think of you; his sympathy and interest in others, and his sensitiveness for the feelings of others.

Tell me all the hunting stories you please – I'm hardened to cruelty. I don't know if there are any jack rabbits here or not – there are lots of little "cotton tails." I told the children a story about "Molly Cottontail" – they were much interested.

This has been an eventful week. Mr. Cloyd came into my room just after recess one day. Some of the children had come in noisily, and I sent them back to come in over again, so we were slow getting started. He came in just as they were taking their books. I counted the "one, two, three," according to instruction (I can't bear it; it's like being in prison), but the class didn't take books as I counted – each child grabbed his book as he pleased. That made Mr. Cloyd "wrathry." He took them in hand, made them take books over and over, and shook the heads of several because they weren't quick enough. He then picked up a little fellow because he didn't get his books in his desk on "three" and spanked him. The boy cried and howled; Mr. Cloyd told him to stop; he couldn't, and Mr. Cloyd spanked him three times to make him stop crying. He made him put his hands down and cry before them all. Then the boy's little sister began to sob – that drew Mr. Cloyd's attention away from her brother, and he pounced down on *her*, shook her, and acted so brutally I was ashamed of him. It disgusted me to see that great man acting so horribly to a little girl – almost a baby – just because she showed some sympathy for her brother.

Then he had me go on with the work, telling me first that I hadn't enough snap – that the children were doing as they pleased. The children were so frightened they didn't know anything, and so was I. I was going to let the boy off without reciting, but Mr. Cloyd called on him – oh, he's heartless. I expected to get a talking to privately, but he's never said a word to me about that or my work since. The old teachers say it's nothing unusual for him to act so.

When we went to breakfast yesterday, I rehearsed my quotation for teachers' meeting as I came downstairs. Mr. Cloyd said, "It must have been short." I said, "It's quite a distance from my room." "Well, if you came downstairs as slow as you came into the dining room, I guess there was plenty of time," he said. I'm sorry His Royal Highness doesn't like my manner of walking. It amuses the girls to have him act so snappish to me, for he remarked at table one day that Miss Barnard was his pet, and they've teased me about it – not before him, of course.

If I admired Mr. Cloyd, and had more regard for his opinion, I should feel badly, but I don't care much. If I'm a failure, I wonder that he didn't find it out before. He's told me repeatedly that if he saw anything wrong with my work he'd tell me. If they don't want me in Cloquet another year, I presume I can find a place somewhere else. Mr. Cloyd in some moods is charming; in other moods he's despicable. We're all more or less Dr. Jekyll and Mr. Hyde, so I ought not to judge. I've told you what I think – now I'll stop thinking about it and try to see the good side of him, and please him as far as I can.

I must tell you what my little Indian said. He put his head under his desk, and when he raised it, he had something in his mouth. "What have you in your mouth, Willie?" I asked. "Gum." I took him by the shoulder and walked him to the waste basket. He spit it out, and I saw that it was apple. "Why, Willie Cadreaux!" I said. "What made you tell me it was gum, when 'twas apple?" He stood with his eyes on the piece of apple for a minute, and said, in a scared voice, "I thought it was *gum*." I disgraced myself by laughing – a good hard laugh it was, too – and, of course, when I laughed, the children did too. A teacher ought not to have any sense of humor, should they? I'm always laughing in the wrong place. I should've been severe and warned against telling wrong stories. The children will think it's cute to tell lies now, I suppose. Did I tell you that this boy's sister said, "A wife is what a man has to cook for him."

The children were talking at recess. One said, "I saw a live elephant." Another said, "That's nothing – *I* saw a live *clown*." Most of them believe in Santa Claus. They wrote letters to him – I'll send you one.

People sometimes ask me the queerest questions. Mr. Cloyd said something once that shows he knows some of my people died of consumption. He also said, "I know a great deal more about you than you think I do." Mr. Thompson asked me what my mother's maiden name was – what does he care? Why don't they ask me what my great-great grandfather's business was, and his religious views? 'Twould be more sensible.

I must stop – there goes the supper bell.

With my dearest love,

Anna

Here's one of the children's Santa letters – isn't it darling?

Dear Santa Claus,

Are you coming to Cloquet this year? I will watch for you. I want to make someone happy just as you do.

Will you please bring me a horn, and a sled with a horse, and a jump-and-jack, and a pare of skates, and a drum, and a boy doll, and a ball, and a schoolbook.

Eddie McMulrey

DECEMBER 23, 1896
Oronoco to 1012 8th St. S.E. Minneapolis

My Dearest:

I'm just "home from the ball." It's very early, but the spirit moves me, so I'm going to write.

Today was Uncle George's birthday, and there was a clan gathering, and we younger folks came in the evening after supper. We had quite a good time.

I don't like your Mr. Cloyd, what I know of him – I dinna like him at all. Don't try and tell a lot of good things about him next time – it cuts no ice. 'Twas hard for you, dear, wasn't it? I wouldn't like to have seen your face, and that's saying a great deal. He's a grand inquisitor, isn't he? It's a hideous feeling for a sensitive child not to be allowed to hide his face at time of need. 'Course, I'm just a kid, comparatively, and never learned such things out of books – but I was little and sensitive once. I never had such a thing as that to go through, but I know how he felt.

You can't talk back, can you, because you're a lady? I dinna like him, I say. Don't let things bother you more than you can help. You're a sensible little girl – although we did agree once that we were both not sensible, and then rejoiced at the fact.

I will try to be gentle about you as I can – it won't be hard, knowing you. That's one of the things I pray for always, as I told you once. (I would hate to have anyone but you read this.)

Friday is Christmas. I wanted to send you something good for reading during vacation time. I couldn't go in person, but I sent a list with Mother half as long as my arm, and then they had nothing I wanted at the store. What can I do? Here's an idea – if you're downtown, would you be kind enough to stop at Donaldson's or somewhere and get *Prairie Folks* by Hamlin Garland, or the little book of short stories by R.L. Stevenson – *The Merry Men and Other Tales and Fables*? There are only two stories in this last that are any good – "Thrawn Janet" and "Olalla" – but they make up for all the others, I think. Well, get it, and, as Uncle Grant says, "Let me pay the shot." Pest that I am – 'tis a queer proposal, isn't it? Don't do it if it's too much bother. You're not offended, are you? I wouldn't hurt you for the wide world, dearest. If I couldn't have got these, I would look at Stevenson's *Child's Garden of Verses*, perhaps the *Moss-hags*, or Kipling's *The Courting of Dinah Shadd*, *Soldiers Three* and others.

I'd like to see you. I'm getting a little bit sleepy, but only a little, for this is a wakeful sort of night – one when a body's cheeks are a little hot and he can stay awake all night. I'm enjoying myself this year – it's good to be at home. The mill work seems a "snap" to me, and I'm exercising quite a bit, as I intended.

Dearie, if I ever say anything that hurts or grates on you, know that it's because I was stupid. I never mean to.

With my dear love,

Roy

DECEMBER 29, 1896
Minneapolis to Oronoco

My Dear Roy:

We have a hard time finding what we want for each other this Christmas, don't we? I hunted and hunted for *Auld Lang Syne*. They said it wasn't to be found in St. Paul or Minneapolis, but last night I found one copy – the only one in the store. It looks a bit dusty, but it's the right one. I wanted to give it to you because I like it so well; and perhaps, when you're old, and my "prophecy" is fulfilled, you will come across the book, and be reminded of *our* days of Auld Lang Syne. I looked at the Glass Block for the books you spoke of – the only one they had was *A Child's Garden of Verse*. I'll look somewhere else.

There's a Teachers Association that meets in St. Paul today and tomorrow. Mr. Cloyd and several of our teachers and I are coming down. I wish I hadn't said so much about Mr. Cloyd. I expected to get lectured at the next teachers' meeting. Instead, he spoke of his own faults, and said that almost every morning as he came into his office he thought of something he had done the day before that he ought to be ashamed of.

I don't believe you know how hard it is for a teacher to keep gentle. If I have helped you to be gentle, it will be *you*, now, who are helping me. No, dearest – I'm not offended. I believe we have always gloried in the fact that we do things differently from anyone else.

I go back to Cloquet Saturday. We're invited out this afternoon, so I must stop.

With my love,

Anna

CHAPTER 23

Brave, Persevering Spirit

1897

William McKinley inaugurated as President.

Rudyard Kipling publishes *Captains Courageous*.

H.G. Wells publishes *The Invisible Man*.

Edmond Rostand publishes *Cyrano de Bergerac*.

"Katzenjammer Kids" – the first American comic strip – is created by Rudolph Dirks.

Henri Rousseau exhibits his painting "Sleeping Gypsy."

Queen Victoria celebrates her Diamond Jubilee.

Ronald Ross discovers the malaria bacillus.

J.J. Thomson discovers the electron.

JANUARY 6, 1897
Oronoco to Cloquet

My Dearest Anna:

I've just read your letter. Been thinking lots about you the last two or three days – no harm saying so, is there?

I'm glad you liked *Days of Auld Lang Syne* – I liked it too. I read *Men of the Moss Hags* last winter. I don't like Maisie as well as May Maxwell, and I like the Wull-cat Will. Of what different things those two Scotchmen write, eh? I finished *Daniel Deronda* last week. Yes, I like it pretty well – oh, more than that. Grandcourt wasn't altogether despicable, was he – he was "no fool." But I hated him worse than if he had been altogether despicable. Poor Gwendolen – I like her and feel sorry for her.

I won't say any more, for I'm pretty dry in my literary chat – so different from my customary brilliant remarks (!). I want to read *Charles O'Malley* – you've heard of it – an old book – one of Charles Lever's, I think.

People away at school, teaching, etc., know how to appreciate holiday time best. The family has been together several times this winter. It seems good – I'm enjoying myself very much in a quiet way. I'm very well, and the work seems nothing – we usually get through early.

I went hunting last week with Charlie after "jacks." We got a six or seven-mile walk, and didn't find any – I didn't break my heart over it. I'm sorry, but I'm afraid I'm not so bloodthirsty as Caligula – not a hero. I like to hunt well enough, but not so well as Charlie – in him it amounts to a passion. Where I'm strong is in liking so many things (or perhaps 'tis a weakness). A body can do anything if they want to hard enough.

If you were teaching in Minneapolis, and I were there too, and I could see you once in a while – it would be something to look forward to. It wouldn't hurt me at all – how could it? But you were thinking to go to California – dearie, do as you think best. But it would be so very good to see you oftener than once or twice in nine months. But you must leave me altogether out of your decision.

It's getting late. You mustn't take to drinking to excess, Anna. Several times in your letter you have mentioned various bouts in which you participated – glycerin and whiskey, etc. Don't be offended – I only want to warn you against *excess*. "Moderation in everything," saith Eugene Sandow – remember this in your orgies (!).

I would give anything to see you. I'm glad you didn't take cold coming from Carlton. May all blessings come to Mr. Lewis for taking such good care of you.

With my dear love,

Roy

JANUARY 14, 1897
Oronoco to Cloquet

My Dearest Anna:

The folks are over to Uncle George's, and I'm staying with Blanche and the boy. They're in the sitting room, blowing bubbles. Of course, we think Volney someway belongs to us all. He is a very *bright* little chap. It's wonderful how rapidly he learned to talk when he started, and the destructiveness in him – how he likes to *hammer* – it takes one person all the time to watch him!

I'm kinda tired tonight. We put in sharp rolls day before yesterday, and took up the stone to dress it. Today was the biggest feed day of the winter yet, and I had to do it alone.

I hope you are feeling better now. I wish you *were* strong as an Amazon (if you want to be). I would want to be Hercules – so's to line up with you. It wouldn't be necessary to be *that* strong. Yes, you would be a power. I like you as you are, though – I admire your brave, persevering spirit, dearie. You are and do more good than big, strong people.

How like a great raw boy I talk. I've been disliking myself today, Anna. There *are* people, aren't there, who could let their lives be turned inside out so's you could see all about them – what they thought and everything? I wouldn't want to be turned wrong-side out. But people might see *good* things they didn't know of, as well as bad, couldn't they? I feel sad and humbled and angry with myself. I'm going to try and do the right thing, my good angel, and be as I said I would that last night when you kissed me on the forehead. One hates to fall below what they think they are. Please don't think I'm a monster of some kind or other, dearie.

How shall I get back on track now, so's not to be abrupt? I don't care if I am.

I liked Jamie Soutar best of all the Drumtochty folk – I think you did too. Jamie could see right through people – the true and the fake – and people felt it too. I'm glad you marked it – I like to notice things that strike you.

I expect I write tedious letters. It's been so long since I saw you. When I opened your letter I was alone by the fireplace, lying close to the firelight to see. Dearest, why didn't you come then?

Roy

I've just read this over, and I ought to tear it up and try again, but I can't seem to write anything as I'd like to tonight.

JANUARY 17, 1897
Cloquet to Oronoco

My Dearest Roy:

We're having quite a blizzard today. It snowed all night and is still snowing. I went to church – only 19 people. Mr. Johnson asked in church study how many books there are in the Bible. No one knew. "How many in the Old Testament?" he asked. "Thirty-six," I said. "How many in the New Testament? "Twenty-seven," I answered. "Then how many in both?" he said, looking at me. I put them together and got 63 – that wasn't right, I thought, so I stared back and said nothing. Then some of the others spoke up for me, and said 63. Then he said the first number was wrong – there are 39 books in the O.T. Miss Gelstone said I ought to have told him that we don't go higher than 10 in the first grade, and he shouldn't ask me such hard questions (!).

The storm is growing worse – I think we'll not go out tonight.

I finished *Men of the Moss Hags* yesterday. Maisie wasn't so human as May Maxwell, was she? She didn't seem so real. I've been reading *Cranford* today – a little book Mother sent me. I never heard of it or the author – Mrs. Gaskell – before. It's quite an interesting book about the people in a little English town and their efforts to be aristocratic. Shall we read another book together? You say what it shall be this time.

Roy, I've almost made up my mind that I'll go to the U. (You said, "You can do *anything* if you want to hard enough.") It won't be next year, or the next, but perhaps the year after that. I'd like to go two years, anyway. I believe I can, and I'd like to know more just for my own sake. Mr. Cloyd wondered why I hadn't gone before. He asked me how it came about that I didn't try for a position in Minneapolis last spring. He must think I'm inclined to aim high – higher than I can reach, likely. I know there was no hope of getting into Minneapolis last year – perhaps there won't be this year.

Mr. Cloyd visited my room more than ever before this week. He's been "doing the grades." He held a special meeting and talked about our work in general, then said he would like to see each teacher alone, and make some criticisms of her work. The rest said they'd take their dose there before us all, but I said I'd rather not. So I went over alone after supper. He laughed as I came in (he was feeling good) and asked me what I thought he would say. I told him, and he said I should write that out, and he would sign his name to it. Of course, he says I haven't enough "snap" (not severe enough) and don't insist on the essentials in writing – that is, sitting straight and holding the pen in the proper position. Is there *anyone* in this wide world who holds the pen properly? I always wrote according to my own sweet will, and sat as I pleased, in spite of my teachers. I wrote an exam at the Normal last year sitting on one foot. Mr. Cloyd says careful attention to those things will make quite a difference in my room. He's pleased with my work, on the whole.

I'm teaching *Hiawatha* to the children. I read parts of it to them, and tell the legends, and put drawings on the board of Indian things. I wish you could hear one little boy say, "Ewa-yea! My little owlet!" He's such a tiny fellow, and he looks so cunning in his little sailor suit with long trousers. He stands as straight as a captain, with his hands behind him, and his voice makes me think of a little silvery brook. Couldn't you teach it to Volney? Tell him the stories and legends about the moon and see if he likes them. Our Bible reading hasn't been together lately. Shall we read Acts? I finish the third chapter tonight.

I'm feeling better. I'm not very hungry yet – been living mostly on lemons, and people think I'm getting pale on that kind of diet. Mrs. Thompson recommends more wine. I have tried to follow your advice, and as my room-mate can tell you, I have not drunk to excess but once, when my fellow teachers put me on a trunk behind the curtains, and kept me there until I got over it.

I have to write a paper on loyalty for a church program to be given by the Christian Endeavor Society. Wonder why they give me such subjects when I never belonged to a church? I presume if I did I'd be loyal to it without a great deal of pulling.

I wish I could have come to you as you lay there in the firelight. It says in *Cranford* that letters are as far from talk between friends as dead, dry flowers in an herbarium are from bright, living flowers. That isn't strong enough. I think if you were here I could make you feel very sure I don't imagine you to be any kind of a *monster*. Whatever it is that troubles you – remember that I can sympathize, for I'm very weak in some ways that I thought myself quite strong in.

I'm not half as good as I ought to be. I wish I were better for your sake – I'm going to try harder.

Anna

JANUARY 21, 1897
Oronoco to Cloquet

Dear Anna:

Half the nine months is gone, isn't it? We'll have to get acquainted again, but that winna be hard or severe.

It snows outside. It was too cold to write in my room, so I'm down here at the table where it's warm and "comfy." I'm tired tonight – ground out at the mill, and then boxed with Lou and a couple other fellows until dark. I like to box, for I have such a 'ard 'ead and sweet temper (!).

I hope you are so you can eat something besides lemon juice – should think you'd run out of energy? Wish you could go to the U. You would like it immensely, wouldn't you though? I think you would find the bright side there.

I haven't heard from Zim this year. Ernest came into the mill a while ago, and I asked him if Frank was home Xmas tide. He said he was, but added that "Frank was stuck on a girl." I axed him was he hard bit, and Ernest said 'twas even so. Poor lost boy – would that I could rescue him. Nay, is better so – who can war against the fates. That's the reason he's neglected his pard – I should have known as much before. Guess I'll write and tantalize him.

We're having fine weather here – it's been a beautiful winter. Do you notice the cold much more there in Cloquet than here?

Yes, we will read something together again. I'll think what. It's very true what you said about letters – and the longer it is without seeing someone, the weaker they seem. Still, they're better than nothing.

I just finished Acts, but I'll read them again. I was reading Matthew. You're very good, dearest – the best of the best to me.

JANUARY 23, 1897
Cloquet to Oronoco

Dearest Roy:

Oh, I'd like to be home today. I've got another hard cold – I could hardly speak above a whisper yesterday. I thought in the morning that I couldn't teach. I usually go to school before 8, but yesterday I sat here in a big easy chair until nearly 8:20. I thought how comfortable I'd be at home – I'd sit by the fire and be waited on, and probably have Dr. Dugan come down, and he'd know what I needed and wouldn't ask 400 questions; how I'd read and just be "comfortably sick." But it was nearly time for the first bell to ring, so I pulled myself together and went over to school. I had to begin talking in a whisper, but my voice cleared a bit after a while, and I got through the day all right.

The children seemed sorry for me, bless them, and wanted to "help Miss Barnard." You wouldn't think such little things could be so thoughtful. They would watch me, and often anticipated what I wanted – or what I wanted them to do. How can there be people who disbelieve in the goodness of human nature? Then the janitor – he really is the best janitor I ever saw – came as I started to dismiss my lines. He met me in the hall and said, "It's too cold for you here, Miss. I'll see to your line." And he did – in good shape, too.

I sent for the doctor last evening. Two of the teachers went. His office is not a block from here, but he was at home – and what did those girls do but go to his house, nearly a mile away. It was nearly 40 below – they almost froze. 'Twas so cold the doctor wouldn't come out, but sent a prescription. I tell you, I'll try to be good to people. The girls pretended they weren't cold – they didn't mind the walk and all that. It was so good of them.

There was a Masonic dance last evening – the teachers were all invited. Here, a Masonic dance is made up of the best people. I intended to go, but couldn't, of course. We teachers had planned to visit a lumber camp today, but had to give it up because of the cold. We were going to take dinner with the lumbermen. Mr. Cloyd has a Kodak, and we would have had some pictures.

It's 20 below. I'm missing all the good things because of this cold. Besides the dance, there was a lecture on Ian Maclaren and Robert Burns by a Scotchman from Duluth. I like to hear him talk – he's such a warm-hearted, kindly old Scotchman. Mr. Bolton went and was much pleased. Mr. Bolton just returned from his home in Amherst – it seems good to have him back again. Don't be *jealous* – you'd like him – he's such a pleasant, unassuming, frank fellow. He never will push to the front like Mr. Cloyd – he hasn't the energy nor the ambition. But he has much more kindness and consideration for people, and is more truly a gentleman than Mr. Cloyd ever dreamed of. Dearest, I think I have told you that you have that fine side – more than anyone I ever knew.

There was a miserable little dog shut up in the post office last night – he howled and scratched all night long. (Our room is over the post office, and you can hear every sound.) It fairly makes your teeth ache to hear that never-resting door go bang! bang! all day long. I'm going to teach the children how to open and close a door!

I'm growing like the writer who was said to have written a chapter on the appearance of a doorknob ....

We had considerable excitement here – Mr. Cloyd *danced*! He even asked us to teach him, and said he intended to go to the Masonic dance. He's always been very much opposed to dancing – raked over the high-school girls for going to dances, and one year was very active in getting people to pledge themselves not to dance. All Cloquet wonders at the change, but he only says he will surprise us more before the year is out.

(I spoke too soon – he's changed back again – he did *not* go to the Masonic dance, and he says no more dancing. How wearisome.)

I'm eating good square meals now. It's queer I'm so hoarse and cough, and yet feel so well. Folks think I ought to be sick in bed, but I go down and eat beans and potatoes and beefsteak and milk, and when they ask me "how I feel," I begin my answer in a voice as hoarse and coarse as some lumberjack, and after many breaks and quavers, end in a whisper. I'm almost ashamed to try to speak in the dining room, for fear strangers will realize that awful voice belongs to me.

Don't be too hard on Frank. You may fall in love yourself someday, and then you'll be better able to understand such things. Take this advice from your old grandmother – deal gently with the lad. Remember Jerome K. Jerome's words – "'tis like the measles!"

I have commenced *Romola*. I finished *Cranford* and have read a little book, *Coffee and Repartee* by J.K. Bangs. I think I told you about reading *The Houseboat on the Styx*.

My shoulder is beginning to ache, and I guess your eyes will ache by this time too. Good-night, dearest, dearest.

Anna

You asked about the cold. I don't feel it so much as I did in Rochester, for the house is heated by furnace, and I have only to walk across the street to go to school and church. But the children come to school crying with the cold sometimes. And today it's been so fearfully cold I didn't even go as far as the P.O. It's been 12 or 13 below every day. I'm as hoarse as ever. Had the doctor tonight, and he gave me another kind of stuff – has chloroform in it. Dr. Brunelle is French – don't like him – he drinks. But he's the best there is in Cloquet. Ugh – he got after my "nervous heart," as he calls it. Don't wonder it's nervous when he listens to it – I'd jump and kick and tear around if I were my heart too.

That California plan has been in my mind pretty strong, but because I care so much for you, I want to stay here. On the other hand, for your sake, I must go. Oh, it's hard to decide. I feel something pulling me, but it's so much easier to drift and let things decide themselves. I wonder how it will come out.

FEBRUARY 1, 1897
Oronoco to Cloquet

Dearest Anna:

You poor child – how's your throat now? I'm awful sorry for you, and can help you not a bit. I've worried about you – please take care of yourself. I know you do that as well as you can. Oh grandmother mine, when do you suppose she you spoke of will come to me, and what will she be like?

I guess this warm change will penetrate even to Cloquet. It was dreadful cold here too – how I hate such weather when a body just *exists* – trying to last through in hopes of better things. The warm change seems so good.

I had a long letter from Zim last week. It was a letter to his pard, whom he imagines it safe to tell things to. I'll try to be worthy of the trust. He walketh on air, I reckon. I laughed deep and low to myself when I read it – good old soft-hearted Zim.

I read most of *Oliver Twist* again. I read *Romola* quite some time ago. I remember Tito Melema the best of them all –Tito was a coward and afraid to stand unpleasant things. Do you like J.K. Bangs' books? I don't much. I've read some of *Houseboat on Styx* and *The Idiot*, but they aren't very much fun for me. It's like the funny columns in a newspaper – it isn't the kind of fun I like, and I've never read one of them through. I like some things of Stockton's pretty well. I read a book of short stories by him that Mary got from the library.

I'm very well, and doing just the same as I have been. I was alone part of the time today – Fred went to town with the rest of the "Woodmen," and everybody else in our establishment is putting up ice for next summer's campers.

I had another letter from Miss Sperry – queer sort of letter, but characteristic. I asked her what kind of a medic she thought I'd make if I tried hard, and here's what she said: "Now, you do write very entertainingly, always – but never, I think, have I found a passage richer in humor than that hesitating, half-bashful jest about being a *medic* – if you *tried hard*! My poor young friend – who hit you with a brick, or is it the heat? Try to forget it, do – *the idea*! You a *medic* – horrors! However, this is only my opinion." Isn't my idea stupendously impractical, according to her reaction? But you thought differently, yes?

I do so hope you're better. I wish so much I could help you. Good-night, dearest.

Roy

Do my letters seem cold? I'm not cold a bit, but letters are cold things. I liked your last letter – only that you weren't well.

FEBRUARY 7, 1897
Cloquet to Oronoco

My Dear, Dear Roy:

I must write you today, for I guess my last letter was very *blue*. I'm better – I went back to school the next day. Mother saw Dr. Dugan, and he sent me some medicine that is helping the cough, but the troublesome hoarseness still stays by me. What if it should never go away, and I should always talk in this deep, growly way?

We had quite a scare last night. Miss Gelston, our little teacher, fell downstairs. She was going down the back stairs and her foot slipped. She slid under the railing and went feet foremost down to the ground – about 16 feet. She's going to school tomorrow. I don't see how she could have been hurt so little, but she's very small and light.

I'm like *Romola*. I wonder if I'm not a bit of a coward – I can sympathize with Tito. I'd have hated awfully to go back and free that old man, wouldn't you? You would have done it, though.

I like Bangs' books in the way I read them – *The House Boat* while we talked and ate popcorn in the parlor, and *Coffee and Repartee* a little at a time before supper. I didn't care enough about *The Idiot* to finish it, and I think we didn't finish *The House Boat*.

I've been reading a little book – *What is Worthwhile?* Some things in it I like very much. She says good things about friendship – things I often think about when I'm away from you, and fear that being away so much, we may grow apart. She says a real friend will never get away from one, or try to, or want to. "Love does not have to be tethered – either in time or eternity."

No, your letter wasn't cold, dear. What did I say to make you think so? I've been reading Miss Sperry's letter over again. I laugh today, for it *is* like you. There is the Donatello, the Wild Huntsman, and all the rest in you. It's *you* – I'd know it – only it's like your shadow or something – the *real* you isn't there. The strength, the power, the *man* in you, is left out.

I've talked with Mother about the California plan. She says Dr. D. thinks southern California is the best place for me, but it's *so* far away. He said there was no benefit in our southern states, except as far as Florida, and there you find malaria and dampness and, in all probability, I would get bilious. Colorado wouldn't do at all because of the high altitude, which would give my heart too much to do. So southern California, Arizona or New Mexico. Oh, I've no idea what to do. We must keep talking about it, yes?

Lovingly,

Anna

FEBRUARY 7, 1897
Oronoco to Cloquet

My Dearest Anna:

I wrote a letter to you earlier, but it didn't suit me. Wish I knew how you are today – I've been thinking, thinking of you. Yesterday I felt lonesome all day, though I was working and hadn't ought to have felt so. Have mercy, dear, and write me just a little often when you're sick, so I may know how you are. I wish Dr. Lane, who helped you last year, could see you. Do you think this Frenchman understands as well?

No one but strong people ought to live in these country winters – nearly everyone gives out a little along toward spring. Oh, I'll be glad for that first spring breath we'll feel in the raw March wind – it winna be long. Sister Mary is sick today – has had a terrible cold for several days, and today she's sick and faint and limpsey. Baby has been sick same way – had the doctor out three or four times.

This has been sort of an unfortunate week for me, though we've had plenty to do. One day I had a "spat" with Fred – nothing serious, and neither of us remembers things more than we can help. But I feel shy of someone after a squabble like that, and I *won't* quarrel – I hate it. I didn't mean to flare, but Fred is peppery, and I'm not an angel. Oh, 'twas nothing – Fred's a good fellow and doesn't mean all he says when he's angry. Then Friday I tried to "put up" more than I ought to, and started to tear loose the latissimus dorsi – that long muscle along the side – from its lower attachment on the ribs.

Then worst of all – your letter saying you weren't better. My poor, sick little girl – I wish so that you are better. But what's the use of my wishing – if wishing did any good, what things I could wish – that you lived on an island in the Pacific and I lived on another island nearby.

Miss Sperry doesn't know me as you do. I sent what she said so you might see how queerly she writes things. What Miss Sperry thinks makes not a particle of difference, while *your* opinion – well, that's altogether different. You haven't pushed me, Anna. It was my idea, dear – you told me you wanted me to do what I thought I could do best and wanted to do most.

Charlie and I were down the river awhile this afternoon. When I got back home, Mary was sitting in the firelight, and I took hold of her hands. She looked languid and limp – she said my hands felt good and cold. And I dreamed it was someone else who was hot and weary and faint, and kissed her good-night, and felt very tender, and all the time I dreamed it was someone else.

Dearest, you are *everything* to me. Good-night.

Write. If I could only send my life to you to help you, I would do it. Don't teach, Anna, when you're not able – don't work until you drop. Think.

FEBRUARY 8, 1897
Cloquet to Oronoco

My Dearest Roy:

I'm out of school sick, in spite of Dr. Brunelle's doses and all the remedies of everyone in the house. I'd give a good deal to be home today, with no thought of school and work crowding upon me. I haven't slept well for two nights, and I coughed so hard and so often yesterday that I could hardly teach. I'm in Miss Hay's room. The banging of that post office door was too much for me – I couldn't sleep. Some of my children came to see me this noon and reported great performances by their classmates. I *must* get back tomorrow.

I think I've never felt more *blue*. I think now that the question is decided – if I can get a school in California, I'll go. I'd like to talk with you about it, but I don't know as there's much to say. It isn't sensible to stay here when the doctors say my lungs are getting weaker with each cold. I've been hoarse for so long the *children* are beginning to talk hoarse! I guess the Board won't want me another year when I have such an effect on my school.

I wonder if Miss Sperry and I see different sides of you, or why it is we think so differently. I was a bit angry when I read what she said. I'm not now. I wouldn't for the world urge you to study medicine if that's not what you want to do – you must do what you think best.

Lovingly,

Anna

FEBRUARY 11, 1897
Oronoco to Cloquet

Dearest Anna:

Aoi! I was so glad to get your letter and know you were better. It was good of you to write to me so soon. I went after the mail, thinking there would be nothing, but I was hoping.

I'm only going to write just a scrap. Mary is sick yet – been having hard earaches. All the folks here have been sick except Blanche and I, and we've had to eat all the heels and crusts while they had the soft bread. But now our backs will be stronger and our hair curl tighter, won't it?

My hurt side causes me to grit my teeth once in a while when I throw a sack of feed out wrong. It's just the lower fastening of the muscle – "the "articulation" – that was strained – nothing serious.

I read something in the last *Cosmopolitan* about peace, rest and sleep – or some other allied drowsy subject. It hit me as amusing – and it made me sleepy (!).

This isn't a decent answer to your last good letter, though I will do that – just a scrawl to show I'm in the land of the living, and you won't feel as if you were writing to a ghost.

There – I'm not sleepy, and I'm serious as I tell you good-night, and I hope you're feeling better.

It's a disgrace to my badge of honor to send such an epistle as this.

FEBRUARY 12, 1897
Cloquet to Oronoco

My Dearest Roy:

Your last letter was one of the *best* letters. How little I deserve the love you give me. Most men do not love as you do – I'm sure of it.

I've thought of you often this week – even in school – something I think I've never done before, except when the thought would flash through my mind – "I wish Roy could see this child or hear this one's questions." If I scolded, I thought, "What would Roy think!" If they weren't listening, I thought, "Roy would not blame them."

I'm better, dear. We had no school this afternoon, but the high school gave an entertainment, and as one of the "faculty" I had to go. We had a program of the usual high-school order, then a *long* speech by a lawyer. Oh, dear – I'm so used to stirring around I can't sit *still*, and I was tired when 'twas over. The wife of a School Board member invited us to tea. We looked at photographs and talked about children, Cloquet people (not *gossip*), magazines and dancing.

Now I'm sitting by the register and wearing my old slippers with the yellow bows ('member them?) and my comfortable dressing jacket. This last you've not seen – it's soft warm flannel, cream in color, with blue and a bit of brown. It's trimmed with my mother's wedding gown – soft brown silk – and I feel very comfortable and not a bit like going to bed, though it's almost 10 and I ought to, as I have lots of work for tomorrow. How I'll revel in *not* "taking good care of myself" next summer. I can let you and Mother do that, and how lovely it will be.

I was sitting last night, finishing my work, when the boys came up and wanted to dance. Some of the girls had gone to bed, but those of us who hadn't hurried into our work-a-day gowns again went to the parlor. The boys were just in the mood for it – Mr. Bolton especially. He's small and light, and he was moving in time to the music and whistling or singing softly. He has a beautiful voice – not very strong, but sweet and full. We sang some; then we all sat on the stairs and ate apples. The boys sang "Good-night, ladies" and left us. What a lot of fun people can have out of nothing. I haven't felt so gay for a long time. Do you remember how I felt last spring? Hope it will come again.

Don't worry about me, dear. I have my usual weight – 110 – and my usual appetite, and people tell me how well I look. So you can see I can stand a cough. I hope your side is well again. You must take care of yourself.

I wish the Someone Else (they're singing "Auld Lang Syne") were here in the firelight now.

With my dearest love,

Anna

FEBRUARY 14, 1897
Cloquet to Oronoco

My Dear Roy:

We're having some trouble in school. A boy refused to obey the seventh-grade teacher, Miss Ferguson. She sent for Mr. Cloyd, and the boy defied him. Mr. Cloyd whipped him, and while he was still at the boy, the gang struck, and Miss Ferguson dismissed the school. Those boys were very much excited, and spread great reports around town. In a few minutes a crowd of men gathered on the sidewalks and around the post office, and two of the biggest toughs in town came in and ordered Mr. Cloyd to let the boy alone. Mr. Cloyd sent them out of the building. They went – if they hadn't, I guess Mr. Cloyd would have thrown them out. He's big and he could do it, and he's furious when he's angry. He has arrested the men for disturbing the school, and they have their trial tomorrow night. Some of the teachers have to be witnesses.

I can't help but admire Mr. Cloyd in this. I don't think he knows what fear is. This is such a rough place – *I'd* be afraid to venture out after dark if I were in his place. He's a queer man. In some ways, I like and respect and admire him. In other ways – well, I've told you how I feel. I pity his wife, if he even has one – how she would have to watch his moods and fit herself to them. If she were ever sick, 'twould all be her fault, because she didn't know enough to take care of herself. (He even tells *me* he would never let such a cough hang about him 24 hours.) I believe he would lock her up if she wished to do something he didn't approve of.

Miss Roth and I feel silly tonight. We disgraced the faculty by giggling in Christian Endeavor meeting. I told her a story last night, and my voice was hoarse enough, so I made it most as deep as yours. She nearly had hysterics. She says that was the cause of her silliness today.

Oh – we are to have an old colonial party Friday evening. We're going to dress in costume, or as near it as we can.

With my love,

Anna

FEBRUARY 18, 1897
Oronoco to Cloquet

My Dearest Anna:

If you thought my letter before last was good, the next was enough to antidote it, I bet. I'm sorry I sent it. I hadn't ought to write so untidily, and I beg your pardon.

I'm glad you're feeling so much better. I didn't expect you to keep writing twice a week – only so I was informed while you were sick, that's all – if it wasn't too much trouble. The folks, Volney and Mary are better. The little king staggers as he runs, but he's much improved, and Mary's back at school. The baby calls her Minimo, although he can say her name well enough. He just coined it.

Faith – I hope you *will* have your spring fever, though I wunna be there to see. You'll only be convalescing from it when I see you in June!

Night before last, when I came over about 9 o'clock, there was a bracing wind, but not cold, blowing from the southwest. I believe there was a touch of March in it. The moon was wonderfully bright, and the stars big, and the sky so blue – you never saw a deeper blue night sky in the depths of summer. I went south half a mile, perhaps, where I could see over the white country, for I had been in dusty work that day. Everything looked so cold and clear and white that it sort of oppressed one – made you feel lonesome a wee bit, and exalted too. Sometimes the bigness and coldness of things does press on one like a nightmare, doesn't it? Perhaps you never felt just that way. I like big, broad views.

Now, now – I must come to earth and tell you how I've been working – grinding rye while my elder brother helped decorate the hall for the great Woodmen dance tomorrow night. There's a strong lodge here – almost all the boys around belong – 40 or 50 members. Sometimes I partly wish I belonged. Fred is clerk and a *great* Woodman. He's better and younger than he used to be – he didn't use to look as well as he does now. He hunts and dances; plays with the kid – little Volney likes him better than anyone. Charles and I get him to singing once in a while – get him started on some old song and he will sing it all. He used to be in lots of minstrel shows and home talent plays long ago. He would have made a good variety actor, I think.

You wrote me a while ago about something you read on friendship and people growing apart. I have thought of it too. Of course, love isn't tethered, and one always would love what the other was in the beginning. Still, I think people might grow apart having likings and new hopes and thoughts that the other one knew nothing of or cared nothing for. We *will* keep together all we can, won't we? Oh, we never will get *far* apart. I will try and come wherever you are – won't you? Perhaps you'll get higher than I can come – I know you're higher now in lots of ways. But women are better anyway. And I'll try and be a gentleman, dear – even if I'm not quite up to your standards.

Oftentimes I've thought it's very important to just like *good* things a great deal better than mean, sordid things. Burns didn't live right, exactly – he had more to resist than some. But he loved the best and highest. I like Robert Burns. In a late *Arena* there was a good article about him – wish you might read it.

My side is almost right again – the muscle had to fasten on solid where it began to tear loose. I'm sure I diagnosed it right. Yes, I will be careful. I have a mortal dread of being permanently injured, maimed or any such thing – I had rather be killed outright, it seems to me, than crippled or blinded or fixed so I couldn't do as I want to.

You wrote me about all the Cloquet people you speak of, but I've forgotten what some of them were like. You like Miss Roth, don't you? I don't imagine I should if she liked that fellow Heath. I always thought that the best kind of woman wouldn't like him at all.

This is a crazy letter. May all things good be with you.

With my dear love,

Tell me how the "toughs" – those boys – come out. Next time you meet them, give them my respects. If it had been a saloon fight, it probably would have been a snap for this Colossus, whom you all admire and stand so much in awe of – ha! I hate big, overbearing so-called gentlemen, and I like toughs, comparatively. Why? Imp of the perverse, I 'spose.

Wish I could see you in that jacket you told me of. You always look especially *dear* when you're fixed warm. Haven't seen you for so long I hardly dared tell you that.

CHAPTER 24

Ambition

FEBRUARY 21, 1897
Cloquet to Oronoco
My Dear Roy:

Your good long letter came yesterday. Wish you would always write long ones.

This has been a busy week. We had a program Friday. All the grades celebrated Washington's Birthday, and during the week a great deal of time had to be given to drilling the children, decorating the room, etc. We made chains of red, white and blue and draped them on the wall. I mounted pictures of Washington; made red, white and blue soldier caps for the children; made a new table spread for the schoolroom; hunted up poems, stories, pictures and what-not. I'm glad there are no more birthdays to celebrate.

Then people flocked in, expecting something great. The children dressed in their best, and looked at their clothes and at each other, and were so much taken up with that and the company that half of them didn't sing, and the other half wouldn't look at me, but sang to suit themselves – some fast, some slow. They forgot the words and would sing the chorus two or three times over, and once they forgot it entirely, while I sang out at the top of my voice, all alone.

Then there was a party in the evening, so we had to come home and get ready for that, which was no small task, as we dressed (or tried to) in old style. I sent home for my mother's old black silk – has a full skirt and pointed bodice that laces up in front and is like some of the pictures of Puritan maidens' gowns. I wore a white chiffon collar and fixed my hair high. Most of the girls wore large white collars like Martha Washington's.

The girls looked nice, but the boys beat us. They came in knee trousers, brocaded vests, slippers with bows on them, frills and puffs around the neck and wrists, and powdered hair and wigs. We danced the minuet and Virginia reel. As they came in, Mr. Thompson announced each one, giving them all sorts of names. I was Pocahontas; Miss Gelston – Evangeline; Miss Ferguson – Priscilla; Mr. Bolton – John Alden; Mr. Thompson – George Washington; Mrs. Thompson – Lady Washington; and Mr. Lyons – Uncle Sam. We had a fine time – the best I've had at a party for ever so long.

I read nearly all day yesterday. I've not finished *Romola*. I got *A Mortal Antipathy* by O.W. Holmes, and *Idle Thoughts* – several of us read it together. The other girls liked it very much, but perhaps because I'd read it before, it didn't mean as much to me. Perhaps I'm getting old.

I'm glad spring is coming – I'll *feel* things more then. My ambition is beginning to stir already. I went down to breakfast and someone announced, "Miss B is the first one here!" I haven't created such a sensation since I arrived! At first they praised and patted me on the head, until I felt like a cat who has caught her first mouse. Then Mr. Cloyd came in and said my conscience must have troubled me or I would still be sleeping. Whereat Mr. Thompson waxed angry, and said Miss Barnard should rise when she pleased and how she pleased. When I left, Mr. C. sang out, "Glad you're going," and I answered, "I always like to please people." There was a transient at the other table – guess he thought we were queer folks. Well, we are. I never thought when I came here I'd *become* one of these people, but here I am.

I wish I might have taken that walk with you. Haven't we had beautiful moonlit nights this week? Wednesday some of us went downtown after supper. The moon had just risen, the clouds were thick in the east, and the moon shone through them, making a halo; and sometimes the light shone downward into the clouds, making a bright path like the reflection of the moon in the water. Oh, it was beautiful! I thought of you and wanted you to see it. I think I felt something as you did, looking across the cold white fields.

What you say about growing apart is true. I've thought of it so much when I think of California. It's possible for me to go to Minneapolis, where I can be near you; where we can be comrades and closer companions than we can by writing. Next year, if you decide to study medicine, you will change more than you have any year since I've known you. I fear we'll drift apart if I'm in California. But if I stay, I'll have bronchitis – it won't make me very ill, but I'll not be as I am in summer, and then there's some danger in letting it go too far. If I could stay in California two or three winters, I could come back and be entirely free from the cough. I'd rather die than be a burden or a drag on anyone.

Roy, dearest – you don't know me yet. You have a kinder heart, a broader sympathy, and more real love for people than I ever had. You are more honest, and in some ways more conscientious than I. I wish I could make you see this now, for you will someday. Then you will be disappointed in *me*. I'm sure if we try to keep together, and pray for that, God will keep us near each other, though maybe ever so far in miles. I wonder how much God leads us. I can't help but feel that in some way God will show me how to decide, and yet I don't know how far we ought to let things shape themselves. I feel like one who is blindfolded, trying to find some hidden thing. I stand waiting for the pull – the pressure – the something that shows me how to go.

The "toughs" have been to Mr. Cloyd and said they were wrong, and the case is not to go any further. I think our Colossus was in the right this time. I know he's hot-headed – I can't forget his actions in my room that one time. But when a child refuses to mind everyone, and tries to carry things his own way, I can't see what else can be done. If you had only that one child to manage, you could do something different from whipping. But with 40 others looking on to see whether he's going to have his way or not, something has to be done quickly.

I don't believe you know what a rough place this is. People from Duluth say they laughed when they heard there was to be a Christian Endeavor convention in Cloquet. They even said, "Can any good thing come out of Cloquet?" I don't see much of the roughness, except when the children tell me such stories: "My father swears awfully. He's night watchman, and he gets cold, and he swears while he eats breakfast; then he goes to bed and he swears in bed." "My grandfather got drunk last night." "My two cousins got drunk, and one of 'em stabbed the other, and he died, and the other's in jail." All the particulars … it's hard to hear sometimes.

Some of the children have no obedience. I've seen them in their homes, where they do just as they please. It may be that some of the punishment we give them will save the executioner's future work. They don't learn obedience, industry, honesty and truthfulness at home; and sometimes it takes more than talk to make them know we expect those things. I've spanked five children since I've been here, and shaken a great many more, and talked to others as severely as I know how to.

I caught a little fellow cheating the other day. I said the worst things about cheating I could think of, and sent him away, and tried to make him suffer until he could see how I – how we *all* – despised cheating, and wouldn't have a cheat with us, and didn't want him with us until he could feel sorry and ashamed. You'll think me hard-hearted and cruel, and perhaps I am, but I try to do what I think is best for the children, and I'm sure Mr. Cloyd does. We're all so very, very human – we make great mistakes. But we don't any of us mean to be torturers of children, and you don't know how hard it is to be firm and strong, and at the same time, gentle.

It's all right – we understand each other. I had to have my say.

With my dearest love,

Anna

FEBRUARY 24, 1897

Oronoco to Cloquet

My Dear Little First Grade Teacher:

If anyone should be honored for what they do, it's you folks, who take these small savages and start them right. I'm glad you had your say, for I had to laugh at the way you got at me, beat down my guard, and led for my chin! Wusha!

There – my hat's off; my guard's down; I'm very humble. I do swear by the head of Odin's horse to aid and abet all first-grade teachers in everything whatsoever! I'm afraid I've eaten my words too much. Doggone all Colossuses anyway. I don't know why I should have such spleen toward superintendents – I guess it's the vagabond in me, with my theoretical hatred of authority.

Your letter was a good one. I think I could write long letters if I tried, but think you would prefer them as they are – jewels of compactness, elegance and study.

Had a short letter from Walter. He's very busy – five studies, and will have six from now on. Said he was downtown and saw Edwin and Homer – they're studying at the U – dentistry, both of them. All the folks in our class are doing something with their heads 'cept me. Nellie is teaching at Clairmont. Mother was in town this week and saw Clara – she's clerking at Leet and Knowlton's for a while.

I get lonesome sometimes (I *guess* it's lonesomeness). I was so last Sunday – Sundays are long days. I haven't been anywhere for a long time. I might go to church – I've been to church once since I went with you. Will that bother you, dear – to go without you? I think it won't. I haven't bubbled over and had a regular old tear, such as I used to, for so long. I will have yet. When the spirit moves, it comes from within. Yes, I'll be glad when spring comes – "The time of the spring running and of the new talk," as Bagheera and Mowgli said.

I went through the woods Sunday afternoon, and someway the trees and everything seemed nearer to me – more alive – for I was thinking of the beautiful life that would sweep over everything soon.

Yesterday afternoon I didn't work at all. I kept still and warm and tried to cure up a pain I had – a "crick" – sort of a pleurisy in the intercostal muscles – something I've had three or four times during my eventful career. It's sharp pain – brings a body right to time; hurts to breathe when it catches you. It's better today, but this week I'm not going to do more than my work, and I'll be all right next week.

I *do* get lonesome sometimes. A fellow can't be vitally interested grinding feed. I can't get what I want to read. But I box some – that helps. If it wasn't for these things I would get lonesomer yet. When I get squared up, I think I'll go to training hard right along until you come home. There will be lots of work soon, too.

I want to see you so. It will soon be the longest we've been away from each other. I think you should try and carry out that plan of going to California, if possible. Anna, my dearest, you and your being well are above everything else. You won't let me be a hindrance, will you? You know how much I care. We wouldn't grow far apart, I think, for we would both try. You are above all considerations anyway. How I wish I could see you a few minutes – I could tell you more than in a thousand letters. I will see you in June – we won't look farther than that now.

I found that same old copy of *Idle Thoughts* that Volney brought with him that spring. I read some, and at first I thought something was gone, but as I read, some of the same old feeling came over me – bringing back the shadows of sensations and thoughts and that spring. There's always something – I don't know what – something so sweet and evanescent about that springtime. I can't *tell* you exactly – perhaps a musician could play it. How little things – a scent or a sound will bring back so much. A perfume has that power more than anything.

I won't write more. A fellow can work just as well if he notices sunsets, can't he?

I read this over and thought of tearing it up. Letters don't suit me. But it's too late to write another one tonight.

FEBRUARY 28, 1897
Cloquet to Oronoco

My Dearest Roy:

Your last letter was a fine one. I'll keep every one of your letters as long as I live.

I've felt glorious all week. There's not the faintest sign of spring here, but it's time there was. Perhaps that's why I feel so good – people tell me how much color I have in my face, and how near I am to having a double chin. I'm hungry as a bear three times a day – I'm almost ashamed to keep on eating after the rest are through.

It has been very cold this week – 30 and 35 below several times. This morning Mr. Thompson walked through the halls, saying in a tone that could be heard all through the house, "35 below zero! Stay in bed!" We did – for an hour longer. I wish you could be here for a while and see the way we act – you'll be shocked next summer when I tell you some of our antics. Miss Gelston has a new dress – she put it on for us to see. We all went into raptures over it, and two of the girls caught her and started to carry her downstairs to show her to the boys. Poor child – she struggled and clutched at everything and ran from one point to another, like a mouse in a trap.

One of the teachers is engaged. They torment her nearly to death. This isn't enough like a hotel to make people keep still in the dining room, and they say everything there. I never had such a *jolly* time and acted as if I "never had any bringing up" as I do this year. If I'm rough and wild when I come home, know that it's the effect of Cloquet, and will wear off in time.

Miss Roth and I went to a dance Monday night. It was a Masonic dance, and only nice people were there. I waltzed with Mr. Cutliff once – he's the best waltzer in town, and I didn't feel awkward at all. I never waltzed before, except here among ourselves.

Did I tell you I'm reading *A Mortal Antipathy* by Holmes? Miss Roth and I read *The Prisoner of Zenda* yesterday – you've read that, haven't you? It's equal to your *Three Musketeers* for fighting, I think. I never read a book so full of action. It's quite a change from what I'm reading today – Hawthorne's *Twice-Told Tales*. I have time to do some systematic reading if I put my mind to it. I've always read just as I pleased from one thing to another. Maybe I had better read differently this spring.

I'm afraid you have hurt yourself lifting. It won't do any good to tell you to be careful, but I wish you *would* be more careful, dear.

Do you remember the night we came home from Edwin's – we had been to a class meeting? We were speaking of Jerome K. Jerome, and you wished you could write as he did. Miss P. said you would be just a bit like him if you *did* write. I thought of it again as we read *Idle Thoughts*. I wish you would write things as good as Jerome. I wish you would write about the Oronoco people, just as you have talked about them to me – *please do*. If you were here, you'd throw cold water on my enthusiasm, but you're not, so I dare to suggest it.

I won't torture you by such a long letter this time.

With my love,

Anna

MARCH 4, 1897
Oronoco to Cloquet

My Dearest Anna:

When you're feeling the best, you write the shortest letters. I'm awfully glad you're feeling so well – not on account of the letters, though.

I'm good, sooth it's not very much like spring here yet – sleet, snow and rain this evening – but that's March, ain't it? We've been having lots of grinding this week – farmer folk getting in a supply for "spring's work." Some queer people come to the mill.

If I write as you told me to – like Jerome – whom shall I send it to – you? I presume there would be great strife trying to decide whether to submit something to *Arena, Forum, Century*, etc. I'm not meaning to "throw cold water" on your enthusiasm – a body ought to do as little as they can of that. Would you have me write "Neighborhood Types," such as I used to see in *Ladies Home Journal*, by Mrs. Wilkinson or someone? I don't like such things very well for my own use.

I never read *Prisoner of Zenda*. "Where the Barries cease from Thrumming, and the Anthony's hope no more." I presume I should like it. When I was a kid I read Mark Twain's *Gilded Age*. I had nothing to read especial Sunday, so I tramped out to Farnhams to get a book. Mrs. Farnham was Col. George's daughter of Chickamauga fame – 'member that from history? Someway they remind me, these folks, of people of a broken-down family – proud of their ancestry – sort of reserved, you know, such as Scots tell about sometimes.

Lots of people are sick. Howard Clapp, who teaches our school, has been sick. He had pneumonia last winter and year before, and he nearly had it this winter. Can't get over the terrible colds he's been having; resigned and given up his school. I feel sorry for Howard. He came down to the mill late in the afternoon where Lou and I had been boxing. Lou wanted to do some trick thing, and Howard answered kind of petulantly, and I joshed him a little, and then I saw he was blue and discouraged. The other boys went, and he told me about it. He was scared – thought he was getting consumption; hated himself for being around complaining; was ashamed of himself; said 'twould be endurable in a girl, etc. I didn't try to cheer him up – that isn't the best way always – but he knew I was sorry for him. He wishes he was in California three months of the year. He'll be all right when it gets warm. Blues have to wear themselves out, don't they? A body's health is a grand thing, isn't it? Hope I'll never get old. *(Howard would soon be smitten by Roy's younger sister Mary – one of his pupils – whom he would later marry. He taught grade school in Oronoco for three years, then went on to become a geologist, mining engineer, and dean at CalTech in Pasadena.)*

Anna, I haven't a single accomplishment, have I – what most folks call an accomplishment? I wish I knew for certain what work is best for me. Wish I was 18 – hang it all – I'm not so very old, though. I'm not very sorry over the way I used the last two years – no, I'm not sorry.

Wish I could have a talk with you. I want so to see you. Three months. Well, I won't write more, for I'm feeling pretty well myself and won't "torture" you further.

With my dear love,

Roy

MARCH 7, 1897
Cloquet to Oronoco

My Dear Roy:

How I wish we could have a good old talk tonight – speak of all the things we've been thinking of, and the work we've been doing. I'd like you to tell me about some of the people who come to the mill; about the baby; about the woods and pond, though that's nothing but a white level place now. I never saw it in winter, so I think of it as I saw it last. I'd ask you about Mary – if she has the same ambitions and plans that commenced to stir a couple years ago, and if she speaks of them to you, and finds you her best friend. We'd talk about Myrtle Hazard in *The Guardian Angel*, for I've been reading it this afternoon, and am very much interested in her having the "high stirricks," as the old nurse called them.

We have not had any spring-like weather yet. The snow is very deep – up to the top of the fences – and where it's piled up by the walks, you can hardly see over it. But the sunshine isn't so pale, and it warms one in the middle of the day. When it shines into the room it seems like spring, and I hear the sparrows chirping in the morning.

When you write something, send it to *me*!! I'm glad you have no accomplishments. I have none either, so we can sympathize! Since I've been here I've gained the name of story teller. My father and Frank had that name, but I don't believe I like a woman who's always spinning yarns, so I refuse, point blank, when they call on me or try to lure me into telling a story.

I haven't heard anything from California. I guess my chances of getting a school there are pretty small. I'm so well now – perhaps there's no need of going.

Stop wishing you were 18 – a boy of 18 writing such letters to a woman of 22! The idea! I never would allow it! I'm growing old – Miss Lynch said so this morning. She discovered some wrinkles about my mouth – fine, but still visible. Probably you will find me very aged when I come home next spring.

You would have thought me about 10 years old if you were here the last three nights. Wednesday the boys all came up after supper, and we played everything we could think of and as hard as we could play. In Blind Man's Bluff, I bruised my cheek (it's black and blue yet!) and scraped the skin off my arm. The next night the boys took us to a church supper; then we came home and danced. The next night we sang, danced and played Blind Man's Bluff again. I always get hurt. I hit my shoulder on the molding around the window, and took the skin off later on when I ran into the side of the house and fell down.

There's quite a bit of excitement in the house tonight. A young lady who lives with her aunt across the street is very ill. There's all sorts of family trouble – she was hiding from her father when she came here. Her father appeared today and was determined to see her. He was armed, and the aunt and uncle are afraid of him, and refuse to let him see the girl. He's shut up in the lower part of the house at present, and two marshals are watching the house.

Such adventure. I must go to bed.

Lovingly,

Anna

MARCH 11, 1897
Oronoco to Cloquet

My dearest Anna:

I'm only going to write a little, for it's late. We had a big day in the mill today – Fred says the biggest day he remembers. My fingers feel kinda stiff. I like to grind when there's a lot to do.

Do you remember Kaiser, the famous white bulldog with one eye light and the other dark like Hereward the Wake? He's dead. There was another bulldog as big as he, and Kaiser ran on to him when he was chasing a rabbit, and there was a big fight, and both of them got bit some – Kaiser in the forelegs. Teague's little boy threw water on them to part them. But old Kaiser was hurt, so he didn't like to walk, and he lay down all wet in the snow and chilled to death. I hated to have him die so in that way. It's just like a little kid to tell you all about this, isn't it? Well, he was a fine dog – quite a friend. I've wished I was as good a man in every way as he was a dog.

It will seem so good to see you – I'm glad it isn't nine months. I wouldn't worry about the wrinkles around your mouth. I have some too – they're like parentheses – they come from much laughter, I think.

When I wished I was 18, I meant to be 18 and have all my present wisdom and experience. I suppose I wanted you that way too, though you're very nice as you are. All right – I won't wish any more.

Lots of people are sick here with pneumonia and lung fever – perhaps on account of the queer warm weather with its changes.

You're reading *A Mortal Antipathy* – I read that in the fall. There's a book I want more than any other – Rudyard Kipling's *Seven Seas*. You've heard of it – it's poetry. It probably will be a long time before the stupid book people have it. I liked *Barrack-room Ballads*.

Oh, for a talk after I get acquainted with you again! It's too bad to write this way. I'm glad you are so well. What time was it you came home two years ago?

With my love always,

Roy

If you happened to expect a good letter, this is a disappointment, isn't it? I would do better if it wasn't so late and I weren't so stupid.

MARCH 14, 1897
Cloquet to Oronoco

My Dear Roy:

I just finished my letter to Mother – if my letter to you turns out as stupid as hers, I'm sorry for you. Nothing has happened to write about. It ought to be spring, but it isn't, and I guess never will be. It's like a day in January, except the good old sun knows he ought to shine like a spring sun, and is pouring a flood of sunlight across the room – it almost touches my feet.

There was no service in the Presbyterian Church today, so I went to the Episcopal. Do you know, I believe I like the Episcopal Church best of any? I like the ceremony and their hymns. In other churches if you don't like or can't believe what the minister says, there isn't much chance for devotion on your part, except in the hymns. And when, as in so many churches, they sing about everything from "little pebble, little pebble" to the bird with the broken pinion, your soul can't go out toward God in those – mine doesn't, anyway. But the beautiful hymns – which are prayers in themselves – help you, and when you join in the responses you feel you are *worshipping*, not being preached at.

I didn't used to feel so. What is causing the change, I wonder? Do you sometimes feel yourself changing – that you're growing to believe in something you never believed in before, and to sympathize in things you never understood before? I do – all the time. People who do this very much are called inconsistent, I presume, when maybe they can't help it. I feel much like Queen Esther when she went before King Ahasuerus, and her words to her friends – "Fast ye, and pray for me" – keep ringing in my mind.

I have to conduct a lesson on drawing before the whole faculty tomorrow night. I will have my own pupils, and the faculty come to my room. You don't know how I dread it. They are great critics up here, and I realize how faulty my work with the children has been. I have thought about it and dreamed about it until I have worked the nervousness off, as one wears out the blues.

I remember old Kaiser. I'm sorry he's dead.

I came home March 16 two years ago, I think. The time seems to have passed much more quickly since last September than it did two years ago – because I'm working now, I suppose, and I was playing then. It isn't good for one to play so long. I'm happier this year then I was then. There aren't so many things troubling me.

I finished *A Guardian Angel* yesterday. It's almost as fascinating as *Elsie Venner*. Dr. Bolton has been reading *A Marble Faun*. He says I'm like Hilda – principally because I take things seriously. I think I take things quite the opposite. What do you think? I've forgotten about Hilda – I must look it over again. She was good and serious-minded and spiritual and greatly devoted to her art, wasn't she? No, I'm not like Hilda.

Do you feel 'twould take long to get acquainted again? I don't believe we'd act much like strangers if we saw each other this minute. It won't be long until we'll see!

With my love,

Anna

MARCH 23, 1897
Cloquet to Oronoco

My Dear Roy:

As usual, I'm too tired to write a respectable sort of a letter.

I got through my teaching ordeal all right – nothing very serious happened. After it was over and the criticism came, it was much as I expected, and much as was given for the other teachers – children not all attentive; some not following directions, etc. But Mr. Cloyd's criticism was most important, of course. He said my lessons, while they showed thought and a good deal of hard work, were turned wrong end to (Mother always said in my sewing that I got the cart before the horse). I thought I had worked things out very logically, and was proceeding in fine shape from the "known to unknown." He said that I allowed the children to talk in *words* and not in "complete statements." He said some good things about my voice and manner toward the children, and I suppose I can turn my lessons around and hound the children with complete statements until I shall more nearly suit him.

I'm going to apply for a school in Minneapolis if Pres. Shepard will recommend me there. I've written him but not heard back. Mr. Cloyd says he will give me a good recommendation. I'm not likely to get in, but there's no harm in trying. The California plan has fallen through entirely – for this year at least.

I received a letter from Aunt Maliza, and the deed of the farm for me to sign. It's to be sold, you know – most of the furniture and things we had are there yet, and I had to tell Aunt Maliza what things to sell and what to keep. I tried to think of the little things that I cared about, and will have her take them to her house. I dreaded writing that letter – I believe all those things are dearer to me because I'm the only one left, and it rests with me to say what shall be done. And as I go over in my mind – the old furniture and things – there are so many associations gathered around everything. Well, I don't need to tell you – you know how I feel.

We've been discussing religion lately at table. From some things I said, the folks say I'm a Universalist, so we have all denominations, nearly, at our table – even a Materialist.

It's little more than two months and I'll see you again. Then I'll find out if you are X=0, whatever that means. Who *cares* what the value of X is? I've never done *any* equation. You are *you*, and that's enough!

I'd like to see you tonight. I feel annoyed Mr. Cloyd teased me at the supper table. He thinks he's smart – I think he's rude. I sometimes wonder what sort of family he came from – that way down below the surface there's something lacking that you feel at once in well-bred people.

I *must* go to work. Good-night.

Lovingly,

Anna

MARCH 28, 1897
Cloquet to Oronoco

My Dear Roy:

I received your letter this afternoon. I wish I knew more about your thumb – you made so light of it that I don't know how serious it is. Will it ever be like your other thumb? I bet I could have done it up if I'd been there, even though

I've only had experience with children's injuries. It must have hurt, you poor child – can you work? I shouldn't think you could.

I don't think I'm sorry about California. Perhaps I might have made it materialize if I had done my best. Still – I've only missed one day of school. Probably I wouldn't do better in California.

Speaking of – I'm laid up this afternoon. I was all right this morning, and went to church. But a pain gripped me under the left shoulder blade. It's better now, and I presume it will be gone by tomorrow, but it makes me hold my breath. It must be like the pain you had in your side.

Two weeks more – then vacation. I'll write again sometime when I can write a better letter.

Lovingly,

Anna

APRIL 6, 1897
Cloquet to Oronoco

My Dear Roy:

Your letter and pictures came Monday. It seemed good to see all the folks again in the camp picture. I looked at it for half an hour at a stretch, I guess. This will be a "bit letter" – I'm stupid and tired after a day of teaching, and even if you were here, I'm afraid nothing would seem worth saying. I'm glad your thumb is coming out all right. I'm all right too.

The St. Louis River is breaking up too. You ought to hear them tell of the time when all the lumber went out several years ago. It must have been a sight to see the logs being tossed about in that rocky gorge. I used to watch the ice go over the dam in the Mettowee when I was little. I could stand for hours and watch.

We're getting anxious about re-election. I've no idea whether or not they'll want me another year. I *want* to be re-elected. There's such very little chance of my being elected in Minneapolis, that I'm afraid our dreams are wild to think of being together next year.

Only three more days – then vacation for a week. Teaching goes hard these days. I have 48 children, and they're full of spring. I can sympathize, for I know how I used to feel in the spring. They're on the wiggle and jump from morning to night. They come so full of enthusiasm, and their faces show at a glance that they want awfully to be good – but in 10 minutes – oh – it's worse than managing the same number of colts. They've been writing – they were to write to anyone and about anything they wished, and were not to have any help from me. I put the best-written ones up at school, but I'll include some of the funny ones in this letter.

I'll try to write better next time.

Lovingly,

Anna

(Letters from Anna's students)

Dear Miss Barnard,

I can read slow. I can read good. I cannot read fast. I have read two times. I hapet stey hapet school. Love, Alfred

To my dear friend Frances,

I read about Mary and I sore a little bird today. I am going to school. I am good in school. There is lost of girls and boys. Most is boys. Some is girls too. I like to go to school. Love, Lulu

I am writing to my friends and my brothers and my uncle and my mama Hilda and Papa and Annette and Frances Peterson and Miss Barnard. I like all my friends and my teachers and ourselfs and my grandma to. I don't like to do nothing unless you tell me. I won't to write less and read the lesson in my second reader. And I like to work as good as anybody. I like to draw on my slate to. We rede about stories almost to recess to, and I like to play in the mud, lo, and I like to sing into the singing chart. Your friend, Frances Peterson

Dear friend Miss Barnard,

I have write a little letter to my grandma and she sent a letter to me. When she sent me the letter she said that a little baby girl die. When my grandfather die his feet hurt very much.

Aren't those precious?

APRIL 13, 1897
Cloquet to Oronoco
My Dear Roy:

I'd like to have you here tonight. Seems I'm bluer than I've been since I came to Cloquet. I have a cold – that's one thing. And our election comes in two weeks. Mrs. Thompson spoke of different teachers, and whether or not they wished to come back. She heard that "Miss Barnard didn't want to come back." She said she thought that arose because Dr. Allen (one of the Board) said I ought not to come back because of my cough – that some other climate would be better for me, and I ought not stay here. Ever so many have asked if I wasn't going to try a different climate, and have seemed surprised when I said I didn't expect to – not at present, at least.

I think Mrs. T said that to let me know I may not be reelected. (She's on the School Board.) I think my going to a different climate is only an excuse, and there is some other cause for not wanting me – perhaps Mr. Cloyd has not spoken so well of my work all along. But if he's recommending me for Minneapolis, he must believe I'm able to do the work here. Perhaps they think I can't put enough life and enthusiasm into my work with such a cough. Maybe they're afraid they may have an invalid on their hands in another year – Lord only knows what they do think! But if I'm fired from Cloquet, and that's the true reason, I shall be utterly, utterly discouraged. "The survival of the fittest" is a pretty hard law, isn't it – from the little crowded bud on the pussy willow branch to us human folks. I've tried to teach the children to be careful of those "little pussies," and to like them just as well as their big furry brothers and sisters.

I can't understand why the Board should feel so. I've missed only one day, I'm as well as I was last year, and I did a great deal more work this year than last. A cough can't be hidden, and I suppose I've made them painfully conscious of it every time they see me. Well, what must be must be. I feel sure I shan't be reelected. I can tell this to you. You will be sorry, and it's a comfort to tell you, but I can't write it to Mother until it's settled past any doubt.

I got a letter from Pres. Shepard today: "I have written Supt. Jordan in Minneapolis on your behalf, and Supt. Cloyd has certainly endorsed you strongly. But I fear the ruling of the Board at Minneapolis will bar you out, since they require that a high-school graduate has taken the Advanced Professional Course, unless they have extended experience in schools of like grade."

So no one gives me much hope of getting a position there, but it didn't hurt to try.

I have a new spring hat! Wonder how you would like it. It's a small brown straw with a tam-o-shanter crown, a rose next to my hair, some stand-up things on the left side, some violets dropped on the crown on the right side, and some rose buds running all around the underside. You'll see it soon!

Only five weeks of active teaching, but that last week will be worst of all. The preparations for last day (we are to have as elaborate a program as we can get up) and the reports will keep us on the jump.

The crocuses you sent make me want to get out. I asked Mr. Bolton if it wasn't time for trailing arbutus. He says there's two feet of snow yet in the woods, and they don't get arbutus before May. Do you remember when we went out on St. Mary's Hill after crocuses? Did those you sent me grow on our Point?

I have commenced *Middlemarch*. Have you read it?

This isn't a good letter. I'd hate to have anyone but you read the letters I write. I've always felt I could be myself with you, and I am – even in my letters.

Good-night, dearest.

Anna

APRIL 18, 1897
Oronoco to Cloquet

My Dear Anna:

Oh, if I could see you – writing won't do much good. Hope your cold is better. And, little girl – try not to get blue until you're *sure* about your position. Then if it shouldn't be as you want it, everything won't be dark, will it? I'm glad you tell me these things, dear – glad that you *can*. I *do* feel so sorry that you're feeling so, and I love you dearly, *dearly*. Things *do* seem pretty rough on you. It doesn't help a body at all to have someone underestimate troubles. Don't be discouraged utterly – I'm sure you won't, for you're very brave in a quiet way.

I suppose you teach again this week. Don't bother yourself to write me on work days, unless you feel like it. Please don't think I imagine my scrawls do any great good.

I was reading that book you lent me long ago – *Hot Ploughshares* – do you remember? It's good, isn't it? I believe I'm getting to have my old-time zest for reading, such as I had when I first read *Lorna Doone*. *Middlemarch* is in the library – I'll get it.

The crocuses I sent came from the bluffs to the east. There are lots of them on the Point now – *our* Point – where the worms were (!). Mary and I walked out there just before evening. Some of the crocuses were their natural color, and some a different blue. Looked as though they were awfully cold – I guess they were. Your beloved hepaticas are just beginning to show wee buds – I'll send one. Do I remember the time when we went out to St. Mary's hill – faith, I have the note you wrote me! I carried it so long it all wore apart where 'twas folded.

There have been several deaths here in the last month – old people died with a deadly sort of pneumonia. Pa is terribly hoarse and has a bad cold in his lungs – we feel troubled about it. Mother induced him to go to the doctor this morning, after patient effort. He came back and said, with sort of a disappointed look, that "the doctor didn't think he was very bad off." Almost everybody has been sick except me. We have had so little sunshine. I feel better than ever – but then, I'm always so well. I feel stronger – this year hasn't hurt me.

I want to see you. I read over what I've written, and it doesn't tell what I want to, dearest. Try not to get blue and discouraged, my dear little girl – you're all right; you do splendidly; and it's not your fault that you're handicapped somewhat, as you said. You're not sure what these people think or will do – perhaps you imagine a lot.

With my dear love,

Roy

Things will get right someway, I'm sure. I will be strong for two, and you know I belong to you entirely.

APRIL 21, 1897
Cloquet to Oronoco

My Dearest Roy:

It's after 9, and not all my lessons are planned, but I must write you just a little. That last letter of yours was such a good one – you don't know how your letters help. That little hepatica bud fell out the first thing. Yes, they are my beloveds.

I was a goose, I suppose. Mr. Thompson got to talking with me alone Sunday. He asked me if I wanted the school next year. I said I did, if the folks wanted me. He said quite positively that I could have it, for he had never heard the Board or Mr. Cloyd say anything against me, and they have talked us over considerable.

One of the teachers just brought in a bowlful of the worst-looking stuff you ever saw for my cold. They've been concocting it unbeknownst to me. I refused point-blank to take it. Of course, they're huffy. But every one of the teachers has half a dozen or more old grandmother medicines that they *know* will cure me if I'd take 'em. It's enough to try the patience of a saint. Whiskey straight, whiskey and glycerin, whiskey and rum, rum and glycerin, whiskey external and internal, turpentine external and internal, turpentine put on a pillow to inhale (pity me), cod liver oil, Piso's Cure for consumption *(a popular cough medicine – the only brand-name cannabis medicine named in Samuel Adams' now classic book on quackery – The Great American Fraud)*, Dr. King's something-or-other (I've forgotten it), and all the patent medicines I never heard of – mustard plaster; parano plaster; molasses and onions; onions straight; a concoction of hemlock buds, tar and balsam; a hot compress; a cold compress; "a stocking round your throat;" celery compound; potash; salt; another concoction brought to me by the pitcher-full.

I've not stretched this a bit. These were all things that in sober earnest were recommended for my cough, and there were ever so many I've not told about. I presume, now that I have so flatly refused this last, they'll leave me to my own destruction. I wished so last night that Mother was here. She'd drive 'em off, and take me in hand, and I could rest in peace. I 'spose they think it's their duty, and I do appreciate it, in a way.

I'll answer your good letter Sunday. Good-night, dearest.

Your Anna

APRIL 22, 1897
Oronoco to Cloquet

My Dear Anna:

This is just a sham letter to get straightened around with.

I guess spring is sure 'nough coming now. Yesterday and today were the first warm days. I was out in the woods back toward the Point this noon and saw some hepaticas. This evening Auntie and I were out and got some – thought you would like to see some if you hadn't yet, so Auntie found me a box and here they are. Hope they don't altogether wither. I don't believe you have any yet. How relaxed one feels these first warm days – and lazy. I went to sleep on the floor today. The boats are nearly all ready for the summer – painted white outside and green inside, with red trimmings.

The folks that were sick at our house are better. Poor Baby Volney – they have just let him out today to walk. You should see his eyes when he's out-doors – so big and wide with looking. Pa wheeled him up on the Point to see "rock roses" grow, but Baby liked the wide view best.

I mustn't write you when I'm so void of thoughts. In six weeks you'll be home, probably. I so want so to see you.

I went over and looked at *Middlemarch* and, Anna, I don't like the looks of it. I had no especial reason, but it looked very deep and dry, and I just didn't want it. I got *Lorna Doone* instead.

CHAPTER 25

Played Out

APRIL 25, 1897
Cloquet to Oronoco
My Dearest Roy:

Your letter and flowers came yesterday. You dear boy – no one but you would have thought to send them! No one would have remembered how well I liked them. They were withered some, and the poor little things were so faint that the woodsy smell was all gone. But I put them in water, and this morning when I got up I smelled again, and the faint, fresh perfume was there. They revived soon after I put them in water. One of them is standing straight up in the saucer, looking at me! Some of the little buds are just open-ing. The crocuses – great, strong fellows – didn't stand the trip half so well. I can't coax them to open.

The arbutus are out. They are *so* sweet – I wish I could send you their fragrance. Do you remember when John Alden said of them: "Modest and simple and sweet – the type of Puritan maidens"? There's something peculiar about the fragrance of spring flowers. They're so sweet and true and natural – something forgetful of self, and growing as God wishes. The roses and sum-mer flowers lose that. The lilies of the valley have it.

This afternoon the boys came for us to go visit a sugar camp. It's a lovely walk through the woods. I couldn't go – I wanted to so much. Mr. T. said he'd take me to ride instead, so we went to Carlton. I wore my winter coat and Mrs. Thompson's fur cape over it. We met people walking without any wraps – I wasn't any too warm, but I felt foolish.

Did I tell you Mr. Cloyd told me to dismiss the children early for a while? It makes it a good deal easier for me. Besides the time spent in teaching, it saves preparation of two subjects – General Lessons and Science. These took the most time to prepare. Mr. Cloyd means to be good to me, though he also scolds and acts cross when I have a cold. He said rather gruffly, "It would be better for the school if you came at 9 and stepped out at 3:30, than to have a substitute."

I resigned my Sunday school class too, and have not been to church for three Sundays. I feel much better today. I wrote Mother to see Dr. Dugan, and he sent me some medicine, which is helping me, I think. One kind is to keep me from coughing so much, and I slept the best last night that I have for two weeks. I stayed in bed until noon Saturday. There was a dance nearby, and I couldn't sleep a wink nearly all night.

The folks here are as good to me as they can be. Mr. Cutliff brought me a jar of maple syrup from the camp. He's such a kind-hearted fellow – he was sorry for me when I told him I couldn't go. I've missed more things this week – the dance, the walk to Carlton, a tramp over the rocks and around the falls, and the camp this afternoon – isn't it a shame?

My Minneapolis plan has gone nowhere. My application came after the appointment had been made. It wasn't my fault – Pres. Shepard sent a good recommendation, and so did Mr. Cloyd, but they were sent too late. I'm not disappointed, for I hadn't dared think it possible I should get a position there. I guess I'm to be here another year, if I'm fortunate enough to be reelected. They decide tomorrow night. If I'm fired, I'll let you know.

Roy, I haven't had any spring fever at all, yet I heard a robin early this morning – 'twas the first I've heard. I like to lie still and listen to it, but it didn't set things stirring – neither do the flowers. They're sweet, and I love to have them near me, but I'm tired and listless – I don't even want to talk.

With my love,

Anna

APRIL 30, 1897
Oronoco to Cloquet

My Dearest Anna:

It's late and I'm going to write just a little. Baby Volney is desperately sick. He was feverish last night, and this afternoon he had a convulsion. I was up to the house when I heard Blanche speak to him, but he had such a queer look in his eyes – looked at you so steady and queer, when you know he saw nothing at all. I went after Pa, and Fred after the doctor, and while we were gone Baby stiffened out and carried on. I didn't like to see Blanche when I got back. He's sleeping now, but restless. I was doing no good over there. I hope so he will be better in the morning. Poor little chap – he has such a great brain and nerves – out of proportion to the rest of him. What would Blanche do … no, I won't think of it.

I read your last letter while I was in the boat among the willows. Anna, dearie – it made me ache to think how tired and fagged you are. It's a shame – made me feel edgeways. Perhaps spring isn't there in strong enough force yet.

I wish your school was through – I presume you're more tired out than I can conceive of, poor child. I'm sorry your Minneapolis plan didn't materialize. If Pres. Shepard did as you thought – slowed the process up a bit – it seems to me a "shabby" thing to do, as my papa would say.

I've been feeling sort of blue here for some cause. I've been banging myself up lately – hurt my wrist boxing, and now it's lame. (One does get a spell of bruising in boxing, you know.)

I'm glad you liked the flowers – and you said I was a dear boy, and I liked that too. Yes, I like the spring flowers best – nothing strong and overpowering about their fragrance – just wholesome and dainty and sweet. Saturday I was over in "our woods" for a while. You should have seen the hepaticas – the ground was blurred purple with them. If you could be here for a week and rest, you would hear the robins in the morning, and things "would stir," and when you looked away with the wind blowing in your face, you would look glorious as I have seen you.

With my dear love,

Roy

How cramped my writing is tonight – it looks as if a boy about 12 wrote it. My hands were sore, and I was careless and hurrying. Oh – Volney is a little better.

MAY 2, 1897
Cloquet to Oronoco

My Dearest Roy:

Miss Lynch just brought me your letter. I'm anxious about the baby, and so sorry for him and Blanche. I'm glad summer is coming – he'll be better if he can be out in the sun, I presume. I'm feeling better – I sleep nights now. The folks laugh at the way I sleep – I sit up straight, wrapped in a blanket, and read with my eyes half-closed until I get sleepy. Then I turn out the light, keeping as still as I can. By and by I feel myself dropping off, and then I fall over – you know how you do when you're almost asleep?

I took a walk in the woods yesterday with some of the children. It was warm and sunny. We found some hepaticas and one spring beauty and two little violets. There's a tiny blue violet that grows here – I never saw any like them before. The hepaticas were scattered and looked frail and white. There was a piney smell – the trees were thick, and some had that grey moss clinging to them and hanging down like the trees in Maine. Wish I could find hepaticas like those you tell me of. They grew like that at home in the east. Mr. Lewis found some arbutus Saturday. It grows three miles from here. I want so to get some, but don't feel equal to a six-mile tramp. I've had some all week – the children bring them – but I want to pick them myself.

The Board met last Monday night and I was reelected! Mr. Lewis, Miss Gelston and Miss Johnson were not. There's so much needed in a teacher besides actual worth to get in, isn't there? I haven't the faith in people that I used to – Miss Johnson was worth *two* of me, but people didn't like her as well. Miss Gelston is too much of a lady to be appreciated here. They are going to try to get on without a teacher in Mr. Lewis' place.

Don't worry about me – you know I often get played out a bit, but I'll be all right soon. I always come up with a bound. I'd like the week in Oronoco, but I don't believe even June, if it should come suddenly with all its roses and frogs singing in the evening, could make things "stir." I'd only want to lie in a hammock in the sun and think of nothing.

There are only three Sundays more in Cloquet. I want to stop and visit schools for a week in Minneapolis – it's my only chance to improve, you know. Then I'll be home.

I'll send some arbutus. I've been weaning it and it's limpy.

With my love,

Anna

MAY 7, 1897
Oronoco to Cloquet

My Dearest Anna:

I wish now I had written you last night. Things aren't much altered, and I'm the same fellow – but there's a difference tonight, and I feel out of sorts about things. Lots of little things, and thinking about such, pile up and seem large sometimes, don't they?

Baby Volney is better. The doctor couldn't tell what was the matter because he didn't develop any very definite, conclusive symptoms. The doctor thought he had pneumonia, but it was *measles*, and he's coming along all right so far. I had to laugh – every old lady would tell the doctor it was "worms," and that would make him so disgusted. They all had a remedy.

And speaking of such – your tale of manifold ills in the shape of remedies! You're a sensible body not to take such a track – 'tis all nonsense. I never took anything but food or exercise or quiet. Oh, of course, remedies are all right – but that list eclipsed anything I ever heard of!

Thank you for the picture. Seems as if you and Miss Roth look awful prim and sober and school-marmish – dreadful so. I was a little bit awed.

It's getting along toward the nicest time of the year – the leaves are out just a little. Thoughts and ideas and hopes seem to be different – glorified this time of year, don't they? Except like tonight, when things don't seem that way at all. I'd like to talk to you this evening. You're very far off, and I can't write what I'd like to tell you – it would be foolish to try. I'm very glad you're feeling better – awfully glad. It's been a hard pull. I'll be relieved when you're through.

I must stop. I haven't written you a blue letter this year before, have I?

MAY 10, 1897
Cloquet to Oronoco
My Dearest Roy:

I've been wicked – I didn't go to church. In the morning, Mr. Anderson drove down and said Miss Roth and I could take his horse and carriage for a ride. The boys at the house looked envious, and made remarks about how it wasn't safe for two girls to go off alone – that we couldn't drive, etc. But we refused to have a driver, and I managed the horse. It's the first time I've had reins in my hands since I left home.

After dinner the boys came for us to go out to the Indian reservation after arbutus. I was well enough to go this time. We had a lovely walk through the woods and past two small lakes. We would stop sometimes and sit on a log and talk and eat wintergreen berries, which were growing all about us. At last we came to the arbutus. I couldn't find it at first – we would see the leaves, but no flowers. But you part the leaves and brush away the dead ones, and there you find the delicate pink waxy flowers, and oh – they are so sweet! It's fun to find them. I couldn't bear to come away and leave them.

We were pretty tired when we got home. We had walked about six miles, the boys said. We were too tired to go to church in the evening, of course, but I had a glorious sleep. I didn't cough once, and I felt fine today. We're going on a fishing trip Saturday. There are a good many pretty lakes near here. We're going to visit the mills some night this week – they're lighted by electricity and work all night.

Two weeks more after this! I still close school early. In spite of all his faults, Mr. Cloyd is good to me, isn't he? I will be so glad to see you, dear. I've never been away from you for so long. If it wasn't for visiting primary work in Minneapolis, I should come straight home. Oh, I do want to talk to you –

perhaps I could help you out of the blues. I think you wouldn't be blue if you were here tonight – I'm better, and it's spring, and I'm coming home soon, and I feel quite happy. I wish you could tell me about the things that trouble you. You must when I come home.

I'm not *altogether* "school-marmish," and I don't think you'll feel awed a bit. For fear you may, I'll send you a snapshot they took of me – the "old lady with the birdcage" (your grandmother, you know). The other folks were going for a walk. I had a cold and couldn't go, but I fixed up as if I was. My hair was coiled on top of my head, and my hat toppled every which way. I took the afghan for a shawl and went down to show off to the girls in the dining room. The boys heard the laughter and came to the door to see. The one with the cigar is Mr. Cutliff. At his left is Mr. Watkins, and the one behind him is Mr. Watts. His hair is wild – it's a standing joke. It's light and fluffy and everyone makes fun of it. Miss Gelston is over by the table. I hope to have the picture back – it's the only one I have.

Am glad the baby is better. The spring hasn't been the same to me this year. Perhaps I shall feel it in June, when work is over and I'm started for home. The children have been bringing me anemones, blue and white violets, cowslips and dandelions. I sent some arbutus home last week. I wanted to send some to you, but I thought of Charlie and your breathing and all and didn't dare.

I'm still reading *Middlemarch*. I'm not deeply interested – it isn't a good book for spring.

With my love,

Anna

I forgot to tell you about the trip to the log jam up the river. For nearly a mile the logs are jammed in as close as possible – they reach from shore to shore. We went up on the train, and the boys came in a handcar. I walked across the river on the logs! We took our supper and ate on the bank of the river. Mr. Wentworth brought Miss Roth and me home on a railroad velocipede. It was lovely – cool and fresh, and the frogs were singing, and the moss beside the track was a bright green. I thought of you and wished you were there.

MAY 14, 1897
Oronoco to Cloquet
My Dear Anna:

I wrote you last night, but it didn't suit me. I didn't want to send it, and so did the devouring flame act this morning. Your letter and picture came

– thanks – that looks all right! Yes, I'll keep it for you – guard it as I would ma' honor, as they say in the plays. How long it seems since I saw a play. Seems a long time since I had a really good time. I've been pretty contented for me, but lately – this last week, especially – I've been kinda down-hearted sometimes. I don't want to live like a turtle. I haven't been off-duty but once last July and the day after Thanksgiving, since I came home last June. Maybe that's the problem.

I'm very glad you're feeling better – glad you're coming home. You mustn't put off or give up your visiting schools in Minneapolis. It will be good to see you and talk wi' you. I haven't had a talk – a *regular* talk – with anyone for an age.

Baby just came out and asked me was I writing to a man. I told him to a *lady*; he asked *who*, and where she lived, and now he's asking me questions galore.

Day before yesterday as I came over the bridge, I remembered it was three years ago since we all came out here. It was very much such a morning. I ground alone that afternoon, with a prospect of raking leaves and tidying up the side hill. Queer how I hate little puttering work, isn't it? What a love of a gardener I would have made!

I guess this is long enough, considering the quality. My letters aren't very sparkling, are they?

I'll see you soon, I hope – you don't know how I want to.

With my dear love,

Roy

MAY 16, 1897
Cloquet to Oronoco

My Dearest Roy:

It's warm and "summery" today. I have on the light green waist I wore to the class play last year, and have been walking without a wrap. The trees are beginning to get feathery now, and as you look off toward the reservation, the hills look quite green. We took a walk before supper – there's a fine view of the river and woods from the top of some of these hills.

Tuesday evening we girls felt in the mood for a dance, so we asked the boys up. We had a good deal of fun. It's probably the last dance we'll have before we go. Wednesday evening the boys came for us to go to the mills. They're lighted by electricity and run day and night. Mr. Wentworth (one of the boys) showed us his father's mill. We looked in the place where the slabs are burned – it's a great tall tower with wire netting over the top. The slabs are torn into small pieces and carried into the tower, where they fall on an iron grating and are burned. There's a terrible draft through it – it almost drew my umbrella wrong-side out when I put it in to see how great the draft was. I never saw such a fire. The burning slabs are blown about, and when the new ones come in, they crash down – my, it's awful – and think of it going night and day.

Two weeks from last night I will be in Minneapolis, and then home – and you. I've been thinking of you a great deal lately. I'm afraid you'll wonder who that old woman is when you see me – I feel awfully old.

The high school played *East Lynne* last evening. They did well, but 'twas awfully funny to see a little fellow arrest someone twice his size; to have the villain pipe out his lines in a fine soft boyish voice; and to see the lover stand in the middle of the floor and say loving things to his sweetheart way across the stage. We laughed in the most pathetic parts, and when the curtain went up on the last scene when the heroine dies, we all cried.

It's almost dark. I'm still reading *Middlemarch*. I've not been particularly interested in it, but I'm sure I shall always remember how Dr. Lydgate started out with such high aspirations – so proud and independent and free – and became in debt and went down and down, until he would have stooped to anything almost for the sake of money.

I can hardly see the lines, so I must stop.

With my dearest love,

Anna

MAY 20, 1897
Oronoco to Cloquet

Dearest Anna:

Two or three more letters – and then something better! I expect you're dreadfully tired and worn, you poor little girl. I'll be sorry to have you so fagged, of course. I'm not going to write much these days. *You* may write as long as you please, however. I wonder what you'll think of me – where you will be. Oh, I'm thinking of you too – thinking lots.

Yesterday was a rainy day – the best we've had – a soft rain coming and slacking up and going again, and warm too. It cleared up at night for a little while, just at sunset. I rowed awhile and walked through the woods. The air was do damp, sweet and heavy – how things are growing. Then there was a glorious red sunset.

The folks went to town today and there wasn't much grinding. We had a good many boats out, though it's cold today for the time o'year, with a great raw wind and dark sky. Fred and I swiped Charlie Mayo's sailboat this afternoon and went sailing. There was a stiff breeze – the sail wasn't reefed a bit, and we had no ballast except ourselves, so 'twas quite fun. We didn't stay very long. I suppose it's for our interest to have all these fishermen here, but I don't much like to have them traipsing around all the time. Years ago it was all so quiet – Sundays, especially. Now it's different – I dinna like to see 'em all. Some fellows tipped over today. They had been having a gay time, I guess. Fred said they were awfully afraid our editor would get hold of it. Did I tell you we had a paper now? Editor, "devil" and all!

My, I want to see you. Aren't you tired of this prattle? Sayest thou the word and I won't write anymore until I see you. I will if you *want* me to – I just make you this offer through my great mercy and clemency.

I love you dearly.

CHAPTER 26

Closer Than Ever

JUNE 6, 1897
Oronoco to Eyota

My Dearest Anna:

Oh, do I want to see you, Anna! Was so glad to get your letter last night. You see, I'm disobeying you and writing. When do you want me to come? "I wonder if you do." (I like to be formal, you see.)

I'm wanting to see you so much.

With my love,

Roy

I put on sort of civilized clothes today – have 'em on yet – and I did feel mean – oh, so ornery.

JUNE 15, 1897
Eyota to Oronoco

My Dear, Dear Roy:

I wonder if you're missing me tonight, as I am you. I have felt blue and sad, and things are not as interesting as they were when you were here – I mean, *nothing* seems so interesting. You wakened me from my listlessness, dear, but now I'm just as bad again. You have to come and help me out. I don't see what is the matter with me. I *must* get at something and get up some interest.

I looked over your letters today, and arranged them in order, making a package for each year. I counted them too – there are 140. What comrades we have been!

I finished *Sentimental Journey* tonight. You must read it sometime. I think you will like it better than *A Window in Thrums*.

We are *good* friends. I'm so glad we have *kept* friends all three years. The brother and friend and lover are so combined in you that I seem to have lost all three since you went away, and I miss them so. I miss the curly head, too – I wish it were here this minute. Seems as if you had won my heart over again, though it was always yours. I love you so, dearest.

Anna

JUNE 20, 1897
Eyota to Oronoco

Dear, dear Roy:

Your letter came Friday evening. Dinna tear up your love letters again – *ever.* I'm going to carry this with me next year – it made me feel wonderfully happy as I read it, and has ever since.

Instead of growing away from you this year, I think I love you more than ever before, dearest.

When I commenced to waken this morning, I had a vague, undefined feeling of something very sweet and beautiful and broad – something that seemed to wrap me about, and yet was boundless – like sunshine. Then it crept into my sleepy head – "tio Royo love" – and I woke with a feeling of exultation that something so beautiful was mine – my own.

Mother has been a little anxious because I have not gotten over being tired, so she had the doctor come down yesterday. He examined my lungs and heart and gave me some tonic and medicine for my heart. He says not to go to Cloquet next year – he thinks I'd better go to New Mexico, Arizona or southern California. Mother cannot think of my living in the first two places, so I guess I'll have to find something to do in California. I'm going to see Pres. Shepard sometime this week, if he's in Winona, and see if he can find a place there for me. I can probably get Dr. Lane to plead my case, as he advised me to go to California last year.

Doctor said a good deal about my being so thin. He had me weighed, and said to watch and see whether I gain or not. I weigh 101½ – it isn't bad, I think. I weighed only 110 last winter, with coat and overshoes. Doctor says not to do much or walk much. Won't I be lazy? I could've been lazy enough without his "say so," but now my conscience doesn't trouble me in the least. I know I'm *much* better than I was two months ago, or even the first of this month. I'll weigh 120 before the summer is over – I'll show doctor I *can* get fat if I want to.

I wonder if I could get all the class of '94 down here in August. We have never had a class reunion, and I wish we might.

You must come down often, dearie. If I go away, I don't know when I can come back. I thought I had everything settled, and now this has come up to bother me. I'm sure no distance can break our love for each other, and as long as we have that, nothing else matters.

Good-night, dearest.

Anna

JUNE 23, 1897
Oronoco to Eyota

Dear Anna:

I'm writing downstairs – I like better to write you when I'm alone. You write the *best* letters, and that last was one of the best. But somehow it left an ache. Dearie, I love you so, oh so much. I must see you soon. Yes, I'm sure we're closer than ever, and that didn't seem possible, did it?

I'm glad you're not going back to Cloquet – I thought another year there would almost kill you. You must go to California if it's possible. It will be dreadful to have you away so far and so long, but, dearie, you *must* get to feeling better.

You must come up to Oronoco. What would the summer be without you here for a while? You'll come, won't you? Everyone really wants you to. We'll take good care of you, and you won't be "entertained" – I told Auntie you weren't the kind that had to be treated that way.

Oh, it's a glorious evening. Perhaps you went to Winona today. As I came up from the mill this evening, everything looked glorious. There had been a little rain – just so things were sweet and fresh – and then the bright setting sun on the fields, woods and water. It was just a little thing – but a body wants to enjoy little things if they can. I want you with me so.

I've been working pretty sharp yesterday and today. I was alone, and 'twas pretty hot. Just a good day of physical work makes one respect himself a bit more, doesn't it?

This isn't a very good letter. You *dear* little girl – yours was *such* a good letter. I will do something yet, I hope – I want to be worthy to have such a one as you love me so.

Roy

JUNE 25, 1897
Eyota to Oronoco

Dearest Roy:

I wrote Pres. Shepard to see when he would be there. After that comes a dressmaker, and then I'll be free to come to Oronoco. I suppose I'll have to take an examination if I go out-of-state. Pres. Shepard wrote: "I'm inclined to advise that you yield and change your climate, rather than run the risk of spending the winter in Minnesota." I doubt he can find a place in California for me. I wish I knew someone there.

Doctor was down again yesterday. He said the first thing: "Your color is better." He says my pulse behaves better too. He talked with me quite a while about my work. He thinks it isn't so much the climate as the *work* – that is – I could stand the cold better if I wasn't working. I'd rather go to a place where the climate is warmer and I can *work*.

It's so easy for people to say "let things go" and that I can't do what other people can. Oh, it makes me *wild*! They (at least Doctor) seem to expect me to be perfectly contented to be a fourth or fifth-class teacher, when I could be *first* class – I *know* I could – Mr. Cloyd said so – if I could only work half-time. Doctor asked me if I did much outside of school hours. He seemed surprised that a primary teacher should have such preparation outside of class. He said he supposed a good primary teacher had a "knack of interesting children and managing them" and that was all there was to it! *Really*! I wonder what he would think of a physician who had a "knack of doctoring folks"!

My mind goes from one end of the chain to the other and back again. I *can't* do what others can, and I never shall be able to. I've been home nearly a month, and I'm not strong yet. What a grumbler I've been. I could stand it better, I think, if I were old.

I'm afraid I ought not send this letter to you. You will feel badly because I'm so impatient, but I want to tell you because you can understand and sympathize. I don't want to be told that "things might be worse" and all that. I know they might, but I want someone to see it all and feel it as I do – and, dearest, I know you do. I'm selfish to let you suffer too. You said you were no "fair weather folks," and it's very sweet to know you can understand – you're the only one who does.

I'm feeling blue today. I have a headache. I'm really much better than I was when I came home. I hope this burst hasn't alarmed you. I get to thinking sometimes – thinking way ahead – and I guess that isn't good for one.

I wonder if you can come down and spend a week from Sunday – oh, that will be the 4th! Good-night – here's a kiss, you dear, dear boy.

Anna

JULY 5, 1897
Eyota to Oronoco

My Dear Roy:

Your letter came Saturday – it was such a short one. I'll have to forgive you, though, for you are working, and I'm of all idlers the idlest.

I went to Winona Wednesday. I took dinner with Mrs. Van Anders and then went to see Pres. Shepard. He was very cordial, and said at once that he thought he could help me. He is to meet a number of superintendents from California, New Mexico and Arizona at the Educational Association in Milwaukee this week. He advised me to go there, and he would introduce and recommend me to people from those states.

He seemed to think there was not much doubt that I could get a position, and I had about made up my mind to go to Milwaukee when I thought I'd see Dr. Lane. He helped me out of a good many colds while I was in Winona, and was always very kind. I laid the whole thing before him – how I have not been well in Cloquet, and how he and other doctors had said I might be better in California. He listened to it all, then examined my heart and lungs, and then told me to go home and go to bed. He said all the discouraging things he could think of, I guess – said I wasn't in any shape to teach, and wouldn't be for a year; that I should stay right at home and not do a thing and lie still as much as possible. He was kind – said he hated to say all he did to me. He said he would see Pres. Shepard and explain it to him, and that when I'm better and able to go to California, Pres. Shepard would help me as willingly as now. Dr. Lane kept at me until I promised him I would take his advice and stay at home.

I've had dreadful times to myself, but I guess I've made up my mind to it now, and I shall be happy, in a way. My father used to try to make me see that it wasn't circumstances – it was *myself* that determined whether or not I should be happy.

Don't worry about me, dear – there's no tuberculosis or anything of that sort about my lungs. Doctor said the "vital forces" of my system were low – heart, lungs and nervous system – so I suppose rest will fix me all right.

I haven't read much lately but magazines. I'm reading *Men of the Moss Hags* aloud to Aunt Matt. Do you remember *Butterflies – A Tale of Nature* by James Lane Allen? I've seen a good deal of him in magazines lately. It says of him in the last *Bookman* that he's one of the few living men who may yet produce something classical. Have you read Robert Louis Stevenson's *St. Ives*? If you haven't, you must read it next time you come to Eyota. It's in *McClure's* – it isn't finished yet.

Come down when you can.

Lovingly,

Anna

JULY 11, 1897
Oronoco to Eyota

Dearest Anna:

I was glad to read that letter even after just seeing you. You wrote that you had dreadful times "to myself." It *is* hard – I knew when you told me – guessed from your look how it was. You must try and be happy as possible. Oh, listen to me preach, would you! Forgive me. Don't think you are no use, though, for it isn't true. I'd like to help you if I could, but I'm so bungling I just say the same thing over again. I want to see you – I'm *always* wanting to see you. Wonder how many times I've said that in 140 letters.

When I got to Rochester Thursday night, of course I had lost connection with train or coach, so I walked home. It was pretty warm. It was well I started as I did, for I was overtaken by a man who waited for the cool of the evening, and he brought me within three miles of home – lucky, wasn't I? Then *that* three-mile's walk I had more company – a fellow walking in to get his wheel. He talked all the way; told me about his bicycle trips – the talk broken only by my polite and pretty ejaculations of wonder, amusement, etc. It's very easy to keep some people talking, isn't it? I believe they like it lots better than to have anyone else talk to *them*.

When I came into town I heard the water roar. It was up – smelled like a June freshet and was the color of chocolate. I ground the next day and the next, but didn't have a great deal. Friday noon I felt – ugh! – as if molasses and dusty feed had been poured down my back, and after dinner I rowed around the Point and cooled off some. Saturday it rained and there wasn't much to grind. Henry and I cleaned out down below in the mill. In the afternoon I was over to Charlie's, and hunted around there and found the magazine that had "The Godmothers." I'm going to read it to you when you come.

Speaking of – when?

Today there have been but few picnickers, but the Mayos are up in force to stay a couple weeks. I helped clean out the boats this morning. Just at evening I rowed over and – oh, such a sunset. How good the coolness feels. Won't it be a great night to sleep?

With my dear love,

Oronoco to Eyota

Dearest:

If all the time you're away seemed as long in proportion as the first two or three days, what an endless time it would be.

It's been rather slack with grinding today, though now I start to write I've nae doot there'll be plenty. I'm writing on a stool at the east mill window in the middle of the afternoon. These are fine days, aren't they, for all the heat? Nearly all the boats are out, and campers keep coming. I think there must be some Eyota people picnicking here today. There's a Plainview bunch of campers just gone. All the fellows wear those soup-bowl hats and look "alike," as Mother says – "medium-hathe, red-har, long-favored."

I've tended boats and ground and read quite a bit today. Gadzooks and Grammercy! I've been reading *White Company* by Arthur Conan Doyle. So the White Company was a band of English archers.

"And we'll drink all together

To the gray goose feather

And the land where the gray goose flew."

It's all about knights, pages, tournaments, ladies, archers, etc. It's pretty well-done and all right to pick up for a bit.

I got even with the hornets in the boathouse. Uncle and I went down to look them over and get 'em in a sack. Couldn't do it – they were right against the wall. So I lighted the sack and held it under until everything was burned. I'll teach them to act so.

This isn't a good letter, even as my letters go. It will do to break the ice, though. Now write to me, dear, for I miss you so – it seems an age. I love you dearly.

Roy

I went over to Uncle George's just at evening – rowed Mable up to where her umbrella sank, and she played Sousa's "Ben Hur" for me. Did you ever hear it? I liked it. You can see the whole chariot race – all the incidents, and the steady beat and roll and work of the race goes on underneath. It's fine this evening – coming back to the cove there's a broad path leading down through the corn, and the strong sweet smell of it.

Good-night, dearie, *my* dearie. There's no one like you.

AUGUST 5, 1897
Oronoco to Eyota

My Dearest Anna:

It's late. I went over to help at the pavilion awhile – some Zumbrota people wanted to dance, and I've just now got back. The folks have all gone to bed. I write now because perhaps I won't get a chance tomorrow.

Pa bought nine more boats. About 60 people came from Zumbrota to camp; the band came with them. More campers here now than last year. No camp so nice as Idyllwilde, though – never will be, I guess. As it gets along in August about camping time, seems as if there's something lacking. It will get more intense. I'm lonesome right now.

Fred and I tossed up to see who should tend mill and who campers. It fell to me to tend mill. We've a little building over there now for oars and office, and there's a little pier where we keep all the boats now. It's lots nicer. Fred sat there at the doorway of his dwelling fixing oars – reminded me of "The Ancient Arrow-maker." I've worked pretty well today – done quite a lot of things. Day before yesterday I felt glorious for no particular cause.

Well, I'll bring *White Company* to you sometime. You don't imagine you'd like it, do you? Perhaps you would. The people aren't like those in *Three Musketeers*. I've been reading a little criticism on "Choir Invisible." I hope we may read that together sometime – imagine it's good.

How I hate to say good-night and then go. When I get squared around I'll write good letters.

With my dear love,

Roy

AUGUST 10, 1897
Oronoco to Eyota

Dear Little Girl:

Just got your letter tonight. You can *too* grumble if you want to, and if that's what you call it. Don't you want to do the fair thing? Think of the stupid blue letters I've written *you* – turn about's fair play. Never let that bother you the least bit.

I've had sort of a headache today – that's unusual with me. It'll feel good in the morning. I'll get a good sleep in my own room here at home in a great broad bed where there's lots of room.

We've been pretty busy. Sunday was a great day. I wish we had twice as many boats and three times the barn room. The Zumbrota band is camping here, and they played a good deal. In the evening – you remember what a beautiful evening it was – they went out on the water, took torches with them, and played and sang. It was very pretty. I was lying on the bank tending boats. Saturday night, despite the rainy day, we had a big dance – pretty good decent one too. We must keep them so. Oh, it was fine as I rowed home, with the big moon's bright track in the water. I thought of you – of course I did – and wished for you.

There were four dances last week, and will be four this week. That Zumbrota camp have hired the pavilion – they are the nicest people here. And they have the most fun of any too – an uproar goeth up from them all the time! They dressed a fellow up in a wrapper and broad hat, got in procession with the band at the head, and one of them went ahead advertising and talking endless truck like a showman, all around the other camps.

No, I don't think the lake in Rochester will hurt us at all. I heard Dr. Mayo say it wouldn't too, so you have authority from two good sources, haven't you? Besides, we don't depend altogether on Rochester. I hope we will reach out further. Wish we had a good summer hotel – could run it ourselves.

I'm going to study this winter. We're going to the state U next year, aren't we?

Dearie, I'm so glad you're getting to enjoy things better – awfully glad to hear you *say* it. I've a grudge against anything taking all the fun out of things for you. Doubtless I shall settle the score someway, sometime – even as I burned out the hornets. My poor little girl – I know how you fret and chafe. Tell me all about it, dearest – it isn't grumbling. It's hard, of course, but it isn't *useless* to lie still this year, for it's to get stronger. Next summer things will look different. And I can come see you just as the first spring weather arrives – how I will love you. You will enjoy the wind and everything – the smell, the uplift – just as you once did. That will be partly worth idling for now, won't it?

It's cooler, isn't it – feels like late summer? I noticed the goldenrod for the first time tonight. I'm glad you aren't way far off. I hope you won't get *very* lonesome and weary this week. I think of you so much. I'm so glad I have *you* – you are everything.

Roy

AUGUST 12, 1897
Eyota to Oronoco

Dearest:

Your letter came yesterday. I'm always saying how good your letters are, but that one seemed *especially* dear. You *dearest* boy – I'm happy now, with your letter here, and I've been thinking how good and true and gentle you are. And, dearie – life seems wonderfully sweet and beautiful to me, because you love me so.

Hasn't it been beautiful today! Mother brought Aunt Matt down, and we sat out on the lawn and ate nuts and pears and drank lemonade and fed the chickens. Mother and I lay on the grass, and Grandma reproved us for matting it down so!

I was weighed today – 104½ – a gain of 4½ lbs. since I came home.

I've been reading "The Reds of the Midi." It's a story of the French Revolution – how the Marseilles Battalion marched to Paris and attacked the Castle of the King. You must read it. It's by some Frenchman – I never heard of the author before – but I guess it's quite true to history. It's stirring! He tells how they marched – 500 of them – sunburned and dust-covered, dragging their cannon and forge. The men were harnessed to the cannon, and "like oxen pulled with head and shoulders." Every muscle was stretched and strained; they were bent nearly double, and the sweat dripped from them; but still they sang "The Marseillaise" and shouted "Vive la Nation!"

It makes me feel like a Frenchman to hear the Marseillaise. I don't wonder they went *wild* as they sang it. The description of the way they marched into Avignon, and later into Paris, is fine. As they marched through Paris, not only 500 but a thousand – 10,000 – 20,000 – were singing with one voice. Wouldn't you like to have been there?

Yes, I've noticed the goldenrod too. This was about the time I am thinking of going away. I'm kinda glad I'm *not* going away from *you*, dear, after all.

Your own Anna

AUGUST 15, 1897
Oronoco to Eyota

Dearest Anna:

This has been the quietest Sunday I've had in a long time. It's been rather cold and dark and drizzled some, but I haven't minded it much – it was a change. Wonder if it's been a long day for you. Perhaps you've been reading about the "Reds" more.

That last letter was such a good one. I got it last evening just before supper, for I ground a little late. Then I read it before I went over to the pavilion. It sent something of the feeling over me that a glimpse of yourself does. It doesn't do any harm, dear, to tell me when you like my letters. They seem so dull sometimes that it does me good to hear it.

Friday and most of Saturday Pa was away, and I tended boats and resort. It was a change from grinding feed, and I rather liked it, for the new boats had come, and I had plenty for all.

Friday as I was getting oars, someone behind me said, "Boom-get-a-rattrap," and I knew it was some of the folks – Thad and Mary, Mrs. Titus and Bob. I was awfully glad to see them. Thad's the same; Mary looked rather thin and coughed. She's had a great cold and bronchitis. Bob's eyes droop at the corners, and 'e's a gurt broad-faced lad. They want to come camping. Late in the afternoon I rowed with them, looking up a site. Wish you were coming too. Miss Mary seems so much nicer – more delicate someway than ordinary people.

I want to see you – I *must* soon.

We had another big dance last night. It's hard to manage a big lot of people so they will all be satisfied, isn't it? Someone lent a book to Mary – Riley's *Neighborly Poems*. Some of them I had never read. I like "When the Frost is on the Pumpkin and the Fodder's in the Shock" – you probably have read it. Mabel stayed all night with Minimo last night – Mabel was stuck in her Caesar. She asked for help, so this afternoon I went over. It was that 14th chapter – "oratio obligua" – you remember. We both worked at it and hammered it out. A body does get rusty. Mabel hasn't had enough Latin grammar – had the declensions and a lot of translations, but didn't know hardly any rules – never heard of the deponent verb or ablative absolute till she began this Caesar.

Mary's going to school – don't know where she's going to board yet. She's getting her traps ready; got the cloth for a red wrapper. Guess she got that partly on my account – brought it out for my inspection.

At one of the camps there were a couple of boys – one about 17 or 18, and the other a kid. They stayed around the oar-house a good deal. I never saw such a fellow who seemed so full of hatred for everyone as that older chap. Everyone who came along, he had something to say about them and hate them for. He was mean to his brother – rough and foul and brutal – and the kid was getting just like him, though perhaps he wasn't naturally so. He must have been so mean that everybody hated him, and that soured him, and he hated everybody – probably himself. Didn't seem to be *anything* he admired. He was a queer savage. Perhaps he would like you better if you treated him well, though he didn't show it. It seemed a shame to get the kid that way.

Write to me soon. Wish I could see you now. That was a lovely letter. I love you dearly.

AUGUST 17, 1897
Oronoco to Eyota

My Dear Anna:

Mary says you intend to have the reunion next Friday. I don't know as I could get away that day of all others, because if it don't rain, I expect it will be the biggest day of the season. Queen City band gave a concert and dance with 14 pieces in the orchestra, a baseball game and a balloon ascension. However, if it's only me who can't come, don't let that interfere with your plans.

Had a long letter from Zimmerman tonight – he's in summer school. He sorta plans on my coming back yet – makes me a little homesick. Said he saw Miss Peck and Jessie, who said she wanted to see me more than any of the old ones. There – ain't I complimented?

I had rather go next year when I'm better prepared. I'm going to be near *you* this year. I'm so glad, dear.

AUGUST 17, 1897
Eyota to Oronoco

My Dear Roy:

I'm not feeling very well today, so I'm taking comfort here on the lounge. I have the pillows piled up high, and have on a comfortable old red wrapper. I have a nice warm fire too. Oh, it's great to be able to lie around when you feel like it, isn't it? I'm glad I don't have to pull myself together and go off to school. I'm losing ambition fast – what will I be at the end of a year?

I wrote Walter two or three weeks ago at Hamline, but didn't hear from him. I was worried. Then here comes his letter this morning! He says he moved and things got out of place, and my letter escaped him "until he got to work to attend to his correspondence." We couldn't have a good time without our old philosopher, so I'll write to folks and change the date of the reunion.

I finished "The Reds of the Midi." I've been reading Hall Caine's *Deemster* some today. Your last letter was a *good* one too. I *like* them long.

Lovingly,
Anna

AUGUST 24, 1897
Eyota to Oronoco

My Dearest Roy:

I've been looking for a letter from you for the last two days – what has happened? Why don't you write? I've been sick since last Tuesday. I feel pretty well now – just a trifle weak, is all. Doctor said it was something like the grippe.

Walter says he will be here Aug. 28, unless something awful happens. You *must* come some way, and you must stay for Sunday.

It seems such a long time since I've seen you, dearest. I want to talk with you more about going to school. I'm inclined to think you better go this year if you can. You can make up the extra work in the two years, and that will be better than staying out another year. You can't make it all up at home anyway, can you? Something might happen, and you might never go if you don't go this year. And there will be so many of your club back – oh, you *must* go! You said in your letter that you were going to be near me this year. Roy, dearest – you're not going to let that keep you away from school, are you? I'm going to ask you this when you come down, and you must answer me truly. You know I'll *keep* (as you always say of yourself), and you must not take me into consideration at all in what you do.

I seem to dread and feel sad over these signs of fall as much as I ever do, and I'm not going to work either. You must come soon – I want you, dear. We were together some the fall of '94 in September – do you remember? The leaves were falling from the vine over the summer house, and the plums were ripe. I wish you were here.

With my love,
Anna

AUGUST 25, 1897
Oronoco to Eyota

My Dearest Anna:

It isn't long since I wrote you, but it seems long someway. We looked for you Friday and Saturday. I didn't know but you would feel better with the fine weather and perhaps come out.

As a result of my traipsing off helping campers, a man had to bide quite a while for his grist. I heard of his being there in an angry frame of mind, and went down prepared, and laid myself out handsome, and his anger, if there was any, faded away in thin air.

The folks seemed to want me to come and see them often, so I did – often as I could. I took dinner there Sunday. We had green corn and apple pie and beef steak and potatoes, and it seemed like the old days.

I like such weather as we've been having – it feeleth like fall. It seems strange to think I can come and see you now – always before, in the fall time, we've said good-bye and gone opposite ways. It seems *very* good, dearie.

I hope you're feeling better. I'm thankful you aren't "pulling yourself together" every day and going on, on to the death. Anna, I love you – oh so much – right now.

Roy

SEPTEMBER 5, 1897
Oronoco to Eyota

Dearest Anna:

This letter shall be a nondescript one – written on odds and ends, bits of bone and parchment – for he who writes is shut out from his own place and writes on whatever he finds in his room.

How are you? I've rather been expecting a letter – perhaps you've been feeling the same way.

I wanted to write today, but I was doing other things until this late hour. You see, Mary said this was the last Sunday she would be at home for a while; wanted me to do as she wished, etc., so I have done so in great part.

What a delightful, sparkling letter this is! Well – Oy's sleepy a little.

Louie brought over his *Munsey's* last week and I read "The Christian" up-to-date. I like it – a lot. I fell in love with Glory. Mary has a fine copy of *Les Misérables*. I've read a little in that. I've had a good day today. A week ago we were together. You were good to me when I was stupid. I wish reunions came oftener – I want to see you *dreadfully*, and it's been only a week – "week's a long time."

It's fine weather for all the heat. This morning I was all right and clean, and I sat and read quite a while. Then I sauntered out to think and look around. I met Crossen down by the mill. He's the barber here until school commences. He's a Hamline man – graduates next year. He used to room across the hall from me. (About the only bright spots in that Hamline life were your letters to me, dearest. Oh, there were other things, of course, but those were best. You've been very good to me.) We decided to go out. It was a fine morning. We went up to the headwaters and then up to the rocks, where you and Clara and I went. Guess I haven't been there since. Crossen talked quite a lot. When we were done, he said he'd had a very pleasant time – he would remember for a long time. I'm glad – I was feeling all right, and didn't make myself *very* obnoxious, perhaps.

Hope you're feeling well, dear. I think of you so often.

I've been a little dissatisfied with myself some this week. Sometimes I wish I was in Alaska. It seems as if I've never done *anything* except work pretty well sometimes. But I've never done anything that seemed to count for much.

Try not to get utterly weary of my letters.

SEPTEMBER 5, 1897
Eyota to Oronoco

My Dearest Roy:

I believe I wrote you a year ago today from Cloquet. I would probably be writing you from Cloquet today, if it hadn't been for Dr. Lane.

I've been in Rochester all week. Aunt Hattie and I commenced to fix things for Clara and her room. She's working hard at her German. Aunt Hattie and I made a puff, a comforter and pillow shams. We hemmed sheets and towels and made lots of things. I enjoyed helping her get ready.

Monday we all went for dinner to Miss Knapp's. I wasn't dressed for such things, but I went. We got to talking about Hall Caine's books and *The Deemster*. Uncle Henry and Mrs. Edgar thought those books might not have a good influence upon young people, and objected to their being in the city library. Mary and Thad and I took the other side – we thought it would be a *very* good book for a boy to read – that he would see in that story that it isn't the *punishment* that law inflicts, but the *remorse* that follows the sin – that is, the awful consequence of sin. The punishment by law may be escaped (every boy knows that without reading Hall Caine), but Caine shows that he can never escape *himself* and his own thoughts. Mrs. Edgar thought the harm was in putting bad things into the heads of children. She's an old teacher – she must know something about it. They talked about all sorts of things, and I thoroughly enjoyed it.

I had a stiff neck Tuesday and Wednesday – it's the most ridiculous thing to ail one, but it hurts, and you like best to keep still.

Van Smith came calling – I haven't seen him for some time, and he's changed some. He wore white duck trousers, and looked as dainty and clean and cool as a girl. He has a camera and showed us pictures of his room. He's furnished it in oriental style – Indian tapestries on the walls and draped from the corners to the middle of the ceiling. There are all sorts of pretty knickknacks, incense burners, shaped stools and tables, an oriental lamp and sofa pillows – elegant ones. He had a picture of a palm he's been growing. He talked of music and musicians and composers; he's been reading books on metaphysics and psychology. I think he leans a bit toward Christian Science. He takes an art magazine and has his walls covered with studies from the best artists. He told us how he got things together for his room without it costing very much. He's been reading a translation of the Koran, but he likes Riley and Kipling in spite of his love for the ancient. He's like a girl in caring to talk about only what he likes.

What a lot about Van Smith! I presume you're intensely interested (!). I wonder what *you* would think of him. I never talked with a boy like him before – he seems like a *girl*, but he doesn't seem quite "dependable."

I'm sorry you've been feeling blue. I wish I might learn how to drive it away. Then perhaps I might have a "second sight" like Dan's old nurse in *The Deemster*, and I'd know when you were blue and how to drive it away – wouldn't that be fine? Well, you're all right – it doesn't matter so much what you *do* as who you *are*. You're all the world to Someone just as you are, and Someone knows she'll never be disappointed in him.

There's a story in the *Ladies Home Journal* – "The Spirit of Sweetwater" by Hamlin Garland. Clara and I read it and we liked it. The hero of the story has the same effect on one as a strong fresh bracing wind. It's a western too.

Clara spoke of you – Mr. Titus said he had heard of Roy Allis and would like to meet him. Uncle Henry and Aunt Hattie have a plan – they want me to come there and stay with them. They say they *really* want me – that the girls are going away and they will be lonely. I think they're doing it mostly on my account because they think *I'm* lonely here and things trouble me. I talked with Aunt Matt about it. She thinks I'd better go. I've not spoken to Mother and Grandma yet. I think they won't care. I'd rather be there than anywhere. What do you think?

I haven't read the last *Munsey*, but I like "Glory" too – my, she was a real girl – a friend. I should admire her. I'd be very fond of her, but I'd be ashamed of her sometimes – would you? She's very real, isn't she?

I haven't written such a long letter all summer, and it's a tiresome letter too – I'm sorry! I won't do so every time. Write again this week, dearest. I'm so glad to get your letters.

With my love,

Anna

CHAPTER 27

Glorious Fall

SEPTEMBER 9, 1897

Oronoco to Eyota

My Dearest Anna:

I'm all alone, squared round and ready. Auntie and Mother are out calling, I guess. How pleasant this new coolness is – it came so quickly. I went over to the grounds to keep Lou company while he was waiting for some fellows to come in. We took a couple sets of oars and rowed up the south branch so Lou could get his supper, and I didn't notice 'twas cooler, but that I rowed with less mental exertion.

Now I'll read your letter again. There – take that promise back – I like long letters too! Who *is* this Van Smith, and what doth he do? I've heard others speak of him.

The vagabond has been stirring in me. Of course, best of all, I'd like to go to Alaska, but I have no 160 acres of land to sell like my pop had when he raised his stake to go to California in '49. I've wasted my youth getting larnin' 'stead of chopping cordwood, logging, etc. Ah me. I hope I may go to school next fall, but barring that – I'll go vagabonding! The folks are going to California pretty sure to visit family, I guess. Well – I'll be a good steady lad and take care of myself, but it'll be because I hope for better things. It's no way for a so-called gentleman to work away like a turtle and let the moss grow on his back, now is it, Miss Barnard?

I brought up Walter's geometry when I came. Wonder if it wouldn't be a good scheme for me to get a certificate to teach school? Beshrew me, but it might be a useful thing for the aforesaid restless vagabond gentleman. I've been so dreadfully dependent – I've worked well enough, but I've never been cut loose. Perhaps it would be a good thing – of a verity, it singeth in my ears and raiseth my heart. But this winter I'll work and study some – take care of myself. The folks will go away and come back rested. And I shall see you this year, dearest, no matter wha kens. It's so good to know there is *you*, and that you are who you are. Dearie, I don't want you to be disappointed in me. It would be the worst of anything.

We've been threshing this warm weather. It's always hot weather in that upstairs room in the mill. Wonder if Van Smith would look dainty and sweet at that? Sometimes one gets into the spirit of such things, and glories in being a strong, hot, reeking animal that cares not at all for anything. And then sometimes one has other *unrealized* longings to be dainty, cool and sweet.

Writing's a kinda unhandy medium for telling things, isn't it?

I went swimming last night with Louie and Rube – oh, it was nice. I took off most of my suit so's to have it dry to come home in, and it felt glorious after the heat and dust to stretch out and feel the coolness all around and over you. We had a great time. We rowed over to the grounds to get Rube a cot so he wouldn't have to sleep on the floor. We yelled awful – no – we shouted *moderately*, and we danced in the moonlight before the houses of the man-pack. Rube is awfully "steeple-shouldered" – about as broad as my hand in the shoulders, and wide-hipped, and over all his fragile garb he had a long linen duster of Fred's. He looked astonishing. We called him Cimourdain after the stern, ascetic old priest in *Ninety-three*.

I've been reading up some of the back series of *Corleone* in *Munsey*. I like it, but somehow there seem to be so many words that I get tired of it. Does it affect you so, or did you never read anything of Marion Crawford's?

I don't see why it wouldn't be all right to stay with the Titus people, because they want you, and you like best to stay there. I think it would be nice for you. You wouldn't have to stay there all the time.

How folks are getting off to school now – Mabel goes Saturday night, Mary Sunday, Mary Pettit Tuesday. And "Oy, he makes the wheels go round." Never mind that I'm not going – I don't.

I wonder what I've written. I'm glad you're not in Cloquet – awfully glad. I want to see you, and I love you with my whole heart.

Roy

SEPTEMBER 12, 1897
Eyota to Oronoco

My Dearest Roy:

Isn't it nice and hot! I've gloried in wearing white dresses nearly every day this week. I want to hold on to these warm days and glorious nights, for I know they'll be gone so soon. It doesn't seem like September and time for school – that is, to be working again. I wish you were here and we could enjoy this weather together. The folks are half dead with the heat, and I flourish like a "green bay tree." I suppose I'm wicked to so delight in what is a trouble to others – including you, working in the heat – but it won't last long.

Yesterday Mother and I mended sacks. We worked from dinnertime till dark. We sat in the woodshed, and as the sacks were dusty, we wore old gowns and aprons and capes. The only needle work I'd done before was embroidering silk. It was fun to work at the sacks for a while, where you could hurry along and take long stitches, and all you had to work for was to make it strong.

I'm starting a conversational German class. And I've read *Margaret Ogilvy* – Barrie's book about his mother. They must have been great friends. A book like that makes me feel that others have had something I never had and never *can* have. I often think I would have been very different if I could have had my mother and been with her all this time. She was very spiritual, they say, and sweet and good, and she thought everything of us. And she was bright and cheerful, even when she was sick. I wish I could remember back to the time when she was gay and merry, as they say she was.

We can't see how things work. I may have been influenced by her – they say I look and act like her. I'm not complaining – I have you, and you are *everything*. Oh, Roy – I'm *so* glad you're near this year – I'm afraid it will spoil me forever going far away again.

Eyota people are the queerest in all the world! Mrs. Wright was in Friday – she said it was the anniversary of her wedding day, and she thought Mr. Wright ought to celebrate, so she persuaded him to celebrate by going to St. Paul while she "tended shop" back here in Eyota! I looked at her ready to laugh, but her eyes were honest – she saw nothing funny.

A week from tomorrow is your birthday – can't you come down the Sunday before?

With my love,

Anna

SEPTEMBER 16, 1897
Oronoco to Eyota

Dearest:

I won't be able to see you Saturday – I'm sorry. Likely I'll come next week if you let me. Fred has gone to Kasson to play at a fair, and tomorrow we thrash, and the fish chute is just being commenced, and my pa must see to that personally, so I must be here.

I wish I could have seen you in a white dress this summer. Well, I like to see you just as well when you look warm. You're a regular salamander! Wonder why you like the heat so well. I like warm weather better than winter, but I like the "in-between" such as we have now best.

I've ground steadily all day – a splendid day – one of the kind I like. The north wind sent waves down the pond, and the spray flew from the dam, and I could hear the strong wind in the trees all the time, and the bright sunlight too. When it's so warm, and I work in the dust, I don't half sleep at night. I work at something in my head, half-asleep. The other night I shifted my pillow to the foot of the bed, with a vague idea that it would seem cool to see the sky.

Charlie sent after a great 44-caliber Colt's revolver – weighs 2½ lbs. It came tonight. I want one – that's the American weapon. I'm reading *Les Misérables* yet; soon I intend to study some.

I want to see you *dreadfully* again, and so I will soon. I always imagined you were like your mother – you're very gentle and spiritual too, dear. I want to be very good to you – I hope I may do it the right way.

With my dear love,

Roy

SEPTEMBER 17, 1897
Eyota to Oronoco

My Dearest Roy:

Perhaps you had better bide a wee. Mother and I are helping Delle all we can, and Grandma is so sick this morning. Delle will be through this week, and next week is all free. Come if you can – I want *so much* to see you.

That last letter was wonderfully good, dearie. This has been a blue day, and I want to write to you for a minute and be "comforted." The nerves have been on the outside again today, and little things have seemed unbearable. Something was said that struck my cry strata, and I've been letting myself go – I couldn't help it – and now my head aches, and I'm weak and faint. My head wants to go down to our old place, and I want to hear someone say that he understands, and I'm not acting sulky and childish.

It's a comfort to know you *do* understand, and you're so considerate. Roy, *my* Roy – good-night.

With my love,

Anna

SEPTEMBER 19, 1897
Eyota to Oronoco

Dearest:

Mother and Grandma have gone to church and I'm alone. I wish you were here. Mother and I took a long drive this afternoon – we went to Marion and beyond to the "Hog's Back." This charming name belongs to a ridge between two valleys. The road is very narrow in places, and you can look down the steep banks more than a hundred feet to the river. It's quite a wild, pretty place. Perhaps we'll go there sometime. It was a fine afternoon – there was quite a strong wind and the air was fresh and clear. There was the fall sunlight too. Such days are beautiful, but they make me want to cry.

You're as busy as ever at Oronoco. I'd like to see you tomorrow because it's your birthday, but I can wait. Delle is coming Tuesday, and will be here sewing all week. If you could come Saturday, it would be all right. You could come anytime, you know – only if we can't be outdoors, Delle is always in the *way*, and we have to talk like sensible beings.

The German class has met twice. I think we'll enjoy and get some good from it. How does Mary like school, and how does she get on away from home?

I've been reading *Adam Bede* again. I read it when I was 14 or 15, I think. I've changed since then – I have more sympathy with people now, even if I've lost some of my confidence in them. Perhaps finding unexpected weakness in the best of people has helped to give me more sympathy for everyone. I don't believe I'll read any more of George Eliot or Thackeray or those writers who make you feel the terrible struggles and temptations and suffering of humanity – at least not until I'm at work again. Such books are depressing now. It makes me want to get out in the air and sunlight and take good deep breaths. Guess I'll read Robert Louis Stevenson and go back to my books for children and Barrows' books about birds and flowers.

What *are* some books that are good and fresh and wholesome?

I've been reading again the note I wrote Friday night. I thought at first when I read it I wouldn't send it, but I will. We must tell each other of the things that trouble us. Here's a kiss for your birthday, dear – one on your forehead, one on your lips.

With my dear love,

Anna

SEPTEMBER 21, 1897
Oronoco to Eyota

Dearest Little Girl:

I never have been with you when you needed me most. If I could only have seen you when you were so down, and I'm *glad* you sent that note. You *must* tell me all things – and, dearest, you know I'm right *with* you and *for* you always, even if I'm not there in person. I *want to be there*, though. I'm glad you wrote to me so, dearie – very glad. We stand together.

I like these fall days. I guess I can feel a little of what you mean when you say they make you want to cry. Tonight is just fine. I imagine you sitting out on the porch. I love you for all times of the year, dearie.

I went back toward the water just at night. As I walked over the grass and stirred leaves, the faint smell and all things together brought feelings up to me – too shadowy to be thoughts. Strange, isn't it, about sensations? Perhaps they are shadows of the first sensations we had when we were little children – when things were altogether new.

I've been reading more of *Les Misérables*. I believe I will bring *White Company* to you to read. It's fresh and free – mainly action – and no mind analysis, and the foes all flesh and blood. What have you read of Scott? His books are fresh and wholesome. His women aren't so real, but his men are very much alive and human – a body can generally get hold of them. If you like him and haven't read them, try *Waverly* or *Quentin Durward*. *Waverly* gets better the deeper you get in.

Mary was home the weekend. She likes school pretty well, I guess, but glad to get home. Said she cried about her Latin twice. She'll be all right – likes Miss Peck and Mr. Overholt. I looked at the course of studies. Things are different now from what they were in our time – more compact, ironclad – only one course.

Yes, yesterday was my birth-day (on my forehead and lips – you are just adorable, dearie). I ground all day and didn't get through. The stone is up; Fred is dressing it. We've been thrashing – yes, we've been quite busy this week.

I'll go over and mail this, and then I believe I'll trot around the drive a couple times. I haven't done any of that, and I think I'm getting lazy.

My, I'm glad you are near. There's *no one* like you.

With my dear love,

Roy

You deserve a better letter than this.

SEPTEMBER 24, 1897
Oronoco to Eyota

Dearest Anna:

I'm tempted to come see you tomorrow in the evening, in spite of your warning. It's just come into my unreasoning head that I want to see you *very* much right off. I'm queer. If I should do so, and it wasn't right, you'll tell me, won't you? And I'll go straight back. Fred will be gone last of next week, and the week after part of the time, so I'll be busier then.

There's no telling what I may do. You said to come if I could. Oh, well – I'll just push the dumbbells a while and go to bed. I worked sharp all day. Good-night, dearest, my own dearest.

Roy

OCTOBER 1, 1897
Eyota to Oronoco

My Dearest Roy:

What a beautiful day this has been! I've been in tune with the weather all week, and full of a warm, quiet happiness that was half-sad too. I believe all nature hates to have these days go. The trees have been still, as if trying to keep the leaves – their children – with them as long as they can. The maples ae turning from within – their inner leaves are yellow, but the outer ones are still green. I've been dreamy, like the days, and hardly know what I've done since you went away.

I've not read much – a little in *White Company*. I like what I've read, but I'm not in reading mood. *The Review of Reviews* has a review of "The Christian" that's better than the one in *The Bookman*. It says of Glory: "She stands out – lithe, red-lipped, sunny, with buoyant life lustily coursing through her veins; a full-blooded, beautiful pagan, and withal, a very sweet-natured, kind-hearted girl." That's just Glory, isn't it? I'm anxious to finish the story. I'm afraid Glory isn't coming out as I thought she would.

I seem to be running over with happiness tonight, and can think of nothing except how good I feel, and I wish you were here. I love you and miss you as I always do.

With my dearest love,

Anna

I've been reading *St. Ives* by R.L. Stevenson – it's running in *McClure's*. You must read it. St. Ives was a Frenchman, and my! what adventures he has, and how he gets through them. It's better than *Kidnapped*.

OCTOBER 3, 1897
Oronoco to Eyota

My Dear Anna:

I had a dream that it was fall-time. I was mistaken (just dreaming) – see the hepaticas I've enclosed. The smell of the woods and water is maddening when one has to work. Today has been glorious. Mary and I went rowing and wandering this morning.

You should be with me. I think you would like me tonight. I'm *different*.

With my love,

OCTOBER 6, 1897
Eyota to Oronoco

My Dearest Roy:

Poor little hepaticas – are they dreaming, or are we? Isn't this a glorious fall? It's the best since I can remember. How the wind must blow the spray over the lake. I'd like to look out the south window of the mill today. We ought to be together this month.

> "Oh, suns and skies and clouds of June,
> And flowers of June together,
> Ye cannot rival for one hour
> October's bright blue weather."
> *(From Helen Hunt Jackson's poem "October")*

I'm *living* again now. I've been out here on the porch all afternoon. The wind blows a gale, and I have to hold tight to this paper. The sun has come out again – how yellow and mellow it is! Grandma went to Chatfield this afternoon to stay several days. She's been telling Mother and me how to take care of the house and what to cook while she's gone.

I've been reading *The White Company* – I like it. I read "The Christian" in the October *Munsey's* last night. I'm disappointed in Glory – she didn't love John Storm half as much as he deserved. I'd be willing to go to the ends of the earth with you – but then I've no "career" to give up as Glory had. And besides, John Storm wasn't such a "lover" as you (!). If it were you instead of John Storm, I'm quite sure Glory would have gone. You *must* read it. I believe she was as bad as the girl in *The Light That Failed* was to Dick. (No she wasn't, for Dick was lovable even if he *did* swear, and John Storm isn't, for some reason – I wonder why.)

Mother and I had a good time Sunday. We drove about 20 miles on a new road through the prettiest woods, and came out on the edge of a bluff. There was a magnificent view – the air was hazy, and everything was softened by it, and away off everything melted into a blue gray smoke.

Mrs. Doty called one day and saw "The Voyage of Maeldune" beside me. I was reading and learning from it as I sewed. Mrs. Doty asked what it was, and I read a couple verses. I could see she didn't like it. She asked what *I* liked about it – I said the beauty, the rhythm. I couldn't tell her exactly what is so *charming*. She said if I wanted to learn something, why didn't I learn "Thanatopsis"? Think of "when thoughts of the last bitter hour come like a blight over thy spirit" instead of "the red passion-flower to the cliffs, and the dark-blue clematis, clung." My! No comparison. I'll love my Tennyson and Riley, with his "Ringlety-jing and what shall we sing" and "rhymes and chimes;" and Fields and his "Rock-a-bye Lady;" and "China Plate and Calico Cat." No matter what sober-minded people think – it's like the little boy's lamb I told you about – if "me like it" that's enough.

Good-bye, dearie – here's a long, long kiss.

Anna

OCTOBER 7, 1897
Oronoco to Eyota

My Dearest Anna:

I need to write to you – that was a splendid letter! If I'd been tired or cross, it would have taken it all out of me. Oh, yes – it's been glorious weather – the mornings and mists and blue sky and water – oh, so fresh when it's early; the days and sunsets and moonlight evenings and smell of leaves. I feel so well – I knew you would get to "living" again.

I've been alone in the mill for nearly two weeks – Fred has been sick. I'm troubled about him – he has a terrible headache at times, and a fever that rises and falls. He looks thin and doesn't eat. I hope he gets better soon. Typhoid hangs around and reduces a person that way sometimes before it lets go. The poor lad is so nervous, too – I'm afraid he will worry and fret himself into a fever. He acts as if the whole universe rests on his shoulders. He'll get better soon – he must.

Yes, the spray was flying yesterday afternoon. I wasn't very busy – I read some in *Les Misérables*. No one was at work on the fishway. Pa had gone to town and I was seeing to things.

I've had some sharp runs this week, but didn't mind. When a body wants to work fastest, to do the most, I've learned you don't want to "tear" yourself, but work still and stubborn all the time – keep everything in front of you. Everyone knows this, of course, but perhaps they don't realize it.

I've written only a scrap since I last saw you, haven't I? The little hepaticas, yes – I was with Mary over in "our woods" of the old days. It was beautiful – they were on a slope among the colored leaves, with the yellow hazy sunlight over them – poor little folks. I suppose they thought it queer and different from what their folks had told them of life.

I saw Miss Peck up at the high school. The schools were just out as I came up, and a long line of folks came down the walk, but hardly anyone knew me. It seems strange to have people you don't know look at you in familiar places. Miss Peck and I had quite a talk. She asked about you, and said good things I winna tell. She wants to see you very much. She said I had grown and improved, in – it seems a queer thing for me to say – a *spiritual* way. She said I seemed much more *pliable*. If it's true, it's on account of you, dearie – because of my loving you these years. One couldn't do that without being better. I think she could see the change.

Miss Peck likes my sister Mary – she says she has a hard time over her Latin. Miss Peck said she came to her in "anguish of spirit" the other day; Miss P said she had never seen *me* in that frame of mind over Latin – she had seen me *angry* and *stubborn*, but never *sorry*. She said Mary was very conscientious and persevering in her work – more than I used to be.

Then I went up to where Mary lives. She was feeling very sorry – there were tears in her eyes. She thought she wasn't doing well in school, and wanted to walk with me. I comforted my kleine sister best I could. I 'spose it made her want to cry more, but perhaps it didn't do any harm after a while, I hope. Just told her she was all right, and not to take things so much to heart – they didn't cut much. Talked in an elder fashion, if you can believe it!

Then I walked three miles and met a great three-seat surrey with all Cass McCray's family, and hopped in. I had forgotten it was the day they were pulling up and going back to Pennsylvania. I was sorry to have them go. Those brothers always have been together – this will be real hard to leave Joe behind. It was pitiful to hear them talk to each other about commonplace things, when you knew they could think of nothing else but leaving. It was a nice ride home all alone on the big soft back seat. I didn't talk to Joe – could see him wipe his eyes once in a while and then speak to the horses. Sometimes I think he looks as much like a man as anyone I ever saw.

I finished "Choir Invisible" – liked it immensely, clear-through.

This is an awfully long, rambling letter, I'm afraid. That was a splendid letter you sent. You are wonderfully nice – the *dearest* little girl. I wish I were as I want to be, for your sake.

With my dearest love,

OCTOBER 10, 1897
Eyota to Oronoco

Dearest:

Was *my* letter the cause of such a wonderfully good letter from *you*?! Wish my letter *could* take the tiredness away from you.

I'm glad you had a talk with Miss Peck – Roy, that's *fine* what she says of you. And, dearest – you can't think how it touches me to have you say that *I* have helped. Poor Mary – I know how she feels. You must not let her feel she's no earthly good, as I did when I couldn't get my "examples" done. No one realized how I felt, I guess, but Clara was my good angel. I hope I can go to Rochester soon – then I shall see Miss Peck, and, oh, I won't tell you a *thing* she says – *then* you'll wish you hadn't been so tantalizing!

We have a new minister – Mr. Dodge – a young man. He looks like a sensitive sort of a fellow – as though he needed to have people stand by him to do his best. I couldn't help but feel sorry for him today – he will have so much cold water thrown on him. I'm afraid it will drive out the earnestness – the enthusiasm – he seems to have. I have more sympathy for young people just starting out in their work or in a new place since I went to Cloquet and started in among strangers. How chilling a little carelessness or indifference can be, and how wonderfully good a little encouragement is. I'm going to help what I can.

I want to see you very much tonight. Good-night, dearest, dearest.

Anna

OCTOBER 13, 1897
Oronoco to Eyota

Dearest Anna:

Was my last letter so good? I'm a little tired tonight – not *dead* tired – just comfortably tired. I ground until after dark, and then have been lazing around at different things. Fred is getting better – he's awfully thin for the time he's been sick.

I read the latest chapter of "The Christian." It troubled me a little when I read it. I'm not ashamed of Glory, or disappointed – I like her, and can sympathize with her in lots of things. John Storm is so unselfish and earnest and self-sacrificing, you're ashamed to say anything against him. But he seems *determined* to be a monk of some kind. Why doesn't he do it then, and not try to drag warm-hearted human people into it, who want to love and live so much? And then Storm, of course, had to fix it so he couldn't tell her he loved her – he would make up for it in the next world. How could he tell such a one as Glory that he couldn't have understood her? He was super-humanly selfish – one feels ashamed to speak against him. But I don't like monks. I sympathize with Glory a lot, and I stand by her. It isn't always loftiness of character that makes people "likable," is it? You said, "Dick was likable, even if he did swear." Wasn't he likable because he *did* swear? I guess my philosophy is a little weak here.

I'm glad you like "Voyage of Maeldune" – very glad. Most people wouldn't. I'm glad we can like things together. I read it first last fall. And such a child or barbarian I am – that it rang in my head and made me feel so good and exultant and strong. I imagine that's how those old fellows used to feel after a great rattling saga or *The Song of Roland*. Did you ever read *Roland*? Every verse ends with that old, old war cry of the North – Aoi! I remember reading how a captive Norman sang it to Hereward and his men in an English forest.

I'm afraid this is a stupid letter, and I'm getting sleepy and haven't time to redeem it if I could. I want to see you so much. I love you always.

OCTOBER 21, 1897
Oronoco to Eyota

My Dearest Anna:

I've a lot of writing I ought to do – five or six letters – and I've come up to my room to wrastle with it. But before I "wrastle" I'll write to *you*. It's *different* with you (though sometimes I'm ashamed of my letters to you). When I write people I should like to write *good* ones.

I'm glad you like *White Company*. I believe you'd like *King Solomon's Mines* too. I've read *Study in Scarlet* – I didn't like it very well – it's something like *Sign of the Four*. Don't let me prejudice you, though.

I'm alone in the mill yet. I rather like it – do everything just as I see fit. The fish chute is done, and it's a daisy. Oh, yes – I remember what a morning it was Sunday. I got up feeling so good. I hadn't been lazy a bit all week – ran and everything – and then I felt just right sitting where it was warm by the kitchen fire and reading so still and stupid and comfortable. But then I had to be interrupted to get a boat.

I read some of the *Tale of Two Cities* that Mary is reading in her English Literature class. Remember Sidney Carlton? It was long ago that I read it – the first or second of Dickens' that I read, and he stayed by me better than all the rest.

I went to church with Mary. When I got out I felt as if I was full of energy bottled up. Do you ever feel that way – when you sit very still in unaccustomed quiet, and your muscles feel harder than usual?

I wish you could be here at Oronoco these fine fall days – you never have been. The leaves and woods are very beautiful – there are so many kinds of trees. I think you would like it better than any other time – I do. Saturday I got through work just as the sun set, and took some of it in – the bright yellow light in the tall yellow trees.

I've wanted so much to go to Minneapolis and see the Wisconsin game and a theatre or so (and the folks, of course). But I didn't see how I could do it without trouble – I was afraid to ask Pa. I wanted a change, you see – to do as I used to do once. But I'm trying to make expiation these two years – give back for what the folks have done for me.

I'm feeling very well. Frank Wood left his Indian clubs at the mill. I picked up three or four swings and think they're all right. I'll try and get a book about them, and believe I can learn a good deal – I think I'm improving. *(These bowling-pin-shaped clubs were exceptionally popular for both men and women during the health craze of the late Victorian area. Gymnasia were built just to cater to club exercise groups.)* I have more sense too, than I had two years ago. If I could only get so I feel I'm doing something well and strongly to a purpose. I don't want you to be disappointed in me a bit, *ever*.

I want to see you so – I want to *talk* with you. Dearie, do you think I might come a week from Saturday? I love you with all my heart.

Please don't think I'm egotistical because I stud this letter so thick with I's. My – how they bristle!

OCTOBER 28, 1897
Oronoco to Eyota
Dearest:

I'm going up to see the Wisconsin game after all. Things came around, so it seemed I could go all right. But I'm half-disappointed – I was planning on coming to see *you* Saturday, you know, and it seems so long this month. But I'm afraid Wisconsin will win this year from what has already happened. I'm a mascot, so I want to be there – do you see, dearie? Minnesota *must* eat up those Badgers.

But I will see you soon. You know I'd rather see you than a whole lot of football games, but I can do both, and this seems the only chance I'll have to get back there.

With my dear love,

NOVEMBER 3, 1897

Oronoco to the home of Thomas Henry Titus (Anna's uncle), *528 W. 2nd St. Rochester MN*

My Dearest Anna:

I'm back. Did you read about it – that horrible Waterloo of a game? It was awful, wasn't it? I'll tell you about it when I see you. It seems so long – can I come see you at the end of the week?

I got home Monday night – had a good time – saw all the people, the game, and a couple of theaters. Otis Skinner was playing Prince Rudolph. I didn't see Miss Sperry – she came home sick with nervous prostration.

By the way – I saw your Mr. Cloyd while I was in Minneapolis – actually ate next to him a couple times!

Isn't it beautiful weather? How I want to see you. I haven't the heart to write, for I want something better. Write me, dear.

With my dearest love,

CHAPTER 28

Looking for the Cows

NOVEMBER 5, 1897
Rochester to Oronoco

My Dearest Roy:

What a snowstorm – the old woman of the sky is surely picking her geese this morning.

I'm in Rochester "helping" Uncle Henry in the bank – doesn't that sound big? The reality is Uncle H. is good enough to let me putter around the bank and make believe I'm doing something. I take up a good deal of his time asking questions, and I get things out of place, and shut up important papers in books, and make mistakes – all that and more in a few hours! Yesterday from 3 to 6 p.m. was my first experience.

*Young Roy on
the Zumbro River*

Yes, I thought you would stay longer in Minneapolis, so I didn't write. I read about the "Waterloo." I'd like to see Mr. Cloyd. I liked him and disliked him, but I'd rather see him than lots of people I did *not* have a "dislike" for – does that make sense? Did you tell him you knew me? Probably he thinks I'm still in Cloquet. What did you think of him? Did he act conceited, or did he have on company manners and act very pleasant and agreeable?

You may come and see me here, you know – as if I were at home. You will be in *soon*, won't you? Then we can *talk*.

With my love,

Anna

NOVEMBER 8, 1897
Oronoco to Rochester c/o T.H. Titus

My Dearest:

I got home at 1 a.m., I think *(Roy was walking from Rochester to Oronoco – about 11 miles each way).* I don't know what time I started after I left you. Nothing very interesting happened, except that for some cause I got ravenously *hungry* after a mile or two. The north wind helped it, and for three or four miles I thought what was there in the dark houses I passed that would do the most good – buckwheat cakes and "fillin'" things. Auntie left me crackers and a wee bit of meat and fruit – tasted awfully good. Then I slept.

I thought of you as I told you it would be. It was so very *good* to see you. I was just a trifle tired this morning, but I'll have a great sleep tonight. My papa didn't know I was going yesterday, or he would have had me take our horse Fanny. Guess I will use her in the future.

We had a rather busy day in the mill today, and ground up a lot of things ahead, for the masons come to build that wall tomorrow, and we can't run the rye stone while they're at work.

I'm not going to write more – you may write *me* a long letter, though. Wish I might see you. I love you "lots."

With my dear love,

Roy

NOVEMBER 14, 1897
Oronoco to Rochester

My Dearest (she who writes wonderful letters!):

Mary was having a bad day, so I didn't broach the subject of coming to visit you. And I don't like to come so often without some plausible pretext. But may I come next week, please? I'm wanting to see and talk to you as you can't imagine. I'm glad you didn't think to have me take something to eat when I left – it would be prosaic, and that would be worse than hunger, I guess. I'm awfully glad you aren't so drefful *practical*. What a head for *dreams* you have.

What a letter, dear heart, you wrote me! I'm going to tell you again what I think of you when I see you. I'd been grinding all day and into the evening and got your letter and carried it a little and read it. Then I went out where it was still in the moonlight and thought of things – the effect is with me yet, my dearest. Do you know it's going to be very hard to be away from you very long at a time – harder than ever? I wish lots of things.

We've been hard at work this week. The old wall is going up pretty fast, with six or seven men at it most of last week, and it will take three or four days yet. I could grind but one run while they were at work, for the dust smoked them out, and there came a great rush, so we've been grinding evenings as well as days. Fred has been fixing up his "house" for winter, so I've been alone in my glory, except in the evenings.

Clara Titus (Anna's cousin), Anna, and Mrs. Hattie Titus (Anna's aunt) at the Titus home in Rochester, Minnesota

Isn't it a typical November today – dark and gloomy, and such a black night as it is outside? I've been pretty quiet most of the day – been reading more in *Tale of Two Cities*. You've finished *Choir Invisible*. 'Member his telling about the old road through the forest – that road where John Gray waited for his man – and who and what had traveled it, coming from all directions from the north, and the "warm, moon-loved southern mountains." I liked that, didn't you?

My own dearest – I love you so much. It would be different if we were both there, I guess. I hope you're going to be in Rochester quite a while. You like it there, I think – 'tis good for you.

The pond froze partly the other night. Hope we get some good skating – then you're going to honor us wi' your presence again – I hope you'll come.

I hope it will be another such day as this when I see you – the contrast, the bleakness and dreariness – and then – being with you.

With my dear love always,

NOVEMBER 18, 1897
Rochester to Oronoco

You Dearest Roy:

It's going to be hard to be away from you very long. Dear, let's not think of another year, but just be happy together this year. You must come as often as you want – never mind the pretext. We'll say you're looking for the cows. I half expected you last Sunday. Aunt Hattie was playing, and Uncle H reading in the library, and when it grew dark and I knew you wouldn't come, I let the tears come. I've wanted you so much, but there's only two days more before I see you.

Hasn't it been spring-like today? Mother and Grandma were up yesterday. Grandma gave me *Lady of the Lake* – quite a pretty little book. *Rodney Stone* is all right – I liked it. I'm reading *Choir Invisible* aloud to Aunt Hattie. She's very must interested – enough to leave her work and sit down "to see if he was killed." You remember the fight with the wildcat? I liked the old road, same as you did – that phrase about "the moon-loved, passionate southern mountains" struck me as it did you.

I'll see you soon. Here's a long, long kiss to tell you how I love you.

Your own,

Anna

NOVEMBER 23, 1897
Oronoco to Rochester

My Dearie:

You're nice to write me so. I got home about 1. I was a little tired, and the north wind wasn't so balmy, but it was all right. I saw but one person – a fellow went by on a bike and said "hello" and that it was a raw night. The lunch you gave me helped out wonderfully, and Auntie left a lunch too. I was in good shape to sleep. Auntie always calls to me: "Are you all right?" as I come upstairs. It seems to bother Papa – my walking to see you when we have lots

Mary (Roy's sister) and friends Mabel and Clara on Lake Shady in Oronoco

of horses. He said to me, "I mourned all day about your walking." It seems very good to have you so near, dearie.

You say I may come and see you Sunday if I feel like it. I *always* feel like it, Anna – *always*.

I've been pretty busy today. This afternoon I had some sharp work, and the dust was dreadful thick. We were sacking up buckwheat flour and grinding it.

I've thought of you lots, my dearest, since I left you – thought of you on the sofa and the firelight 'till I could almost feel your warm cheek. How I love you. As I think back about things before I knew you, they seem tame. You and the thought of you are suffused through and around everything – all good things.

Tomorrow is Thanksgiving. I watched them stuff the turkey. They dasn't tell little Volney it's one of the turkeys outside, because he cries and says he don't want any of them killed – "They won't roost in the trees." So, of course, Blanche and Mother had hard work to keep me from telling him all about it, and I told him it's a *vast* hen, and he rests satisfied.

Mary came tonight. She brought *Rodney Stone* – thank you – it was kind of you to think about that, dearie. I finished it. When I read of the smith's battle, I knew I had the best of it, and the rest would be windup. I didn't care so much for the story, but I liked some of the people and incidents.

It's long past 11 o'clock and I'd better pull up. I want to see you – it seems to get stronger and stronger, this want. I remember my coming home Thanksgiving time three years ago, when you were out east. You are near now – I'm so glad.

Pardon my stupid letter. You write the best letters – that was a *dear* ending.

With my love,

Roy

NOVEMBER 27, 1897
Rochester to Oronoco

Dearest Roy:

You are the *best* boy. You weren't going to tell me what a horrible blunder I made – sending a letter to you without sealing it – and I have been in agony ever since, for fear it fell out and never reached you. I got to thinking of it down at the bank, and made some awful mistakes there in consequence. I could feel my face burning, and wondered if anyone noticed. I don't believe I'll ever do such a thing again.

I can remember with what a shock I discovered that people killed things. I'm thinking of Baby – a calf we had. I came upon my father and Frank killing her. It was such a pretty, soft-eyed calf, and I knew its mother would miss it. I thought my father and Frank must be monsters, but I knew they were not, and that was the hard part – to understand how they could be what I had always believed them, and yet kill a calf. I remember how I ran screaming to my mother. It was a dreadful time for me. I had other similar shocks when I found that Frank was making a collection of birds' eggs. I talked to him about it, and he gave me some small comfort when he explained that he never took but one. But I thought *other* boys might take one until they were all gone, and then the poor bird wouldn't have any eggs, and I argued and wept about it.

I guess I've told you how I came upon some boys killing frogs and skinning them. I screamed and cried and fussed, and the boys told me I must not tell the teacher or they'd kill and skin *me* and hide me under the dark bridge. My, I was scared!

I remember what you wrote to me about coming home Thanksgiving when you were at Hamline – how you stood in the moonlight and listened to the church bell. Uncle Henry has gone to Beloit, so we need "a man in the house" on Sunday – you better come!

With my love,

Anna

NOVEMBER 28, 1897
Oronoco to Rochester

My Own Dearest:

I wanted so to see you today, but it wasn't so I could. Wonder, were you disappointed? I hope so, and I'm sorry. It's been a wretched day for me. I had a bitter old tantrum with myself, such as I haven't had for a long time. Is a fellow altogether a puppy if he's like a child once in a while? I've been feeling very puppified.

I'm coming to see you next Sunday, if I may – you'll write me if you'll be there, won't you? You don't know, dearie, how glad I am that there is *you*. I feel better even as I write.

I had some sharp work the day after Thanksgiving – a big day, and my brother was away playing. I think we are going to have lots of work.

Today ended rather tragically. Along toward dark – it was deep dusk – Pa came to the door breathless, and said to get Fred and three or four men – that one of the young horses was in the pond over by the pavilion. Pa went for ropes, and I ran over there and up to the barn and got two or three planks.

I could hear the poor beasts breathe and moan – they had been in at least three hours in the ice water, barely touching the bottom – just their noses out – think of it. There were two – big strong Jerry, and a beauty of a colt – a year-and-a-half old. No one had come yet. I could do nothing more until they came, but I just talked to them and pulled their ears. It's piteous to see animals suffer that way, and not be able to get them out. How they breathed with every breath so hoarse – 'twas a groan – and Jerry's old head was white with ice, and the poor little colt was more feeble.

Then the others came, and after a pretty sharp struggle we dragged the little one out. It took some time, and his heart was barely beating, and he died right away. The rope choked and there wasn't enough of him left to do without that oxygen. Then old 1,200-lb. Jerry – we ran the plank under him and lifted him so his shoulder wouldn't strike, and then pulled hard and long, and the ice broke behind him as he dragged along. Pa and I were out next to him in the water, and I was drefful wet, and Jerry lay stiff as a mackerel, and they said he'll never get up there, but if he was on land, he might. And then Jerry's great constitution rallied, and up he got all his lone and looked around, and then went straight for the barn at quite a good stiff trot, and when I got back with blankets, he was eating oats at a desperate pace. I presume he had been thinking of them all the long afternoon. I guess he will come out all right, though, of course, he was frightfully chilled. He's a queer kind of fellow – looks so big and hearty and sort of burly, and rules all the other colts. But the poor little fellow – I suppose he was forced under more than once, 'cause he was weaker, and the bigger horse would get his head across his neck.

What a long yarn I've spun, but you like horses. I thought how sorry you would be for them, dear Gentleness, and you wouldn't mind.

Thanksgiving day I skated an hour or so. The ice was hardly strong enough, and then came the snow and spoiled it all. It's cold out, isn't it? As I came over the bridge I saw the moon very low down – looking yellow as a summer moon. It made me feel sort of lonesome – I'm lonesome now – have been all day. You love me, don't you? I will see you soon – I must.

With my dear love,

Roy

DECEMBER 8, 1897
Oronoco to Rochester

My Dearest:

I got home all right, but it was dreadfully late. I had to put away the robes and take care of my nag, and 'twas after 2 before I was ready to sleep. I might have come faster, but it was such hard going that I had to speak to Fanny every time to get her out of a walk, and she doesn't need encouragement ordinarily.

I felt woe to leave you – lonesome, *so* lonesome just after I left. And this was such a little time I was to be away. You don't think me childish or foolish, do you, dear? Don't you remember that time I had seen you but a little, and I was late for the stage (as I usually am), so I had to walk, and after I got out a ways it seemed as though I *must* just see you again for a minute – and I would have done it too, but for the shame of coming back. I guess I *am* a little like a child now and then. There's *no one* like you.

Everything has been going lovely – quite a lot of work. We've got a great new steel range! It's a daisy – so big we couldn't get it into the house through the door, and those who brought it fussed and figured and 'lowed we'd have to tear a side out, when "out of the mouths of babes" came wisdom, for once, and I suggested the window, and we did it even so. I'm glad we have it for the folks – Mother and the house folk have been working at great disadvantage.

Hasn't it been a fine day, and last night it was grand, and there was a fine sunset? You probably were busy then, and didn't see it.

Write to me, dearest – soon. This isn't a good letter, but it ought to be, for I *mean* a whole lot. I love you so much.

DECEMBER 10, 1897
Rochester to Oronoco

Dearest Roy:

Your letter came Thursday – to the *bank*! I didn't want to read it with the boys standing around and likely to notice my face as I read, so I left it on my desk unopened until after my work was done and the boys were gone. Then I went in the little office and read it.

I remember that holiday time so well, and how I felt after I left you. I went with the girls, you remember, and made some New Year's cards. I felt as though I was in a dream. My heart was with you, and I answered questions and ate and listened to music, which made my heart ache worse than ever at leaving you. I can't remember what I wrote you when I went back to Winona – I only knew I wanted you – oh, so much – and there was nothing but work before me, and the dreaded Geometry. Then I was feverish that night – just because I was so lonely.

How different it is now. I certainly *ought* to be happy. I guess I am. Only I want to *teach*.

I saw Miss Peck for a few minutes tonight. She asked when you were in town and why we did not come to see her. We must go – we gave her the right to be interested in us, and she really wants us to come.

I was going to tell you, dearie – that letter you wrote after I went back to Winona was the best *love* letter you ever wrote. I took it to Cloquet with me, and kept it in my writing desk when I was in Winona, and I read it until I almost knew it by heart. I'm going to read that letter to you when you are old and grey-headed.

Good night, dearest, dearest.

Anna

DECEMBER 14, 1897
Oronoco to Rochester

My Dearest:

I came home easier than I have before – I guess, dear, it was the lovely start I had. I was some tired, of course, but done up not a bit. Auntie asked me if I didn't want to send you a piece of smilax and a carnation, so here they are. Why is it that I didn't want to do it? Tell me, thou who knowest all – it seems a wee sentimental.

We had a lot of grinding today – late start and didn't get it all done. Uncle Grant's here – staying until after the holidays. He said to send his regards – he felt badly he didn't come to see you at Cloquet. He oftentimes kisses people 'cause he's an affectionate man. I'm glad he didn't come.

I'm a vagabond to talk so. 'S the feller says, if this so-called letter exhaleth the odor of carbolic acid, don't mind it much.

I'm a beast – I ought to write a good letter, for I've thought of you so many times. Each time I think of you, dear, I see your face against my arm with the – no, I won't make you self-conscious.

I love you always.

Roy

DECEMBER 15, 1897
Rochester to Oronoco

Dearie:

I'm all right – feel as well as ever. I saw Miss Peck tonight –went with her downtown to the dressmaker's. She's such a busy woman. She's getting ready for the Educational Association – she's secretary and has to conduct a discussion on Latin. Someone asked for her picture, for they wished to have pictures of the "principal" educators of the state for publication. Miss Peck thinks it's a great joke to have them ask for her picture.

I went to prayer meeting with Aunt Hattie tonight. When we came home it was snowing hard and the wind howled. It's a night to enjoy a fire. I'm glad I'm not sitting by a register over a post office in a hotel tonight. It's lots better here, but I wish you were here too, dearie.

The smilax is all right – I'm glad you sent it. Do you remember the time your Aunt Minnie sent flowers to me when I was in camp? It was nice of her to think of me. Remember me to her and give my regards to your Uncle Grant.

Oh, I had such a dream of you. A lot of people were going down the street with handkerchiefs over their ears the way you wanted to wear yours – single-file, with shoulders hitched up and hands in their pockets, as if they were half frozen – and such solemn, immovable faces. Then I discovered you were one of them, and the dream dissolved. What comical dreams I've been having of late, and why should I dream that, rather than anything else of you?

If it's pleasant, come on Sunday, for if I go back to Eyota, it will be a long time until I see you. I can't account for it, but I seem to grow more in love with you, dear, as I see *more* of you.

I wish you'd finished what you started to say. I'd try and not be self-conscious!

My dearest love,

Anna

DECEMBER 19, 1897
Oronoco to Rochester

My Dearest:

I thought I better not come today, though I wanted to hard enough. I've thought of you lots – wondered where you were and what you were thinking when the light faded, and wanted so to be with you. I've been rather restless – it's been a gray day. I walked around a little, wrote a letter and read just a bit – *Maud* – I had hardly looked at it since we read it that hot dry fall you went away. Last night I was thinking of you when I went to sleep, and you were tangled into my dreaming, though I can't remember how; and this morning when I woke, I was thinking of you first thing. I'm afraid I'm getting very hopelessly in love too.

I think I can come to Eyota Saturday. Mother's going to have Xmas dinner, but perhaps I could get away in time to make that train. I don't want the stretches to be longer than we can help this year. I'm glad I'm not away to school; I'm glad you're well and not far away, wearing yourself down. I'm happy tonight, even if I'm not close by you, and things will come right.

I've been fussing around with Mary today. We ransacked the garret, hunting up and reading old papers. She seemed to kinda want to be with me, and we had quite a time. She's glad to be at home. I like Minimo. I like my *folks* fairly well – that's 'cause I'm part German, ain't it? The folks all have been under the weather with colds and things – they're all right now. I really think the chances for their California trip get better. My, I hope they do go.

Tomorrow there's a meeting at Mr. Petitt's for some sort of play-acting for Christmas Eve. It's going to be about Queen Esther. Minimo and I are wanted to take part. It's many a year since I last trod the boards.

Do you suppose everyone writes stupid letters like this sometimes? I suppose so. I have missed you, dearie.

With my dear love,

DECEMBER 29, 1897
Rochester to Oronoco

My Dear Roy:

Walter Bowers is home. I've not seen him, but saw a notice in the *Bulletin* that he's here. A friend told us he saw Walter and someone he thought might be his friend Roy Allis. I didn't feel like asking more, but I wondered why you didn't visit me when you were here?

I found a good deal of work at the bank when I went Monday. I made some dreadful mistakes, which made John cross, and I shed a few tears behind his back when no one could see.

Yesterday I got another Christmas present – from Aunt Maliza. It was done up in a box, which I remembered used to be in Grandma's room. Grandma used to make boxes and cover them with wallpaper and do all sorts of little things to keep herself busy. It seemed very strange to have that box in my hand, and to think how Grandma had made and kept it. I tore away the paper in the bottom of the box to see the stitches Grandma took, and there under the papers was a blot of ink, and in it the impress of my father's cuff button, just as plain.

You can't think what a feeling it gave me to find that so unexpectedly. It must have been made 15 or more years ago – I suppose sometime when my father was writing he spilled the ink and got his cuff on it, and then Grandma took the back of the tablet and made it into a box. I miss him so.

With my love,

Anna

DECEMBER 30, 1897
Oronoco to Rochester

My Dear Anna:

It's midnight. I just read your letter and want to send a wee reply. I just came home from a party, and last night I was to another party at Uncle Grant's – ain't I getting gay? Tonight I walked home with Ann Rice (you know her) and talked with her at the door and knocked the bucksaw down once – ain't I dissipated – and probably waked the folks. *(Ann Rice went on to become a local legend – a teacher, notary public, postmistress, and clerk of elections. When women received the right to vote, she was elected the first justice of the peace in Minnesota. A prolific writer, she contributed to all the major local newspapers, becoming a reporter for the* Rochester Post Bulletin *when she was only 14. She wrote a comprehensive history of Oronoco in 1948 when she was nearly 80, and served as director of the Olmsted County Historical Society from 1926 to 1951.)*

You're good to write me about Bowers. As I was trotting down the street pretty near the post office, he hailed me, and I ran over and shook hands. I wanted him to come home with me, but he couldn't – he had to go to a great teachers' convention in St. Paul. He was going up on the morning train, so I decided to stay overnight with him and go home on the train wi' him. We went up to your uncle's house, but didn't see you. Then we got some nuts, and sat behind in the sleigh on a box and talked and made merry and ate and sang. Then we went back to his house and talked and slept. Bowers waked me up by grinding his teeth, according to his custom as of old. It was good to see him again.

I got home in time to start grinding. I didn't feel quite up to snuff somehow – heartily sick of myself all through. I'd like to be someone else awhile and see if they felt the way I do. I must be an unhealthy bein'. I felt better next day with the beautiful spring weather – wasn't it fine? And work and exercise help – I can't get along without it.

It was strange about the mark from your father's sleeve, dear – of course, it affected you.

With my dear love,

CHAPTER 29

Restless

1898

First horseless carriage seen in Rochester. The first locally owned automobile – a four-horsepower steam car – belonged to Dr. Charles H. Mayo.

U.S. declares war on Spain over Cuba.

Henry James publishes *The Turn of the Screw.*

H.G. Wells publishes *The War of the Worlds.*

Pierre and Marie Curie discover radium and polonium.

First photographs taken using artificial light.

JANUARY 3, 1898
Rochester to Oronoco

My Dearest Roy:

Haven't I begun '98 well! The first time I write 1898 is in this letter to you. Clara went this morning on the train. She won't be back until June. Aunt Hattie feels sober, and I keep still. What a hard, hard thing it is to be away from those you are fond of, always.

Walter called on me yesterday. He likes his work and is digging at it as hard as ever. I went to the Methodist Church Sunday. It was communion at the Presbyterian, and I don't exactly like such services. Walter looked at me funny because I run away from such things, but he says he does too. Well, I'm glad I went to the Methodist, for I saw Walter there, and we didn't stay to Sunday school, but came home and talked until after 1. I like Walter – he's all right – I don't care what *anyone* says.

Isn't this wonderful weather? Both Clara and I've been reading *Quo Vadis*. I don't know what to think of it. I don't *like* it, but I'm interested.

Oh, it makes me restless to have everyone going off to work and not go too. I don't believe I *can* keep still much longer. I wonder if I shall have to teach always in order to be satisfied.

What a letter you wrote – I read part of it to Clara, and she laughed good over it – especially the part about talking with Ann Rice and knocking the bucksaw down. Why didn't you and Walter come around to the house and call Monday? He didn't seem to know why.

I thought you were *never* going to write this last time. Write *sooner* next time.

With my love,

Anna

JANUARY 5, 1898
Oronoco to Rochester

My Dearest Anna:

It isn't exactly warm up here tonight, but I like to be off alone when I write to you.

No, I don't suppose you will be satisfied unless you're teaching always. Nevertheless, you're not going to teach *any* at all this year, s'help me – do you understand? I have spoken!

I'm some in the doldrums just at present. I suppose I should be more ashamed of it than I am. I tend to be too sentimental, methinks, but not very masterful.

I finished the book Sunday, and liked it ever so much better than *A Window in Thrums*. I read quite a bit in *Quo Vadis*. It seemed to me – what I read – that the people were *made* folks, and it all seemed to smell sick and bloody and rank – not my interest.

Yes, it's been fine weather. Feels like the last of February, doesn't it – when it's 'most time for spring vacation, and you get out of some class you hate, and the wind flows over you, and a ripple runs all through you, and you feel *good*, and you like your pard and everybody. Such times as that Bowers would say, "You get a breath of fresh air, and away you go."

With my dear love,

Roy

JANUARY 7, 1898
Rochester to Oronoco

My Dearest Roy:

Your letter came yesterday morning. You say I shall *not* teach, and then in the next breath tell me you're not "masterful"!

Can't you come to Rochester Sunday? I want to see you, dear. Hasn't this been a beautiful week – so spring-like and warm? I almost went back in my old spring wood. Did you see the sunset tonight? The west was beautiful – not brilliant – but lovely soft shades of pink and gold and violet. It's been so warm and bright – I've enjoyed going out. I'd like to take a tramp on snowshoes tonight.

I'm reading *English Lands, Letters and Kings, from Celt to Tudor* by Donald G. Mitchell. I like it, and haven't had much time for *Quo Vadis*. *English Lands* is so good and fresh. I'll finish *Quo Vadis*, for I want to see what becomes of them all, but it isn't – *clean*, is it?

Uncle T. and I just had a little finger wrestling – he with his little finger, and I with my middle. Aunt Hattie is here too. We've been cutting up all evening, and this isn't much of a letter, but I'll see you soon and we'll *talk* the rest. Dearest, dearest – good-night.

Anna

JANUARY 11, 1898
Oronoco to Rochester

My Own Dearie:

Has the headache been slept away, as you promised me? I write soon, you see.

I came home all right – about 1 a.m. when I arrived, but it was later by the time I'd taken care of the nag and everything. It was very bright and light, with white fleecy clouds, but I was lonesome, and didn't see the brightest side of things. A body feels that way – generally late at night and alone, I think – and sometimes, too, when I've been with people, and I don't like myself after – am sort of dissatisfied and disgusted. I wish I was very conceited – well, *some* conceited. It's a wonder *you* don't get disgusted with my telling you about me. Probably you do, but are too kind to tell me so. And I *talk*, yes, and what good comes of talking? Oh, I'm a broth of a boy, to be sure (deep sarcasm).

I've been busy all day, and we have some grinding left over for tomorrow – the more the better. Punched the bag some – keeps me from getting tired when you're mogging along easily. It's drudgery sometimes, but when you're exerting yourself *hard*, there's something of the spirit in it, and it *isn't* drudgery. I don't mind grinding at all, only one's *head* gets tired of it, and you always feel better at night when you've done a bit more than is necessary.

I know some people call this weather raw and don't like it, but it's not disagreeable to me.

Last evening I went over to Lou's for a minute to take a magazine back. There was a good damp, fresh wind. I was thinking of you – it's good to know there is *you*, dearest. You love me well as ever you did, don't you?

Write to me soon, if you feel like it. I love you so dearly. Don't think me stupid – though I *want* you to, if I *am*. Seems so I'd rather be *true* than anything else.

JANUARY 12, 1898
Rochester to Oronoco

My Dearest Roy:

I hated so to have you go last night, and I think you did too. It seemed I had seen so little of you, and hadn't said what I *wanted* to – all we did was *surface* talk. I watched you from my window upstairs as you drove past the front of the house, and drew back the curtain, thinking you might see the light and look up. I'm better today – a little weak and not hungry yet, but all right. I'll go to the bank this afternoon.

I'm glad I shall see you again before long. Perhaps it will be warm, and we can take a walk, and I'll be your "bon comrade" again, and not a languid sort of woman looking like a dishrag. You're the best, kindest, gentlest boy in all the world, and I'm proud of you, dear. I'm (hide your face, but I must tell you) glad to have Uncle Henry know you better and how much of a man you are.

I've been reading *English Lands, Letters and Kings* to Aunt Hattie this morning. I'm doing my usual work at the bank. I wish just now that I had the garlic for my heart – which, by the way, is full of love for you, dearest, dearest of all, and thankfulness to God because He has given me such love – the warmest, sweetest, tenderest, truest.

We got a letter from Thad, saying Mary burned her hand badly – a lampshade caught fire. The doctor, who comes to see her every day and wants to keep her in bed most of the time, thinks the burn may leave a scar. Their hired girl left the day she was burned, and Thad says Mary suffers a good deal and is homesick for her mother, so Aunt Hattie is going tomorrow morning.

At first she felt she shouldn't go – that I would overwork myself first thing if she went away. We finally convinced her that I had some sense, and May and I are just aching to run the house alone. So at last Aunt concluded we could get along without her. It's amusing to hear her caution each of us about how to look out for the others. She tells me if Uncle H gets sick or troubled or anxious, I must let her know at once. She tells May that she must be sure to do the heavy work before she goes to school.

You dearest boy – perhaps *you'd* be happier if you were conceited, but *I* shouldn't, so have regard for me and don't try to "develop" conceit. Yes, probably I do get disgusted hearing about you, just as you get disgusted hearing about *me*.

Yes, I love you as much as ever, dearest. Here's the kiss I wanted to give you last night and couldn't. God keep you, my darling.

Anna

JANUARY 14, 1898
Oronoco to Rochester

Dearest, Dearest Anna:

I read your letter time and again – what a letter! I was afraid someone might look into my face while I read – I'm sure they could see the uplift there. But I didn't send mine – what I wrote didn't touch the right spot. It wasna what I wanted, and I burned it all up. But I kept *your* letter, dearie, where I could reach it all night.

Wish one could do the things one wants to do without being foolish. If it were that way, I would have come to you last night just to tell you how delicious you are, my dearest – the way it ought to be told – oh, I could do it just right. There's no one like you – no one so good and gentle and sweet. I love you more than everything.

I *did* hate to leave you – I guess we felt the same way. And I *did* want to kiss you good-night. It seemed as if I hadn't seen you at all. I've thought about you lots, and wondered if you were all right. You and May are keeping house all by your lone by this time. I can imagine how Mrs. Titus would tell you all what to do – Mither does the same way.

Mary came home tonight. She's a queer one sometimes – someone asked her if there was gold up here, and Minimo said yes – there was some. He asked her how much to pan, and she said she had heard it yielded "two dollars-and-a-half a pan." I wonder what she thought we were grinding feed and summer resortin' for if we could've made that much panning. I suppose she had heard Pop say, as I have, that down at the old "gold diggings" he thought it would pay wages – perhaps $2.50. *(Gold was discovered in the sands of the Zumbro River at both Rochester and Oronoco in 1857-1858. Oronoco became a base of operations. The Rochester Democrat reported: "Remarkable pure gold equal in richness to the best of California products." Prospectors swarmed in, but the entire operation was washed away in a cloudburst in 1859.)*

I have another of Conan Doyle's books – *Micah Clarke*. I don't know how good it will be. I won't write more. I wish this were a good letter, and it isn't very. But yours was lovely, Anna. I don't deserve it, dearest. I'm going to try and be worthy of you, love – *more* worthy, anyway. I always pray for that. One never prays for anything without honestly wanting it, do they?

I want to see you, Anna, and I love you dearly, *dearly*.

JANUARY 17, 1898
Rochester to Oronoco

Lover of Lovers:

Oh, your letter – you told it "the way it ought to be told, but thee may'st tell it again if thee likest." I can't tell you how good it was, darling.

May and I are getting on in fine shape, except she became sick and languid, so I've been housekeeper, cook and nurse all in one. May has never minded petting since she was a little thing, and I enjoyed "mothering" her a little. She's all right now.

Mother wrote that George Alden was in St. Marys Hospital, so I went up to see him. He has a tubercular swelling in his hand and wrist, and had just had it operated upon. Dr. Charlie injected some kind of fluid that eats away the swelling, and the operation has to be repeated a good many times. George seemed very glad to see me. He said the days and nights had been pretty long – especially when his hand pained him so he couldn't sleep. I took him "Choir Invisible." He will have to come back several times before all is well.

May has come home, and we must fix things for dinner. I'm quite a cook! Wish you had been here yesterday to see how we cooked the roast. We put it in before we went to church. Uncle Henry asked us in church if we had shut the damper – of course, we hadn't. When we got home the fire was out and the stove cold, the water boiled out of the roast, and the meat barely half done! We had to get it going again – it was pretty good.

We've had a little yellow-and-white cat come to us. I was planning what to eat with May – "Guess I'll make a turnover and use up this pie crust. And we'll have baked apples and that will use up the whipped cream. And then we'll have scalloped potatoes and French toast to use up the old bread." And then May said, "Yes, and we've borrowed a cat to eat up what's left." And Uncle H said, "I think we had better borrow a baby to use up the rest of our *time* – especially nights." We thought that was all pretty funny.

I've burned my arm and grated my fingers, but have had no serious accidents or failures in my cooking – except the pancakes that wouldn't rise and were sour, and we put in five spoonfuls of soda to make them rise and get sweet, but they still failed, so we gave them to Mrs. Baron's pigs, and had cut-up potatoes and toast and coffee and doughnuts and bread and butter.

I had an encounter with a mouse this morning. He was on a shelf in the cellar. He didn't see me until I had looked at him quite a while, but when he did, he jumped to the top stair, fell on his side, got up and went down to the cellar quite leisurely.

Do you think you can subsist on my cooking for a day? If you think you can, you may try it next Sunday. Write to me soon.

Anna

Mary seemed to be getting better, but then we heard she has been much worse than they let us know. The skin has all come off from her hands, and the doctor thought he would have to try skin grafting, but now the new skin is coming on. She's very weak from so much suffering and anxiety. They have no girl to help – Thad has been everywhere to find one.

We had lots of fun last night – May dressed up in Uncle H's clothes, and then I helped him fix up in *her* clothes – dress, cape, hat and veil. Wish you could have seen them. (Don't speak of this last – perhaps they wouldn't like to have it told.)

JANUARY 22, 1898
Rochester to Oronoco

My Dear Roy:

I can't write but a minute, for I must go to the bank soon. Come tomorrow, yes? May is baking some apples especially for you. Aunt Hattie is busy helping Mary – she won't be able to use her hand for a long time, and I guess Aunt H will stay a while.

You better take the horse here. I always hate to have you take that long walk at night, dear. I'm not afraid, but it's so lonesome, and a horse is company.

Anna

JANUARY 25, 1898
Oronoco to Rochester

My Dearest:

I didn't intend to write you tonight, but I wanted to speak to you. I hope that cough has begun to stop tearing you up – dearie, I so hate to have it hurt you. You will write me soon and tell me –that you like me just as well as ever?

I got home all right. It *was* kinda long and lonesome. I didn't hurry much. Wish I could walk the whole 24 miles in the daytime, when it was *toward* you. There was a fog, and the frost gathered on my eyelashes. Faith, Anna – I'm always so lonesome when I leave you, and it seems to me that I'm stupider than common. You mustn't get disgusted wi' me, for I'm not altogether so queer as I act.

I was sleepy tonight and needed a tall rest. We've been busy in the mill today – had 240 sacks.

I'm coming to see you again soon. I love you very much, dearest. I feel very tender toward you tonight, though the letter doesn't show it, and reads like a boy's. You don't seem disappointed in me, and you're just the dearest, truest, noblest girl in the world. We will always love each other just the same, won't we? Yes, more.

Roy

JANUARY 27, 1898
Oronoco to Rochester

My Dearest Anna:

Oh, I want to see you. I guess I will come Sunday, 'thout something unforeseen happens. Yes – I think I can "subsist" on your cooking!

Had quite a bit of work today. I've finished reading *Micah Clarke* and liked it pretty well – about that Protestant uprising in the west counties in England under the Duke of Monmouth. You remember Monmouth's Rebellion – John Ridd went to get Tom Faggus safe back from trouble and his encounter with Kirke's "lambs"?

When I heard you had lent my "Choir Invisible" I was very wroth, and today I did wreak vengeance (!) – I lent *Rodney Stone* to George Farnham, who has brought things to me to read.

Isn't it a fine winter, and it's half gone sure? And then spring, and you'll be out here when the hepaticas come.

I've been restless for a couple of nights, and had dreams about having to go to school and not being prepared. One isn't troubled so much in reality as in dreams – there it's multiplied many times – so many that the product is very much like a nightmare. It was terrible.

Mary's getting burned is so terrible. She must have hung to that burning shade pretty gamely. A body's hands are about the tenderest, most sensitive part too.

I want to see you *very* much.

Roy

I hadn't much to say, so this, for the most part, is a vain letter, composed of empty words.

JANUARY 27, 1898
Rochester to Oronoco

My Dearest Roy:

Your letter came yesterday. May and I are running things all alone. I have been fixing fires most all morning. The fire here in the dining room has gone out twice; and the one in the parlor wouldn't warm up, though I fixed all the drafts right, and shook and poked at it, and May did too. In between fixing fires, I ran and put wood in the kitchen stove. Wasn't it cold last night? A little morning glory that came up in a dish of English ivy I had froze last night.

I'm glad you wrote soon – I'm always wondering if you get home all right. I don't want to wait two weeks before seeing you again – can't you come next Sunday? I haven't really seen much of you for a long time, it seems to me.

I have read some in the book Miss Peck spoke of – *A Man's Value in Society*. It reads like she talks. I finished *Quo Vadis* and the first volume of *English Lands, Letters and Kings*.

I had a fine sleep last night, and I'm sleepy today, but I don't cough so much. Sleep seems to be the best thing for my cough.

I haven't told you what you said I must be sure to tell you. I could tell it best if you were here, but you're not – so – put your head down, dearie, and close your eyes. There – my arms are about your dear head, so close – and I love you, love you, love you.

Your own,

Anna

JANUARY 31, 1898
Oronoco to Rochester

My Dearest Anna:

I wanted to come and see you Sunday, and then it was sort of a bad day. I thought of you – wondered if you'd expect me in the afternoon. I hope I may come next Sunday.

Mary brought me *By Order of the King*. It's very Hugoesque, but not nearly so good as *Ninety Three*.

Isn't it cold tonight? This is the winter I don't like. There wasn't a great deal of work in the mill – guess it was a bad day out on the prairie. I couldn't see the hills for the blowing snow. It didn't seem so bad yesterday afternoon – it was cold and blustering, but the snowflakes were light as frost, and the wind seemed merry somehow.

I'd like to go to Alaska with three or four good folks. I wouldn't be a good leader because I haven't any experience – and so not enough confidence – but why wouldn't I be a good follower? Can't do it, though – haven't any cash. A couple of the boys intend to go, but I don't believe they will – they're not very good at bringing plans to a finish.

Next time I see you, I want to tell you about some things. You're better than everything – just glorious – but I want to be so you won't despise me, ever. Good-night, dearest.

Roy

I hope I may have you to myself next time. You won't have to lead Christian Endeavor, I hope? Am I naughty to wish so?

FEBRUARY 2, 1898
Rochester to Oronoco

My Dearest Roy:

Yes, I looked for you Sunday – I watched for you nearly all day. But you'll come next Sunday. I won't lead Christian Endeavor or anything, and we will talk and see something of each other.

If you had come last Sunday, you might have had some of my first bread! Now I shall be an "experienced" bread maker before you come again. I baked bread yesterday and I'm going to bake Saturday. It isn't as good as Aunt Hattie's, and I know it isn't like Blanche's, but it isn't sour or hard. I made cinnamon rolls too. The edges wouldn't stay tucked in – May suggests gluing them next time (!).

I've been showing May how to do an example. She gets impatient and thinks there's no use of it and doesn't want to try, just as I used to. She's in good spirits and in advance of the lessons. She is still at *Ivanhoe* by spells. She generally goes to sleep over it, and said one evening as she closed the book, "I haven't got much more to read." She wants to read it because I urged her to, but it isn't any use – she doesn't care for it. She liked *John Halifax* and read *Marcella*. I'm going to try to find something she will like, for she asks me what to read.

Isn't it nice to stay in the house by a warm fire and hear the wind howl, and know that you haven't got to go out in the cold? I haven't had the luxury of a stove for two winters – nothing but registers, and last winter that square, bare-looking room in Cloquet, with that hideous picture on the rickety easel. I won't have things so next time I go away – I'll take things to make my room look nice if I have to have a carload.

When Uncle Henry came home from church Sunday he sat down, looked around and said, "Why, where's *Roy*? I *miss* him." You must come Sunday, dearie, and no Miss Peck or Christian Endeavor shall interfere.

With my love,

Anna

FEBRUARY 7, 1898
Oronoco to Rochester

My Dearest Anna:

I write soon, because I feel under a cloud. I thought this morning: "You great silly – you didn't hook up that tug!" How foolish – to leave that un-hitched. It was colossally idiotic. The horse must've wondered what I meant – I never did such a thing before. What a stupid, stupid thing to do! What do you think of me? You have me at your mercy.

I came home all serene, of course. It was a wonderfully fine, soft night – wish you might have come with me. It took me about two hours, I guess. I unhooked the tugs when I removed the harness from the beast. I consider this a good thing to do (unhook the tugs from the carriage *before* the horse is led away!).

Going to rain tonight, isn't it? Fred saw four crows today, and you know what that means *(old superstition – four crows meant wealth)*. We carried some boats up the hill into the boathouse for painting – got as warm as July. We didn't have a very big day in the mill. I didn't take much exercise because I had been short of sleep. I used the 70-pound weights and boxed two or three lads after I was ground out. That's what I do on a day when I get time and ain't lazy.

I tell you about this because you seemed anxious about my exercise routine. You don't know how good it was to know you cared that way. You were *splendid* yesterday – my, I love you, dearest. Just yesterday – it seems more than that.

With my dearest love,

Roy

FEBRUARY 9, 1898
Rochester to Oronoco

My Dearest Roy:

I laughed all yesterday afternoon over your letter. Yes, I'll forget if it will make you happier – or at least remember it only when you're naughty and need to be reminded of how inexpressibly funny you looked, driving off so serenely in the moonlight, with one tug fastened, and the other flapping in front of Fannie. What do I think of you? Next time you come, I'll tell you ….

How spring-like it's been all week. I didn't go to the bank yesterday, and think I won't go today. I've been sneezing and feeling as though I was coming down with a great cold, but it may not amount to anything.

I made bread yesterday again. Uncle Henry is at the hospital today – he's one of the examining committee, and will be there all day. Glad I'm not teaching today. It's so nice to be lazy, but it's spoiling me. I'm petting myself altogether too much.

You haven't convinced me that you're not taking too much exercise, and I *am* anxious. I'm pulled in two directions – it's glorious to have you so strong – I'm proud of your strength and love you for it. And I'm *afraid*, too, and almost wish you wouldn't do so much. Do you see?

You must be careful, dearest – it's for my sake.

With my love,

Anna

FEBRUARY 11, 1898
Oronoco to Rochester

My Dearest Anna:

I was glad to get your letter – glad you're so lenient with me. It *must* have been funny about the horse. I wring my hands whenever I think of it.

These two stormy days there has been almost nothing in the mill. Fred's away and I've been flooded with loafers who come to box and kill time (I won't let them box when there's any work). I'd think it would be awful tiresome to wander around that way with no work to do. I've been idle in my day, but I wasn't loafing.

I've been wondering if that great cold did settle down on you – how I hope it hasn't, dearest. So many people are sick – Mary came home tonight with a hard headache, and Aunt Minnie has been under the weather, too. Mother had another gathering this week of those she was "indebted to" – a dandy supper – best she ever made. The old folks here have been very gay and festive this winter, with parties galore.

I'm glad you care about the physical business we talked of. Yes, I imagine you feel you're getting very weak and effeminate from your way of living, but it won't hurt you to be comfortable a little.

Mary brought back *Soldiers of Fortune*. I've been reading some in *Ten Thousand a Year*. I like some of it – it's all right – but the "females," he calls them, don't seem to be real folks.

It won't be very long until I see you again. I'm wanting to.

With my love,

Roy

FEBRUARY 15, 1898
Rochester to Oronoco

My Dear Roy:

We're all here in the dining room, writing for dear life. May is writing a geography paper. Uncle Henry is writing hospital reports, and as soon as he gets them in shape, I copy them. I'm writing to you while I wait for the next paper.

I made doughnuts this morning and bread and cinnamon rolls Monday. I can't think what to have for desert tomorrow. I went with Miss Peck to Epworth League class, and learned about Methodist missions and art. Aunt Hattie doesn't say anything about coming home. Uncle H says he thinks he will send her her sunbonnet and parasol and other summer things.

We've been very gay since you were here. Uncle H and I went to a minstrel show, and he proposed that we go to a masquerade ball after prayer meeting tonight. It's so cold I don't think I want to go. I didn't work in the bank for three days – my cold was struggling for a chance, but my extra vitality (owing to this lazy life) drove it out. I have just a touch of rheumatism – a pain under my shoulder blade that catches now and then. I hope you haven't been anxious about me.

Yes, dearest – I *do* care very much about the "physical business." You must come Sunday when we can talk. It's only days until then!

With my love,

Anna

FEBRUARY 18, 1898
Oronoco to Rochester

Dearest Anna:

I'm going to write just a wee bit. Had a big, awful, dusty day today – I'm dusty without and within, and sleepy and got a sore throat. I've got to get up in the morning and grind out what I left over before the grists get there, and I've a cold.

I thought you were never going to write me. I hope I may see you Sunday. I won't write more, for I'm so sleepy. Good-night, dearie.

With my love,

Roy

FEBRUARY 21, 1898
Rochester to Oronoco

My Dearest Roy:

I missed you Sunday, but didn't expect you when I saw how deep the snow was.

I went up to St. Marys Hospital after I got through at the bank, and asked Mary to go too. We met Mrs. Burchard and several of the Sisters. We went around through the halls and saw something of the rooms, the women's ward, and the operating room. Mary makes me think of you some – an expression she'll say once in a while, such as, "This smells like sick folks," and the way she looked at the operating table with sort of a horror that seemed to see all the people who have been laid there.

I guess I wrote you Uncle Henry has been sick and out of the bank – headache caused by indigestion. He's been under the weather ever since, and last Saturday saw Dr. Stinchfield. The pain where I hit him when we were horsing about has grown worse, and he couldn't take a deep breath. Doctor examined the spot and said the blow had evidently shocked his heart. It was a little irregular in its action – *that*, however, might be due to indigestion. Doctor said, "It must have been a pretty good *thump*!" Uncle H then told him who my teacher in fightin' was (so you are implicated!). Doctor thinks it isn't anything permanent.

I'm reading *Harold* by Bulwer Lytton. Have you read Tennyson's *Harold*? If you haven't, let's read it together some day.

You haven't had much to do today, probably – the roads being so bad – so you're not tired and dusty and sleepy tonight. The days will seem long until Sunday – you will surely come then, yes? Good-night, dearest.

Anna

FEBRUARY 24, 1898
Oronoco to Rochester

My Dearest Anna:

Your letter came last night – I was glad to get it. I was just about to send an appeal to you, for it seemed a long time since you'd written.

I haven't been quite well – not sick, exactly. I might have come to see you if it hadn't been for that. I've had a terrible cold, and my throat was pretty sore – same disease as Mary had, I guess. Makes me cough nights and I feel a bit "bum." I'll straighten it out directly. I'm not going to have a cold anymore – I have spoken!

We've had a good deal of grinding. Day before yesterday was the biggest day in the mill I ever saw. Fred was away and Henry was off hauling logs, so my Pa and I held down the grinding. In the evening Henry and I didn't get through until nearly 11. Pa was pretty well fagged.

That seems so queer that you struck so effective a blow on your uncle. A mighty fine fighter – what a girl you are! I sorted over your letters Sunday and divided them into years. I had to open a good many to get the dates, and, of course, I read some of them. They took me back. I want to see you, dearest. When I knew I couldn't come Sunday, I wanted to see you more than ever. I'm queer about such things. I'll come next Sunday, unless you forbid.

You're reading *Harold* – I wonder if you like it. I did when I read it, but perhaps now it would seem very mail-clad and heroic. I'll ask you about it when I see you.

And I hadn't better write more, had I? Good-night – I love you dearly.

FEBRUARY 28, 1898
Rochester to Oronoco

My Dearest Roy:

You were in my dreams all night, and when I woke this morning. I hope you weren't lonely or blue last night as you went home. I wonder if you thought of the things I told you to.

I have felt the spring gladness – it will soon be here! I think the pussy willows will be out in a couple of weeks – watch for them.

I've been reading *English Lands, Letters and Kings* again – about Steele, Addison and Swift and Queen Anne. I read the Mormon story in January *Harper's*. It's horrid. I read two about New York in the days of the Dutch governors.

There's nothing to tell you, but it seems very good to hear from you soon after I see you. I was happy yesterday, dearest. I hope we can have a great many such days the rest of the year when the thought of "good-bye" doesn't hang over us.

I love you as I did yesterday, and I do always.

Your own,

Anna

CHAPTER 30

Worthwhile To Be Alive

MARCH 3, 1898
Oronoco to Rochester

My Dearest Anna:

Your letter came last night. I was waiting for it – ran back to the mill to read it by the west window. Oh, so good to get the letter after I've just seen you, and to know it's from you, *you*. And you say the things, dearest, that somehow touch the right spot.

What a happy Sunday we had! I remembered what you told me, and I wasn't blue or lonesome as I've been before lots of times. It was hard going back home. The little snow that had fallen made everything uniformly white, so it was difficult to pick and choose my road as I did coming down. I went slowly, and it was about the usual time when I got squared round for sleep.

I'm glad I was in your dreams – that's such a pleasant place to be. I thought of you too, as I slept. Your dear, sweet presence seemed to be round me yet, and I would half wake and half remember all and be glad and contented and asleep again.

I haven't much to tell. Had considerable grinding this week, but not so much as last. This afternoon was slack. I was alone in the mill, so I boxed a bit – half an hour, perhaps. I've read a little book of short stories by R.L. Stevenson called *The Pavilion on the Links* – it isn't as good as the others I've read.

I felt the spring that morning you spoke of – the fresh air and the sky so bright, springy blue, with the clouds all blown away. I left the mill door open and felt radiant. I'm glad spring is coming too – it will be glorious to see you the last of April – as if it wasn't always glorious to see you, darling.

This isn't a good letter, but never mind. I'm all right – and how I love you!

Roy

MARCH 4, 1898
Rochester to Oronoco

My Dearest Roy:

I wish you were here now – I want to see you so. This hasn't been quite so happy a week as usual, and it seems a long time since I saw you. My sense of humor has come in to help me out of what would otherwise have been a hard place. I'll tell you about it when I see you.

Uncle Henry has a new bookcase. It's oak – five feet high – and reaches from the east window in the library almost to the dining room door. He's arranging his books according to subjects now. You ought to hear him whistle and sing – he can't carry a tune and has no idea of time!

I had another letter from Florence this week. I asked her last fall to get me fleece-lined underwear. Now aren't you fascinated with *that* news? The calico cat just jumped up in my lap – she wants to be petted. She's so affectionate. Don't you wish you had her there with you?

I see in the last *Review of Reviews* that Julian Hawthorne has gone to Cuba to study and report the famine. He says it's worse than that of India. There's a summary of the Cuban trouble *(the Cuban famine preceded the Spanish-American War, which begins in April)*, and a great deal about Zola and the Dreyfus case *(Zola fought with others for exoneration of falsely accused and convicted army officer Alfred Dreyfus, who was charged with treason)*. I believe now I understand what all the trouble is about. Uncle H said he hoped I would explain it to him too.

Yes – it's spring! Look for the pussy willows every day. Oh, it's worthwhile to be alive! I'm glad I'm here and have you to love me – wonderfully glad. I love you so.

Anna

We'll write as often as we want to, even if it is every day. Your letter was an awfully dear one.

MARCH 7, 1898
Oronoco to Rochester

My Dearest Anna:

Yes, it's springy, and it seems so good! I heard the crows calling yesterday, and a flock of ducks "lit" in the deep hole. I took a walk around the woods over to Uncle George's and across the pond, up by the islands where the willows grow; then through the woods along that southern shore where we read one time (when you were going away next morning – how I remember), and farther up where we went for those yellow daisy-like flowers long, long ago. The sun felt warm and the wind raw, so I took off my coat for the one and put it on again for the 'tither. I went farther, rambling just to be outdoors, you know, and came and visited Jim White's dogs – pacified the low-browed suspicious bulldog, and waxed friendly with the other. The water's up – been running over the dam for some time, and I could hear it drowsily up here in my room where I'm writing now. At night it sounds hoarser – more angry.

I dreamed last night of being in a very great school where Dr. Charles Mayo was one of the instructors. You were there too. Strange things happened, but I've forgotten. I remember I helped you on with a cloak, and you spoke to me in the kindest way. I wish I could remember more of it.

I've struggled through *Ten Thousand a Year* at last. It seems dull, most of it – and the good women in it faint away generally, or sob, and turn pale, or their expressive eyes swim with tears. It's tiresome. I read it because George lent it to me out of the kindness of his heart. I read "My Favorite Novelist: Three Essays" by Walter Besant in the last *Munsey* yesterday. I rather liked it. Say, Anna – have you read *Huckleberry Finn*? I know all about the Dreyfus business – read it in *Cosmopolitan*. Don't know about Zola's connection with it – you'll have to post me too on it.

All right – it's agreed – we'll write to each other whenever we choose then! I knew I could, but it was nice to have you say so too. We shall be great comrades. And I'm going to try and tell you all things. There's no one like you, Anna – no one.

We've had quite a busy day, and tomorrow will be a great one because it's town meetin', so I must to sleep. I'm wanting to see you so just now. We will write often; we will be great friends. I love you dearly.

This is another of my kid letters – with little bits of separate short sentences strewn along, just as I would talk. Only when one is talking, he fills in with other things. Bowers used to criticize that in me when I'd write one of my very rare essays. I wouldn't fix them, and probably they were a trifle primitive, albeit somewhat breezy.

MARCH 11, 1898
Eyota to Oronoco

My Dear, Dear Roy:

I came to Eyota from Rochester night before last. They need me here, so I came suddenly. I can't see you Sunday – I'll let you know when I *can*, and explain why I'm writing as I do when I see you. Until then, I know you'll "bide."

I am thankful – so thankful, Roy – that I have you. Write to me often, dearest. I hate to send you this queer letter, but I'm all right, and perhaps I can see you a week from Sunday. And you trust me – I know that.

Your own little girl,

Anna

MARCH 13, 1898
Oronoco to Eyota

My Own Dearest:

I'm going to write just a little tonight. I've been thinking of you much to-day – wondering what you were doing; wishing you were with me. I was glad to get your letter – everything is right when *you're* "all right." Trust – of course I trust you, dearie – absolute and unlimited. I hope things aren't troubling you, but I'm afraid they are. I'm so glad there is *you*, darling – what would anything be without you? We stand together, you and I.

Mary is home this week. We went walking in the woods this afternoon – to the place where you and I cut our names in the bark of a tree six years ago. We make a trip there about this time in the spring every year or two. Mary said if we could have looked forward these years, we couldn't have seen things much different. We stopped at Aunt Minnie's coming back to see if she had anything to eat. She had a banana, and I broke it in two and gave Minimo the biggest piece. Then we went down to Reifsnider's, and I looked in the cupboard and saw a piece of elderberry pie, so we ate that too, and said nothing. We came home then, and went down cellar when Blanche wasn't there, and ate crackers and preserved things until we thought we'd never be hungry again. We hadn't any more relations to forage on, so we had to quit!

We sawed up a lot of wood yesterday, and I got a rap on my forehead from a flying stick that made me see stars and union jacks, but it was all right after a minute. My hair helped shield me some, and then one's front head is hard.

Come close, closer, while I tell you good-night, and that you're the best and truest and sweetest in the world, my own, and I love you – *love* you – you know how much.

MARCH 14, 1898
Eyota to Oronoco

My Dear, Dear Roy:

I've just come home from Rochester. I saw your father and mother going to the hotel, and I went to see them. Your mother looked tired and weak, so I didn't talk long. Then I went to the house and saw my folks. Little Bob has got over the croup and feels like himself again, Mary says. I never saw such a happy baby – a round, roly-poly fellow, and just bubbled over with fun. He's just the opposite of Volney, with his grave, serious face. Bob never will be pretty, but he's funny.

Sunday Uncle Henry and I drove out in the country. I was thinking of you, dear. Your letter was such a good one. I got it on my way to the depot, and took it to Rochester with me. It's so good to have you say you trust me and have faith in me. Roy, you are the noblest, purest – the *manliest* man! You don't know what it means to me now, to believe in you as I do – I am glad, *so* glad. Yes, things are troubling me. I can't tell you now, but you said something that touched the right spot when you said, "We stand together, you and I."

I'm afraid you're not careful of yourself, dear. You get hurt so often, and I'm afraid you'll be seriously hurt (this sounds "grandmotherish," but I love you, dearie). I'm near you, darling. I touch your hair with my lips.

Anna

MARCH 23, 1898
Oronoco to Eyota

My Own Dearest:

I just loafed around after I got to Rochester. I didn't quite feel in the mood for going to see people. I saw Martin Beatty in the Post Office while I waited for the stage, and talked quite a while with him. He intends to go to the University next fall if finances are right. He urged me to go – said I ought to do it. Said, like the Celt he is (all Celts have kissed the blarney stone), that if he had half my constitution and head he would surely go. And I hid my face – at which he vowed, of course, that he wasn't saying it to talk nice, and I laughed at him. I hope he will go – I think it will be good for him. His ideas about being better able to help people and himself made me think of the days of my youth, when I talked thus and thought I would be able to "live more." Dost remember? Well, perhaps I was all right in theory (I'm not sneering a bit).

I saw Gertie Miller in the same place, and she asked me if I was on a "vacation." Someone else said something of the kind. Can I never shake it off? People always think as a matter of course that I'm eternally in school. It's nearly as bad as your trouble about teaching.

The folks all inquired about you. I'm not very busy today. Henry and Fred are dressing stone, and I do the grinding on the rolls. They're dead-sharp and tear it out pretty fast. Mother has been sick and feels "pretty slim" yet, as she says – I guess the doctors don't know the cause of it.

I've thought of you lots, as I always do. I hope things aren't torturing you, dearest – you mustn't let them more than you can help. You're so precious to me, darling. I hate to think of your suffering. I tell things kind of awkwardly sometimes, but you understand how I feel – I *love* you so much. We will counteract everything in time with our great, strong love, won't we?

MARCH 27, 1898
Oronoco to Eyota

My Dearest Anna:

So you've been to Winona and back, I guess. By this time you have seen Dr. Lane – this doctor who speaks the inexorable truth – and you feel good, or are in despair. And if despairing, how great is that despair today – this bleakest, dreariest, lonesomest day of the whole year? I am wanting much to know what the verdict is about you – write me soon.

I've been wandering around "like a lost goose" today. It's been such a dismal day. I read some, but didn't have much to read. I rowed up to the rocks and back. We put a boat in last night – it wasn't especially pleasant, for there was a raw wind and a rainy cold mist. There's a piece of elderberry pie in the kitchen that will be a fitting finale for the day. I was busy last week. Mary came home for a week's vacation Friday. I rather expect Bowers to come and see me this week.

I think you show your good taste in not liking my last letter, for I imagine, somehow, you didn't. I'll cut this short, for I've not much to tell. Write to me soon and tell me all, won't you, dearie?

You know what I would say if I were there next to you.

MARCH 27, 1898
Eyota to Oronoco

My Dearest Roy:

It's so dark I can't see to write at the writing desk, so am writing at the little sewing table at the window. I didn't go to church this morning, and I'm going to write a lot of letters. I won't *get* any, I suppose, unless I *write* first, for I owe almost everyone a letter.

I had a long talk with Dr. Lane Friday. He says I have made "very satisfactory improvement" this year, and he has no objection to my teaching next year – provided I stay in this part of the country where I can have "proper care," and that I take things easy and not put every particle of energy that I possess into my work. I talked with him in regard to the future. I want to talk it over with you when you're down. I saw Pres. Shepard, and he said he would be pleased to recommend me to any primary school in any state. Wasn't it nice to hear him say that, after my being out a year? And I'm *so* glad I can teach! I should feel I was really doing wrong if I disobeyed Dr. Lane, or went contrary to his advice.

I saw most of the Normal teachers I knew. I went up to Mr. Holzinger's room – he's as sunny and kindly as ever. He said his wife had been very sick, and his little baby had died. But his face brightened again soon, and he said, "We're all alike – we all have our troubles."

Uncle Henry says if I apply in Chatfield he doesn't think I would need anything more, with two of the School Board and Pres. Shepard behind me, but I'd rather have Mr. Cloyd's approval too. Then if I don't get it, I will have done all I can; and if I *do* get it, the Board will be so much more likely to stand by me in case of trouble, if they remember that I was well recommended – see? I'd like to be in Rochester best of any place, but they have reelected all their old teachers, so unless some of them resign, there won't be any place for me.

I've been reading some old letters from Aunt Matt and her sister to Grandma – when they were girls and teaching in country schools near Preston. They are interesting, and Aunt Matt says I may keep them. I want to read them to you sometime. They had dreadful times – "boarded 'round" and lived with all sorts of people. Think of a family like mine, living in only two rooms and a tiny attic, and only six chairs in the house.

If you come down when the crocuses are out, we'll hunt for them. I suppose arbutus is out, or soon will be, in Cloquet. I am reading *Westward Ho* and like it. I read part of Frank. R. Stockton's *The Stories of the Three Burglars* today. What a stormy day it is.

Your letters are such a comfort. Come down when you can.

With my dearest love,

Anna

MARCH 29, 1898
Oronoco to Eyota

My Dearest Anna:

I'm so glad Dr. Lane could say what he did – glad it's true, and glad you can do as you want to. It's nicer to congratulate you than condole. I'm very glad, dearest – you're a dear to write me soon when I was waiting to hear how it went.

I'm alone in the mill. Fred's painting up at the house. Got to take the stone up again and see what's wrong with it – the spindle got too heated up this forenoon. It's a nasty business, and I've had done with it for the day. The winter is making its last rally, I guess. It seems as if all the seasons make a struggle before they leave us. Last evening I was out – it was sharp and clear and cold, but the sky looked hopeful of spring.

I'm going to write you whether I have anything to say or not. I've worked pretty well today and feel just sleepy – not tired – only just the edge taken off so it's comfortable, you ken. I love you more than everything, and I'm wanting so much to see you.

Roy

Don't I tire you, *ever*?

MARCH 31, 1898
Eyota to Oronoco

My Dearest Roy:

I was glad to have you write so soon. You're so wonderfully good, dearest. You poor boy! You've been "condoling" with me for one thing and another nearly all the time since my country school. I really believed you would think me good for nothing if I made a failure of that school.

I wrote to Chatfield, asking more questions – now all I can do is wait. I've been dressmaking this week. I put a new front and back into my brilliantine waist, so now it's like the boy's jackknife – the same old knife he'd had for years, only he put in a new blade and handle. I fixed over my old, much-darned reefer jacket dress that I wore in school most of last year. I always feel in the schoolmarm "Johnnie, stand!" mood when I get it on. The effect is like the sound of fire bells to the superannuated horse with the milk wagon – you remember Will Carleton's poem?

Whatever made you think I didn't approve of that letter of yours? I did – every bit of it, and especially when you say we will counteract all bad things with our strong love.

I read some more in *Westward Ho*. It's good – very good – fresh and free and strong, as you said. Amyas Leigh is great, isn't he?

Write me often, dear. I *am* tortured a good deal, but I hate to always be complaining. While I have you, nothing else matters much. Here's a kiss ….

Your little girl

APRIL 3, 1898
Oronoco to Eyota

My Dearest Anna:

I want to see you. I wish I might, and your hair would be braided just for the time. I love you – I never could love anyone else, because there could be no one like you.

I was glad for your letter. I don't know why I thought you didn't like mine – possibly it was a little spleen against myself.

Mary and I were walking this afternoon. We went through the woods and out on the bluff and found some crocuses – game little fellows, struggling up in spite of the frosty nights. It was nearly sunset, and I heard a robin below, singing the fit song they're always singing at evening, and it seemed pleasant. I expect the hepaticas to come soon. I think each spring seems lovely, partly because of the other springs gone by.

Things are looking pretty warlike, aren't they? Probably next week we will know something. I'm interested – we're all Uncle Sam's men.

I remember that country school you went to. You used to write as if I were looking on and weighing the balance, and how blue and discouraged you got sometimes. I thought of you back then – how would I be held now?

I'm glad you like *Westward Ho!* Isn't that an antipodes to *Quo Vadis* and the like? Yes, Amyas Leigh is just great – a gentleman, wasn't he? So straight and true and every way strong. I liked that book very much.

Aunt Minnie and I went to a play last week, got up by home talent. It was pretty good. Ann Rice and Ella Wurt were in it. Ella has a very clear carrying voice and did well. Lou was villain and said "Ah ha" and "How, my fine lady," but his fierce mustache slipped down once while he was executing aforesaid paroxysm of demonic glee, and that changes the effect on the audience rather suddenly if they notice it.

I wish you were here, dearest – I want you. I hate so to have things bothering you. You needn't be afraid of "complaining"– it isn't complaining with me, you know.

With my dearest love,

Roy

APRIL 6, 1898
Rochester to Oronoco
My Dearest Roy:

Those crocuses are the first I've seen. They smell like the warm hillside on a spring day, and are almost living things – like kittens. I've been putting the soft, downy little things to my lips – they seem wonderfully fresh and cool.

You see I'm writing in Rochester. My home is here now. I came up Saturday to see Uncle Henry about living here. I went back Monday to pack up and came back here last night. It's been hard, but things had become unendurable. I had to say my say to Mother – I told her that I was coming and the reasons.

While I was in Eyota I received a telephone call from John Chermak in Chatfield. He said their primary teacher had resigned. The Board had not yet acted upon her resignation, but he wanted to know, in case they accepted it, if I would take her place and be ready Monday. I said I would, so you see, I'm waiting – not knowing whether I'll stay here or go to Chatfield. I haven't unpacked all my trunk, and I'm going to spend much of my time, until I hear from John again, visiting primary grades.

I want to see you before I go, but if I go, it will be Saturday. Can't you drive in Friday night? I'm so glad – so very *glad* – to have a friend like you, Roy – so strong and true and loyal. I'm going to tell you what I've done when I see you. You're better than I – you wouldn't be so hard – so unforgiving. You'll blame me. I blame myself, but it can't be undone.

If I hear from Chatfield, I'll write you.

Anna

APRIL 7, 1898

From: State Normal School at Winona, Minnesota

President's Office

To: Miss Anna Barnard, Eyota MN

Dear Miss Barnard:

Supt. E.J. Donaldson of Chatfield wants a primary teacher for next Monday. I have recommended you. As you are so near, my suggestion is that you make a personal application. I think you can get the place. Let me know your action and the result.

Cordially,

Irwin Shepard, Pres.

APRIL 7, 1898

Rochester to Oronoco

Dear Roy:

I'm elected in Chatfield at $40 per mo. for the balance of the term! Begin Monday! Am going tonight to see teacher and get the hang of the work. Visited schools this morning. Am sick abed at present – I'm tortured physically and can't hold my hand steady or write decent – so sorry. Must stop. I can't see you tomorrow.

With my dearest love,

Your own A

CHAPTER 31

In It Again

APRIL 10, 1898
Chatfield, Minnesota, to Oronoco

My Dearest Roy:

I came to Chatfield Thursday evening and made my way up to Mrs. Chermak's – do you remember her? I visited school the next day, talked the work over with the teacher, and got the hang of things somewhat. I met the superintendent and most of the teachers – they're all very friendly. Two of them were in the Normal when I was.

The school room is large – bright and well-ventilated. I have over 50 children. None of them are over 6 years old, and many of them only 5. There's one curly-headed 5-year-old that I fell in love with. It must have been mutual, for he trotted across the room for me to help him put on his coat. He has long brown curls and brown eyes – he reminds me of that picture of you when you were little. There's a Roy among them – I'm sorry – I wanted that name just for you. School hours are from 9 to 11:30 and 1:15 to 3:10. I am to send home the youngest at 10:45 and 2:25.

It seems so good to be in it again. I expect to be ready for vacation when it comes, but I want to work now. I'm sorry I came away just before the hepaticas are out, but I don't want to give this up if I can help it. I want you to come to Chatfield while I'm here. I'm not so far away that we can't see each other. I'm going to board here at Mrs. Chermak's. It's quite a distance from the schoolhouse, so I'll take my dinner at Miss Atchison's. Several of the teachers board there.

It's so very pretty here. Chatfield is in a valley – there are bluffs covered with woods near the river. Mr. Haven – one of the Board members and Uncle Henry's friend – invited me to his house last evening. We had a nice time. Have been privileged to join two literary societies and Christian Endeavor, and invited to attend Salvation Army meetings. Wouldn't I look nice in one of those bonnets? May I join?

I hope I'll have a letter from you soon. You'll write to me often, dearie, won't you? Be careful – send my mail to Box 70. There's another Anna Barnard here; also another Frank Barnard. The postmaster is known for being careless, and he might not see which mail is for which Anna.

Hasn't this been a beautiful day? How I wish we could spend our spring together, but I think of you with every breeze and cloud, and the birds and the spring smell all speak of you. Even the children and the people I meet make me wish you could see them too.

Good-bye, dearest,

Anna

APRIL 11, 1898
Oronoco to Chatfield

Respected Lady:

Oh, the *deuce*, Anna – *she's* got it – my letter – that *other* Anna, named like you. I wish so you had told me not to write. I got your letter Thursday night and wrote you that evening – how did I know there were *more* of you? I feel sorry and – drat! – get hot and scarlet when I think of anyone but you reading that letter. I suppose one shouldn't write things that everyone couldn't see, but no one does that. I will get cut to ribbons about it. Do you know this person? If I ever see her, it will mean unlimited chocolate creams, of course. I'm dreadfully sorry – I'd give anything if it hadn't happened. Possibly you got it all right, but somehow by your letter I'm sure of the contrary. I'm so sorry – you don't blame me, do you? Well, it can't be helped now. What's she like – the other Anna? Do I keep on, now I've started the correspondence so furiously? Oh!

Walter stopped off last Tuesday on his way down from Hamline. He's same as ever, of course. Mary came home Friday. Sunday we went over in "our woods" (don't care if the other one *does* see that) and gathered quite a lot of hepaticas.

'Course we want you to come visit. Aunt Minnie has been planning it all winter. I wish it might be next Friday, but the household is torn completely to pieces with a great, thorough housecleaning – the old "10 days" kind – and probably you wouldna want to eat on a barrel. Auntie hated to have me tell you "we were cleaning house" after we'd talked of your coming, so I won't. We must make it work somehow.

I've had a bit of a "thorn in the flesh" – my old biennial "kelch" in the thorax. Perhaps you know the thing – it catches you and you feel like coming to your knees. It's gone now, as it always does. You're feeling better, aren't you? I've been worried. Write me soon, if you can. The hour is early, but I fear I've already trespassed too far upon your time and patience.

Yours most sincerely (ain't that stilted),

Roy W. Allis

Because I mock a little, don't imagine I'm any less chagrined over that occurrence.

APRIL 13, 1898
Chatfield to Oronoco

My Dearest Roy:

School work piles up over my ears. There's to be a great "grade entertainment" and I have not done a thing toward it. Miss Marvin, the former teacher, promised to send me her plan. It came, but isn't complete enough for the superintendent and me to use, so I've got to get up something out of my own head. I'll have to send tonight for whatever I need, and spend Saturday getting things into shape. I have a pretty scheme for the children to sing and represent violets – a flag song and a rainbow song. Haven't the music for any of it, so I'll have to trot around and see to costumes – oh, it's *lots* of work. I didn't know if you were expecting me Saturday, but thought I'd better write and tell you I can't come.

My cold isn't very bad, except for singing and drilling children. Have been looking for a letter for several days. Did you write to the "other one"? I suppose it's her turn now (!).

Lovingly,

Anna

I've just read this over. It sounds blue, but I'm not – I'm very happy. I like the pressure of work, and it's good to be in it again.

APRIL 14, 1898
Chatfield to Oronoco

My Dearest Roy:

I've been here a week – seems shorter than that. Your letter came all right this time, but I've not yet got the other one. I laughed good over your letter. You poor boy – you're always in trouble of some sort when *you* suffer horribly and *I'm* amused. I was a bit anxious about that letter. I didn't know what the other Anna was like, or what she would do with your letter, so I asked Mrs. Chermak to ask her husband if she had received any letters that didn't belong to her. He said she hadn't – though she probably wouldn't share such a letter with him if she had. There's a Barnard family in the country, and I guess it must've gone there. I *want* that letter the most of any.

I thought it a little strange you were so slow about answering, especially after what I'd written, but thought it was due to my moving about so – you wouldn't know just where I'd be. Don't bother about the letter anymore, dear. If someone has got it, I'm perfectly willing they should know I have such a lover as you – especially as they found it out through no fault of ours.

School goes fine – nearly 60 children. Must go to sleep early tonight – I'm going to take care of myself this time. Good-night, dearie.

Anna

APRIL 17, 1898
Chatfield to Oronoco

Dearest Roy:

It's 2 p.m. and I've just wakened from a nap and feel as one does if they sleep in the day time. I went to a party last night – the teachers and high school were entertaining. Had a pleasant time. I have a good deal of sympathy with them in all things – moreso because of you than anything else. You can't sympathize with happiness and lightness and gaiety without having had a taste of it, and I did that last year – all because of you.

I never was in a place where people were so determined to know who I am, where I'm from, what I've been doing, and who my folks are. Seems almost everyone in some roundabout way asks one or all of those questions.

I have the cloth for the black dress I told you about – brilliantine skirt, black shirtwaist, white collar and bright ribbon tie. It's at the dressmaker's, and I expect to have it this week. Do you remember the hat with the white crown that had a fit and twisted all out of shape? I gave it a dozen coats of shoe polish, and it's now a nice *black* hat. And I have a *new* hat – it's small and black and tilts to the right. There are some dark red roses on the left side next to my hair, and quills and ribbon that stick up just above them. It's rather a jaunty little hat when it's all by itself, but I'm afraid it loses its character on my serious head.

I have to train the children to take part in some school entertainment before school is out. Mr. Keser – a man who boards where I do – asked me a good deal about myself and what I'd been doing. I spoke of being in Cloquet, and then having been in Rochester at my Uncle Titus's. The next day there was a little item in the paper in regard to Miss Marvin's successor, saying I had considerable experience in Cloquet, and was a relation of Mr. Titus of Rochester! People never asked any questions in Cloquet – I was so far away from home they didn't care who my folks were. I was simply Miss Barnard from the southern part of the state, and if they liked me I was all right, and that was enough.

I've got on all right with my work – have about 54 little ones. They seem to like me. I have some of the nicest boys. I've become very interested in a little girl in my room – I wish I could adopt her. Her mother is dead, and her father is a rough sort of a man. People say the child was dreadfully neglected and abused and made as rough as her father. One of the Salvation Army girls got hold of her and kept her while she was here. May is about 6 – just as sweet and affectionate and pretty as can be – she makes me think of a kitten. The first day of school she ran up to me, reached up her little arms around my waist and said, "I like you, Miss Barnard, and you won't go away, will you?" Miss Marvin went away, so I think she's afraid I might. When they lined up to go home, she reached up to be kissed. I thought she must come from a home where the love in her nature had a chance to develop, so I was surprised when I found what her home had been.

There's a little boy who reminds me of Volney – he has a serious, sensitive, earnest face, and is *so* good. I fell in love with him, and when I questioned folks in regard to him, I found that *his* father is rough and taught the little fellow to swear like any pirate, so people kept their children away from him. He's learning better, they say, since he's been in school. I have some wonderfully sweet children.

I have been to supper and Christian Endeavor since I commenced this. I'm writing up here in my room. Cuba the cat is lonesome and has come upstairs too. She's here on the table playing with my pencils. She found a wasp crawling up the curtain and took it into her head to poke and smell him. I was afraid the wasp would sting her, so I killed it. I always think when I kill anything that I never will again.

Mr. Van Smith is a vegetarian. I sit next to him at dinner. He's dreadfully fastidious – you ought to see him writhe if anything disagreeable occurs at table. Mr. Keser was trying to amuse the baby in the way people do, by smacking his lips and chucking, and Van nearly had a fit.

I'm invited to join two literary societies – I think I'll go to one. Did I ever tell you I used to think Uncle Henry thought I was a bit lazy and could do a great deal more if I had a mind to? Well, I'm surprised – he really seems anxious for fear I'll do too much. He tells me not to let people get me into too much work: "Tell them you're not strong and can't do so much, and have broken down from overwork once." I believe his opinion of me has changed. He never has seen me when I'm working. I'm *very* careful, and intend to be. I don't care if people think me lazy – I know best what I can stand. I didn't have but one cold all winter, you remember. I've taken cold only one week of school – isn't it queer how colds and school go together? I think this won't be much of a cold – it's just in my throat and makes me "hack" a little.

I'm still reading *Westward Ho."* I like it, but have so much to think about that I don't read very much. I can't believe there will be war, because I hate awfully to have it. It seems a dreadful thing, now that it's so close.

I may have to work at school Saturday. How are the hepaticas – will they be out then? I haven't picked any this spring, though the children have brought them. And tell me if you all really expect me to come.

A little boy came Friday with a beaming face. He said, "Miss B – I've got a live crab for you in my pocket." He brought it out, and another boy said, "I can bring you one bigger'n that." Now I have two of them in a tin cup!

I love you more than ever.

A.

APRIL 20, 1898
Oronoco to Chatfield

My Dearest Anna:

It's late, and I'm going to write just a little, for I'm intending to see you Friday night. You'll try to come then, won't you – if it doesn't look so *dreadfully* bad weather that you can't ride? I'll be waiting for you, whether you come or not. Auntie is expecting you and wants you, and I want to see you *so* much. It seems very long since we saw each other.

I was glad to get your letter. If all one's life could be emotion of some kind, it would be easy to live, wouldn't it? Interesting, anyhow. You are good, dearie – a little pearl of a girl. But I've sworn off making love letters after that episode. Well – I'm sure I'll break through once in a while – how can I help it?

Yes, it looks warlike. It's a terrible thing, of course, but there are worse. I wish I was a midshipman or something on the "Indiana" *(one of three battleships that served in the Spanish-American War).* I think if there is fighting, the main part will be on the sea. But we may have a chance – land folks, I mean. It would be more interesting than the "kickoff" in a Wisconsin game, wouldn't it?

Good-night, dearest. I wish you would've had that lost letter – it was a masterpiece. I'll always tell you this, even if it wasn't (!). Try and come, if possible. I want so to see you.

APRIL 24, 1898
Chatfield to Oronoco

My Dearest Roy:

Both your letters came yesterday. I read the "right" one first, and then the other. I think I never knew you cared so much, darling. I somehow thought the whole trip to see you all was to favor me, and in giving it up because of work, I didn't realize I was hurting anyone but myself. I'm sorry, dearest – so sorry you were disappointed. Can you ever forgive me, dear, for being so selfish – for forgetting how you would care? I did get a lot done – it goes so much better on Saturday than put in after a day of school.

I won't forget again, dearie. It's so wonderfully sweet to have someone care to have me with them – it means more to me than anything else. I love you so, dearest. You'll think I'm a "Maysie" – always thinking of my work and indifferent to "Jack" – but I'm not. Oh, I'll make you *know* I'm not someday.

I'm not overworking, dear. I have chosen something very easy for my grade's part for the exercises – that is, as easy as it could be and have them do well. The only trouble is, my cold has grown worse, and it's hard to teach them the songs. All the other teachers are so busy, I hate to call on them to help me. I won't be fagged out, dear – the time is short, and I'm taking care of myself, at the risk of being thought lazy.

I want you to come to Chatfield soon. Carrie's house is full. She has three boarders – her father, a high school boy, and myself. If it weren't for that, I should want you to come here, but you can engage a room at the Madina House. Then we can have the evening together and Sunday. You could go back Monday. There are some woods about a mile from here – Dark Valley, they call it. We could go over there Sunday and hunt for flowers. Do you like my plan? Will you come? You must come before school is out. And then, if you and Aunt Minnie will ever ask me again (after saying I would come and then didn't), I'll come.

The dress I told you of is finished, and I wore it to church today – also the new hat. I like them very much – I hope you will.

You *are* a help to me, dearest, dearest boy. Without you there would be no one who cared – no one who would trouble themselves over me. I love you more than ever just now. I imagine I have pushed your head down on the sofa pillow. My arm and hand feel the warm, dear weight. My other hand touches your thick, beautiful, curly hair – I'm pushing it back from your forehead. Dearie, do you feel my lips, my breath? Then your clear, true eyes – I love them so – and your lips ….

My lover – you have all my heart.

Your own little girl

Oronoco to Chatfield

My Dearest Anna:

You wrote me the loveliest letter, darling. It was the best and sweetest and truest of all things – like being near you. It's glorious to have you love me so – there's no one like you.

Of course, I was disappointed at not seeing you – how queer that you didn't know that. I must make you understand that I'm "fond" – oh, more than fond – of you; you haven't realized the sense of it yet. You're just the dearest, *dearest* little girl, and I don't deserve a thousandth part of it all. I was so worried that you were sick, and then I was *afraid*. I'm sorry you're hoarse – it must be dreadfully hard to sing. And I was sure you were working at high pressure. I don't like to have you killed off, and I was angry with *everything* for a bit. I was wonderfully glad of the letter, my own.

It's getting like spring – the water even smells as it does at this time when things begin to show. The woods are beginning to look hazy with buds. Sunday was a lovely day – I was thinking of you. I've been having a good deal of work. There was a dance in the pavilion Saturday night.

And the war. I intend to be in it if it's to be of any size. I wish I knew whether it was or not. I'd like to see some active service, above all things. I read about an ex-college military organization in the state – Shattuck, Pillsbury and the U all drill some, you know. But I would hate to lie around in some garrison for a year or so. Well, one must take his chances with that. If it's of any size, I intend to enlist – that's right, isn't it? It's a queer war – we haven't anything in the line of land or such to win, have we? It's something like a crusade – I like that. It seems as if things might have been done more gently. I can't see the way things were put to her – how Spain could back down without fighting; without shame. But we are on the side of humanity – on the right side – and we'll all stand together when we're in it once.

I won't come to Chatfield this week – possibly next. I hate to bother you – you're sure it would be all right? I'm wanting you so *dreadfully* right now, darling, and I love you with all my life.

That was a wonderful letter – how I love you, Anna, my own little girl. Do you mind my telling you so often?

APRIL 27, 1898
Chatfield to Oronoco

My Dearest Roy:

Your letter came today. Someone brought it to me at school, and I didn't want to wait, so read it with the children about me. It was wonderfully good and *dear*.

But, Roy – you said what I've been expecting to hear you say (knowing you so well) and fearing so to have you say it. I *don't* want you to enlist. Perhaps I would if there was great need of you, but there isn't – so many are volunteering. Wait for a couple of years, at least. There will be greater need for the best then. If you should go now, it would take several years out of your life – just when you ought to be beginning your life work. If you were in the army four or five years, you would come back with no business set up, and nothing in particular to do. You would be too old to make a beginning, and your life wouldn't be as helpful as it would if you had spent those years – or at least part of them – getting ready for your work that will come after the war. I *can't* have you think of going – for a couple years, at least.

Come to Chatfield – I want to have you *tell* me about it, and why you think you ought to go. Of course you won't "bother me," dearie – I wouldn't have asked you if I thought you would.

My cough is no worse. Dr. Lane sent a package of digitalis and a message that it was my heart that caused the trouble, and not to take cough medicine. I'm not good for much if I can't teach without coughing.

I'm quite tired, so good-night, dearest, dearest.

Anna

APRIL 30, 1898
Oronoco to Chatfield

My Dearest Anna:

I'm disappointed, of course, that you can't come. Curse the schools – how I hate things sometimes. You will kill yourself – you're overworking, I presume, just as of old, but it can't be helped, I suppose. Only I love you, you know.

What dark weather we're having – it probably wouldn't be pleasant for you to come visit, even if everything else was favorable. I'm so sorry about your cold – it's the way you were before, and you'll be all fagged out and careless about everything at the finish of school. Now I'm croaking like an old raven – I'm in a savage humor, I guess.

I haven't been reading much because I've had nothing I cared to read. Last Sunday was a lonesome day – dark and raining – and I lay down indoors, and then wandered around in the wet woods. What good am I? You needn't take the trouble to answer this stupid letter – it doesn't deserve a reply.

Aunt Minnie brought me a little bunch of flowers to send you, and wished me to tell you how sorry she was not to see you as shortly as she expected. I'm in the mill alone – there isn't a great deal of work just now. Some days there'll be a good deal, and then slack ones.

I'm glad you wrote me about the hat – how it tilts to one side and the rest. I liked your long letter – you are the *dearest* girl. I've nothing to write yet. I keep maundering on. I'm not a bit of help to you – sulky and savage. I ought not to send such a mess to you. Forgive me when I'm blue and bad. And Anna, dearest – try to spare yourself what you can.

With my dear love,

Roy

MAY 1, 1898
Oronoco to Chatfield

My Dearest Anna:

And it's May. I'll be glad when school is out – very glad. I think likely that's the cause of your cough. You can hardly help but work hard, but you also said you weren't much good unless you could teach without coughing. It would be a whole lot of good if you didn't teach *at all*, but I know you need to. I hope you'll get better soon.

So – the war. You're funny – put it off for a "couple of years, at least." I laughed – you evidently think we're in it for the long haul. My child – I imagine it will be over in much less time than that *(Roy was right – the war began in April and was over in August)*. And you said I should tell you why I thought I "ought" to go. I guess "ought" doesn't have so much to do with it – I *want* to go, and you know me well enough that that would pull me harder than the other – is it not so?

I got a letter from Zim – rather tender and advisory (I'm a beast to speak so) – telling me it wasn't my duty to go at the first call; that the state didn't want its college men to go yet (the deuce) when the fellows from our homes are going. After that is when he thinks we would do the most good. He spoke of my "gifts" (say, didst ever see anything of those same gifts, Annabel, that people sometimes speak of?). Zim's good, anyhow.

You see, I should like to see some of it before I die. Someone must go, and I'm young, with a superb digestion. And I don't know anyone whose time is less valuable to himself. It would be the daintiest, most considerate thing for my friends, if I could get comfortably knocked on the head at the present stage of the game. (There – if that isn't maudlin sentimental, true or not, I dinna ken what is, do you?) But I'm not going to throw this away. I want to be in it if it's a big scrap; otherwise, I don't. I thought of joining the "Zumbrota Guards" *(Minnesota was the first state to mobilize for the war)* – they've gone already, but thought I'd wait to see the caliber of the affair. Don't trouble, dearie – I've never done anything of this sort, and probably never will.

I've been working pretty hard. Fred's painting a man's house. Kit went over to Zumbrota to see her brother off with the "Guards." He's got some false teeth though, and I shouldn't wonder if that would knock him out when it comes to the examination. I wandered around today – listened to the band practicing and boys playing ball. Took a little exercise 'cause it was Sunday and I wasn't working, and read some of *Vanity Fair*. Did you like it?

I want to see you, dear. I guess I'll come next Saturday, if you want me, and are sure I won't be troublesome. I hope the cough is better, darling – wish I could help you. Anna, I need you more than you know. Don't ever think, dearest, that you're worthless – nothing is farther from the truth. I love you. You are everything.

Roy

MAY 4, 1898
Chatfield to Oronoco

My Dearest Roy:

Come Saturday for sure – I shall be looking for you. I've been counting the days. Chatfield is such an "early to bed" town – you'd better engage your room before you come, or you might be obliged to lodge in the woodshed or cellar. I'll send you a map I've drawn – study it carefully, and you'll see where to cross the street from the train. After walking about Chatfield, you'll appreciate my kindness in telling you where to go. Remember I'm at John Chermak's. There are a number of Chermaks, and if you mention Barnard they'll send you to the other one. (I'm afraid if you did, you'd disappear like my letter!)

I tell you – Chatfield is an uncanny place. I'll save up the rest of my inspiring ideas until I see you. I shall never doubt the "gifts" Zim speaks of.

Lovingly,

Anna

We talked in school today a little about war. The children have such funny notions. Cuba, Spain, islands, soldiers, sailors, battleships, battle and war are either meaningless or very vague terms to them. A small boy said we were fighting the Spaniards because we wanted to go to Heaven!

CHAPTER 32

Draw Up Closer

MAY 9, 1898
Chatfield to Oronoco

My Dearest Roy:

I want to write to you before I sleep tonight. I'm thinking how I hurt you yesterday, darling. I've been able all day to see more and more how cruel I was – how selfish – all taken up with what I had been through and the marks it left on me. How could I feel so toward you – you who have been such a gentleman – such a knight always, and so good – so wonderfully good to me? Are you sure you feel the same? Have I fallen some – am I less a woman than you believed me? I wish I could look into your eyes to see the answer, but I'm afraid to.

I've been unusually tender with the children today because of this. Instead of scolding them, I've drawn some tear-filled eyes close, close to me, and it's been a comfort.

I'm so glad we had this talk last night. I had given my heart to you before, but now I think my very soul is yours, and my love comes something near worship. I have known a hero – the bravest, strangest, truest hero. I'm not worth his care, but he *does* care for me, and this is worth all the struggle of living.

It's only 8:30, but I'm tired – my cough has been troublesome today. I'm so sorry that I hurt you, dearest – do you forgive me? Is it all as it was before? If we stand together, our love shall be something more than human. Such a good year it's been. I've been thinking, thinking – sometimes it seems best that we should *not* stand together, and then it seems best that we should be true to all we have felt and believe of our love. I can't tell how it will be decided. We will try to do whatever is right.

I'm writing this here at school. This has not been a hard day – the air is so good and clear, and the children have been happy and good. They seem to *like* me – some of the parents have told me so, and the children act as if they did. You don't know how good it is to have the *love* of the children, when you're trying to teach them. I have seven large bouquets of apple and plum blossoms and bluebells. The air is so fragrant!

Good night, Roy, my knight.

Your own little girl

MAY 9, 1898
Oronoco to Chatfield

My Own Dearest:

I came straight to the Oronoco Station and worked in the mill a little after 10. Oh, I was heartsick and lonesome, with a feeling that something had happened, and an ache somewhere. I came down through the woods, for we had talked of things that seem bitter and cruel and hard, and I'm glad we did now. Anna, I so want you to be happy and untroubled, and we will be very happy, dearie – sometime. We will have a sadness with us, but that will go away too. We will be good children, and everything will come out all right. But we must stand together, you and I – there is no happiness for me without you.

I wish you could have been here this evening – I believe you would've liked me. I have my fighting clothes on. If we ever work together, I think you will get to like me better, for then I'm not so sulky and egotistical.

I wonder if you're tired today, and what you're thinking. You're the bravest and truest and noblest of women, Anna. I love you more than ever. It's only three weeks before I see you. How glad and thankful I am there is you. We'll stand together always, always.

Such a poor letter, but how can one write such things? I love you dearly and always, my own.

Roy

MAY 12, 1898
Oronoco to Chatfield

My Dearest Anna:

Your letter came tonight – oh, it was good to get it. I never wanted something from you more. Forgive you? Of course I do, darling. And will you forgive me – for speaking out roughly? I was rude – I wasn't thoughtful the evening before. *I* was wrong dearie, not *you*. Don't think more of it – it was so much better to let me know how you felt, and I'm glad you did.

Of course, I'm the same as always – *just* the same. I wish you were here – wish you could see deep enough into my eyes to see how you are to me. I want to *tell* you some things – things I won't try to write. I've been thinking of you all the time since I left you – seen you as you've looked a thousand times since I first met you – your looks, your eyes, your voice. You've been so gentle and good to me always. You're so dear to me, Anna – I love you so.

All things will draw up closer, dear, if we take them right. We'll make our love stronger, warmer, holier, and we'll stand together. Do you ever think how I need you? You think too highly of me – I'm not a hero – I just love you. And, of course, the children love you – people *always* like you!

Your picture is on the wee table here in my room, and by it a shell full of moss and hepaticas, all faded and dry now. Auntie put them there when they were fresh because you like them.

Things will come right – I will be a man yet. Be careful with yourself, won't you? May all good things come to you – dearest, holiest little girl.

MAY 15, 1898
Chatfield to Oronoco

My Dearest Roy:

A week ago we were here in this room talking. It's a warm, nice day – just as it was then. I wish you were here now. We will be together as often as possible during the summer.

The birds are very thick around here. The grove is so near. I have seen several rose-breasted grosbeaks, and yesterday the thrushes sang all day in the oak trees near the house. I just *love* this springtime.

Your two letters this week were wonderfully good. You are the kindest boy! I have nothing to forgive you for – the fault was altogether mine. I shall claim it and not allow you to take any of it. You write the dearest, sweetest letters.

I wish I could know beyond all doubt what would make your life the happiest, the fullest, the richest. You remember we talked about what you wanted your life to be – one of broad experiences and emotions. I'm afraid I'll cramp your life, instead of helping you live the kind we planned. I must talk with you again. I cannot, I *must* not let you sacrifice your happiness for my sake. I wish I could know what is best for you. I never heard you as I do now. Perhaps Miss Peck is right – she says we're not left alone to decide these questions. But it seems as if we are sometimes?

I brought some apple blossoms home from school, and the room is fragrant with them. There's a phoebe singing near the window, and the sun streams in — it's beautiful out. I wish we could go for a row up to the rocks.

Good-bye, dearest.

Anna

MAY 18, 1898
Oronoco to Chatfield

My Dearest Anna:

Last evening was perfect, wasn't it? Like the "land o' faery." I was out on the water rowing Rube around, while he got together the torch and things for a fishing excursion. It was springtime — almost intoxicating, the air was all so sweet. I love it too. I like to feel the cool, soft air touch me all over, with the heavy winter things all gone. I'm glad summer's coming and your school will soon be through.

Sunday evening tied 12 boats together and towed them back to the grounds. We rowed up to the rocks after that, and the frogs were singing and the whip-poor-wills calling. Do you suppose I was thinking of you? Last night I went to a show. It was the slimmest affair I ever saw, and 'twas funny to see the folks all look at each other, for they didn't know what they were doing.

I had a pretty good run at the mill this forenoon, but 'twas slack this afternoon, so I took to straightening up. I have spasms of cleaning up and being neat. I'm not chronically afflicted that way, I'm glad to say — no, I guess I'm *sorry* to say. I could be much worse. I was careful to leave a little undone, for if I didn't, I knew I should feel so blame virtuous no one could live with me in any comfort. I'm still reading *Vanity Fair*. I like it much better than I did before. Thackeray knows how to say things that will touch you.

Yes, dear — we will have another talk — we won't write it. Things will come out right. I'm thinking of you — love you so much.

Roy

MAY 22, 1898
Chatfield to Oronoco

My Dearest Roy:

This has been a busy week — two more weeks of school. Our literary class is holding a picnic next Saturday. I am to whistle! The program is to be a funny affair. I'll tell you about it after it's over, and I see how it goes.

I went to Eyota Saturday to see Dr. Dugan. I've taken more cold, I guess, and cough more than usual. Doctor gave me some medicine – it hasn't had any effect so far. Eyota looks as usual. George is at Ft. Thomas, Chickamauga. Aunt M has the flag he had when he was a little fellow out on the house. One other boy from Eyota went. The boys have suddenly changed from boys of no particular accomplishment to heroes, in the eyes of Eyota, I guess. The papers say there will be a second call soon – you won't go, will you?

How beautiful it was toward sunset this afternoon. I put on a jacket and hat and sat out on the porch. I thought perhaps you were out on the river. I want to come out for a day and have a row up to the rocks and the North Branch, where we get lost in the woods when it's dark. I never hear whip-poor-wills except when I'm with you at Oronoco.

Uncle H says he's saved reports of board meetings for me to copy when I get home. I'm glad I'll have something to do at first. He tells me now and then of business matters – things that are not to be told. It seems wonderfully good to be treated as a woman who can understand and be trusted with things – especially by a man like Uncle Henry.

I love you dearly – your letters are so good. I'm sweeter because of them.

With my dear love,

Anna

MAY 24, 1898
Oronoco to Chatfield

My Dearest Anna:

It takes longer for letters than when you were in Cloquet – why is that? I was afraid something was wrong; then I would think – she's just busy.

I've been wagging on as usual – everything's all right. We had a pavilion dance Saturday, and someone had to stay with Mither and baby through the evening. I did – I had rather stay with them than do the dance. I was up until 3 reading the rest of *Vanity Fair*. It was getting light just the least bit as I came over – like the rainy Sunday when you were here, when it cleared off so bright. I must've been walking when you were sitting on the porch. I walked to the Point and saw things looking so bright and fresh, and the sky so pure and clear.

Three more weeks of school – I'm sorry. And I'm dreadfully worried your cough is worse. But it's getting hot, and you'll be flourishing again with the summer. We'll go up the North Branch when you come, and let it get dark. Do you remember one night we were up there when the moon was so bright, and you were feeling splendid – you sang to me a little? I remember just how you were.

I've no wonder Mr. Titus gives you his papers – you're a woman *very much* to be trusted. It's queer you like me – I'm glad you do. I want to see you and get your atmosphere. I'm glad my letters do you some good. I'm not what I ought to be – I've not lived the life that would make me the most good to you. But I'm not very old, and I can progress some yet.

It's fine to see so much life come on with the warm rains and the heat, but I like fall the best. It's nicer to feel the life in one's self than in growing things, and *you* are always best then. How you are tangled into everything – all in four years.

Next Monday is Decoration Day. I hope you'll keep liking me – I guess I need it. I love you so dearly and think of you every hour. I wish I could help more. Do I tire you, Anna? Don't you feel disappointed sometimes at my letters? Be honest.

Roy

I'm going to try and help you, dear – I'll see you often this summer. You're a wonderfully brave, noble woman. Try not to get discouraged. I'm sure things won't be so hard for you after a bit. I love you always.

MAY 25, 1898
Chatfield to Oronoco

My Dearest Roy:

Your letter came to me quickly – it was so good. Did you sit up all night taking care of your mother and baby? I think my cough is some better. I'm not so tired tonight.

This weather makes me think of the river and the woods; I remember dimly singing some up on the North Branch. Let me be your "bon comrade" in all things! I'm never disappointed at your letters – *honest*. I wish you could know how glad I am to get them, and how very good they are.

I've been reading in the *Ladies Home Journal* an article about Robert Browning and his wife. They were as much in love as we are – it's very beautiful to read about such love. The trouble is that people are so weak and human. I don't know what the trouble is, but it seems these days that almost everyone has been engaged two or three times, and it's very easy to get over one love affair and take up a new one. I may have lost some of my faith in human nature, but I haven't lost any of my faith in *you*. Good-night, dearest.

Anna

MAY 27, 1898
Oronoco to Chatfield

My Dearest Anna:

I wonder if it's the genuine article when people "get over" a love so easily. I should think it would be a hardening process – to do it over and over. If it *wasn't* the real thing, and one found out, that would make a difference. But if it were otherwise – how would it be to feel you were planting the same sacred soil over and over? Seems it would get so it wasn't sacred anymore, and it's bad to lose holy ground – there's so little – don't you think so, dear? I know what you mean – lots of times it's spurious, fair-weather love – vain and selfish. I would hate to get over an honest love, wouldn't you? Even worse to entirely get over it and be as well as before.

I have been out on the water hardly at all – I'll wait for you. This stretch of three weeks seems the longest of any. I haven't been busy today, so read some more Thackeray – "Lovel, the Widower" – little story in the back of *Vanity Fair*. I didn't care for it, especially. I'm out of reading matter, and evenings are a little tedious. I think I will have things a bit different next year, after I get settled – I wasn't this year.

I'm glad you're even a little better with the cough. Wish you were through with school.

I'll see you pretty soon. I love you, dearie – always.

MAY 29, 1898
Chatfield to Oronoco

My Dearest Roy:

A week from tomorrow and I shall be in Rochester. Your letter sounds as if you're as anxious to see me as if I had been away six months. (It's very nice!)

Our literary picnic is over, the Board has met for election of teachers, and my year report is made out and handed in – three important things over with. Oh, say – I'm reelected! The picnic was a success – I think I enjoyed it best of anything since I've been here. We did a play – I was a little girl and played with a doll. I wore a short white dress, with the waist very high – almost under my arms – and white stockings and slippers, and had my hair braided in two braids and tied with white ribbons. I spoke a piece of four lines, and whistled! The whistling was supposed to be the best I could do, but I got out of breath; then scared; then more out of breath, and my lips got all dry and wouldn't work. But people were very nice, and told me I did well – just because I'm a girl and not supposed to know how to whistle, I suppose.

I've been quite gay the past two days – don't know why. There's some merriment within me that bubbles out once in a while when it's uncalled for. I think it's the time of the year.

Good-night, dearie. I love you – love you so.

Anna

JUNE 7, 1898
Rochester to Oronoco

My Dearest Roy:

I'm here in Rochester – came last night on the evening train. It seems nice to be here, but there isn't the "let up" – the feeling of relief that usually comes with the end of school. I'm not tired. It seems very good to be in the mood for doing something, instead of feeling so languid.

One of our neighbors is building a house and barn on the lot below us. It shuts off the view to the east, and it's horrid to have it there. Aunt Hattie feels badly, but she tries so hard to make the best of it that it seems funny. She says, "Well, we won't be troubled by those weeds growing there, as we have been!" And: "I'll set out some roses and shrubs on the edge of the lawn, and that will help hide it!" – as if a rose bush could hide a barn! She always makes the best of things.

Could you drive over tomorrow? Come and take supper with us and spend the evening. I want to learn all about birds this summer. I noticed so many about Chatfield. I want to watch them and find out what some of them are. If you have any books or magazine articles about them, bring them over.

I'll see you so soon I won't write more.

Lovingly,

Anna

JUNE 8, 1898
Eyota to Oronoco

My Dear Roy:

Your letter came this morning. Don't wait till the last of the week – I've been waiting nine long months, and I don't want to wait a day more, do you? Come *tomorrow*. Of course, I am here *any* time, but I want you *tomorrow*!

It's so good to be home – to wander around outdoors and sleep all I want and do just as I please. We'll be lazy together and do just what we want (if we can find what that is). I have so much leisure that I hardly know what I *do* want to do.

I'll watch the trains tomorrow.

Anna

JUNE 11, 1898
Eyota to Oronoco
My Dearest Roy:

I locked and bolted the door you went out of last night, then closed the window in the parlor, put out the lights and went to bed. This morning Uncle Henry found the parlor door partway open – I forgot to close it. See the effect on me you have? You were in my dreams last night, dear, as you are so often after I've seen you.

I miss you and I love you.

Your own little girl

JUNE 12, 1898
Oronoco to Rochester
My Dearest Anna:

I was glad to get your letter – 'twas good of you to write so, dear. I would've liked to have come down today, but I thought it was too soon.

I didn't have to walk the streets homeless and desperate Friday night – I sallied out and found Frank, and he seemed glad to see me. Then the harp player wanted to come out and fish. I brought him out, harp and all – the harp across our knees – and off we went on the water. Must've been a sight to see.

I've had quite a time today – I've fascinated everyone. I had it in my head that white duck trousers would be good in the mill in the summer – cool, and wouldn't really get soiled any more than anything else, so I "blowed myself" for a pair. I fixed up last night, resurrected my worn belt, put on a dear little white tie and white cap – everything white "sine macula" – and people have been paralyzed. I'm decidedly the warmest thing on the ahvenoo. You should see me!

Don't trouble yourself, Anna, about things. I love you – just *you*, always. We'll talk things over and face things together, won't we? It's fate. I say not to trouble, but I know you can't help it. Don't fret more than you need to – things will come out all right.

I haven't done much today but pick strawberries and stroll around and rest a little. I must see you soon – when? I love you always.

JUNE 19, 1898
Rochester to Oronoco

My Dearest Roy:

Isn't this a glorious day? I've been watching birds this morning. When I come to Oronoco I'll have a better chance. The robins and blue jays predominate here, though I've seen a catbird, a red-headed and a golden-winged woodpecker, a purple grackle, and a wood pewee. It's the wood pewee that has that sweet little mournful song: "de-ar-ee, dear." He used to sing up the hill near your aunt's house last summer – do you remember?

Things must be fine there today. It's so bright and fresh after the rain. I'm reading *Vanity Fair*. I wanted to read it again. You *must* come tomorrow. We shall be looking for you.

Anna

JUNE 23, 1898
Oronoco to Rochester

My Dearest Anna:

I got home all right with poor old Fanny. I started at 5 and reached home a little after 9. I thought I wasn't going to make it – she wasn't quite right, but we made it home. She's in the pasture and improving. Aunt Minnie was troubled when I didn't come home at the usual time – didn't sleep and worried something might've happened to me. Seems good to be back in my room here. Bowers always grinds his teeth until I almost fly out of my skin.

Walter rode up Tuesday on my bike. I haven't ridden it yet to speak of – just over to the grounds and back in a roundabout way. Hot afternoon today – a lot to do, and oh, wasn't it warm?

There's quite a moon out tonight. I *must* see you. I love you always.

JUNE 27, 1898
Rochester to Oronoco

My Dearest Roy:

It's been a little over 12 hours since I saw you, and you've been in my thoughts most of the time since. You were in my dreams all night. The dreams were very vague and sweet – I would wake enough to know I was happy and contented, and then go off to sleep again. It was a good night to ride home, after all – how bright the moon was soon after you went.

Clara has been unpacking and I've talked with her a little. It's good to have her home.

I hope you'll ride over some night soon. My, it's good to have you so *near*.

Lovingly,

Anna

CHAPTER 33

Sadness and Longing

JUNE 30, 1898
Oronoco to Rochester

My Dearest Anna:

I've held off writing because I was expecting to ride in and see you last night, but it didn't work out. I really want to see you this evening. It's raining. I hope the roads get into shape quickly. It would be nice to see you twice close together.

I had no trouble coming home the other night. The shower just touched me a little. The moon was under clouds most of the time, but I got along all right. I saw something strange – a rainbow in the east, caused by the moonlight. Such a ghost of a rainbow it was – I never saw that before, did you?

I've been reading *Soldiers of Fortune*. Meanwhile, I sent for *Summer in Arcady* yesterday – shall we read that? I'll bring it when I come. That was a good criticism you showed me on R.H. Davis – I've always liked to read things he wrote.

I've been pretty busy, and we will be very busy July 4th. Do you remember when I came to see you last July, just at evening? You were sitting out on the porch, and you told me how you couldn't teach that year, and looked quiet and sorry, and then said we would see each other oftener though. I want to see you now, dearie.

With my love,

Roy

JULY 1, 1898
Rochester to Oronoco

My Dearest Roy:

I guessed the reasons why you didn't write – I never saw such "beastly" weather. I had a letter from Aunt Matt today, enclosing some of George Alden's letters. They're interesting. George says they have received orders to be ready to start at any time, but he has no idea where they're to go. He's pretty sick of the life, and wants to get at some fighting, though he thinks it's hot enough in Georgia, and if it's so much hotter in Cuba, he'd rather stay where he is during the summer. I'll read the letters to you when you come.

I wish you were here, dearie. I have something to tell you when I see you, if Clara says I may – it's good! I'm the only one in Rochester that knows it besides Clara – I feel big!

I'm sitting in the hammock facing the house. May sits in the wooden seat, and I stop once in a while to help her with some fancy work. Clara and Uncle H are gone. How I wish you were here.

Wasn't it beautiful last night? I hated so to come in the house.

It's going to rain and you can't come tonight – *plague* take the weather! I hope you can come tomorrow – you *must*!

Your own,

Anna

JULY 4, 1898
(*From* Oronoco, Past and Present, *by Elsie Boutelle*)

> "By July 4th – in just six days – the Oronoco dance pavilion has been built – 80' x 30', with maple floors. An orchestra was procured and played into the wee hours of the morning … as dancers filled the floor …. The pavilion was finished, except the roof, and sheeted today. At 2 a.m. a torrent of rain descended. Ann Rice said: 'Although it dampened the clothes of the dancers, it dampened their ardor not a bit.' Ladies wore long dresses and high shoes. Boats were soon put on the lake. There is a barn for horses, and an icehouse, where great masses of ice are stored for use by campers …. Resident cottages are built in the village and occupied by many Rochester young people, including Drs. William J. and Charles H. Mayo, Drs. Henry Plummer and E.S. Judd, J.H. Kahler and Burt W. Eaton."

JULY 6, 1898
Oronoco to Rochester

My Dearest Anna:

I thought of riding in this evening, but a stupid person came to the mill late and I've felt sleepy. Very likely I'll come tomorrow, 'gin it don't rain – *again*.

I had rather a hard trip home Sunday. The birds were singing before I got to Oronoco. I heard the clock strike 4, just before I fell asleep. The next day we were all at it hard, and again the birds were singing, and the moon ghostly as I went home. It's nice to see the morning come in the summer time, don't you think so?

Things went off as well as you could expect the 4th – better, I guess. It wasn't very pleasant weather, of course. Oh – there was a crowd the first of the night – such a select company. I'll tell you about it when I see you.

I'm sleepy and warm, so this letter is dull and abrupt. I'll be all right tomorrow, and hope I may see you. I love you so.

Roy

JULY 8, 1898
Rochester to Oronoco

My Dearest Roy:

I ought to be doing some work, but I want to write so you will get this this afternoon.

If you haven't ordered *A Kentucky Cardinal* or *Aftermath*, don't do it. I got them last night and am keeping them to read with you.

Walter called last night – had the best visit with him I've had since high school times. He was more in the mood for talking than I've seen him in a long time. You ought to have seen his face wrinkle all over when I told him you rode over in an hour Sunday, and I was afraid you would hurt yourself riding so hard when you're not used to it! He said he didn't think you were in any immediate danger from too much exercise, unless your habits had changed since Hamline days. However, he would use his influences to stop you if I wished it.

Come when you can. I'm looking for a letter this afternoon.

With my love,
Anna

JULY 12, 1898
Oronoco to Rochester

Dearest:

We have had beautiful days, haven't we? I rode over to Uncle George's this evening, and as I talked with them on the porch, I could see the sun go out and the fields all white with the oats.

Walter came out yesterday and went back this afternoon. I was busy all the time he was here. The boys are dressing the stone – the rolls are dull at present, and grind like a coffee mill. The grists keep ahead of me, and it tires me to be so slow. I spoke to Walter about my writing, and he said *of course* I could write, and urged me some. I told him you thought I could, and he said, "If you weren't such a blame *idiot*, you'd *know* you could."

I hope the roads look good – I'll see you soon. You know I love you always, but I don't want to tire you.

With my love,

Roy

JULY 15, 1898
Rochester to Oronoco

My dearest Roy:

Your letter came Monday. I was glad to get it – Sunday was a long, restless day. I looked for you until almost night, and you were in my mind all day. I was thinking about what's right – what will make you happiest. The tears come when I think of how much I want to be to you, and how little I can be. I love you more than ever, darling. I'm glad you talked with me as you did Friday. I understand you better – I'm coming closer.

Frank Zimmerman was at church Sunday evening. He walked up with me and took lunch with us and talked awhile. I feel acquainted with him just because he is your friend. He spoke of you.

I met with the Red Cross Society and rolled bandages for wounded soldiers yesterday. I never thought *I* should do that, when I have heard our mothers and grandmothers tell what they did for the soldiers in the Civil War. I'm going to work in the bank this afternoon.

You *must* come Sunday – in time for dinner. Three more days – it seems so long. I love you, *love* you, darling.

Your own,

Anna

JULY 16, 1898
Rochester to Oronoco

My Dear Roy:

I was shocked beyond measure to find you at the circus, and here in the afternoon, and you never came up to see me! I thought you'd surely come to the house one of those times. My, wasn't it grand? Did you see the long line of elephants – each holding the tail of the one in front? Wasn't that pretty? And ye gentle knight, riding your snow-white charger, right behind ye calliope that played "A Hot Time in the Old Town Tonight."

Then the brave gentleman that sat beside the hippopotamus and didn't look scared a bit. And ye lord in ye dress suit and silk hat, accompanied by ye stately lady riding ye milk-white palfrey, and the beautiful ladies with lovely parasols, riding in perfectly elegant carriages, and the handsome men besides them. Oh, oh – wasn't it heavenly! And now it's all over, and we won't have another such circus for several years.

Come over tomorrow and we'll read *Aftermath*.

Anna

JULY 19, 1898
Rochester to Oronoco

My Dearest Roy:

Isn't this a glorious storm! Clara and I watched it until it rained and we had to come in. She's watching it now from the bedroom window – ready to tell us when to go down cellar. Aunt Hattie is making a cake; May is ironing; I'm writing, so Clara thinks she must look after the family. Grandma collects all her valuables in her apron and opens the cellar door when a storm comes up. When I was little, I used to go around and fill my apron with all sorts of things – stove pokers, old shoes, etc., and stand behind her, waiting for the word to go down cellar.

I took a nap yesterday afternoon – from 2 until nearly 5! I felt fine afterward. May and I took a walk up the hill. It's dark and shady there – almost like a walk through the woods – and we came down through a meadow. The grass had been cut, and it smelled like the country, and I listened to the soft *swep, swep* of our feet through the grass. I like that sound. When we told where we'd been, Clara said, "You couldn't *hire* me to go through there this time of night!"

In the evening we read *The Adventures of Francois* in the June *Century*. Does anyone in Oronoco take *The Century*? If they do, get it and read it – very interesting. I got *The Flute and Violin* from the library last night – it's a number of short stories that came out in *Harpers* and *The Century* several years ago. One of them – "Sister Dolorosa" – I remember reading back then.

I had a letter from George Alden yesterday. They're dreadfully tired of doing nothing except drill, and want to go somewhere – they don't care where.

George writes that he earned a dollar sewing on a button. I'd like to know how he learned – I never knew he could sew!

Come when you can. I love you, darling – dearly, so dearly.

Anna

JULY 20, 1898
Oronoco to Rochester

My Dearest Anna:

And why does he write this time o'day? He should be at work. I have an excuse – I haven't been well the last couple days – haven't worked at all. I know now how you felt when you put your head down on the table and wanted to just keep still. Caught a cold – sore throat, fever and headache. But they're about gone today, and I'll be at work tomorrow. I don't feel myself yet.

Sunday night after I left you, I faced northwest and saw a storm coming pretty rapidly. I didn't know it was going to drift around and break away, and I rode hard six or seven miles. I was going pretty fast or it wouldn't have happened – I struck a bit of sand and took a header – the only hard fall I've taken. Glad no one was there to see me – a body hates to fall. I got up all hot and bothered about doing such a thing, and I think that road hit me harder than I thought at the time – I felt so sore yesterday. And I ain't *hungry* – *now* I know you're terribly worried (!). (You see – I don't get a chance to talk ailments very often, and when I do, I wax very hypochondriacal. There!)

Isn't today refreshing – oh, it seems so good – and all the woods seem to look deeper green and sturdier and to have "taken a brace."

I've finished *Hugh Wynne* and like it very much – I liked his mother.

I may or may not see you until Sunday – I'm sorry, dearie – every week counts now. I'm thinking of you *so* much. I love you – *all* of me.

JULY 21, 1898
Rochester to Oronoco

My Dearest Roy:

I was helping to get dinner yesterday when your letter came. When Clara passed me my plate, there was your letter with the potato and meat!

I'm sorry you've been sick. I'm afraid you rode too hard going home. I'm really anxious about it, dearie – you must be more careful – you pitch into things so hard. I'm afraid you work harder with your wheel than you realize.

Clara has a dressmaker, and I'm awfully sorry for her – I'm afraid she has consumption. She hasn't been well since early in the spring. She coughs and is so pale and thin. She weighs only 105 – she used to weigh 140 – and is so languid, when she used to be sprightly. It seems a dreadful thing for her to keep at work. I should like to *torture* her husband in the worst way – the idea of letting her *work* – not only for herself, but for *him*! She said Dr. Will told her she must stop or she couldn't live three months. It fairly makes me *wild* – to think her people will let her kill herself. Someone ought to *make* her stop. I think I feel worse about it because I might have been where she is if someone hadn't made me stop.

What beautiful weather this is! The valley off to the south is alive now with yellow and green patches.

I'm glad you like *Hugh Wynne*. I knew you would like his mother. We all went to the orchestra concert Tuesday. I enjoyed everything the violinist from Chicago played. There's nothing in the world that can express every human feeling as a violin. Sometimes he would make it bubble over with rollicking fun; then it would grow homesick and tired and sleepy. Sometimes it was a merry child, and sometimes a gay, girlish girl dancing. And the last that he played – oh, it was the sweetest little home spirit – sunny and cheerful and smiling and contented. But behind it all there was heartache. I wish you had been there – it sent cold chills creeping, as fine music will.

Come before Sunday if you can, but you must not hurt yourself. I love you, dearest.

Anna

JULY 29, 1898
Rochester to Oronoco

My Dear, Dear Roy:

I wish you were here tonight. I'm homesick for you – "a feeling of sadness and longing" that nothing can drive away tonight, except one dear boy. I want to come close – to touch the strong arms, and put my head in the dear old place, and then feel the arms close around me. I love you so, dearest. Perhaps you will come tomorrow night if the roads aren't rough.

I had such a funny dream last night. Charlie Reifsnider called on me. He looked very serious, and began at once to tell me that I was making a very great mistake in keeping you so long – that your mother disliked me *very* much to have you out so late. It made such an impression on me that I resolved on waking to never keep you late again.

Uncle H asked this morning, "Is Roy worse than usual?" I said, "I didn't ask, but I didn't think he looked any *worse*." And Uncle said, "Well, I thought he *must* be – he went home so *early*."

We have some kittens. They're under the porch, and I can't get at them. I fished one through the lattice work. It's grey and *so* cunning – I wish I could bring them all out so I can pet them.

I've read some of the stories in the book you brought. I read "Without Benefit of Clergy" aloud to Clara – what a pitiful story it is. I also read "The Mark of the Beast." Clara's too practical to enjoy such stories – she wants to talk them over, and they won't bear talking about. Aunt H heard part of it and doesn't approve – thinks it's wicked.

Oh dear – I *miss* you so.

With my love,

Anna

CHAPTER 34

Haunted Ground

AUGUST 3, 1898
Oronoco to Rochester

My Dearest Anna:

It's late – I couldn't come tonight 'cause of roads, but they'll be all right tomorrow, so you'd best write or telephone if you don't want me. I came home in about an hour last time – it was very light, and I rode all hills, and mocked and vaunted at the dogs.

I want to see you. It's camping time. I rowed over and spoke to Frank on the grounds just at evening – I have hardly been over there this summer. It was getting dark, and I strolled up through the old camping place. There are no campers over there – it is as it was that first year, and I went up on the hill where the hammock hung, and sat on the stone where you used to sit and read, and it was all haunted ground. I love you so dearly, Anna.

Roy

AUGUST 6, 1898
Rochester to Oronoco

My Dearest Roy:

Did you get home before it rained? I woke sometime in the night and heard it raining. It seemed to me I had been asleep a long time, but I never can tell anything about time when I'm sleeping. I asked Uncle H when it began to rain, and he said, "Just after Roy left."

If the roads don't dry up today, take the other horse and come tomorrow – he won't founder, probably. If he does, you may sleep in the barn with the kittens. I shall look for you Sunday.

Your own little girl

AUGUST 11, 1898
Rochester to Oronoco

My Dearest Roy:

Clara has great news from Beloit! She's very quiet, but May and I prance around and try to express her feelings for her. Ed Brown – her fellow – is coming day after tomorrow!!!

Will your new suit be done in time for Sunday, and have you some nice cuffs, and a clean pocket handkerchief, and a very biled shirt? And be sure your shoes shine! If you look very nice, Clara will allow you to look through the keyhole at the fatted calf – I mean the prodigal – I think he's Mars or Cupid or some other little heathen god! I'm saving the kittens as an offering to him.

Aunt Hattie and Uncle H intend to drive to Eyota Sunday morning, so I'd like to have you go to church and have dinner with us. Such excitement!

With my dearest love,

Anna

AUGUST 14, 1898
Rochester to Oronoco

My Dearest Roy:

The morning work is done, so I'll fill in a few minutes writing to you. I forgot to tell you of the lawn social here on the Titus's lawn tomorrow night – can you come?

I've been thinking about my visit to Oronoco. I hate to change your mother's plans, but I also hate awfully to leave Clara to wash dishes and pare potatoes while Ed is here, and she would have to if I go away this week. Would next week work? I hate to be so changeable.

I intend to go to Chatfield Aug. 31 – I'll need a new dress.

Come tomorrow night if you can, but don't ride fast – and if you're tired, don't come at all. I'm really worried about you, dearest.

With my love,

Anna

AUGUST 15, 1898
Oronoco to Rochester

My Dearest Anna:

Mither says she would like you to come next week Tuesday – can you, dearie? We want you to stay some. At the end of this week is a day of great food preparation for a band contest, and it wouldn't be as nice with so much cooking going on.

I love you as always.

Hastily,

Roy

SEPTEMBER 1, 1898
Chatfield to Oronoco

My Dearest Roy:

Here I am in my room in Chatfield! I have put my table in front of the two west windows, and I get a good breeze once in a while. The family call – "Hello, Miss Barnard!" – has commenced, and although I've not been out of the yard, I've been warmly greeted by several little lads. My trunk is unpacked, and things are in order in room, closet and bureau drawers. My pictures aren't up yet, and my writing desk hasn't come – once those are fixed, I shall be settled.

I went to Eyota yesterday to see everyone. Mother acted nervous and ill at ease all the time I was there. I didn't take my things away as I'd intended – Grandma looked sick and worn, and I hadn't the heart to take down my pictures and books. Aunt Matt says Dr. S says Mother is developing very serious heart and nerve trouble – she looks very thin and worn.

I'm very sorry for Grandma – awfully sorry. The rest have brought things down on their own heads, and I have no sympathy for them. That sounds dreadfully hard, and I ought not to have said it to you, dear. You have sympathy for *everyone*.

I must see the dressmaker this afternoon. Write to me soon, dearest. Give my love to all and write me about everyone.

Lovingly,

Anna

SEPTEMBER 5, 1898
Chatfield to Oronoco

My Dear, Dear Roy:

Your letter came today. Darling, dearest – do you have to *see* me to know how to write? I want to be the same to you always, darling, and you spoke of what I said that time. I'd give anything if all that had never been – you'll never fully forget that. You'll always think that if I felt that way once, I may again, and you'll always be afraid of it. I'm haunted by my dream – when I was tearing my heart in pieces because you wouldn't forgive me, and you said you could say the words, but you couldn't mean them. Try to understand what I'd been through when I said that, dear. I think if you could fully understand, you'd forgive me – but even then you'll always be a little afraid of me, and a bit uncertain.

I have arranged to take dinner at the hotel instead of Miss A's. It's nearer, and I'm planning to save myself all I can. I had only 37 children today – I'm sure of having about 45, I think.

I love you, love you.

Anna

SEPTEMBER 11, 1898
Chatfield to Oronoco

My Dearest Roy:

I received a telephone message from Uncle Henry Titus yesterday, saying that Uncle Henry Barnard was dead, and the funeral would be Tuesday at 1 o'clock. If it were summer and no school on my hands, I would try to go east, as I might be some help to Aunt Maliza and make it less lonely for her for a while. But I couldn't stay, so there's no use in going.

School went all right last week. I had only 38 pupils. I may have more – that's a small school for 1st grade. Mr. Donaldson says they have a fine 1st grade teacher in Preston, and he would like me to visit her school, so he's offered to teach my room for a day and let me go.

I've just been for a ride. I've been thinking how fine the river must be, with the fall, woodsy smell. I'd like to be with you today. You must come to Chatfield while this fine weather lasts – before the roads are spoiled with fall rains. I'd like to see you next Sunday, if you can come then. On your way, go to Uncle Henry's and ask him to show you on the county map the best road down here to avoid the sands and hills, if you can.

What you say about my plan is lovely – I never was quite sure you approved of "Miss Barnard, 1st grade teacher." I think you've quite ignored her heretofore, and given all your attention to Anna – little girl, bon comrade and a very ideal woman, whom you put on a pedestal and paid your devotion to. You're all right, dearest – not so haphazard as you think, and you *do* have order and system about your work – I can see that.

Write me often, dearest. I'll promise anything if only you'll promise not to be afraid *ever*.

With my dearest love,

Anna

SEPTEMBER 16, 1898
Chatfield to Oronoco

My Dearest Roy:

It's 7:45 – I can't write much before school, but I want to tell you that you *must* come if you can. The roads will dry up and be all right, won't they? I'll have a place for you to "wash" if you're hot and thirsty.

I have a hot, irritated throat this morning. It wants to cough, but I don't let it 'cause it hurts. I'm awfully afraid it's the beginning of a cold. Come if you can.

Anna

SEPTEMBER 23, 1898
Oronoco to Chatfield

My Dearest Anna:

I've read your letter three or four times – it's so good to know you think such things of me, even if I can't see it that way. It was sweet to have you tell me so, dearie – praise is so good from you.

It was a pleasant day to ride home. I came out from Rochester at a good rate – I was warmed up and felt like it, and the road in the smoky light looked so yellow and smooth and inviting. I was in the mill in the afternoon – not very busy, and was glad. I sat down in the back room and read some of *The Reds of the Midi*. I liked it, as you did, and remembered what you wrote me after you read it. Warm people from the south there, weren't they? I haven't finished it yet. It's better because you like it too.

Barrack-room Ballads came night before last – I wanted that. I have it down in the desk at the mill part of the time. That's the first thing of Kipling's I ever saw. For some reason I like "L'Envoi" – the last poem. A scrap of it has haunted me ever since I read it in Minneapolis.

Otto wanted me to ride over to Pine Island with him last night to see the Andrews Opera Co. It was a nice ride over wi' the moon. Otto led the way, and I kept five or six rods between us, so if there was an accident to the foremost man I wouldn't run into him. Coming back I led, and struck a bit of sand, and it switched me over to the other side of the road and he took me amid ship. He struck his tire against my pedal, I guess – something popped, and he was punctured, and we walked the remaining three or four miles. He wanted me to ride on, but, of course, I wouldn't do that. It was after 12 when we got home.

Tuesday I went thrashing – took care of our half of the grain – and, Anna, it was my *birthday* and I didn't know it. I felt kinda bad about it next day. I got muddled as to the days of the week.

Tonight was such a free, breezy night, wasn't it? I wanted you so much. I rode over to Uncle George's. Mabel remarked it was a fine, restless night – nice on the water – so we swiped someone's boat from the cove and went out. The wind blew – there was a storm brewing, and the clouds were lurid from fires. I went to the house and swiped some peaches, 'cause we were hungry. On the way home Mabel wanted to row a bit. She let her oar slide out and didn't notice it while she was fixing her shawl. 'Twas dark enough we couldn't find it, so I swiped oars from the boathouse so we could get back. Mabel worried about that oar, and what if the owner wanted to go fishing in the morning, and I said tomorrow I will craftily search the shore.

It's almost 11 o'clock, and I've written a stupid letter in reply to yours. I'm glad there's you – so very glad. I'll write a good letter sometime. I wish you were here. I love you entirely.

You will write Sunday and tell me how you are feeling?

OCTOBER 4, 1898
Chatfield to Oronoco

My Dearest Roy:

I said I'd write and tell you how Monday went – it was all right. So was Tuesday. I'm feeling quite well – better than I did before I gave out. I still cough, but I'm not so hoarse, and I have a superb appetite – I'm taking a tonic and eating like a thresher. They take me to school and take me home, which is a great help. Everyone has been wonderfully good.

I've been thinking of you this evening, and I love you so. You're so strong and tender; so gentle and so much a man. Roy, I almost worship you. I wish you could know how I think of you.

I'm anxious to see you again – the time seems long since you were here. I wish you could have been here when I was sick. I thought of you – so full of vitality and strong, warm life. It's so very sweet when I think of life with you.

I love you so, dearest, dearest.

Anna

OCTOBER 14, 1898
Chatfield to Oronoco

My Dearest Roy:

I read your letter just before the children came in this morning – it made the day better. I *do* want you to write twice a week, dearie – you needn't be afraid I will tire of your letters. I've been afraid to write to *you* too often, for fear you would tire of answering. We will write as often as we must, for we are never going to be tired of each other, if we live a thousand years.

I have felt well all week. It makes me happy, dearest, to know you've been merry again – your letter before sounded so blue, and you were anxious about me. I have on a new red wrapper – I know you'll like it. I also have a new dark blue serge shirtwaist. I wear my bright jeweled belt with it, and you ought to see the children feel and pick at it!

I've been having a dreadful time with an 8-year-old boy. He's been troublesome from the beginning of school, but I hoped he would, after a little, do as he ought to please me. I think most of the children mind simply because they want to please, but this boy doesn't care a rap, evidently. I talked with Mr. Donaldson about him, and we both thought he needed a "spanking." He offered to do it for me, but I thought it would be better to attend to it myself. So Wednesday I spanked him. Thursday he acted up, and I shook him. Today he tried to be smart, and I spanked him again. He isn't mischievous – it isn't an overflow of animal life – it's something *contrary* within him. When I say to the children, "Please don't do that – it disturbs the school," this boy is *sure* to do it, and look at me with his little green eyes and a silly grin on his face.

What can I do with such a boy? You know boys. I ought to get him to *like* me, of course, but I don't know how to do it, and I don't think simply liking me would be enough either, for I believe he would walk over his own mother.

I'm reading *Children of the Ghetto*. I like it quite well, what I've read.

I'm almost certain you haven't run away this week, for the roads are very muddy – at least here. It's rained every day this week except Tuesday and today. I hope you can go next week. Stay away long enough to have a good time and do all you want to – you need some fun!

Did I tell you? I brought a couple of my drawings from Eyota, and have them in my school room – the horse's head and the thistles. I also brought a picture of Evangeline with some cows – I used it to cover a bad place in the plaster. Mr. D came in just as they were done, and said, "Oh, those are pretty enough to frame!" My room is quite pretty – you must see it when you come.

This is the last of my paper, and there isn't *nearly* enough room to tell you how I'm loving you right now, dearest, dearest.

Anna

OCTOBER 18, 1898
Oronoco to Chatfield

My Dearest Anna:

Your letter came tonight – my, I like them often. Of course, I haven't run away yet – the roads don't look much like any such venture just now. When can I? If I don't do it, I'll be sorry for myself, and that's an uncomfortable feeling. Yes, it's been raining the same here – the water has crept up 14 inches. Hasn't it been gloomy? I've read quite a bit, for I haven't been very busy.

Otto and I boxed some yesterday and today. It's hard work for Otto, with his height and reach. Of course, we aren't at all scienced, but we manage to make it interesting. I'm lame in places tonight. I think it better "sport" than shooting squirrels and the like – think you not so too, Anna?

It seems lonesome without Baby Volney. Fred misses him. Baby is funny – whatever there is, he wants the proper owner to have it. The other day at dinner, I sat next to Blanche. When she got up and went into the kitchen, I at once confiscated her meat and had it nearly eaten when she came back. You should've seen the boy's face, with his lip like a crescent moon in a storm sky! They couldn't stop him – down he came and began to belabor me and cry. It was comical to see him, but I thought afterward that if *I* felt like that, I wouldn't like to be laughed at.

I finished *Great Expectations*. I have Holland's *Arthur Bonnicastle* now, and think I shan't like it much. *Rodney Stone* is here, you know. I read some of it again on the rainy yesterday.

How I'm wanting to see you. And I'm so glad, dearest, my own dearest, that you're feeling well.

I'll write soon. I love you entirely.

Roy

This letter doesn't seem good, as I read it – abrupt and school-boyish. But you won't mind. I hope you're not having any more trouble with your emerald-eyed boy. I guess you know much better how to do with him than I. I wonder what kind of a school I would teach. Mabel said if I taught, she would go a hundred miles to visit me!

OCTOBER 24, 1898
Oronoco to Chatfield

My Dearest Anna:

I hope they won't change your school as you said. You *must not* kill yourself, no matter what. If you do, I shall act up enough to burst my heart. You mustn't do what hurts you, dear – for *your* sake and for *mine*. Perhaps it will come out all right – can you protest?

There's nothing at all sure about my trip now, with the weather and all. It's tedious gloomy living, this weather, and I want to see you so much. Otto and I went down to the mill this morning and boxed stripped down and had quite a time. Then we dressed up and went to church. Mr. Pringle spoke – I like him. He shook hands with me, and I told him my name, and he thought he had heard of me. I thought likely, and said I was quite famous. He asked me how I skinned my nose, and I said, "Boxing." He asked was I good at it, and I said, "Not particularly – the nose speaks for itself." We had a very intellectual talk – quite a feast for the soul.

Mother had a letter from Mary tonight – it sounded blue. Her knee isn't so well. She saw Dr. Will, and he told her about the joint there, and how the muscles weren't strong enough to hold it firmly in place. I'm sorry for her – I'll encourage her what I can.

Oh, child – I think you write better than I. You should have been the writer and I the play-actor. I wish I might see you every day or so – that you could be near me all winter. Then we would see what comes about. We must do the best we can as it is. I'm anxious to see you.

With my dear love,

Roy

NOVEMBER 6, 1898
Minneapolis to Chatfield

My Dearest Anna:

Thursday morning I woke early for some reason, and looked out and saw the bright stars and moonlight, and I guess the spirit of "Odin the Goer" came slowly upon me, for I dressed a little, went down and looked at the weather, finished dressing, wrote a couple notes, took a glass of milk, got out my wheel, came up through the woods, and tied a note on the door, saying how I'd clean run off. Then I mounted and rode. The moon was beginning to fade from the morning – oh, 'twas very romantic – and I looked back and shed ye usual parting tears, of course.

I rode to Zumbrota, and when I got there, Charles fried some bacon and three eggs and got peach sauce for me. We walked around a bit and he rode a couple miles with me. I came to Northfield a little after noon – a good ride, though my wrists ached a little. Spent most of the evening there. Same as ever, is the professor, who inquired after everyone, including thee. It was cloudy and looked like rain, and there was a south wind at my back, so I didn't wait longer, but rode a little after 8 o'clock and got to St. Paul for dinner.

I had ridden fairly hard and was dreadfully hungry. I went to the Clarendon Hotel, but I should have loafed around a little first, for the dinner went against me, as it does sometimes when one goes too long – you aren't so hungry as you thought. I rode over to Minneapolis after dinner down Summit Avenue on the cycle path to St. Thomas, then up the riverbanks to the U, taking it real easy – it's a pretty path. I wished it was a tandem and you were with me – yes, when I get a 25-inch thigh, I will have you and a tandem.

My heart beat a little faster as I rode near the U. I didn't see anybody I knew for a couple of hours – all new surroundings and unfamiliar faces. I looked for Buck's Bicycle Shop (Buck that I used to go to theaters with), but it's gone – the Klondike is there now – "a stranger fills the Stuarts' throne." I went down to Sam Reynolds – the ski-u-mah barber – with my broken heart, and got shaved, and he was glad to see me, and said "the old ones are pretty well gone, but old Sam's always here," and said to a man how wide I was, and I was glad to see him.

Then I saw many of the folks and my brother-in-law Howard, who was quietly and heartily glad to see me. We went to the play *Pudd'nhead Wilson* and it was splendid – a good play, and everybody did his part right, and I was delighted. It was like old times, and I enjoyed it and was happy and looked at the old drop curtain and heard the old orchestra and thought some of the old thoughts over again about you and all – dreamy boy thoughts.

I stayed at Windsor House that night, and heard the rain beat when I awakened, and was comfortable and glad I wasn't riding or living in a hollow tree. I loitered around next morning; went up to the library and the U and had a great, clean, staunch dinner with folks. Bimeby we went down to get Mary Pettit to go to the game – U of North Dakota against Minnesota. She's a ND girl, you know, and she was glad to see me, and we got some ND colors and rooted for ND hard – unpatriotic, wasn't I? Force of circumstances, wasn't it? And I saw little Peterson – a senior now – mining engineer – one of the old ones. Stayed all night in Howard's room on a cot he rigged up for me – he's doing the royal act for me, and I'm letting him work his will.

This forenoon I called on Miss Sperry. I had rather see her than all the rest, of course. And she was so unaffectedly glad to see me, and I to see her. She's having a very gay, pleasant time doing just what work she pleases.

My – what a letter I'm spinning you. I'll hold up now and let you recover. I wish I had a letter from you, but I'll have to wait until I get home – don't know just when I'll start back.

Good-night, darling. I'm having a pleasant time, but I want you. I wish you were here to say good-night. You can't tell it by the letter, but you'd *like* me tonight, I believe. I love you so.

Roy

NOVEMBER 13, 1898
Chatfield to Oronoco

My Dear, Dear Roy:

Here's just a line to you, dearie, before I go to sleep. I had the sweetest dream of you last night, and I woke loving you so. I've been loving you all day, and thinking and thinking of you.

Carrie gave me *Laddie* on my birthday – you must read it – it's the sweetest story.

Good-night, darling – my own Roy – my knight – the finest, noblest, truest. You have all my heart.

Anna

NOVEMBER 14, 1898
Oronoco to Chatfield

My Dearest Anna:

Well – I arrived home about 5 o'clock this afternoon. Stayed quite a while, didn't I? I'm glad I did. It was nearly 11 o'clock Sunday when I started to ride. I went out to Fort Snelling on the cycle path, and ferried across the Minnesota River and on to Northfield. It was a grey day, with rather wet roads. Howard had given me a good lunch of bread and meat and cookies, and I carried some fruit stowed around me, and dined on the road. Stopped a couple of hours with Charlie Reifsnider and came on. The roads were horrid – snow some, muddy and slippery in places, and so rough. I was glad to get here, for it isn't pleasant riding now.

I had a good time – saw four or five good plays, two football victories, and heard Sousa. I think I struck it pretty well. Mary is home – she was glad to see me. Poor Minimo – out of school. Your letters were waiting – been thinking of them for days. I'm very glad you're having a good time.

Write to me. I'm tired and lonesome – oh, so lonesome – tonight.

I ordered a little book of poems by E. Field to be sent to you *(the book Roy purchased for Anna was probably Lullaby-Land, Songs of Childhood)*. Hope I'll see you soon.

NOVEMBER 15, 1898
Oronoco to Chatfield

My Dearest Anna:

I'm going to write just a line. How did you know, Annabel – just the note I needed to straighten me out and bring me round right again and stop troubling myself? You are so good, dearie. I'm such an unsatisfactory fellow, ain't I? But I'll be different sometime, I hope.

I wonder what you dreamed. How dear you are to me. I shall see you soon – and I love you entirely.

NOVEMBER 21, 1898
Oronoco to Chatfield

My Dearest Anna:

Your letter just got to me tonight. It would be so good to be with you Thanksgiving, and I can as far as I know. Aunt Minnie says she will let me off.

It's such a good night tonight – not to be living in a hollow tree, with the wind and ice and snow. 'Tisn't long 'til Thursday. Good-night, dearest. I love you entirely, and how I want to see you.

WEDNESDAY, NOVEMBER 23, 1898

From the Olmsted County Democrat newspaper: Anna "came from Chatfield the evening before Thanksgiving, fully expecting to return for the next Monday of school. On the advice of her physician, however, she remained in Rochester, and a substitute was served temporarily."

FRIDAY, NOVEMBER 25, 1898

The Chatfield Democrat: Anna "was forced after Thanksgiving Day to temporarily, as it was then supposed, relinquish her duties on account of failing health. Arrangements were made by which Mrs. B.C. Gillis should take her place until she should recruit her health, and Miss Barnard went to the home of Mr. and Mrs. T.H. Titus of Rochester, where she had resided while attending school at that place, and where she was beloved and treated as a daughter."

SATURDAY, NOVEMBER 26, 1898
Rochester to Oronoco

My Dearest Roy:

The doctor came as I expected, about 5 o'clock. He made a very thorough examination, and said I ought not to teach for a month, at least – and if I was *his* girl, he wouldn't let me teach *at all*. He will see me often during the month, and if I get on all right, perhaps I can go back – perhaps not.

I'm rather weak today – I tired myself out yesterday. I'd like to see you tomorrow, if you feel like driving over with Fannie.

Anna

TUESDAY, NOVEMBER 29, 1898
Oronoco to Rochester

My Dearest Anna:

And are the days going all right, or wearily, or how? Mother and Auntie and Mary were all asking about you.

I came home from seeing you all right, of course – the snow and wind at my back – and I felt real cozy down in my deep collar, with just enough of side roads to make me appreciate being turned away from the bite of the wind full of snow.

I came up to my room to write this 'cause Uncle is downstairs, and he's quite a hand to talk to a body. I had better postpone my attempts to be an author until he's away on the road, I guess. No, on second thought, I better not on that account – I'm altogether too prone to putting that off.

I've been pretty busy the last two days. Did you ever try to get up early and exercise? Isn't it hard? And how different one's mental attitude when the alarm goes off than what it was the night before, and one argues with oneself in the morning, and is easily dissuaded, but it isn't right and is weakening to his character, doubtless. I'm afraid I'll never be the righteous copy-book style of person. Really, one ought to carry things right through when he thinks he should. I ought to write something on "Duty" or "Rules for a Happy Life," hadn't I?

You said I might come and see you Sunday. You are sure it will be all right? Don't mind me asking things over and over, dear. I'm mortally afraid of bothering or tiring you. I get dissatisfied with myself, and then it's natural to think other people feel the same.

Good-night. Write to me, Anna. I love you, dearie – so much.

SATURDAY, DECEMBER 3, 1898

*The **Chatfield Democrat:*** *"Her health did not improve sufficiently to give hopes that she could soon resume her school duties, and by the advice of her physician, she wrote and sent her resignation as teacher to the school board here, but her condition was not such as to cause her friends to fear that death was so near."*

SUNDAY, DECEMBER 4, 1898

*The **Olmsted County Democrat:*** *"Miss Barnard … was apparently recovering nicely and was about the house all day … feeling much improved in health. She ate lunch with her friends after church and retired at the usual hour."*

*The **Record and Union:*** *"On Sunday she was apparently feeling better than she had, and retired without signs of her sudden dissolution."*

CHAPTER 35

Flight

MONDAY, DECEMBER 5, 1898

The Olmsted County Democrat: "At 5:30 this morning, Mr. T.H. Titus was startled from his sleep by hearing a groan. Miss Anna Barnard, who is as a daughter to Mr. and Mrs. Titus, has been in delicate health for some time, and, instinctively, Mr. Titus felt that something had happened to her. He hastened to her bedroom, but the Death Angel had preceded him. Mr. Titus summoned Dr. William James Mayo, but the services of a physician were of no avail. Without waking to consciousness in this world, the sweet spirit of Miss Barnard took its flight. Scarcely three minutes had elapsed before earthly darkness was exchanged for morning in Heaven. It was a peaceful ending of a beautiful life .... Miss Barnard's trouble was complicated, but the weakness of her heart's action was undoubtedly the cause of her death."

The Chatfield Democrat: "The final end came as a surprise and shock last Monday morning at 30 minutes past 5 o'clock. Mr. Titus was awakened by pitiful groans, which came from the room of Miss Barnard. He hastened there, but life was rapidly ebbing away, and in a few minutes all was over."

The Record and Union: "Monday morning Mr. T.H. Titus was aroused at about 5:30 o'clock by heavy groans in a room occupied by Miss Barnard. Hastily going there, he discovered her dying from heart disease, and in scarcely more than a few seconds, she had breathed her last."

The Rochester Post: "Monday morning the home of Mr. T.H. Titus was darkened by the entrance of the Death Angel. The life claimed was that of Miss Anna L. Barnard, who had been making her home there. Her death occurred at thirty minutes past five. Mr. Titus heard groans – the pitiful sounds coming from the room occupied by Miss Barnard as a sleeping apartment. He went to her. Life was rapidly ebbing away, and in a few moments she expired."

WEDNESDAY, DECEMBER 7, 1898

Anna's funeral is held at 2 p.m. at the Titus home, with the Rev. N.H. Burdick officiating.

She is interred in Oakwood Cemetery in Rochester.

THURSDAY, DECEMBER 8, 1898

The Chatfield Democrat: *"A SAD BEREAVEMENT. Chatfield loses an efficient and beloved teacher. Miss Anna Leuella Barnard dies in Rochester.*

"Miss Barnard took charge of the primary department of the school here at the opening of the present year, and her efficiency and kindness won her general esteem and the love of her pupils."

Olmsted County Democrat: *"IN THE MIDST OF LIFE. Sudden death of Miss Anna Barnard*

"Miss Anna Leuella Barnard was born in Granville, New York, November 11, 1874. Twelve years ago she came west to Eyota, but a large part of the time since then has been spent in Rochester. Both of her parents being dead, Miss Barnard was regarded as a daughter by Mr. and Mrs. Titus, and loved as a sister by their children – Mrs. T.T. Creswell and Miss Clara Titus …. She received her education in the Rochester schools, graduating with honors in 1894. Here she made her warmest friendships. Her sweet disposition, unaffected manners, and Christian character endeared her to many …. In her position as a teacher in the Chatfield schools, she was most successful imparting knowledge to children, and continued at her post of duty longer than her physical condition warranted."

FRIDAY, DECEMBER 9, 1898

The Record and Union:

"…. Miss Barnard made her home of late with Mr. and Mrs. T.H. Titus, who, in common with all who knew her, had learned to love her for her many winsome ways and sterling qualities …. She was a most estimable young woman, deservedly popular, and her death is a shock to the community."

Rochester Post: *"A SAD DEATH. Miss Anna L. Barnard Died Suddenly From Heart Failure – The Circumstances of Her Death Particularly Sad.*

"She was an inestimable young lady, and had many friends who will mourn sincerely the loss they sustain in her death."

EPILOGUE

What Happened to Roy

It is difficult to know exactly what transpired when Anna died – how my grandfather came to know of her death; how he reacted; what the days following her death were like for him.

I do know Roy saw Anna the night before she died. I am now reading more letters from the Allis family – hundreds of them, commencing in 1899 (including all the letters between my grandparents when they were courting – another book, I have promised my grandmother). One of the first letters I read from 1899 was from one of my grandmother's friends to her, and she says that Roy visited Anna that night, and that she seemed to be recovering. He went home to Oronoco without knowing the tragedy that would occur the next day. I won't know until I read more of those letters if there will be any more references to Anna – I hope so.

And we know these things occurred in my grandfather's life after Anna's death:

Roy went back to the University of Minnesota, apparently in 1900. The next year he won the Strongman Contest of 1901 – an intercollegiate strength contest in which he beat out 250 other men, including entrants from Columbia, Amherst, Harvard and Wesleyan. According to newspaper accounts of the time, he entered the competition "just for the fun of it," and was called the "new Hercules of the colleges." Further news articles reported:

Roy – winner of the 1901 Strongman Contest

"Allis has never won a reputation in any other department of university athletics. He has never played football. He is not on the Varsity baseball nine … He is a conscientious student, and the development of his marvelous physical powers is a mere incident in his university work. He is a young man with literary aspirations, and recently won second prize in the short story contest between Minnesota and Nebraska U …. Allis will break his own record by a larger margin before the college year ends. The young Hercules' home is in Oronoco, Minnesota, where his father is in the milling business. Before going to college Allis worked in the mill and developed great strength in his shoulders by carrying grain and flour sacks."

The Mayo brothers – Dr. Charles Horace and Dr. William James – offered my grandfather a position at the Mayo Clinic if he completed medical school. He never did. In my father's words: "I'm sure no one ever questioned Dad as being 'just a miller' – he was dearly loved in the community, and the local feed-flour-mill operation was quite common, as well as essential to the communities of the day. He did not *choose* this field of endeavor, I am sure – it was more likely thrust upon him by circumstances which developed when his father was faced with problems in 1900-01, including a flood, which swept away the dam, and I believe there was a fire that destroyed all or most of the older mill. Dad came home at Christmas time in his senior year at the U of M, to lend a hand – and so he chucked what might have been a very brilliant or colorful career, just to be a most considerate and sacrificing son. I don't know, for sure, of course, but from what I know, and from what I heard as a young man – he gave up one helluva good chance to go a ways."

Roy married my grandmother in 1904 – late for the times (he was 30 years old). In my father's words, they shared "a challenging and contentious marriage" for almost 64 years, when my grandfather died in 1968. They owned an 80-acre farm on Lake Shady in Oronoco, and lived their entire lives in the same house my great-grandfather built in 1855. My grandmother was the daughter of a doctor who also served at the Mayo Clinic. The family legend is that she never quite forgave my grandfather for not pursuing the medical profession. But that is another story.

Roy founded a thespian group, took a correspondence writing course, and puttered with manuscripts of plays and books for years. He was a bouncer at the local dance pavilion and boxed – at one time with Fred Fulton, who sparred with the famed Jack Dempsey (Roy decked Fulton for throwing a girl in the lake).

Roy farmed the family homestead (much of the land was eventually sold off to summer residents on Lake Shady – including the Mayos), ran the mill in Oronoco for years, and was long-term clerk of the Oronoco Township Board. He also operated, monitored and regulated the flow of water through the Oronoco dam from the Upper Zumbro River Channel – opening and closing the gates on the dam at the proper times to ensure even flow of water. He operated the dam until he resigned in 1962 at the age of 88 – Olmsted County's oldest employee.

Roy became one of the most colorful figures around Rochester. The *Rochester Post Bulletin* lovingly covered him for decades, and the *St. Paul Pioneer Press* did a full picture story on his physical prowess – still lifting weights, running and swimming every day – when he was 75. In the words of a *Rochester Post Bulletin* reporter, who followed Roy for decades and wrote his obituary: "A friend of mine, Roy Allis, was buried in Oronoco Wednesday, and I shall miss him. He was a good outdoorsman, who taught me how to use an axe, how snowshoes worked, and how to identify the trees growing at the cabin. He was a fund of knowledge on such widely diversified subjects as making maple syrup, trapping passenger pigeons, and canoeing on the Zumbro River.

"In addition to his outdoors knowledge, he was an articulate and well-read scholar, and many 15-minute visits lasted two hours while he settled the problems of the world with some particularly appropriate classical quotation. He was, in the very literal meaning of the word, a gentleman, and one of that fast-vanishing breed – the true individualist."

FINDING ANNA

There have been many surprises along the way as I put together these amazing letters, and help from the most extraordinary people – a testament to the great value of local historical societies, and the sleuthing skills only a real person – a dedicated archivist – can provide. The story of how I came by the letters – and photos of Anna – is almost as interesting as the letters themselves.

Until 2017, even as I transcribed the letters, I had no idea what Anna looked like. I had early photos of my grandfather, but none of her – all of the photos he kept somehow became separated from the letters in my aunt's care.

In 2004 I contacted Russell Dennis, an archivist at Winona State University, who found a graduation photo of Anna's graduating class of 1896. We were so excited! But the photo was a montage, with no one identified! For years we tried to guess which face was Anna's.

In the spring of 2017, deep in the midst of transcribing the letters, I was determined to find a photo. I contacted archivist Krista Lewis at the History Center of Olmsted County. She was unable to find any photos of an Anna Barnard. But she refused to give up. She stubbornly continued to look, and found some old graduation photos of Rochester High School (there were photos back then, but yearbooks weren't created until after 1900). There, in a photo of the class of 1894 – eight students – clearly identified, was my grandfather, and sitting directly in front of him, reading a book, was Anna. It was the first time I saw her face, and I wept.

After I contacted the *Rochester Post Bulletin* to consult their archives, the editor got wind of what I was working on, and assigned reporter Matt Stolle, who wrote a wonderful article in the April 22, 2017, edition, entitled: "I connect with you now – 'Anna letters' tell story of grandfather's tragic first love." That story was replicated in the *Minneapolis Star Tribune*, the *St. Paul Pioneer Press*, the *Faribault Daily News* and, we heard, other southern Minnesotan newspapers we weren't able to verify. Shortly afterward, Stolle was contacted by Bill Gardner – a Rochester resident whose family is from Eyota – who had read the article. Gardner had amazing news. His great grandmother – Winnishiek Early – married Anna's father Lorenzo after Anna's mother died. Lorenzo died six months later, and Winny raised Anna. According to their family legend, Anna "died a week before she was to be married." Gardner had several photos of Anna – including her Normal School graduation photo – and photos of her

The author and her Grandfather Roy (1964)

father and brother. Gardner says his mother believes she still has one of the horse paintings Anna refers to in her letters.

In 2017 I also contacted one of my cousins – Richard Glasenapp, son of my Aunt Harriet (who hid the letters). After Harriet died in 2012, Richard took home many of his mother's boxes of photos and letters. When I told him I was working on a book about the letters, he remembered there were photos in the boxes of a young woman he didn't recognize. Of course, it was Anna.

One last surprise. For years I had a little box of mementos from my father and grandfather – including a tiny pair of spectacles. I never knew whose they were – they didn't appear to match my grandmother's, and were too small for my grandfather. When I finally saw a photo of Anna, I recognized the glasses. They were probably one of the few things Roy had left of her. They sit on my desk next to Anna's picture.

There will probably be at least one more book about Roy and the colorful life he led, and I have promised my Grandmother Lulu that the next book will be about her and her life with my grandfather.

But the legend of Anna has haunted me most of my life. I adored my grandfather – he is probably the most interesting person I have ever met. I am glad to have finally brought this beautiful love story out of the shadows. I was sad when I finally completed reading the letters. I grew to know these two people so well, and the era in which they lived and read and wrote. Their passion for life – and for each other – comes alive on every page.

And I'm sure my grandfather is pleased that his granddaughter went on to become a writer.

The Author

Carol Allis has been writing since her father gave her a manual Underwood typewriter when she was 7. Born and raised in Rochester, Minnesota, she graduated from St. Olaf College in Northfield, Minnesota, with a degree in English education, and has spent her entire professional working life in public service. She first taught junior and senior high English and English as a Foreign Language to Hispanic students. She served as a committee clerk and committee administrator for the Minnesota House of Representatives; media relations specialist for Hennepin

County Medical Center in Minneapolis; communications director for the Minneapolis Community Development Agency; a brief midlife adventure as long-distance education coordinator for Cook County along the North Shore of Lake Superior; public information officer for the Health Care Division of the Minnesota Department of Human Services; and news writer/media relations, outreach and crisis communications specialist for Hennepin County Public Affairs. She specialized in paring down governmentalize into words ordinary people could understand.

Her greatest accomplishment has been raising two precious sons and shepherding amazing grandchildren. Her first book – *Poems for Ordinary People* – was published in 2012 just before she retired. Allis lives near beloved family in Minnetonka, Minnesota, with husband Peter (a retired history professor) and an unbelievably old cat (who knows all her secrets).